World Facts

ISBN 0-75258-484-7 (Paperback)

This is a Parragon Publishing Book
This edition published in 2002
Parragon Publishing
Queen Street House
4 Queen Street
Bath BA1 1HE, UK

Printed in Indonesia
Created and produced by
Foundry Design & Production

Cover design by Blackjacks

World Facts

GENERAL EDITOR:
Dr James Mackay

Contents

Contents

Key to Abbreviations

ac	acres	FM	Field Marshall	mm	millimetre
Adm.	Admiral	Ft	Fort	mph	miles per hour
approx.	approximately	ft	feet	mps	miles per second
b.	born	g	grams	Mt	mountain
bn	billion	Gen.	General	nau mi	nautical miles
bpm	beats per minute	ha	hectares	nm	nanometre
C&W	Country and	hp	horsepower	PM	Prime Minister
	Western	in	inches	Pres.	President
Capt.	Captain	kcal	kilocalories	R&B	Rhythm and
cc	cubic centimetres	km	kilometres		Blues
cm	centimetres	kph	kilometres	Sec.-Gen.	Secretary General
Col.	Colonel		per hour	sq km	square kilometres
Com.	Commander	kps	kilometres	sq mi	square miles
corp.	corporation		per second	St	saint
co.	company	l	litres	v	versus
cu ft	cubic feet	m	metres	yds	yards
cu m	cubic metres	m.	million		
d.	died	MD	Managing		
est.	established/		Director		
	estimated	mi	miles		

How This Book Works

A N 'ENCYCLOPEDIA' has been defined as a work containing general information on all branches of human knowledge, and this is precisely what this book is all about.

More than a just a home reference work for students, teachers and the whole family, the *World Facts Micropedia* is also enormously entertaining – a browser's delight. The alphabetical arrangement of subjects allows myriad opportunities for exploring all manner of facts. Look up Civil War and you may find yourself diverted by the history of the cinema or Classical Art. And so it goes on; the permutations and juxtaposition of unrelated facts is endless, edifying, thought-provoking and stimulating.

Packed into this mini-encyclopedia is an immense range of facts, figures and statistics; bringing together the mundane and the marvellous, the amazing and the downright bizarre. In this fast-moving world of ours, it is important to have the facts and figures at our fingertips: they tell us what we need to know about our world – and beyond.

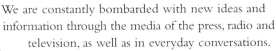

We are constantly bombarded with new ideas and information through the media of the press, radio and television, as well as in everyday conversations. The type of facts found here can settle arguments, win quizzes and provide answers for the most inquisitive of minds.

The entries have been organised for easy reference within around 500 carefully selected subjects ranging from

Actors to Zoology. All aspects of the natural
and human world are covered, from the
farthest reaches of prehistory to the
present day. This is not only a
tremendous source book for
contests of general knowledge,
but it has also been designed to
provide factual depth in support
of the National Curriculum,
presenting morsels of information
in the most palatable, digestible form.

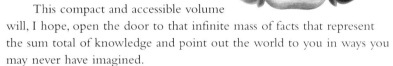

This compact and accessible volume
will, I hope, open the door to that infinite mass of facts that represent
the sum total of knowledge and point out the world to you in ways you
may never have imagined.

Some people may systematically read this book from cover to cover,
but for most readers it is something to dip into at random and then
explore related entries, assisted by the detailed index that spins an intricate web of related subjects.

JAMES MACKAY

ACTORS

'Frankly, my dear, I don't give a damn,' **Clark Gable** (1901–60) said at the end of *Gone With the Wind*. The 'King of Hollywood' was one of its greatest stars for 30 years.

'I have always hated that damn James Bond. I'd like to kill him,' prolific Scottish actor **Sean Connery** (b. Thomas Connery, 1929) said of his most famous film persona (1962–71, 1983).

1950s *Rawhide* TV actor, cult spaghetti-western star (*A Fistful of Dollars*, 1964) and maverick cop (*Dirty Harry* series 1970s–80s), **Clint Eastwood** (b. 1930) extended his range to include directing (*The Unforgiven*, 1992).

A distinguished stage actor, **Sir Laurence Olivier** (1907–89) epitomised the 'English school' of acting in a successful, prolific film career (*Wuthering Heights*, 1939, *Henry V*, 1944, *Richard III*, 1956, *The Entertainer*, 1960, *Sleuth*, 1972).

Actor and drama teacher who founded the Actors' Studio which taught The Method (1950s), **Lee Strasberg** (1899–1982) himself appeared relatively rarely in films (most notably *The Godfather II*, 1974).

Debonair British-born romantic lead from the 1930s with a light comic touch, **Cary Grant** (b. Archibald Leach, 1904–86) became one of Hitchcock's favourite actors in the 1940s–50s (*North by Northwest*, 1959).

Dirk Bogarde (b. 1921), romantic lead in British 1950s films, collaborated with Pinter and Losey (*The Servant*, 1963, *Accident*, 1967), starring in European films (*Death in Venice*, 1971) before retiring to write.

◀ *The rebuilt Shakespeare's Globe Theatre, London.*

Distinguished actor (on stage from 1922, on screen from 1930), **Spencer Tracy** (1900–67) developed the screen image of a tough, honest, well-humoured guy in such films as *Adam's Rib* (1949), *Bad Day at Black Rock* (1955) and *Inherit the Wind* (1960).

Famous as stage and screen actor and father of an acting dynasty, **Sir Michael Redgrave**'s film successes included *The Lady Vanishes* (1938), *The Browning Version* (1950) and *Goodbye Mr Chips* (1969).

From variety stage and *The Goon Show* (1950s), **Peter Sellers** (1925–80) became an international film star by exploiting his uncanny ability to project himself into characters (*Lolita*, 1959, *Dr Strangelove*, 1963, the *Pink Panther* series, 1963–77, *Being There*, 1979).

Gérard Depardieu (b. 1949), prolific French film actor (*Danton*, 1982, *Jean de Florette*, 1986, *Cyrano de Bergerac*, 1990, *Green Card*, 1990), is an international heart-throb, despite his portly girth.

Humphey Bogart (1899–1957), playing gangsters in 1930s movies and classic *films noirs* (*The Maltese Falcon*, 1941, *Casablanca*, 1942), became, as tender-hearted tough guy (*The African Queen*, 1952), a Hollywood institution.

In a brief film career tragically cut short by death in a car crash, **James Dean** (1931–55) defined post-adolescent confusion (*East of Eden*, 1955, *Rebel Without a Cause*, 1955, *Giant*, 1956).

Jack Nicholson (b. 1937) has established a unique screen presence, notably in *Easy Rider* (1969), *Five Easy Pieces* (1970), *Chinatown* (1974), *One Flew Over the Cuckoo's Nest* (1975), *The Shining* (1980) and *Prizzi's Honor* (1985).

US film star Humphrey Bogart. ▶

Actors

James Cagney (1899–1986), Irish-American star of 1930s gangster movies (*Angels with Dirty Faces*, 1938), became one of Hollywood's most memorable stars (*Yankee Doodle Dandy*, 1942, *White Heat*, 1949, *Mister Roberts*, 1955) before retiring (early 1960s).

Kenneth Branagh (b. 1960) is the natural successor to Olivier as actor-director in notable Shakespearean stage and screen productions (*Henry V*, 1989, *Othello*, 1995, *Hamlet*, 1996).

Marcello Mastroianni (1924–96) was perhaps Italy's most famous film star, particularly for his work with Fellini and Antonioni (*La Dolce Vita*, 1959, *La Notte*, 1961, *Eight and a Half*, 1963).

Marlon Brando (b. 1924), archetypal 'Method' actor, defined modern American style in such movies as *A Streetcar Named Desire* (1951), *On the Waterfront* (1954) and *The Godfather* (1972).

Max Von Sydow (b. 1929), Swedish actor originally distinguished as a member of Ingmar Bergman's stage and film repertory company (*The Seventh Seal*, 1956, *The Face*, 1959), found international success in such films as *The Exorcist* (1973).

Michael Caine (b. Maurice Micklewhite, 1933) has been one of the most successful, prolific British actors (Hollywood and internationally) in such films as *The Ipcress File* (1965), *Sleuth* (1973) and *Educating Rita* (1983).

One of the later generation of actors influenced by Strasberg's 'Method', **Al Pacino** (b. 1939) has a powerful screen presence, notably in *The Godfather* trilogy (1972–90), *Serpico* (1973), *Scarface* (1983) and *Carlito's Way* (1993).

◀ *British actor Michael Caine.*

One of the most versatile modern American film actors, **Dustin Hoffman** (b. 1937) has played a variety of character roles (*Midnight Cowboy*, 1969, *Tootsie*, 1983, *Rain Man*, 1988).

Original romantic screen idol, **Rudolph Valentino** (b. Rodolpho d'Antonguolla, 1895–1926), whose sudden death caused several suicides, starred in silent movies such as *The Four Horsemen of the Apocalypse* (1921) and *The Sheik* (1921).

Originally a distinguished stage (particularly Shakespearean) actor, **Sir John Gielgud** (b. 1904) was slow to adapt to the cinema. Since the 1960s he has compensated by playing a prodigious number of film roles.

Paul Scofield (b. 1922) is a distinguished stage actor whose relatively rare film roles have included *A Man for All Seasons* (1966), *King Lear* (1969), *Henry V* (1989) and *Hamlet* (1990).

Sir Alec Guinness (b. 1914) developed from being a distinguished stage actor to a stunning film character actor (*Kind Hearts and Coronets*, 1949, *The Bridge on the River Kwai*, 1957, *Star Wars*, 1977).

The most beloved and enduring of Hollywood stars, **James Stewart** (1908–97), played hesitant, honest heroes in such films as *Mr Smith Goes to Washington* (1939), *It's a Wonderful Life* (1946) and *Vertigo* (1958).

Welsh stage-screen actor, **Richard Burton** (b. Richard Jenkins, 1925–84), had a brooding screen presence matched by a colourful lifestyle. His most memorable film is perhaps *Who's Afraid of Virginia Woolf?* (1966), with Elizabeth Taylor, to whom he was twice married.

Elizabethan actors and playwrights. ▲

ACTRESSES

'I want to be alone', **Greta Garbo** (b. Greta Gustafsson, 1905–91) said in *Grand Hotel* (1932). After early retirement the Swedish star of *Queen Christina* (1933), *Camille* (1936) and *Ninotchka* (1939) left millions of worshippers.

A leading star of the silent screen (*Male and Female*, 1919), **Gloria Swanson** (1897–1983) made a stunning comeback as a caricature of herself in Billy Wilder's *Sunset Boulevard* (1950).

Anne Bancroft (b. Anna Maria Italiano, 1931) has distinguished herself in a variety of films (*The Miracle Worker*, 1962, *The Graduate*, 1968, *84 Charing Cross*, 1987, *How to Make an American Quilt*, 1995).

Bette Davis (b. Ruth Elizabeth Davis, 1908–89) was the most enduring and intense of classic Hollywood's dramatic actresses from the 1930s (*Dangerous*, 1935) to the 1980s (*The Whales of August*, 1987).

Brigitte Bardot (b. Camille Javal, 1933) was a huge star of the French cinema in the 1950s and '60s as blonde 'sex kitten' in such films as *And God Created Women* (1956). She retired in the 1970s, becoming an animal-rights activist.

Broadway diva, singer, actress, director, **Barbra Streisand** (b. 1942) is one of the few genuine female Hollywood stars since the 1960s (*Funny Girl*, 1968, *What's Up Doc?*, 1972, *The Way We Were*, 1973).

Child star, 1960s icon of the Cleopatra look, eight times married, Hollywood veteran **Elizabeth Taylor** (b. 1932) has lived her life in the limelight, memorably in *Who's Afraid of Virginia Woolf?* (1966).

Dame Judi Dench (b. 1934), showered with awards for her work on the stage over the past 30 years, was nominated for a Best Actress Academy Award (1998) for *Mrs Brown* (1997).

Daughter of Sir Michael, **Vanessa Redgrave** (b. 1937) is arguably Britain's finest stage and screen actress (*Mary Queen of Scots*, 1972, *Playing for Time* (TV), 1981, *Wetherby*, 1985, *Howards End*, 1992).

Enduring and gifted Swedish actress **Ingrid Bergman** (1915–82) was star of such noirish Hollywood films as *Intermezzo* (1936), *Casablanca* (1943), *Gaslight* (1944) and *Spellbound* (1945).

From child star in *Wizard of Oz* (1939) to America's leading voice of show business (*Meet Me in St Louis*, 1944, *Easter Parade*, 1948, *A Star Is Born*, 1954), **Judy Garland** (1922–69) was loved by the world yet lonely.

From impish, kookie, hooker roles (*Irma La Douce*, 1963) to cantankerous old women (*Madame Sousatzka*, 1988), **Shirley MacLaine** has had a glittering career as actress, singer and dancer (*Sweet Charity*, 1968).

Epitomising gamine chic, Belgian-born of Anglo-Irish-Dutch parentage, **Audrey Hepburn** (b. Audrey Hepburn-Ruston, 1929–93), star of *Roman Holiday* (1956) and *Breakfast at Tiffany's* (1961), was ambassador for UNICEF.

From being a child star (*Bugsy Malone*, 1976, *Taxi Driver*, 1976), **Jodie Foster** has become one of the leading actresses of the 1980s and '90s (*The Accused*, 1988, *Silence of the Lambs*, 1991).

▲ *Swedish actress Ingrid Bergman. UNICEF ambassador Audrey Hepburn.* ▶

German actress and singer **Marlene Dietrich** (b. Maria Magdalena von Losch, 1901–92) wowed Hollywood from the 1930s with her deep husky voice and magnetism (*The Blue Angel*, 1930, *Shanghai Express*, 1932, *Destry Rides Again*, 1939).

Hollywood's most famous child star, **Shirley Temple** (b.1928) performed in short films aged three and later famously in *Little Miss Marker* (1934), *Curly Top* (1935) and *Heidi* (1937).

Jean Harlow (b. Harlean Carpentier), platinum blonde, was the most sensational star of the early 1930s (*Hell's Angels*, 1930, *Public Enemy*, 1931, *Red Headed Woman*, 1932, *Red Dust*, 1932).

Joan Crawford (b. Lucille le Sueur, 1906–77), in spite of her adopted daughter's book *Mommie Dearest* (1978), which painted her as a monster, was one of Hollywood's most adored leading ladies, specialising in thwarted ambition (*Mildred Pierce*, 1945).

Katharine Hepburn (b. 1907) has become the most durable American actress, especially in emancipated female roles (*Pat and Mike*, 1952, *The African Queen*, 1951, *The Lion in Winter*, 1968).

Marilyn Monroe (b. Norma Jean Baker or Mortenson, 1926–62), the century's ultimate tragic sex symbol, was a fine comic actress (*Gentlemen Prefer Blondes*, 1953, *The Seven-Year Itch*, 1955, *Some Like It Hot*, 1959).

Meryl Streep (b. Mary Louise Streep, 1951) is famous for her ability to steep herself in a role, notably in *The French Lieutenant's Woman* (1981), *Sophie's Choice* (1982) and *Out of Africa* (1986).

◄ *American 1950s sex symbol Marilyn Monroe.*

Michelle Pfeiffer (b. 1957) is one of the brightest American film actresses of the last two decades (*Dangerous Liaisons*, 1988, *The Fabulous Baker Brothers*, 1989, *Frankie and Johnny*, 1991).

Not so much actress as archetypal sex symbol and Hollywood phenomenon, **Mae West** (1892–1980) wrote most of her own stage plays and scripts (mostly full of *doubles entendres*), starring memorably in *She Done Him Wrong* (1933).

One of France's greatest stage and film actresses, **Jeanne Moreau** (b. 1928) brings a bittersweet quality to all her roles (*The Lovers*, 1959, *Jules et Jim*, 1961, *Louise*, 1972).

Sarah Bernhardt (1844–1923), the legendary French stage tragedienne, appeared in a number of early silent films including *La Dame aux Camelias* (1911) and *Queen Elizabeth* (1912).

Scarlett O'Hara in *Gone With the Wind*, **Vivien Leigh** (b. Vivien Hartley, 1913–67), famously married to Olivier, was Britain's greatest stage and screen actress from the 1930s to '50s (*Dark Journey*, 1937, *A Streetcar Named Desire*, 1951).

Whoopi Goldberg (b. Caryn Johnson, 1949), star of *The Color Purple* (1985), *Ghost* (1990) and *Sister Act* (1992), is the most successful ever black American actress.

ADVERTISING

Advertising can be seen by economists as either a boost or a hindrance to perfect competition, since it attempts to make **illusory distinctions** between essentially similar products.

Elizabeth Arden (1884–1966) developed and merchandised a line of cosmetic products and also utilised new techniques of mass advertising to introduce her products to the public.

In 1986, after acquiring 12 companies in 10 years, the British firm of Saatchi and Saatchi became the **world's largest advertising agency**.

▲ *Coca Cola – one of the 20th century's success stories.*

In 1992 an estimated $131 bn was **spent** in the US by about 250,000 national advertisers and 1,750,000 local advertisers, a figure that was almost 4% higher than 1991's $126.4 bn.

The **Advertising Standards Authority** (ASA) founded in 1962 recommends to the media that advertisements, which might breach the British Code of Advertising Practice, are not published.

The **UK's national advertising budget** was £6 bn in 1988 (newspapers 40%; television 33%; magazines 20%; posters and radio taking the rest). The UK government spent over £120 m. in 1988.

Top spending industries in the US are automobile ($3.6 bn); retailers ($2.9 bn); food industry ($1.78 bn); restaurants ($1.3 bn); entertainment industry ($1.1 bn); telephone industry ($733 m.); finance ($552 m.); alcohol ($552 m.); toiletries ($537 m.); and medicines ($525 m.).

AFRICA

Africa has an **area** of about 30,000,000 sq km/11,550,000 sq mi. It occupies 5.9% of the world's total surface area and 20.1% of the total land area.

Africa is sometimes called the 'cradle of humanity'. Remains of creatures that were the **ancestors** of present humans are among the oldest verified.

Africa's **lowest point** is Lake Asale, Ethiopia, 156 m/512 ft below sea level; and its **highest** is Mt Kilimanjaro, Tanzania, 5,895 m/19,340 ft.

Street life the Gambia. ▲

In terms of zoogeography, Africa south of the Sahara belongs to the **Ethiopian Realm**.

The **climatic and vegetation zones** of Africa are distributed symmetrically north and south of the equator. A belt of tropical forest is flanked by grasslands, then, to north and south, by desert regions.

Three **Precambrian shields** (platforms) of metamorphic rock form the ancient heart of Africa. Surrounding them are vast areas of ancient undisturbed sedimentary rock.

AID AGENCIES

Created to help the starving in Nazi-occupied Greece during the Allied blockade (1942), **Oxfam** (Oxford Committee for Famine Relief; chair: Joel Joffe) relieves poverty and suffering worldwide, particularly in developing countries.

Established by the Geneva Convention (1864), the **Red Cross** assists the wounded and prisoners of war, war-related victims, refugees and the disabled; aids victims of natural disasters; and organises emergency relief operations worldwide.

Live Aid raised funds to ease famine in Ethiopia. ▶

Founded by lawyer Peter Benenson (1961), **Amnesty International** aims to free prisoners of conscience, ensure fair trials for political prisoners and opposes the death penalty.

Horrified by BBC South Africa correspondent Michael Buerk's 1984 report on Ethiopia, musician Bob Geldof (b. 1954) launched **Live Aid** (13 Jul. 1985) the greatest live global music event ever televised, to provide aid for famine victims.

Human Rights Watch (1978, founder: Robert L. Bernstein) monitors and publicises human-rights abuses by governments, especially attacks on those defending human rights in their own countries.

Known worldwide by its panda logo, the **World Wide Fund for Nature** (WWF, 1961; Pres.: Duke of Edinburgh, b. 1921) protects endangered species and tackles all environmental problems threatening any form of life.

With 115,000 sponsors, London-based **ActionAid** (1972: founder John Batten) helps children, families and communities in the poorest countries in Africa, Asia and Latin America.

AIRCRAFT

In 1967 the first Anglo-French

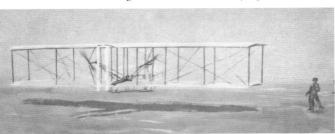

Concorde prototype was unveiled. The new supersonic, drop-nose jet would cut long-haul flights by a half. It is still in service.

Louis Blèriot made the **first channel crossing** in 1909 in a monoplane of his own construction. The 37 km/23 mi crossing took 35.5 minutes.

Strenuous efforts were made by Cayley, Wenham, Stringfellow, Henson, Penaud and Tatin throughout the 19th c to create a **flying machine** but all to no avail.

The **fastest aircraft** is the Lockheed SR-71A, a reconnaissance or spy plane capable of speeds up to 3,715 kph/2,308 mph. It has a ceiling of 26,000 m/85,300 ft and a range of 4,800 km/2,980 mi.

The **first successful flight** was by the Wright brothers in Dec. 1903, flying 260 m/853 ft in 59 seconds. The following year they managed 38.9 km/24.17 mi in under 40 minutes.

The **first transoceanic flight** was made in 1919 by a flying-boat between Long Island, US and Plymouth. Stopping three times, it took 23 days.

The first **ultra-light experimental aircraft**, *Voyager*, completed a non-stop round-the-world trip in 1986. It had two engines and was designed by Burt Rutan.

The Wright brothers making their first successful flight. ▲

AIRFORCES

Bombsights and standardised bomb fittings made it possible to strike targets more accurately. By 1918, 254 tons of bombs had been dropped over England, causing 9,000 casualties.

Hugh Trenchard, first commander of the **Royal Air Force** (1918) and Giulio Douhet, commander of Italy's first aviation unit (1912–15) were the main proponents of early air-fighting power.

In 1915 the German **Fokker E-2** appeared, which featured a machine gun synchronised to shoot through the arc of a spinning propeller, opening the era of air combat.

In the **Gulf War** over 2,250 UN combat aircraft flew 88,000 missions and dropped 88,000 tons of bombs, against Iraq's 500 Soviet MiG-29s and French Mirage F-1s.

In the **Six-Day War** between the Arabs and Israel, victory was clinched in three hours when the Arab forces lost 452 aircraft. Air power was now a dominant force.

In Vietnam **helicopters**, initially used for observation, transport and medical evacuation, became significant combat weapons; the C-47 cargo planes were converted into gunships.

Successful balloon flights in France led to the world's first air force: the **Aerostatic Corps** (1794), which briefly conducted aerial reconnaissance for the armies of Revolutionary France.

The UK and Germany developed the Hawker Hurricane, **Supermarine Spitfire** and Messerschmitt Me109 fighters; and the Junkers Ju87 (Stuka), the Bristol Blenheim and Heinkel He111 bombers.

The US entered the war after Japanese carrier-borne aircraft attacks on **Pearl Harbor** and the Philippines. These attacks destroyed most American land-based aircraft in the Pacific.

World War I **combat aces** included Germany's Baron Manfred von Richthofen (Red Baron), Georges Guynemer (France), Albert Ball (UK), Billy Bishop (Canada) and Eddie Rickenbacker (US).

AIRSHIPS

Stanley Spencer's 22.8 m/75 ft airship was the **first British airship**. It made its maiden flight at Crystal Palace in 1902. It had a capacity of 2,500 cu m/88,300 cu ft.

The **airship duration record** is held by the US Navy ZPG-2. It flew non-stop from Massachusetts to Florida in 1957, some 15,205 km/9448 mi in 264 hours.

The *Akron*, a US airship, carried a record 207 passengers in 1931. However, the **transatlantic record** was achieved by the ill-fated *Hindenburg* in 1937.

The **earliest airship flight** took place in Paris in 1852. Henri Griffard's steam-powered coal-gas airship made it as far as Trappes.

The **largest-ever airship**, the 219 tonne *Graf Zeppelin II* (LZ130), made her maiden flight in 1938. She was dismantled in 1940.

The R101 was the **largest British-built airship**. It crashed in 1930 in France killing all but 6 of 54 on board. Its maiden flight took place the year before.

The rigid airship *Hindenburg* was one of the largest airships with a length of 245 m/804 ft. It burst into flames, killing 36 people as it attempted to land at Lakehurst, New Jersey in 1937.

ALTERNATIVE THERAPIES

Acupuncture is an ancient Chinese medical technique involving the use of thin needles to manipulate the flow of energy in channels (called meridians) throughout the body.

Alexander Technique is a method of correcting established bad habits of posture, breathing and muscular tension which its founder, F. M. Alexander, maintained to be the cause of illness.

Aromatherapy involves using the essential oils of plants for medicinal purposes. Essential oils have a variety of medicinal properties, including anti-bacterial, anti-inflammatory and fungicidal.

Bach Flower Remedies form a system of therapy using the 'hormones' (extracts) of flowers and other plants, which work to alleviate the emotional and mental causes of disease. Developed by Dr Edward Bach.

Chiropractic is a technique of manipulation of the spine and other parts of the body, based on the principle that disorders are caused by problems in the functioning of the nervous system, which the therapy can correct.

Herbalism is an ancient form of healing using plants and their derivatives for medicinal purposes as opposed to the 'synthetic' equivalents found in drugs.

Homeopathy is a system of medicine based on the principle that symptoms of disease are part of the body's self-healing process. Very dilute doses of a natural substance that would cause illness in a healthy person are administered.

▲ *Robert E. Lee at Gettysburg.*

Hypnotherapy is the use of hypnotic trance and post-hypnotic suggestions to relieve illness and stress-related conditions, to break habits and addictions and to encourage well-being.

Naturopathy involves a number of therapies, such as diet, natural medicines, hydrotherapy, osteopathy and lifestyle counselling, to encourage the natural self-healing processes of the body and restore the body to health.

Nutritional therapy involves treating imbalances, deficiencies and illnesses with food and nutrients, including vitamins, minerals, amino acids and other elements of nutrition.

Osteopathy is a system of physical manipulation used to treat mechanical stress. Osteopaths are usually consulted to treat problems of the musculoskeletal system, although overall health will benefit from treatment.

Reflexology is the manipulation and massage of the feet (and sometimes hands) to ascertain and treat disease or dysfunction elsewhere in the body.

Shiatsu is a Japanese method of massage derived from acupuncture, which treats organic or physiological dysfunction by applying finger or hand pressure to parts of the body remote from the affected part.

AMERICAN CIVIL WAR

A powerful Union weapon in the American Civil War was the **naval blockade** of southern ports, cutting off the industrially backward Confederacy from the world.

A turning point in favour of the Union during the American Civil War, the Battle of **Gettysburg** (1–3 Jul. 1863) left 43,000 dead and wounded.

Abraham Lincoln's **1860 election** as US president triggered the southern secessions prefacing the American Civil War. He was perceived as advocating the abolition of slavery.

Confederate forces fired the opening shots of the American Civil War at **Ft Sumter**, South Carolina when a resupply of federal troops was attempted (12 Apr. 1861).

Confederate Gen. Robert E. Lee surrendered to Union Commander Ulysses S. Grant at **Appomattox** Courthouse (9 Apr. 1865), ending the American Civil War.

The **American Civil War** (1860–65) was caused by the secession of eleven southern states over constitutional and economic disputes.

Union Gen. **William T. Sherman** marched across Georgia (1864) during the American Civil War cutting a 60-mile swathe of utter destruction.

Virginian **Robert E. Lee**, a widely revered figure, commanded the Confederate Army of Northern Virginia in the American Civil War.

AMERICAN FOOTBALL

Jerry Rice of the San Francisco 49ers holds the National Football League (NFL) record for the **most touch-downs** in a career. His tally currently stands at 165.

Joe Montana of the San Francisco 49ers is the only man to win the Super Bowl **Most Valuable Player** (MVP) Award three times, in 1982, 1985 and 1990.

San Francisco 49ers defeated Denver Broncos 55-10 in Super Bowl XXIV in 1990 to record the **highest team score** and widest winning margin in Super Bowl history.

The rules for American Football were codified in 1874 and called the **Harvard Rules**. The first match under the new rules was Harvard University v McGill University, Montreal.

The **Super Bowl** (est. 1967), the challenge between the American Football Conference (AFC) and National Football Conference (NFC) champions, is held in Jan. every year at the end of the regular season.

Walter Payton of the Chicago Cubs holds the career record for **most yards gained rushing**, 16,726 between 1975 and 1987.

AMERICAN POLITICAL SCANDALS

In 1937 US president Franklin D. Roosevelt lost public approval with the **Court Packing Scheme**, a proposed Supreme Court reorganisation that would have made the body friendlier to the New Deal.

Irangate involved senior members of the administration of Pres. Ronald Reagan (1981–89) who sold arms to Iran despite a worldwide ban.

Scandals plaguing US president, Bill Clinton (1993–), allegedly part of a conservative plot, begin with an investment in **Whitewater**, an Arkansas land development.

Secretary of State Albert Fall, first US cabinet officer imprisoned (1922), was convicted for accepting bribes in exchange for oil leases in the **Teapot Dome** scandal.

Senator Edward Kennedy's presidential aspirations were dashed in 1980 because of the **Chappaquiddick** scandal (1969), a car accident in which a young woman drowned.

◀ Bill Clinton was the first US president to be impeached in 130 years.

The scandals of Richard M. Nixon's presidency (1969–74), resulting from a break-in at Democratic campaign headquarters (17 Jun. 1972), are known collectively as **Watergate**.

The US has had its share of **political scandals**, but since the 1972 Watergate incident (Nixon administration), the American press has obsessively pursued alleged misconduct.

AMERICAN REVOLUTION

A turning point in the American Revolution, the British surrender at **Saratoga** (17 Oct. 1777) led France to form an alliance with the colonists.

As the largest colonial city (population 400), **Philadelphia**, Pennsylvania was the centre of the American Revolution and was the US capital from 1790 to 1800.

Britain's thirteen New World colonies staged the successful **American Revolution** (1775–83) over issues of taxation and representation in Parliament.

Following British occupation of Philadelphia (in the American Revolution), Gen. George Washington moved into winter quarters at **Valley Forge** (1777–78), losing 2,500 men in harsh conditions.

Loyalists, or Tories, comprised a third of the colonial population and suffered political exclusion and social isolation.

The opening battles of the American Revolution, known as 'the shot heard around the world', occurred at **Lexington and Concord** (Massachusetts) on 19 Apr. 1775.

The **Second Continental Congress** of the American Revolution opened in May 1775 and adopted the Declaration of Independence from Britain (4 Jul. 1776).

First US president George Washington. ▶

The **Yorktown** campaign (30 Aug.–19 Oct. 1781) won independence for the colonies in the American Revolution with the surrender of British Gen. Charles Cornwallis.

AMERICAN SOCIETY OF COMPOSERS, AUTHORS, AND PUBLISHERS

The **American Society of Composers, Authors, and Publishers** (1914) links creators and users of music and is the only US performing rights licensing organisation.

The American Society of Composers, Authors, and Publishers protects its members by **licensing and paying royalties** for the public performances of their copyrighted works.

The American Society of Composers, Authors, and Publishers has a membership of **more than 75,000** composers, songwriters, lyricists and music publishers.

The **board of directors** of the American Society of Composers, Authors, and Publishers is made up of writers and music publishers elected from its membership.

AMPHIBIANS

A. R. Wallace discovered the **Flying Frog** of eastern Asia whose highly developed webbed feet act as a parachute as it sails from tree to tree.

In 1914 D. M. S. Watson discovered the **tetrapods**, primitive four-legged animals with long bodies and flattened tails, which inhabited water alongside their fish ancestors.

Linnaeus applied the term **amphibia** to a class of vertebrate animals (frogs, toads, newts and salamanders) able to live on land and in water.

Newts are small tailed amphibians. All of the species are aquatic during the breeding season; some later take up life on land while others remain permanently in water.

Tailed amphibians include the brightly coloured **salamander**. Far from withstanding fire, as the Greeks believed, it is found only in damp places.

The name **frog** is applied to tailless amphibians as a whole, ranging from the European frog to the giant *Rana goliath* (25 cm/10 in) of Cameroon.

◄ *Diamond-cutting is one of Amsterdam's main industries.*

The three **canals**, the Heeren Gracht, Keizers Gracht and Prinsen Gracht, with tree-lined quays and old houses, form the chief thoroughfares of the city.

ANATOMY

A standard study of descriptive anatomy, **Gray's** *Anatomy* has been used by medical students for more than 100 years. It was first published in London in 1858 and an American edition followed in 1859.

Anatomy is divided into several sub-disciplines. **Gross anatomy** involves studies on structures that can be seen with the naked eye. Histology is the study of tissue structure and cytology that of cell structure.

AMSTERDAM

Amsterdam began in 1204 as a dam on the River Amstel. The town received its first charter from Guy of Hainaut in 1300 and developed rapidly as a trading centre.

Amsterdam is located in the province of North Holland, on the south bank of the Y, an arm of the Zuider Zee, and is a major rail and canal centre.

Amsterdam's chief industries are diamond-cutting, sugar-refining, ship-building, brewing, distilling and the manufacture of soap, oil, glass, tobacco and leather goods.

The **population of Amsterdam** is 695,162 (est. 1991). Huguenot refugees from France (1685) settled in De Jordaan district and there is a large Jewish quarter.

English surgeon John Hunter (1728–93) was noted for his precise anatomical knowledge. Italian anatomist Giovanni B. Morgagni (1682–1771) founded **pathologic anatomy** and French physiologist Marie François Bichat (1771–1802) developed histology.

Most notable among those who strove to advance anatomical understanding was Claudius **Galen** (AD 131–200). Galen's monumental work, *On the Use of the Parts of the Human Body*, served as the standard medical text for 1,400 years.

Soon after the death of Aristotle the Ptolemies, Kings of Egypt, encouraged **dissections**. Herophilus (335–280 BC) dissected about 600 bodies and wrote treatises on anatomy and the eyes and a handbook for midwives.

The first recorded attempts to study anatomy were made by **Aristotle** (384–22 BC), although hieroglyphics and papyri produced from 3000 to 1600 BC indicate that some interest was taken in anatomical aspects of mummies.

ANCIENT DISASTERS

After the **Black Death** in the 14th c, plague remained endemic for the next three centuries. An outbreak in London in 1665 killed 100,000 of the 400,000 inhabitants.

The Middle East and Mediterranean suffered greatly from **earthquakes** in ancient times, notably: in AD 526 Antioch, Syria 250,000 deaths; in AD 844 and 847 Damascus 50,000 and 70,000 deaths; AD 856 Qumis, Damghan, Iran 200,000 deaths.

Massive **flooding** hit Britain and the Netherlands in 1099, 1421 and 1446. Records are unclear, but it is said that over 100,000 were drowned.

Flavius Josephus chronicled the **mass suicide** of 960 Jewish zealots at Masada in Israel in AD 73; rather than face capture by the Romans they chose death.

In the early afternoon of 24 Aug. AD 79, **Mt Vesuvius** erupted wiping out Pompeii, Herculaneum and other towns. They lay hidden until the 18th c.

The event upon which the **Old Testament** flood tale is based may have occurred about 3000 BC, when the Euphrates River inundated a vast area, including Ur in southern Mesopotamia.

◄ Remains of an ancient Egyptian ship.

When the bubonic, pneumonic and septicemic plagues hit Eurasia, 1347–51, some 75 m. people died. This still ranks as the biggest **pandemic** in history.

ANCIENT EGYPT

'He is a god by whose dealings one lives, the father and mother of all men, alone by himself, without an equal,' wrote an Egyptian civil servant of the **Pharaoh** in about 1500 BC.

The **art** of ancient Egypt was extremely naturalistic, with charming portrayals of everyday scenes of hunting and fishing, or scribes and craftsmen at work.

The **civilisation of ancient Egypt** first emerged *c.* 3200 BC and for 2,000 years was astonishingly stable, with a single ruling class and religious and administrative system.

The Egyptians had a huge **pantheon**, with over 2,000 gods and several important cults. Horus the falcon god was also god of the sun, and later the offspring of Osiris.

The final dynasty of ancient Egypt came to an end in 30 BC with the suicide of the legendary queen, **Cleopatra**, and the Roman Empire took its place.

The **Great Pyramid of Giza**, the tomb of the Pharaoh Cheops, built *c.* 3000 BC, is one of the Seven Wonders of the World.

The **Rosetta Stone**, a slab of basalt with inscriptions in Greek and Egyptian hieroglyphic writing, was found in 1799 and made translation of ancient Egyptian writing possible.

Ancient Egyptian art. ►

ANCIENT GREECE

About 800 BC Greek writing developed into a true **alphabet**, using both consonants and vowels, affecting every facet of Greek culture – written laws, literature and philosophy.

Although the earliest cookbooks were produced in Sicily, in wealthy, decadent **Sybaris** (ruled by classical Greece) inventors of new recipes were given a year's copyright.

From the Ancient **Greek language** come many of the words we use today: *demos*, the people, gives us *democracy*; *polis*, the city, gives us *political*.

In the temple of Apollo, near the Greek city of **Delphi**, the famous oracle was interpreted by priests from the utterances of the priestesses.

Plato (*c.* 428–347 BC), pupil of Socrates, had in turn for a pupil the polymath **Aristotle**, whose vast body of work includes treatises on logic, philosophy and metaphysics.

Pythagoras (*c.* 580–500 BC), philosopher and mathematician, was the first to elevate mathematics to the realm of a science and contributed to the development of geometry.

Sappho wrote her graceful lyric poetry on the island of Lesbos in the 6th c BC. Later came the tragedies of Euripides (*c.* 484–406 BC) and the satires of Aristophanes (*c.* 450–388 BC).

Tales of the **Trojan War**, fought in *c.* 1200 BC, were woven into Homer's *Iliad* and *Odyssey* 500 years later, and have inspired artists ever since.

The **Parthenon**, the Greek temple built about 447 BC on the Acropolis in Athens, was dedicated to the goddess Athena Parthenos and is a masterpiece of the Doric style.

With its remarkable flowering of culture and political forms, the **Classical period** of Ancient Greece (500–330 BC) has become the reference point for many subsequent civilisations.

◀ *Greek sculpture of Aristotle.*

ANGLING

Alf Dean caught the **largest** officially ratified **rod-caught fish**, a great white shark which weighed 1,208 kg/2,664 lb at South Australia on 21 Apr. 1959.

The **largest British freshwater fish** caught on rod and line was a 29.03 kg/64 lb salmon caught by Miss Georgina Ballantine on the River Tay, Scotland in 1922.

The largest rod-caught freshwater fish in the US was a 212.25 kg/468 lb **white sturgeon** landed by Joey Pallotta III at Benicia, California on 9 Jul. 1983.

The **longest-ever freshwater cast** is 175.01 m/574 ft 2 in by Walter Kummerow of West Germany at the World Casting Championships at Switzerland in 1968.

The **World Fly Fishing Championships** were introduced by angling's ruling body, the Confederation Internationale de la Pêche Sportive (CIPS) in 1981. Italy are most successful with five titles.

The **World Freshwater Championships** were introduced in 1957 and France have been the most successful nation with 12 team victories.

ANIMAL RIGHTS

Animal rights cover the hunting and trapping of animals, mistreatment of work or sport animals or pets, animal experimentation, factory farming and the threat of extinction to many endangered species.

Animal-rights activists in the 20th c have sought, with some success, to obtain better control over the use of animals in laboratories for scientific research and the testing of products.

In a religion such as **Jainism**, for example, all forms of life are considered sacred and not to be injured, whereas the majority of the Western world considers other forms of life subservient to human needs and desires.

The practice of using live animals for scientific experiments has been opposed by numerous humane societies. In the 1870s a strong antivivisection movement emerged in the UK, culminating in the **Cruelty to Animals Act** of 1876.

The Society for the Prevention of Cruelty to Animals (**SPCA**) is the generic term for multiple separate organisations throughout the world that seek to assure humane treatment of animals.

Animal Sports

The term 'vivisection' is applied to any experimentation using live animals and for several years various groups have conducted antivivisection campaigns to obtain more humane treatment for laboratory animals.

The view of animals as unfeeling creatures of reflex, as exemplified by Rene Descartes' (1596–1650) philosophy of science, has long since been undercut by other philosophical approaches and by better understanding of evolution and **animal behaviour**.

ANIMAL SPORTS

After the Norman Conquest, **falconry** was extremely popular with the nobility. The type of hawk or falcon carried marked a man's rank. Interest declined in the 17th c.

Bear-baiting, a populat pastime in Elizabethan times, was a contest between a bear, chained to a stake, and a pack of dogs. The bear was invariably torn to pieces.

During the Middle Ages extensive restrictions limited the taking of game to the ruling classes. **Stag hunts** with hounds were a popular pastime of the nobility.

Hunters of large game employ four techniques: still hunting, stand hunting, stalking and driving. Wild turkeys are hunted by camouflaged hunters using mouth-and-hand operated turkey calls.

In the US, **buffalo** herds, that once numbered in the millions, were virtually wiped out by hunters; by 1895 only 400 buffalo remained in the country.

The first laws designed to **conserve game animals** were instituted in the 13th c Kublai Khan the Mongol leader forbade his subjects to hunt during animal breeding seasons.

The **invention of gunpowder** in the 14th c and the matchlock musket in the 15th c allowed the bringing down of birds and animals at greater distances.

▲ *The chimpanzee is a member of the primate family*

ANIMALS

An **animal** is any living thing, typically differing from plants in its capacity for spontaneous movement, especially in response to stimulation.

Chordata are members of a subkingdom of animals, including the vertebrates, which have at some stage of development a central nervous system along the back.

Fish range from the *Agnatha* and *Cyclostomata* (ampreys and hagfish) to the *Actinistia* (coelacanths) and *Dipnoi* (lungfish), according to their evolution.

Invertebrates have now been classified by Rudolf Raff according to molecular evidence (ribosomal ribonucleic acid) in evolution from reproduction to segmentation.

Mammalia, a term invented by Carl Linnaeus in 1758, encompasses all suckling creatures from the monotremes and marsupials to the ungulates (hoofed animals).

Reptilia in the broadest sense range from the *Amphibia* (amphibians) to *Aves* (birds), but more narrowly pertain to turtles, snakes, lizards and crocodiles.

The **primates** are the highest order of mammals which includes human beings, apes, monkeys and related forms such as lemurs and tarsiers.

◀ *Iguana, a member of the reptile family.*

ANIMALS OF AFRICA

The **African Elephant** (*Loxodonta africana*) is the world's largest land-dwelling animal, reaching a height of 4 m/13 ft. Unlike its Indian cousin it is untameable.

The **Black Rhinoceros** (*Diceros bicornis*) is a large, ungainly animal, noted for the two horns on its face. It was formerly common all over sub-Saharan Africa.

The **Giraffe** (*Giraffa camelopardalis*) is the tallest of the mammals, its head towering 5 m/16 ft above the ground to browse on high-growing leaves.

The **Gorilla** (*Gorilla gorilla*) of central Africa is the largest of the anthropoid apes, standing up to 2 m/6 ft 6 in. They live on fruit and do not kill to eat.

The **Hippopotamus** rivals the Rhino as the second largest land animal. The name is Greek for 'river horse' but it is actually a relative of the pig.

The **Oryx** (*Oryx dammah*), once found all over central Africa, now survives only in Chad. It is noted for its very long, curved horns.

The **Zebra** (*Equus zebra*) is the wild horse of the grassy plains, noted for its striped coat and tufted tail. They are found in large herds, prone to attack by lions.

ANIMALS OF ASIA

The **Asiatic Elephant** (*Elephas maximus*), about 1 m/3 ft 3 in shorter than its African cousin, has long been domesticated and used as a transport animal in India.

The **Giant Panda** (*Ailuropoda melanoleuca*) is found in the bamboo forests of China. Its rarity and cuddly appearance make it a great favourite in zoos.

The **Great Indian Rhinoceros** (*Rhinoceros unicornis*), once found all over South-East Asia, is now confined mainly to India, Thailand and part of China.

The **Langur** or Hanuman (*Semnopithecus entellus*) is the sacred monkey, found in Indian temples. They have very slim bodies with long tails and limbs.

The **Orang Utan** (*Pongo pygmaeus*), distinguished by its bright red hair and very long arms, is a tree-dweller found in the forests of Borneo and Sumatra.

The **Pangolin** or Scaly Anteater (*Manis crassicaudata*) is distinguished by its armour of overlapping plates, much esteemed in Oriental medicine.

The **Tiger** (*Panthera tigris*) of India rivals the lion in size, strength and ferocity. Its coat of rufous fawn is marked by transverse dark-brown stripes.

ANIMALS OF AUSTRALIA

The **Dingo** or Warrigal (*Canis dingo*) is the native dog of Australia. It is sandy brown and stockily built, with white belly, feet and tip of tail.

The **Koala** (*Phascloarctos cinereus*) is a stoutly built marsupial of eastern Australia, ash-grey in colour. It lives in eucalyptus trees whose tender shoots are its main food.

The **Marsupials** are mammals which for some time after birth are kept in a pouch on the underside of the female's body. They comprise the kangaroos, koalas, opossums and wallabies.

The **Monotremes** are the lowest existing order of mammals and consist of the duck-billed platypus and the echidna which lay eggs but suckle their young when hatched.

The **Numbat** or Banded Anteater (*Myrmecobius fasciatus*) is one of the marsupials. It is found in Western Australia and, unusually, is active in the daytime.

The **Tasmanian Devil** (*Sarcophilus ursinus*) is a marsupial about the size of a badger. It owes its sinister name to its deep black colour and fierce appearance.

The **Wombat** forms the marsupial family of Vombatidae, resembling small bears with a shuffling gait. They burrow in the ground and sleep by day.

ANIMALS OF EUROPE

The **Brown Bear** (*Ursus arctos*) was once found all over northern Europe, though extinct in Britain by the 11th c. It has a massive body, short limbs and very short tail.

The **Elk** (*Alces alces*) is found in the northerly regions, notably Sweden. It is distinguished by large palmate antlers, a long fleshy muzzle and long legs.

The **Fox** (*Vulpes vulpes*) is noted for its cunning. It has a reddish coat, sometimes greyish or beige, with a white-tagged tail and black ears, feet and muzzle.

The **Ibex** or Alpine Wild Goat (*Capra ibex*), once found all over the Alps, is now confined to the Gran Paradiso range and the Engadine national park, Switzerland.

The **Mouflon** (*Ovis musimon*) is believed to be the aboriginal sheep of Europe. Once threatened by the spread of domestic sheep, it flourishes in Cyprus to this day.

The **Otter** (*Lutra lutra*) is an aquatic carnivore with an elongated body, short limbs with webbed feet and a tail half the length of its body.

The **Wildcat** (*Felis silvestris*) is larger and heavier than its domesticated cousin, and is characterised by a flatter head with short ears.

ANIMALS OF NORTH AMERICA

The **American Bison** (*Bison bison*) or Buffalo is the largest mammal of North America. Once roaming the plains in vast herds, they were hunted to the verge of extinction.

The **Beaver** (*Castor canadensis*), national emblem of Canada, is a large aquatic rodent with a flat, scaly tail and webbed hind feet. Its fur was much esteemed for hats.

The **Caribou** (*Rangifer caribou*) is a large Arctic and sub-Arctic deer found from Alaska to Newfoundland. Both male and female have antlers.

The **Cougar** (*Felis concolor*), also known as the Mountain Lion or Puma, was once widespread but hunted to extinction in the eastern states.

The **Raccoon** (*Procyon lotor*) is thick-set with a bushy black and white ringed tail. It has the curious habit of washing its food before eating it.

The **Timber Wolf** (*Canis lupus*) grows to a length of 2.8 m/6 ft. They hunt in packs, tracking their prey for long distances until it is exhausted and easily killed.

▲ *The Raccoon, a native of North America.*

The **Wapiti** (*Cervus canadensis*) is somewhat larger than the Red Deer of Europe. It was extinct in the US by 1877, due to the demand of the Order of Elks for its teeth.

ANIMALS OF SOUTH AMERICA

The **Chinchilla** (*Chincilla lanigera*) is a small grey hopping rodent, the size of a squirrel, found in the Andes of Bolivia and esteemed for its fur.

The **Coati** (*Coati mundi*) is a member of the Raccoon family but distinguished by a light-coloured face and long flexible snout with which it pokes into holes in search of food.

The **Jaguar** (*Panthera onca*) is the largest species of Felidae in South America. Its ground colour ranges from white to black, though the average is orange-tan with black spots.

The **Llama** (*Lama guanicoe*) is the larger of the two domesticated members of the Camel family, indigenous to the Andean region of Peru.

The **Tapir** (*Tapir terrestris*) of Brazil has its nose and upper lip protruding to form a short trunk. It has five front and three hind toes.

The **Two-toed Sloth** or Unau (*Choloepus choloepus*) is completely arboreal, spending its entire life hanging from the branch of a tree.

ANTARCTICA

Antarctica has three snow-free, **dry valleys** to the east of the Ross Ice Shelf. What little snow falls in these U-shaped glacial valleys is blown away or melted by surrounding sun-warmed rocks.

In 1775 Capt. James Cook described seeing part of 'a Continent or large tract of land near the Pole', proving the existence of Antarctica and demolishing the myth of the supercontinent *terra australis*.

In 1939 the US explorer Com. Richard Byrd found **coal seams** only 290 km/180 mi from the South Pole. These prove that tropical forests once grew there.

In 1998 scientists discovered some 100 species of tiny **microbes**, including lice, in ice from McMurdo Sound, Antarctica (average annual temperature –68°C/–90°F), raising the possibility of similar bacterial life on Mars.

The **Antarctic** region extends south from about 50°S, where the cold Antarctic currents sink beneath warm currents from the tropics. The Antarctic Circle, 66°32'S, is the line south of which the sun is not visible in winter.

The first undisputed sighting of the **Antarctic continent** was by Capt.

John Biscoe in 1831. He named Enderby Land after his employers, the Enderby brothers.

The **highest** point in Antarctica is the Vinson Massif, 5,140 m/16,705 ft; and the **lowest point** is the Bently Subglacial Trench, which lies 2,538 m/8,248 ft below sea level.

Until well into the 19th c, British and American **sealers** plundered the Antarctic seas for fur seals and sea elephants. In the 20th c whalers took over, with the same devastating effects on stocks.

ANTHROPOLOGY

Anthropology began as natural history, a study of the peoples encountered along the frontiers of European expansion. **Anthropologists** record customs and collect artefacts to reconstruct the history of cultures.

Anthropology is the study of human differences, cultural and biological, against a background of the nature that all humans share. Most anthropologists study human social life and culture.

Anthropologists study social and biological differences in cultures. ▶

Cultural anthropology is a broad category that sometimes includes anthropological linguistics (the study of language in non-Western cultural settings) and prehistoric archeology (the study of the human past before written records).

Physical anthropology is the specialised study of the evolutionary biology of our species. A central task in physical anthropology has been to document the sequence whereby the human line (the hominids) evolved from early primate ancestors.

Since the 1930s anthropology has been considered directly related to the **social sciences**. Anthropologists analyse and compare societies and their ways of life in search of theoretical generalisations and patterns.

The comparative study of social and cultural systems is commonly referred to as cultural anthropology. This branch of anthropology is sometimes also called **ethnology**.

The core of the **anthropological method** is fieldwork: long residence in a community and intimate participation in its daily life. The observer usually records detailed information on kinship, marriage, social organisation and subsistence activities.

Until World War II anthropologists mainly studied **tribal peoples**: American Indians, Africans, Pacific Islanders and Australian Aborigines. By living among peoples and studying their ways of life, anthropologists developed concepts, theories and methods which informed research on all peoples.

APACHE

South-western Indians, who were **fierce fighters**, the Apache warred with the Comanche and under leaders like Cochise and Geronimo tried to halt white expansion.

The **Apache** are a Native American people of the Na-dené geographical linguistic group.

The Apache believed in **many supernatural beings**. Ussen, the Giver of Life, was the most powerful.

Today the Apache live on reservations in **Arizona and New Mexico** that cover 1.2 m ha/3 m. ac.

Woven Apache **'burden' baskets** are highly prized by collectors.

APARTHEID

Apartheid (in Afrikaans, 'apartness') is the name given to the historic South African policy of 'separate development'; a rigid system of **racial segregation** designed to maintain white supremacy.

Apartheid policy officially came into effect when South Africa's **National Party** came to power in 1948. It officially classified the South African population into whites (13%), Africans (77%), Coloureds (of mixed descent, 8%) and Asians (2%).

During the late 1970s–early 1980s the government relaxed the **apartheid laws** slightly, lifting some occupational restrictions, desegregating some public facilities and repealing, in 1985, the 1948 law prohibiting intermarriage.

Mixed bathing on a beach in South Africa, after the Apartheid régime had fallen. ▶

Hendrik Frensch Verwoerd (1901–66), prime minister of South Africa (1958–66), stood for an uncompromising policy of apartheid and played a major part in setting up Bantu homelands and separate black universities.

In 1990 Pres. F. W. de Klerk committed himself to the abolition of apartheid and said that the homelands would be reincorporated into South Africa; the **Group Areas Act** of 1966 and the Land Acts (1913 and 1936) were repealed in Jun. 1991.

In accordance with the theory of **separate development** (apartheid), the South African government set aside certain areas as homelands for each of the officially recognised African ethnolinguistic groups.

Nelson Mandela (b. 1918), leader of the **African National Congress (ANC)**, served 26 years of a life sentence for sabotage, treason and conspiring to overthrow the white South African government. He sought unity among black groups and a peaceful end to apartheid.

ARAPAHO

In modern times the Arapaho of the US Plains lead an **agricultural existence** and benefit from land leases to the oil and gas industries.

In the 1840s the Arapaho ranged from south-eastern Wyoming to eastern Colorado. The **1849 California gold rush** caused their first clashes with whites.

The **Arapaho** are a Native American people of the Algonquin-Wakashan linguistic group.

The Arapaho based their **society on age distinction**. They venerated a sacred pipe. After 1870 they followed the Ghost Dance prophesying an end to white expansion.

The Plains-dwelling Arapaho, divided into northern and southern groups, were known to other tribes as **'dog eaters'**.

ARCHEOLOGY

Archeology is the branch of the humanities and social sciences that studies the material remains of humankind, and is concerned with tools and other artefacts of human culture.

Archeology is a wide-ranging subject that covers a time span of at least 3 m. years, from the first appearance of **humankind** to the present day.

There are two main types of archeologies: the archeology of everything preceding the earliest period of recorded history (**prehistoric archeology**); and

the archeology from the appearance of writing onwards (text-aided archeology).

The only source for knowledge of humankind during the prehistoric period of roughly 3 m. years is archeology – the material remains. Both archeology and **written sources** are combined to produce an account of human culture.

Archeologists attempt to reconstruct the past by analysing, dating and comparing excavated sites and artefacts. Specialist fields include **Egyptology**, Mesopotamian archeology, classical archeology, medieval archeology and American archeology.

As a methodology archeology has many aspects in common with the **natural sciences** and requires experts such as geologists, geophysicists, mineralogists, botanists, zoologists, physical anthropologists, chemists, physicists and other specialists.

In recent years a specialised field called **salvage archeology** has developed in response to the need for the quick recovery and research of finds resulting from urban expansion and modernisation projects throughout the world.

The purpose of archeological excavation is to discover the basic sequence of occupation of a site and to examine various aspects of the **artefacts** and other remains. Archeologists study the structure, dimensions and stratification of the terrain by combining horizontal and vertical cross-sections.

Hodder Westropp (1866) proposed the term 'Mesolithic', making European prehistory a 5-fold system of Old Stone Age (Paleolithic Period), Middle Stone Age (**Mesolithic** Period), New Stone Age (Neolithic Period), Bronze Age and Iron Age.

◄ *Egyptian art, found on archeological digs.*

ARCHITECTURE

Architecture is the art of building structures. The term covers the design of any structure for living or working in and the style of building of houses, churches, temples, palaces, castles at any period of history.

Byzantine architecture developed from the 4th c onwards, with churches based on a Greek cross plan (Hagia Sophia, Istanbul; St Mark's, Venice); they used formalised, symbolic painted and mosaic decorations.

Classical architecture was developed by the Greeks between the 16th and 2nd c BC, marking the beginning of architecture as an art form. Their use of codification and classical orders was modified by the Romans.

Giovanni Lorenzo Bernini and Francesco Borromini developed Mannerism by introducing curvilinear forms and incorporating sculpture and painting in buildings to give a rich and dynamic style, known as **Baroque**.

Post-Modernism in the 1980s was split into two camps in the UK: high tech, represented by Norman Foster, Richard Rogers and James Stirling, and classical, represented by Quinlan Terry or Michael Graves.

The **earliest buildings** were shelter structures, appearing during the Bronze Age circular bases constructed of dry-stone walling with thatched roofs. All over Europe the same societies erected megaliths for religious reasons: Stonehenge (*c.* 2000 BC) is an example.

The main **genres of architecture** include Classical, Byzantine, Romanesque, Gothic, Islamic, Renaissance, Baroque, Neo-Classical, Neo-Gothic, Art Nouveau, Modernism, Neo-Vernacular and Post-Modernism.

Town planning of whole cities, such as Le Corbusier's Chandigarh in India and Brasilia in Brazil, emerged as a discipline in its own right in the 1950s.

The modern Guggenheim Museum in New York. ▶

ARCTIC

From the Middle Ages to the late 18th c people believed that no one could survive in the extremes of polar cold. Nicholas of Lynn, a Franciscan friar, pictured a **magnetic North Pole** rock surrounded by whirlpools and mountains.

In 1893 Fridtjof Nansen, a Norwegian, took his ship *Fram* into the Arctic ice, where it was frozen in. Its emergence on the other side of the ocean in 1896 proved that ice drifts slowly across the Arctic Ocean.

In 1926 Adm. Richard Byrd, an American, became the first to make a **flight over the North Pole** in an aeroplane, starting from Spitsbergen. He described the Pole but made no attempt to land.

It is not possible to reach the North Pole over ice in a continuous line, as there are always breaks, called **leads**, in the ice floes.

▲ *British naval expedition to the Arctic in the mid-nineteenth century.*

Many areas in the Arctic are snow-free for a few summer months. In these **tundra** areas, lichens, mosses, grasses and bushes grow up to 1 m/3 ft high, and nearly 1,000 species of wildflowers grow there.

The **Arctic** may be defined, taking account of terrain and conditions, as the area north of around 60°N, or further north in places. The polar region itself is an ocean, not a land mass.

The **Arctic Ocean** has an area of 14,056,000 sq km/5,426,000 sq mi, and a maximum depth of 5,450 m/17,880 ft. The largest ocean, the Pacific, is about 12 times as big.

Two explorers claimed to have been **first to the North Pole** on foot: Dr Frederick A. Cook, in 1908, and Lt Robert E. Peary, in 1909. Peary is usually given credit but doubt remains.

ARGENTINA

Although the language of Argentina is **Spanish**, Italians form the largest immigrant group, while Patagonia still has a large Welsh-speaking community.

Argentina (capital: Buenos Aires) has an area of 2,780,092 sq km/1,073,399 sq mi and occupies the south-eastern part of South America.

Argentina exports cereals, animal feed, vegetable oils, machinery, iron and steel, and beef. Silver, from which it derives its name, is still the major mineral.

Argentina, discovered by Amerigo Vespucci in 1502, was a **Spanish colony** until 1816 when independence was proclaimed by Jose de San Martin.

The **population of Argentina** is 32,423,465 (1991 census) comprising 85% European, and 15% Amerindian, mestizo and other ethnic groups.

ARMIES

By the 6th c, after the western empire faded, cataphracts (heavily armoured cavalry), which were raised from landed gentry, became the key element in the armies of the **Byzantine Empire**.

Estimates of both sides' armies at the **Battle of Hastings**, in 1066, range from 10,000–50,000. Crusader armies of sometimes fewer than 2,000 faced Saracen armies 10-20 times larger.

Hannibal transported 30,000 men, horses and elephants over the Alps and defeated the Romans at the **Battle of Cannae** by enveloping and destroying their army.

The Normans sail for Hastings in 1066. ▶

▲ *Napoleon successfully led his own troops against much larger armies.*

In France, the **reforms of Charles VII** established the basic organisational forms of modern armies, and his 25,000-man army stunned Europe with its effectiveness in Italy in 1496–97.

In Mesopotamia armies of foot soldiers using spears and bows were created as early as 3200 BC. Warfare was revolutionised (2500 BC) by **chariots** drawn by asses and horses.

In the 13th c, **Mongol armies** could muster between 250,000–1 m. men, overcoming 300,000 Chinese and 250,000 Persians. The combined forces at Crecy (1346) numbered fewer than 60,000.

In the American War of Independence, the **Continental Army** of George Washington never exceeded 15,000, and the armies joined at Yorktown barely exceeded 25,000 men.

In the early 1990s, the **US Army's active** strength of about 550,000, including 80,000 women, was organised in 14 divisions and almost 50 separate brigades, regiments and groups.

Napoleon opposed 500,000 allied troops at Dresden in 1813 with 300,000. Returning from exile in 1815, he raised another half-million troops as allied armies of some 700,000 converged on Waterloo.

The Persians, under Cyrus the Great, refined the concept of the standing army by using infantry and cavalry and establishing a system of **discipline**.

ART DECO

Although the movement began *c.* 1910, the term 'Art Deco' was not applied to it until 1925, when it was coined from the title of the seminal Paris design exhibition, ***Exposition Internationale des Arts Décoratifs et Industriels Modernes***.

Art Deco grew out of a conscious effort to simplify the elaborate turn-of-the-century Art Nouveau style. A new aesthetic developed as the machine age became dominant. Clean lines, aerodynamism and **symmetry** are some characteristics of Art Deco.

Art Deco, style of design popular in the 1920s and 1930s, was used primarily in furniture, jewellery, textiles and interior decor, although graphic arts were highly influenced. Its sleek, streamlined forms convey elegance and sophistication.

Leading **designers** of the 1920s and 1930s (Art Deco) were Jacques Émile Ruhlmann in furniture, Jean Dunand in lacquer-work, Jean Puiforcat in silver and Lalique in jewellery.

Principal European monuments of Art Deco were Ruhlmann's Paris exhibition rooms, Le Pavillon d'un Collectioneur (exhibition, 1925) and the *grand salon* (1930) of the French liner *Normandie*. Art Deco **design** in the US includes Radio City Music Hall (1931) and William van Alen's Chrysler Building (1930).

Two of Art Deco's earliest designers were the couturier Paul Poiret and the jeweller and glassmaker **René Lalique**. Important influences were the Russian ballet producer Sergey Diaghilev's *Ballets Russes* (est. 1909).

ART NOUVEAU

Annual exhibitions of the Arts and Crafts Exhibition Society, beginning in 1888, helped disseminate Art Nouveau and a new magazine, **The Studio** (est. 1893), helped spread it to Europe.

Art Nouveau borrowed **motifs** from sources as varied as Japanese prints, Gothic architecture and the symbolic paintings of the 18th-c English poet

▲ *Art Deco bangle and ring by Georges Fouquet.*

and artist William Blake to create a highly decorative style with strong elements of fantasy.

Art Nouveau had its roots in the **Arts and Crafts** movement in England (founded 1861 by William Morris), which rejected the shoddiness of some mass-production techniques. Art Nouveau elaborated Morris's manifesto.

Art Nouveau was in decline by 1910 and did not outlive World War I, succeeded by the sleekly elegant Art Deco style. It had never been a widespread style, being costly and unsuited to mass manufacture, but the style experienced a later **renaissance** (mid-20th c).

Art Nouveau, literally 'new art', a complex and innovative European art movement 1882–1910, found expression in a wide range of **art forms**: architecture, interior design, furniture, posters, glass, pottery, textiles and book illustration.

Charles Rennie Mackintosh employed a spare, austere version of Art Nouveau style in his interior design, furniture, glass and enamel work. In France Art Nouveau can be seen in Hector Guimard's Parisian Metro entrances (1898–1901) and the work of Émile Gallé, Louis Majorelle and Alphonse Mucha.

The earliest examples of Art Nouveau include the work of the English architect **Arthur Mackmurdo** (chair designed in 1882) and an engraved frontispiece for a book (*Wren's Early Churches*) of 1883, both of which exhibit the sinuous flowing lines that were to become hallmarks of Art Nouveau.

The **fabric designs** sold by Arthur Liberty in his famous London shop (est. 1875) and the illustrations of Aubrey Beardsley (e.g. *The Yellow Book*, 1894 and *Salomé*, 1894) carried English Art Nouveau to its height.

ARTISTS

Albrecht Dürer (1471–1528) was the most famous artist of Reformation Germany, widely known for his paintings, drawings, prints and theoretical writings on art, all of which had a profound influence on 16th-c artists.

Alfred Sisley (1839–99) was a French landscape painter; as a pupil in the studio of Swiss painter Charles Gabriel Gleyre, Sisley met French artists Monet and Renoir, with whom he founded the Impressionist school of painting.

Claude Oscar Monet (1840–1926) was a French Impressionist painter, who brought the study of the transient effects of natural light to its most refined expression.

Edgar Degas (1834–1917), a French painter and sculptor, whose innovative composition, skilful drawing and perceptive analysis of movement made him one of the masters of impressionism; the female ballet dancer was, for many years, his favourite theme.

Fra Angelico (c. 1400–55) was an Italian painter of the early Renaissance; important early works are the *Madonna of the Star* (1428) and *Madonna of the Linen Weavers* (1433).

Great **17th-c artists** include Bernini (1598–1680), Carracci (1560–1609), Caravaggio (1573–1619), Claude Lorrain (1600–82), Poussin (1594–1665), Rubens (1577–1640), Rembrandt (1606–69), Vermeer (1632–75) and Van Dyck (1599–1641).

Great **18th-c artists** include the following: Watteau (1684–1721), David (1748–1825), Canova (1757–1822), Tiepolo (1696–1770), Goya (1746–1828), Reynolds (1723–92), Gainsborough (1727–88) and Hogarth (1697–1764).

◄ *Claude Monet, by the artist Manet.*

Great **19th-c artists** include Delacroix (1798–1863), Ingres (1780–1867), Turner (1775–1851), Constable (1776–1837), Monet (1840–1926), Renoir (1841–1919), Cezanne (1839–1906), Van Gogh (1854–90) and Rodin (1840–1917).

Great **20th-c artists** include Picasso (1881–1973), Matisse (1869–1954), Kandinsky (1866–1944), Mondriaan (1872–1944), Dali (1904–89), Klee (1879–1940), Pollock (1912–56) and Brancusi (1876–1957).

Hans Holbein the Younger (c. 1497–1543) was a German artist, one of the most accomplished masters of Renaissance portraiture and a designer of woodcuts, stained glass and jewellery. Holbein's reputation is based on his realistic portrayals.

Jan van Eyck (1390–1441) was a Flemish painter who, along with Robert Campin in Tournai, was the founder of the Ars Nova ('new art')

of 15th-c northern late-Gothic painting, which heralded the Renaissance.

Naum Gabo (1890–1977), Russian-American sculptor, was one of the leading practitioners of 20th-c Constructivism. In 1914 he took up sculpture, producing Cubist-inspired heads and busts using cut-out sheets of metal, cardboard or celluloid.

Pablo Ruiz y Picasso (1881–1973) was a Spanish painter and sculptor, considered the greatest artist of the 20th c. He was unique as an inventor of forms, innovator of styles and techniques, master of various media and one of the most prolific artists in history.

René François Ghislain Magritte (1898–1967) was a Belgian Surrealist painter, whose first one-man exhibition was in Brussels in 1927. He is noted for works that contain an extraordinary juxtaposition of ordinary images (magic realism).

Salvador Dalí (1904–89), was a Spanish painter, writer and member of the Surrealist movement. Famous works include: *The Persistence of Memory*, *Crucifixion* (1954) and *The Sacrament of the Last Supper* (1955).

▲ *Portrait of a Princess by 17th-c artist Van Dyck.*

Wassily Kandinsky (1866–1944) was a Russian painter and theorist, whose exploration of the possibilities of abstraction made him one of the most important innovators in modern art.

ASIA

Asia is the largest continent, occupying 43,608,000 sq km/16,833,000 sq mi, 8.6% of the world's total surface **area** and 29.5% of the total land area.

Asia's **lowest point** is the Dead Sea, between Israel and Jordan, 400 m/1,310 ft below sea level; and its **highest** is Mt Everest, on the border between Nepal and China, 8,848 m/29,028 ft.

Geologically, Asia consists of the **Angara Shield**, in the north-centre, surrounded by plateaux and much younger mountains, including the Himalaya, formed within the last 50 m. years.

The earliest **civilisations** and the first farmers flourished in the Tigris and Euphrates valleys of south-western Asia, once a more fertile area.

The **Oriental Realm**, in zoogeography, covers south-east Asia. It is separated from the Palearctic Realm of northern Asia by the Himalayas.

The **taiga**, the belt of coniferous forest north of the steppes of central Asia, is the greatest region of continuous forest in the world.

ASSASSINATIONS

Franz Ferdinand (1863–1914), was the Austrian archduke whose assassination by Serbian nationalist Gavrilo Princip at Sarajevo on 28 Jun. 1914 sparked World War I.

◀ *The Dead Sea, Asia's lowest point.*

Indira Gandhi (1917–84), India's first woman PM from 1966, was assassinated by Sikh members of her own security force on 31 Oct. 1984.

John Fitzgerald Kennedy, the 35th president of the US (1961–63), was assassinated in Nov. 1963 by Lee Harvey Oswald, in Dallas, Texas, provoking outrage and widespread mourning.

Julius Caesar (100–44 BC), a military genius and major figure in Roman history, conquered Gaul and was appointed dictator for life in 44 BC. He was assassinated on the Ides of March.

Leon Trotsky (1879–1940), one of the leaders of the Russian Revolution, was exiled by Stalin (1929) and assassinated in Mexico City in 1940.

Malcolm X (1925–65), an American black nationalist, was for a time the leading spokesman for the Black Muslims to the outside world. He was assassinated in 1965 while addressing a rally in New York.

Martin Luther King, Jr. (1929–68) was a Baptist minister recognised as the leading figure of the civil-rights movement in the US. King, who in 1964 became the youngest recipient of the Nobel Peace Prize, was assassinated in 1968.

Mohandas Karamchand Gandhi (1869–1948), leader of the Indian nationalist movement and known as Mahatma ('great soul'), was one of the greatest national leaders of the 20th c. He was assassinated in Delhi on 30 Jan. 1948, by a Hindu fanatic.

Philippine political leader **Benigno Simeon Aquino** (1932–83) was assassinated (21 Aug.) upon his return to the Philippines from three years of self-imposed exile in the US. Massive demonstrations followed.

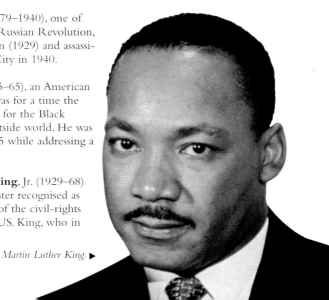

Martin Luther King. ▶

ASTEROIDS

An asteroid or **minor planet** is any of many thousands of small bodies, composed of rock and iron, that orbit the Sun.

Chiron, an object orbiting between Saturn and Uranus, was thought to be an asteroid and is now thought to be a giant cometary nucleus, about 200 km/120 mi across, made of ice with a dark crust of carbon dust.

Most **asteroids** lie in a belt between the orbits of Mars and Jupiter and are thought to be fragments left over when the Solar System formed.

Over 100,000 asteroids may exist but their total **mass** is only a few hundredths of the mass of the Moon.

Some asteroids are on orbits that bring them close to Earth and some, such as **Apollo asteroids**, cross Earth's orbit; some may be former comets that have lost their gas.

Some asteroids have been named including **Ceres**, the largest at 9,400 km/584 mi in diameter, Vesta, the brightest as seen from Earth, Eros and Icarus.

The **first asteroid** was discovered by Italian astronomer Guiseppe Piazzi at the Palermo Observatory, Sicily on 1 Jan. 1801.

ASTROLOGY

Astrologers create charts called **horoscopes**, which map the positions of heavenly bodies at certain times, such as when a person is born.

Astrological beliefs are reflected in **Elizabethan** and **Jacobean** literature. Kings and public figures had their own astrologers; Queen Elizabeth I's astrologer was John Dee.

Astrology is the study of how events on earth may be influenced or interpreted by the positions and movements of the sun, moon, planets and stars.

Astrology originated in the taking of astral omens for state purposes in

Mesopotamia 4,000 years ago and developed into a system for predicting the fates of individuals.

Astrology was a strongly held belief in ancient **Babylon**; it spread to the Mediterranean world and was used by the Greeks and Romans. It exerted a powerful influence in the Middle Ages.

Chinese astrology is based on a 60-year cycle and a lunar calendar. Its signs change yearly and are named after animals; Rat, Ox, Tiger, Hare, Dragon, Snake, Horse, Sheep, Monkey, Rooster, Dog and Pig.

Differing forms of astrology developed in **China and India**, as well as among the Maya, but in the West the coming of Christianity forced it to the sidelines.

Each sign of the Zodiac is believed to represent a set of human characteristics. A **sun sign** is the sign that the sun occupied at the time of a person's birth.

In more modern times many politicians and royalty have turned to astrology. The Renaissance was partly set off by psychologist **Carl Jung** who used archetypal myths and symbols in astrology in his counselling.

The signs are further split into **four elements**. Fire (concerned with will); Aries, Leo, Sagittarius. Earth (material); Taurus, Virgo, Capricorn. Air (thought); Gemini, Libra, Aquarius. Water (emotions); Cancer, Scorpio, Pisces.

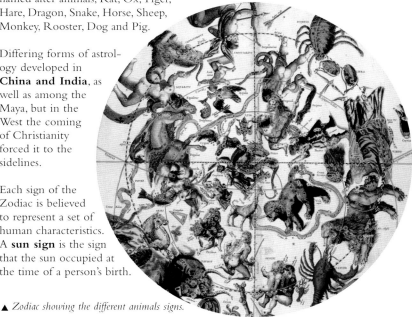

▲ *Zodiac showing the different animals signs.*

The word **astrology** comes from the Greek *astron* meaning 'star', and *logos* meaning 'study'. It involves studying the relative position of planets and stars in the belief they influence events and personality on Earth.

Western astrology is based on 12 signs of the **zodiac**, named after constellations which are; Aries, Taurus, Gemini, Cancer, Leo, Virgo, Libra, Scorpio, Sagittarius, Capricorn, Aquarius and Pisces.

ASTRONOMY

Advances in technology, especially electronics, have led to the ability to study **radiation** from astronomical objects at all wavelengths, from radio waves to X-rays and gamma rays, building up our understanding of the universe.

Astronomy is probably the oldest

science; there are observational records of the heavens from Babylonia, Ancient China, Egypt and Mexico.

By 1609 the laws of **planetary motion** had been discovered by Johann Kepler who had used the new invention of the telescope for his work.

During the 1960s **quasars**, pulsars and celestial X-ray sources were discovered, making it an exciting decade for astronomers, topped off by the first crewed moon-landing in 1969.

In 1838 **Friedrich Bessel** made the first reasonably accurate measurement of a star's distance from the Earth, and Neptune was discovered in 1846 by mathematical prediction of its orbit.

The first true astronomers were the **Greeks** who deduced that the Earth was a sphere and set about trying to measure its size.

The introduction of photography meant **photographic star charts** were produced by 1887, and in 1889 Edward Barnard took the first photographs of the Milky Way.

◄ *The planet Neptune.*

ATHENS

A major centre for banking and **mercantile business**, Athens also has textile mills, distilleries, breweries, factories, shipyards and engineering works.

Athens is rich in classical ruins, notably **the Acropolis** and the temple of Theseus, and many modern landmarks, such as the Olympic Stadium of 1896.

Athens lies at the southern end of the **plain of Attica** overlooking the Saronic Gulf on the south-eastern side of Greece, with a range of mountains to the north.

Settled since Neolithic times, **Athens** was the centre of Greek civilisation from the 7th c BC, though the modern city dates only from 1833 when it became the seat of government.

The **population of Athens** is 885,737 (est. 1991). A further 200,000 live in nearby Piraieus, the port serving the Greek capital.

ATHLETICS

Carl Lewis won a record **eight gold medals** at the World Championshps between 1983 and 1991 – two long jumps, three individual 100 m and three 4x100 m relays.

Dick Fosbury (US) won the Olympic high jump title in 1968 by clearing 2.24 m with a radical new style which came to be called 'the **Fosbury Flop**'.

Lasse Viren (Finland) achieved the **Olympic** 5,000 m and 10,000 m **'double'** twice, the only man to do so, in 1972 and 1976.

◄ *Gold medallist Carl Lewis.*

Mary Rand became the **first British woman** to win an Olympic field event when she broke the long jump world record in 1964 to win the gold medal.

Paavo Nurmo (Finland) won five gold medals at the 1924 Olympics – 1,500 m 5,000 m, 10,000 m cross-country, the 3,000 m team and the cross-country team – the **most by one athlete at a single Games**.

The **longest winning sequence** for a track event is 122 races at 400 m hurdles by Edwin Moses between 1977 and 1987.

ATMOSPHERE

About 51% of incoming **solar radiation** is absorbed by the earth's surface, 14% by the atmosphere. The rest is reflected by the atmosphere, clouds, oceans and land.

Close to the earth's surface, differences in **air** temperature and pressure cause air to circulate between the equator and the poles. This is the origin of surface winds and high-level jet streams.

In the **lower atmosphere**, nitrogen occupies 78%, oxygen 21%, argon 0.93% and other elements, such as rare gases, less than 0.1%.

In the lowest 15 km/9.5 mi of the atmosphere, temperatures decrease with **altitude** at an average rate of 6.5°C per km. Thus upland areas are cooler and have shorter growing seasons than lowlands.

The amount of **water vapour** in the atmosphere is about 14,000 cu km/33,580 cu mi. This is about one ten-thousandth of the total volume of the earth's surface waters (c. 1,400 million cu km).

The atmosphere blocks out many harmful **ultraviolet rays** and protects the earth from extremes of temperature by limiting incoming solar radiation and escaping re-radiated heat.

The atmosphere consists of **layers**, the main ones being the troposphere (up to 10 km/6 mi), stratosphere (10–50 km/6–30 mi), mesosphere (50–100 km/30–60 mi) and thermosphere (100–500 km/60–300 mi).

The **atmosphere** that surrounds the earth is a blanket of gases that enable life to exist. Gravity holds more than 80% of atmospheric gases within about 20 km/12.5 mi of the earth's surface.

The natural balance in the atmosphere may be distorted by the **green-house effect**. Gases such as carbon dioxide build up, trapping heat that should escape into space.

AUSTRALASIA

Australia lies across the **Tropic of Capricorn**. It thus consists of desert and tropical grassland in the interior and equatorial forest in the north, while a Mediterranean climate prevails in the south.

The **Australasian Realm** in zoogeography covers Australia, New Zealand and parts of the East Indies. It has been isolated for so long that it contains animals found nowhere else, such as kangaroos and koalas.

The Australian mainland (that is, excluding Tasmania and small islands) is the **smallest continent**, with an area of 7,614,500 sq km/2,939,960 sq mi.

The first settlers to reach Australia crossed the archipelago of the East Indies – by '**island-hopping**' – about 40,000 years ago during the last Ice Age.

The **highest** point in Australasia is Mt Wilhelm, Papua New Guinea, 4,508 m/14,790 ft; while the **lowest point** is Lake Eyre, in South Australia, 16 m/52 ft.

AUSTRALIA

Although wool and mutton still account for half of **Australia's exports**, minerals (iron, bauxite, copper and lead) are increasingly important.

Australia (capital: Canberra) in the south Pacific is the smallest continent and largest island in the world, with an area of 7,686,848 sq km/2,967,909 sq mi.

Captain Cook charted New South Wales in 1770 and Botany Bay was founded in 1788. The **Commonwealth of Australia** was formed in 1901 from six British colonies.

Remote from any other continent, **Australia** is noted for its unique fauna and flora, including the kangaroo, emu, wombat, platypus and koala.

The **population of Australia** is 17,210,800 (est. 1991) comprising 95.2% European, 1.5% Aboriginal, 1.3% Asian and 2% other. About 27% are Roman Catholic, 24% Anglican and 17.4% other Protestant.

AUSTRIA

Austria (capital: Vienna) is a landlocked state in central Europe, with an area of 83,856 sq km/32,377 sq mi. It is bordered by the Czech Republic, Hungary, Slovenia, Italy, Switzerland and Germany.

Austria is self-sufficient in foodstuffs and exports machinery, transport equipment, electrical goods, clothing and textiles.

In 1996 **Austria** celebrated the millennium of the first documented use of the country's name – Ostarrichi (eastern state), recorded in a deed of Emperor Otto III.

Once the centre of the Habsburg Empire, **Austria** was annexed by Nazi Germany in 1938 but regained its

freedom in 1945, when a republic was re-established.

The **population of Austria** is 7,815,000 (1991 census) comprising 84.3% Roman Catholic, 5.6% Lutheran, 6% non-religious and 0.1% Jewish.

AZTECS

At his meals, **King Montezuma II** (1466–1520), the last Aztec ruler, enjoyed a variety of meat dishes, including turkey, hare and pigeon, and drank chocolate from a gold vessel.

Aztec kings were elected monarchs, presiding over a highly developed **legal system**, with a supreme judge and magistrates' court for each city.

Aztecs are known for their gigantic **architecture**, and their intricate gold, jade and turquoise jewellery. They did not use the wheel and had no domestic animals.

◀ *The Royal palace in Austria.*

For Aztecs **war** was a test of manhood and a religious experience. They maintained hospitals for the wounded, and strictly observed the diplomatic immunity of envoys.

The Aztecs, the war-like civilisation which arose in the 14th c, built their capital city, **Tenochtitlán**, on the lake where Mexico City stands today.

The **Spanish conquistadors'** victory over the Aztecs in 1521 was achieved with the help of an armoury of European diseases, including smallpox, measles and influenza.

Tributes from many vassal states to the Aztecs included taxes, a quota of warriors, and a steady supply of victims for **sacrificial rites**.

Using pictographs, the Aztecs kept accurate records. They employed a complex **calendar**, in which there were 18 months, each with 20 days, and each day had its own god.

▲ *Mexico City, where the Aztec capital of Tenochtitlán once stood.*

BACTERIA

Bacteria are microscopic organisms living in soil, water and organic matter (the bodies of plants and animals). They are important because of their chemical effects.

Bacterial forms occur in three main types: the *bacillus* or rod shape, the *coccus* or spherical form, and the *spirillum* which is spirally twisted.

Bacteriology is the study of bacteria, which developed alongside the microscope. The first to observe microorganisms was the Dutch naturalist A. van Leeuwenhoek in 1683.

Dairy bacteria are employed in the production of curds, sour milk, butter and cheeses, and include *Bacillus bulgaricus* and *Bacillus acidi lactici*.

Nitrification is the process by which plants absorb nitrogen in the form of ammonia. J. H. Schloessing (1877) was the first to realise that this depended on bacteria.

Nitrogen fixation is the process whereby plants (notably legumes) enrich the soil. Such bacteria as *Azobacter chroococcum* utilise the gas dissolved in soil solution.

Sewage disposal in sedimentation and septic tanks depends largely on the action of aerobic bacteria. Since 1913 the activation of sludge has accelerated the process.

BADMINTON

Badminton takes its name from **Badminton House**, the family seat of the Duke of Beaufort whose family and friends played an early form of the game in the 19th c.

Rudy Hartono of Indonesia, with eight victories between 1968 and 1976, has won the most singles titles at the **All-England Championships**.

The **longest recorded match** was the 1997 men's World Championship singles final when Peter Rasmussen (Denmark) defeated Sun Jun (China) after 2 hours 4 minutes.

The men's World Team Championships are contested for the **Thomas Cup**, donated in 1940 by Sir George Thomas, who won 21 All-England titles before World War II.

The most successful nation in Thomas Cup history is **Indonesia** with 10 team titles between 1958 and 1996.

The women's World Team Championships are known as the **Uber Cup** after Betty Uber who represented England a then-record 37 times between 1926 and 1951.

BANGKOK

Bangkok boasts numerous rice mills, sawmills and factories for processing teak, and exports commodities including hides and rubber.

Bangkok is located on the Menam Chao Phya river, upstream from the **Gulf of Siam**. A network of *klongs* (canals) are still used for water-borne traffic.

Most of Bangkok dates from 1800 but includes the **Royal Palace**, the picturesque temple of Wat Arun and the Chapel of the Emerald Buddha, erected in 1785 by Rama I.

The chief city and port of **Thailand**, Bangkok was a small fort and farming village before King Taksin (1767–82) used it as his base against Burma in 1769.

◀ *Dairy bacteria include bacillus bulgaicus.*

BANKING

17th c English goldsmiths pioneered the lending of gold by issuing **promissory notes**. The total value of these banknotes exceeded the total value of the gold.

In 1833 corporate banks in the UK were allowed to accept and transfer deposits; the **issuing of banknotes** became the monopoly of the Bank of England.

The **first modern banks** were established in the 17th c. Notable examples include the Bank of England (1694) and the Swedish Riksbank (1656).

The **Knights Templar** stored valuables, granted loans and transferred funds from country to country as early as the 12th c. They wielded immense power over monarchs.

The world-renowned **Swiss commercial banking system** is dominated by the 'big four'; Union Bank, Swiss Bank Corporation, Credit Suisse and the Volksbank.

There is a national network of over 12,000 **commercial banks** in the US. Only 5% of these banks control over 40% of deposits.

BAROQUE

A third Baroque style developed in Rome *c.* 1630, the so-called **High Baroque**; it is generally considered the most characteristic mode of 17th-c art, with its exuberance, emotionalism, theatricality and unrestrained energy.

Among the general **characteristics of Baroque art** is a sense of movement, energy and tension; strong contrasts of light and shadow enhance the dramatic effects of many paintings and sculptures.

Baroque painting in England was dominated by the presence of Rubens and Van Dyck, who inspired an entire generation of portraitists. British sculpture was influenced equally by Italian and Flemish styles.

◀ *Van Dyck's work reflected the dramatic styles of the Baroque*

Baroque, the style dominating the art and architecture of Europe and European colonies in the Americas (1600s) and in some places until 1750, was launched by the Counter-Reformation of the Roman Catholic church against Protestantism in Italy.

Infinite space is often suggested in Baroque paintings or sculptures; throughout the Renaissance and into the Baroque period, painters sought a grander sense of space and truer depiction of **perspective** in their works.

The roots of Baroque styles are found in the art of Italy. Annibale Carracci and Michelangelo Merisi (called **Caravaggio**) were the two artists at the forefront of early Baroque. Caravaggio's art is influenced by naturalism, Michelangelo and the High Renaissance.

The school that developed around Annibale Carracci attempted to rid art of its mannered complications by returning to the High Renaissance principles of clarity, monumentality and balance. This **Baroque classicism** remained important throughout the 17th c.

Writers such as the 19th-c Swiss cultural historian Jakob Burckhardt considered Baroque the decadent end of the Renaissance. As an art form it encompassed vast regional distinctions, evident in the vastly different **styles** of, for example, Rembrandt and Bernini.

▲ *The Vatican in Italy, where the Baroque style began.*

BASEBALL

Baseball is similar to cricket and rounders. Alexander Cartwright Jr drew up the **rules of baseball** in 1845 and the first organised club was the New York Knickerbockers.

The two US baseball leagues are the American League (AL) and the National League (NL). The annual seasonal winners from each League contest **the World Series**.

In 1961 Roger Maris scored 61 **home runs** for the New York Yankees to break Babe Ruth's long-standing record of 60, also achieved for the Yankees in 1927.

In a **career** stretching from 1954 to 1976 Hank Aaron scored a record 755 **home runs** for Milwaukee Braves (NL), Atlanta Braves (NL) and Milwaukee Brewers (AL).

New York Yankees have been the most **successful team in the World Series**. From a record 34 appearances, they have most victories, 23, between 1923 and 1996.

Pitcher Cy Young had a **record 511 wins** and record 749 complete games from a total of 906 games and 815 starts in his career between 1890 and 1911.

BASKETBALL

Basketball was invented by **Dr James Naismith** at the Training School of the International YMCA College at Springfield, Massachussets in Dec. 1891.

The Los Angeles Lakers won an NBA record **33 games in succession** from 5 Nov. 1971 to 7 Jan. 1972.

Since the inauguration of the **National Basketball Association (NBA)** in 1947 the Boston Celtics have been the most successful club with 16 titles between 1957 and 1986.

The **highest career average** for players who exceed 10,000 points is the 31.7 of Michael Jordan who scored 26,920 in 848 games for the Chicago Bulls between 1984 and 1997.

The **highest-scoring player** in NBA history is Kareem Abdul-Jabbar who scored 38,387 points at an average of 24.6 for the Milwaukee Bucks and Los Angeles Lakers.

The **record winning margin** in an NBA game is 68 points; the Cleveland Cavaliers beat the Miami Heat 148–80 on 17 Dec. 1991.

BATTLES

After three days of savage fighting at **Gettysburg**, Meade's Union army beat off Lee's Confederates in the American Civil War (1861–65). From then the war swung to the Union side.

At **El Alamein**, Montgomery faced Rommel 'the Desert Fox'. The latter lost over half of his army and the Germans were driven out of Africa.

Facing a French force of 25,000, Henry V deployed his 6,000 infantry along a

narrow front and slaughtered the French nobility at **Agincourt** in 1415.

In the English Civil Wars at **Edgehill** (1642), Charles I faced a Parliamentarian army under the Earl of Essex. The losses were even, but the moral advantage was with the King.

In the pass of **Thermopylae**, 1,000 Greeks, under Leonidas, held back a 150,000-strong Persian invasion force. Every one of them died after delaying the Persians for two days.

Lobositz was the first setback for the alliance that pitted itself against Frederick the Great's bluecoats. It was the opening of the Seven Years' War (1756–63).

Napoleon faced Wellington near the Belgian village of **Waterloo**. Before he could crush the Anglo-Dutch force he was attacked in the flank by Blucher's Prussians.

Napoleons' brilliant campaign of 1805 reached a devasting conclusion when he decimated the Austro-Russian army at **Austerlitz** inflicting 16,000 casualties and capturing another 11,000.

▲ *Napoleon Bonaparte.*

Near **Saratoga**, after two ferocious battles with Gates's American rebel army (at Freeman's Farm and Bemis Heights), the British general, Burgoyne was forced to surrender.

The **Duke of Marlborough**'s 50,000-strong army proved unbeatable against the Franco-Bavarian's under Marshall Tallard at Blenheim in this crucial battle in the War of the Spanish Succession.

BEIJING

Beijing is the intellectual, academic and administrative centre of China, with a wide range of light industries. It is also a major tourist attraction.

Beijing lies at the northern apex of the alluvial **Plain of North China**, near the outlet from the mountains of the road to Mongolia.

Formerly Peking or Peiping, Beijing became the **capital of China** *c.* 1267, although the city itself dates from the Chou dynasty in the 12th c BC.

Many imposing buildings were erected in Beijing by successive dynasties, notably the Porcelain Pagoda and the Temple of Heavenly Peace in the **Forbidden City**.

The **population of Beijing** is over 6,800,000 (1990 census), making it the second largest city in China.

The Forbidden City in Beijing. ▶

BELGIUM

Belgium (capital: Brussels) in north-western Europe has an area of 30,518 sq km/11,783 sq mi and is bordered by France, Luxembourg and the Netherlands.

Belgium derives its name from **the Belgae**, a Celtic tribe whom Julius Caesar described as the most courageous of all the tribes of Gaul.

Belgium's exports consist mainly of machinery, cars, textiles, chemicals and steel. It is also one of the major producers of cut diamonds.

Nicknamed 'the cockpit of Europe' because of the wars fought over it, Belgium broke away from Holland in 1831 to become an **independent kingdom**.

The **population of Belgium** is 9,978,000 (est. 1991), comprising 90% Roman Catholic, 1.1% Muslim and 0.4% Protestant. French, Flemish and German are the official languages.

BERLIN

An important centre of the wool and silk trades, **Berlin** produces carpets, hosiery and clothing. Engineering and manufacturing of all kinds are carried on.

Berlin, **capital of Germany**, was founded in 1237. It developed rapidly from 1646, in the reign of the Great Elector Frederick William.

The destruction by fire of the Reichstag in 1933, the parliament building in Berlin, was the pretext for a clampdown on political opponents by **Adolf Hitler** (1889-1945).

The **population of Berlin** is 3,376,800 (1989 census).

BIBLE

Monks in 7th-c England created superb illuminated **Gospel Books**: the Book of Durrow and the Lindisfarne Gospel Book are two of the most spectacular.

The **Authorised King James Version of the Bible**, produced in 1611, immediately won the hearts of the people, and remained for centuries the Bible of every English-speaking country.

The **Bible** is the collection of books, the Old Testament and the New Testament, which Christians regard as the revelation of God's word.

The first five books of the Bible, the Law, are called the **Pentateuch** (from a Greek word meaning 'five scrolls').

The **first printed European book** was the Bible and by 1500 it was being printed in German, Italian and French (the English printed version did not appear until 1526).

The **New Testament**, 27 books written within the century following the death of Jesus, contains the four Gospels, the Acts of the Apostles, 21 letters, and the Book of Revelation.

The **Old Testament** is substantially the Hebrew Bible, and comprises 39 books in three divisions; the Law, the Prophets and the Writings.

There is disagreement among scholars as to whether the **Apocrypha** should be considered as inspired Scripture. It contains 14 books, and dates from *c.* 300 BC.

While he was bishop of Wearmouth Abbey in Northumberland, **Abbot Ceolfrith** commissioned a bible for presentation to the Pope. This is the oldest known complete Latin Bible.

BICYCLES

Alexander Moulton engineered a bike with a **suspension spring** that could be adjusted to the weights of different riders, and a seat that could be adjusted for people of differing heights.

By 1880 a new **safety model** had been developed that was very similar to modern designs. In 1899, the US produced over 1 m. bicycles, but the development of the car industry destroyed the market.

In 1870 James Starley constructed the first **Penny Farthing** or Ordinary Bicycle. It had wire-spoked wheels and later had optional speed gears.

The **first bicycle** was a French-designed vehicle consisting of a beam with two wheels attached. It did not have handlebars and was driven by pushing the feet on the ground.

The **Frankencycle**, built by Dave Moore, is reputed to be the world's largest. First ridden in 1989, it has a wheel diameter of 3.05 m/10 ft.

The style and form of the **modern bicycle** was created in 1840 by the Scot, Kirkpatrick Macmillan, who attached driving levers and pedals to the basic machine, as well as handlebars for steering.

The velocipede became popular in France *c.* 1855; both the wheels and the frame were made of wood. In England this design was known as the '**boneshaker**' for obvious reasons.

BIOLOGY

Biology is the study of all living things and has been practised since the first studies of the structure and behaviour of animals by the Greek Alcmaeon of Croton in 500 BC.

Carolus Linneaus (Karl Linne) established **taxonomy**, or the naming of species, when he published his systematic classification of plants in 1736.

In 450 BC **Hippocrates** of Cos undertook the first anatomical studies of man and by AD 175 Galen had established the basis of anatomy and physiology.

A better understanding of **biological structures** was achieved in the 17th c when William Harvey described blood circulation and the heart as a pump, whilst Robert Hooke used a microscope to study plants' cellular structure.

Retinoblastoma, the first identified human **cancer gene**, was finally isolated by researchers at the Massachusetts Ear and Eye Infirmary in 1985.

The blueprint for our genetic make-up was discovered by James Watson and Francis Crick in 1953 when they described the double-helix structure of **DNA**.

When Charles Darwin first published *On the Origin of Species* in 1859 (giving his theory of **evolution** by natural selection); he was ridiculed, but now his theories are the basis of our evolutionary thought.

Human biologist Charles Darwin. ▶

BIRDS

Birds are feathered, two-legged creatures which developed the ability to fly. They lay eggs and incubate them, usually in some form of nest.

The **Bald Eagle** (*Haliaeetus leucocephalus*), national emblem of the US, is distinguished by its snowy-white head and tail. Virtually extinct except in Alaska, it has now been reintroduced.

The **Condor** (*Vultur gryphus*) is one of the world's largest flying birds, with a wing span of 3 m/10 ft and a head and neck bare of feathers.

The **Emu** (*Dromiceius novaehollandiae*), next to the ostrich the largest living bird, inhabits open country, feeding on fruit, roots and herbage.

The **Macaw** (*Ara macao*), with its red, blue and yellow plumage, is the most colourful of all parrots. With its huge curved bill it can crack Brazil nuts easily.

The **Toucan** (*Ramphastes toco*) of Guyana is distinguished by its enormous bill. In order to sleep, the bird must turn its head backwards and rest it on its back.

The young of the **Hoatzin** (*Opisthocomus hoatzin*) of the South American rain forests have claws on their wings, enabling them to climb trees.

BLACKFOOT

In modern times the Blackfoot tribe of the US Plains farm and ranch in **Montana** and **Canada**.

The **Blackfoot** are a Native American people of the Algonquin-Wakashan geographical linguistic group.

The hostile Blackfoot lived on the Missouri and North Saskatchewan Rivers west of the Rocky Mountains (19th c). **Diminishing buffalo herds** drove them to starvation.

The nomadic Blackfoot of the American Plains based their culture on the **horse and buffalo**. They grew tobacco, used in the eight-day, summer Sun Dance.

The Plains Blackfoot Indians of the US derived their name from the **black-dyed moccasins** they wore.

Egypt by 1500 BC.

Botany is the branch of biology that deals with plant life and includes the study of the properties of individual plants, types and groups.

Bryology is a branch of botany which deals with the study of mosses, horn-

BOTANY

Botanic Gardens are places where plants are arranged according to some system of classification. The earliest was founded by Thotmes III at Karnak,

worts and liverworts. The word is derived from the Greek *bryon* (moss).

Paleobotany or plant paleontology is the branch of botany that studies and classifies the plants of the geologic past, using fossils and vegetation preserved in rocks.

Plant morphology is that branch of botany concerned with the form and structure of plants, including the arrangement and relationships of organs and cells.

Plant physiology is that branch of botany which deals with the study of the life processes and functions of plants, their organs and tissues.

Systematic botany is the study of the arrangement and classification of plants and involves the concept of genera and species, nomenclature and plant evolution.

BOXING

Jane Crouch created history when she became the **first female** to be granted a **professional licence** by the British Boxing Board of Control in Jun. 1998.

Joe Louis (US) is the **longest-reign-ing world champion**. He held the world heavyweight title for 11 years and 252 days between 1936 and 1949.

On 6 Mar. 1976 Wilfred Benitez (US) won the WBA Light Junior Welterweight world title aged 17 years and 176 days; he is the **youngest world champion**.

The 8th Marquess of Queensberry gave his name to the **modern rules of boxing** in 1865 which introduced the ring, rounds and gloves to super-sede bare-knuckle fighting.

Thomas 'the Hitman' Hearns became the first man to win **world titles at five different weight categories**, from welterweight to light-heavy-weight, between 1980 and 1991.

When George Foreman knocked out Michael Moorer to win the WBA heavyweight title on 5 Nov. 1994 he became the **oldest world champion**, aged 45 years and 287 days.

BRAZIL

Brazil (capital: Brasilia) comprises a third of South America, bordering every country except Ecuador and Chile, with an area of 8,511,996 sq km/3,286,500 sq mi.

Brazil exports a very wide range of manufactured goods. The main agri-cultural products are soya, orange juice, coffee and tobacco.

Cabral named his discovery 'the island of the True Cross', but this was soon abandoned in favour of **Brazil**, a tree noted for its dye wood.

Discovered by the Portuguese Pedro Alvares Cabral in 1500, **Brazil** was an independent empire (1822–89) and, since 1946, a federal republic.

The **population of Brazil** is 153,322,000 (est. 1991), comprising 53% white, 22% mulatto, 12% mestizo, 11% black, 0.8% Japanese, 0.1% Amerindian and 1.1% other.

BRIDGES

Eads Bridge (1874) was the first major bridge built entirely of steel, excluding the pier foundations. Designed by James Buchanan Eads, it has three arch spans; two are 153 m/502 ft, the middle 159 m/520 ft.

The **Forth Bridge** over the Firth of Forth in Scotland

▲ The Forth Bridge in Scotland.

(Benjamin Baker, 1890) has two cantilevered spans of 521 m/1,710 ft, which made it the world's longest bridge on its completion.

The **George Washington Bridge**, completed in 1931 with a span of 1,000 m/3,500 ft, is the heaviest single-span steel suspension bridge built to date, and its original ratio of girder depth to span was an amazing 1:350.

The success of the George Washington Bridge design led to the building of bridges such as the **Golden Gate** Bridge, San Francisco (Joseph Strauss, 1937). Its span is 1,280 m/4,200 ft.

The **Konohana suspension bridge** carries a four-lane high-way on a slender, steel box-beam deck only 3 m/10 ft deep. Spanning 303 m/984 ft it was the first major suspension bridge to use a single cable.

George Washington, first US president. ▲

£5

NICKLAUS

The Royal Bank of Scotland plc

PROMISE TO PAY THE BEARER ON DEMAND

FIVE POUNDS

STERLING

AT THEIR HEAD OFFICE HERE IN EDINBURGH
BY ORDER OF THE BOARD
14th JULY 2005

JWN0596969

GROUP
CHIEF EXECUTIVE

£5

JACK NICKLAUS

5 POUNDS

St Andrews Winner 1970 and 1978

Hole	Yards	Par	Hole	Yards	Par
1	376	4	10	380	4
2	453	4	11	174	3
3	397	4	12	348	4
4	480	4	13	465	4
5	568	5	14	618	5
6	412	4	15	456	4
7	390	4	16	423	4
8	175	3	17	455	4
9	352	4	18	357	4

The Royal Bank of Scotland plc

1970—68 1978—71
69 72
69
73
73
72

The single-span bridge under construction across the **Messina Straits** between Sicily and mainland Italy will have a span of 3,320 m/10,892 ft, the world's longest by far.

The **Newport Transporter Bridge** (built Wales 1906) is a high-level suspension bridge which carries a car suspended a few feet above the water.

BRONZE AGE

Bronze tools revolutionised the skills of woodworking and stoneworking and served as a new medium of artistic expression. From the beginning of the 3rd millennium BC, members of the Mesopotamian elite were buried with luxurious bronze objects.

In China the use of bronze was introduced relatively late, probably during the early phases of the Shang dynasty (c. 1600–1027 BC). From 2500–1200 BC, the Aegean civilisations of the Minoans and Mycenaeans established extensive **trade routes** into central Europe to obtain tin and copper.

The **Bronze Age** is the stage of prehistoric cultural development when bronze, an alloy of copper and tin, first came into regular use in the manufacture of tools, weapons and other objects.

The **Bronze Age** marks the transition between the Neolithic Period (a phase of the Stone Age), when stone tools and weapons were predominant, and the succeeding Iron Age, when the large-scale use of metals was introduced.

The Bronze Age occurred at different times around the world. In most areas, the development of bronze technology was preceded by an intermediary period when copper was used (**Copper Age**), which did not occur in some areas (Ancient China and prehistoric Britain).

The Bronze Age spread throughout Europe c. 1800 BC, chiefly through the influence of the **Uneticians** (named after the archeological site of Unetice, in central Europe), a farming and metalworking people living close to the ore sources.

Celtic bronze figure. ▶

The term 'Bronze Age' originated as part of the **three-age system** (Stone Age, Bronze Age and Iron Age) introduced (1816) by Christian Thomsen, a Danish museum curator. The three-age system was later validated through archeological excavations.

BRUSSELS

Brussels (literally 'the place in the marsh') began as a place of refuge for the Gallo-Romans, attacked by the Franks in AD 5th c.

Brussels, capital of Belgium and the province of Brabant, occupies a central position about 112 km/90 mi from the North Sea, in a valley of the River Senne.

The *Grande Place* in **Brussels** is one of the most picturesque public squares in Europe and contains the ornate Town Hall and Royal Palace.

The **population of Brussels** is 137,966 (est. 1990), but including the surrounding region it is 970,501.

BUCHAREST

Bucharest is renowned for its elegant thoroughfares, of which the Calea Victorei, named in honour of victory at Plevna in 1877, is the finest.

Bucharest lies in a slight hollow, traversed by the River Dimbovitza, with a range of low hills on the west and plains on the other sides.

Built by King Mircea (1383–1419) as a bastion against the Turks, **Bucharest** was frequently contested by the Turks, Russians and Austrians.

The **industries of Bucharest** include petroleum-refining, extraction of vegetable oils, furniture, brandy, tanning and the manufacture of machinery, textiles and leather goods.

The **population of Bucharest** is 2,036,894 (1989 census). Before World War II, it had a large Jewish population, but few now remain.

BUDAPEST

Among the many imposing buildings of **Budapest** erected in the 19th c, the finest is the Parliament on the left bank, a Gothic edifice built 1883–1902.

Budapest, capital of Hungary, lies on both banks of the Danube, with a flat plain on the Pest side and beetling cliffs on the Buda side.

Known as Aquincum in Roman times, **Budapest** was the separate towns of

▲ *Budapest and the River Danube.*

Buda and Pesth until 1872 when they united to form a single municipality.

The **population of Budapest** is 2,016,132 (est. 1990), mainly Roman Catholic but with large Protestant and Jewish communities.

Traditionally the centre of the trade in livestock, grain, wines and wool, **Budapest** now has textile, chemical, brewing, distilling and tobacco factories.

BUDDHISM

Although Buddha did not deny the existence of gods, his teachings centred upon the insight that liberation comes through **meditation** and the renunciation of desire.

Buddhist ethical conduct is defined by the Five Precepts, and Buddhists follow the Four Noble Truths. The way to enlightenment is by following the **Noble Eightfold Path**.

Buddhists believe that humans have free will, but that all actions have consequences (*karma*). If desires and suffering (*dhukka*) are allowed to die down, *karma* too dies down.

Bronze figure of the Buddha. ▶

During a life of austerity and study, while meditating under the sacred **bo tree** Buddha achieved his liberation from fear and suffering at last.

From the 3rd c BC Buddhism **spread** throughout India and later into the Far East, the first world religion to spread beyond the society from which it originated.

Siddharta Gautama Buddha was born *c*. 586 BC in Nepal, the latest in a continuing line of buddhas; his life lies at the heart of Buddhism.

Siddharta Gautama was a prince and led a **sheltered life** until one day he re-evaluated his lifestyle and left his family in search of truth.

BUENOS AIRES

At the head of the Avenida de Mayo in the heart of **Buenos Aires** stands the presidential palace, known as the Casa Rosada (pink house) on account of its paintwork.

Buenos Aires, the capital of Argentina, is situated on the low-lying western shore of the River Plate estuary on the north-east side of the country.

In 1536 Pedro de Mendoza founded a settlement, later abandoned and re-occupied in 1586 by Juan de Garay. The origin of the name **Buenos Aires** is unknown.

In addition to being one of the largest ports in the world, the harbour of **Buenos Aires** is entirely man made. Through its docks flow vast grain, animal feed and beef exports.

The **population of Buenos Aires** is 2,922,829 (1991 census) but the greater metropolitan area has a total of 9,967,826, mostly European in descent.

BUSES

About 15,000 US communities have no form of public transportation, and more than 350 m. **intercity bus** passengers are carried each year on a marginally profitable service.

Common during the first two decades of the 20th c were large, **long–frame automobiles** that seated 12–20 people and had bus-like bodies set on a truck chassis.

Frank and William Fageol built (1920) a more **suitably designed bus**. The floor was lowered, the seats were made more comfortable and the brakes and engine were improved.

In 1819 the omnibus was revived with its introduction in Paris and New York. The Latin word *omnibus* ('for everyone') was shortened to the well-known term 'bus'.

The Brazilian city of Rio de Janeiro has the world's **largest bus fleet**. The majority are single-deckers amounting to 6,580 servicing the commuter passengers.

The earliest **municipal omnibus** was brought into service in 1903; it ran between Eastbourne Railway station and Meads in East Sussex.

The motor bus is a descendant of the **horse-drawn omnibus**. The mathematician Blaise Pascal helped introduce (1662) the first known omnibus service in Paris.

BUSINESS

Harrods is the **largest department store** in the UK; its 1994 January sale netted £11 m. in one day, £24 m. in the first four days and £55 m. for the month.

Hugh Nicholson is credited with holding the **most directorships** at one time. In 1961 he was a director of nearly 500 separate businesses.

The business with the **highest number of retail outlets** worldwide is the Woolworth Corporation, founded by Frank Woolworth in 1879, with 8,368 stores. The total revenue exceeds $10 bn.

The **greatest loss ever made** in a financial year was $23.5 bn/£15.5 bn by General Motors. Most of this was caused by changes in the US accountancy laws.

The **greatest profit ever made** by a business in a year is $7.6 bn made by the American Telephone and Telegraph Co. during the 1981–82 tax year.

The **world's largest commercial bank** is the Japanese Dai-Ichi Kangyo Bank Ltd with assets exceeding $450 bn. India's State Bank has the biggest number of outlets at 12,704.

The **world's largest retailer** is Wal-Mart Inc., Arkansas. Founded in 1962 by Sam Walton it has over 2,000 outlets and an annual income of over $67.3 bn.

BYZANTIUM

After the break-up of the Roman Empire in the 5th c its eastern part became the **Byzantine Empire**, which survived for 1,000 years.

Byzantium inherited from Rome a sophisticated central administration, an efficient machinery of justice and finance and a reliable **gold coinage**, enabling the smooth collection of taxes.

Byzantium, renamed Constantinople by Constantine the Great in AD 330, became the assembly point for the **Crusades** and consequently suffered plundering raids by foraging soldiers.

Destroyed in the 5th c BC by the Persian king, **Darius**, Byzantium was rebuilt by the Spartans. It later suffered attack by Greeks, Scythians and Romans.

Eastern Orthodox Christianity developed differently from that in the West, being more mystical and less liturgical. From early days services were conducted in the vernacular.

Embroidery, gold and enamel work, rich mosaics

and vigorous religious images exerted a profound influence on **Italian Renaissance art**.

Heir to the Hellenistic tradition, Byzantium was a sophisticated and wealthy city. Its harbour, later called the **Golden Horn**, was an important port and trading centre.

The city of **Byzantium**, founded c. 660 BC on the European shore of the Bosphorus, was capital of the Byzantine Empire until the Empire's fall in 1453.

CACTI

The **Cholla Cactus** (*Opuntia imbricata*) superficially resembles a tree, with a trunk and branches growing to a height of 4 m/12 ft in Colorado, Texas and Mexico.

The genus **Cereus** comprises about 25 species, mostly found in Mexico, but including the Night-blooming Cereus (*Selenicereus*) of St Helena.

The **Hedgehog Cactus** (*Echinocactus hexaedrophorus*) is common in the deserts of North and South America. Globular with long spines, it produces a very showy flower.

The **Leaf Cactus** (*Epiphyllum* and *Phyllocactus*) comprises 17 species found in Mexico and Central America. They differ from other cacti in being epiphytic.

The **Prickly Pear** (*Opuntia*) is a large group of cacti found all over America as far south as Chile. The large flowers are followed by succulent pear-shaped fruit.

The **Saguaro Cactus** (*Carnegiea gigantea*) is the largest of the cacti, attaining a height of 21 m/70 ft. Named after Andrew Carnegie, they are found in the south-western US.

The word **Cactus** (Greek for a 'prickly plant') was adopted by Carl Linnaeus as the name for a group of succulent or fleshy-stemmed plants, most of them prickly and leafless.

CAIRO

Cairo is a city of contrasts, with modern skyscrapers alongside Roman antiquities, the tombs of the Caliphs, the citadel and over 260 mosques.

Cairo, the capital of modern Egypt, lies on the **River Nile** about 20 km/12 mi south of the apex of the Delta, partly on the alluvial plain and partly on the Mokattam hills.

Originally the Roman fortress of **Babylon**, Cairo was considerably developed by Saladin in 1177 when he erected the citadel or El-Kala.

▼ *Mosque in Cairo.*

The industries of **Cairo** include textiles, namely cotton and silk goods, sugar-refining, gunpowder, leather, glass and machinery.

The **population of Cairo** is 6,452,000 (est. 1990), making it the largest city in Africa.

CANADA

Canada (capital: Ottawa) occupies most of North America north of the 49th parallel, with an area of 9,970,610 sq km/3,849,672 sq mi.

Canada exports motor vehicles, crude petroleum, natural gas, wheat, newsprint, lumber and industrial machinery, mostly to the US, Japan and UK.

Jacques Cartier took possession of **Canada** for France in 1534 but it passed to Britain in 1763. The Confederation, with dominion status, was formed on 1 Jul. 1867.

The **population of Canada** is 26,941,000 (est. 1991), comprising 34.4% British,

▲ *The Canadian Rocky Mountains.*

25.7% French, 3.6% German, 2.8% Italian, 1.7% Ukrainian and 1.5% Amerindian and Inuit.

The world's longest undefended frontier (6,400 km/4,000 mi) lies between **Canada** and the US, and 90% of Canada's people live within 160 km/100 mi of it.

CANALS

In early 1968 archeologists discovered relics of the **oldest canals** in the world, dating from about 4000 BC, at Mandali, Iraq.

In terms of number of transits, 43,287 in 1995, the Kiel Canal between the North and Baltic seas is the **busiest canal** in the world.

The Gaillard Cut, or 'the Ditch', on the Panama Canal, which connects the Pacific and Atlantic oceans, is the **deepest cut** on any canal. It is 82 m/270 ft deep.

The **longest canal** in ancient times was the Grand Canal of China, begun 540 BC, which ran from Beijing to Hangzhou and on completion in 1327 was 1,781 km/1,197 mi long.

The **longest irrigation canal** is the Karakumsky Canal in Turkmenistan. Of its total length of 1,200 km/745 mi, its course length is 800 km/500 mi.

The **longest large-ship canal** is the Suez Canal linking the Red and Mediterranean seas. It took 1.5 m. people 10 years to build (1859–69). It is 162.2 km/100.8 mi long.

CARS

General Motors was founded in 1908 by William C. Durant (1861–1947) providing the organisational pattern for successful large-scale motor-vehicle production over time.

Henry Ford founded the **Ford Motor Company** in 1903 and five years later brought out the famous Model T, the first car to meet the needs of a mass market.

In the 1960s West Germany overtook the UK to become the world's second largest motor vehicle manufacturer, a feat largely attributable to the phenomenal success of the **Volkswagen Beetle**.

In the US, the **Big Three** (General Motors, Ford and Chrysler) controlled 90% of the car market by 1939. The rest was shared by the Middle Five (Hudson, Nash, Packard, Studebaker and Willys-Overland).

Just before World War I, **William Morris** in the UK and Andre Citroen in France began trying to emulate Henry Ford, but they were not initially successful.

The automobile appeared in Germany in 1885, but production on a commercial scale began in France in 1890. **Commercial production** in the US began around the turn of the century.

The heaviest **concentrations of cars** in use are in North America, Western Europe, Japan, Australia and New Zealand, with ratios of 1 car to 2–4 persons. China, by contrast, numbers 1 car per 2,000 people.

CARTOGRAPHY

Contour lines join places that are the same height above sea level. They have been commonly used in mapping since the 19th c.

In **ground surveying**, a tellurometer measures distances by recording the time of travel of electromagnetic waves. A geodimeter uses the speed of light to measure distance.

Large-scale maps show a lot of detail. The larger the scale, the smaller the area shown. Small-scale maps show a larger area in less detail.

Maps are representations on a flat plane of part or all of the earth's surface. All accurate maps are drawn to **scale**, a distance measured on the map representing a constant distance on the ground.

Surveyors collect information for map-making. They measure angles and distances from certain points to various features. Modern electronic equipment measures distances using light or sound waves.

The greatest step forward in map-making for navigation was the creation of **Mercator's map projection** in 1569, on which all straight lines are of constant bearing.

◄ *Henry Ford's GT 40, from 1968.*

The Greek astronomer and philosopher **Ptolemy** (*c*. AD 160) was the first great map-maker. He used different scales and suggested that maps might also show population density and climate.

Topographic maps show the shape or relief of the land using contours, colours and symbols to show features such as water, forests, railway lines and roads.

CASTLES

In 1576 Nobunaga of Japan built a fortress city, **Azuchi**, whose central structure, a seven-story tower, was surrounded by the great houses of his courtiers; the whole was protected by a series of stone walls and moats.

Although the term '**castle**' is often restricted in meaning to the fortified residences of the European Middle Ages, structures with the same dual function were also built in the ancient world.

From the 12th c castle design was influenced by the **Crusaders**, who introduced improvements copied from Byzantine fortifications. European castles became larger and their fortified areas increasingly complex.

In Japan the great era of **castle construction** occurred in the late 1500s under the rule of the warlords Nobunaga and Hideyoshi (the Momoyama period, 1573–1615).

The **motte and bailey castle** (9th c), was the earliest European castle form. Built on a natural or artificial mound (motte) and protected by one or more circular walls (bailey) and often a moat, the castle consisted of the keep, a wood or stone tower and accessory buildings.

The **Tower of London** (*c.* 1074–97) is an extant example of the motte and bailey castle. Its White Tower is the original Norman keep.

▼ *Windsor Castle.*

Windsor Castle has been the premier residence of the royal family of Britain since the reign (1066–87) of William I. The castle, set in a small park, occupies the site of a Roman fort and is surrounded by defensive walls.

CATHEDRALS

Canterbury Cathedral is the seat of the Archbishop of Canterbury. The present church was rebuilt in 1174 under French master mason William of Sens. The Norman nave was replaced in the late 14th c by one in the English Perpendicular Gothic style.

Constructed when Strasbourg was a German city, **Strasbourg Cathedral** is the most French of all German High Gothic churches. The cathedral was

New York's **St Patrick's Cathedral** (1858–79), the largest Roman Catholic cathedral in the US, was designed by James Renwick in a Gothic Revival mixture of English and French Gothic styles but without the usual flying buttresses.

Notre Dame de Chartres, or the Cathedral of Our Lady of Chartres in Paris, is the supreme monument of High Gothic art and architecture. The present church was built in 1194.

begun in 1175 in the Romanesque style; the new High Gothic style was adopted after 1235.

Durham Cathedral is a magnificent example of Norman architecture and one of the most notable Romanesque buildings in Europe. Begun in 1093 by Bishop William of St. Calais, the cathedral replaced an earlier church.

Early in the Middle Ages the church that contained the official 'seat' or throne (*cathedra*) of the bishop was known as the *ecclesia cathedralis*, or 'church of the throne'. We now use the word '**cathedral**'.

Reims Cathedral, built (1211–1311) on the traditional coronation site of the kings of France, is one of the greatest monuments of Gothic art and architecture. Work on the cathedral commenced under the architect Jean d'Orbais and was completed under Robert de Coucy.

St Paul's, cathedral of London and parish church of the British Commonwealth, was designed by Sir Christopher Wren between 1670 and 1675 in a classical version of the baroque style to replace the medieval cathedral of Old Saint Paul's.

▲ *The Death of St Peter the Martyr.*

CAVALRY

Between the world wars, the horse was supplanted in most armies by mechanised equipment. In today's armies **mechanised forces** have taken over all the functions of the cavalry.

Cavalry was used extensively in the US against the Indians and in the Civil War. Increasingly it was found to be **less effective** against repeating rifles, machine guns, trenches and barbed wire.

During **World War I**, cavalry was effectively used only in Palestine and, to a limited extent, in Eastern Europe. Cavalry continued to be used in rough terrain.

Hannibal used cavalry against the Romans in the Second Punic War (218–01 BC), but the Romans finally deployed superior cavalry in the Battle of Zama (202 BC).

Helicopters were used in the Korean and Vietnam wars in a way that was similar to cavalry tactics; the US Army even named one helicopter unit the **First Cavalry Division** (Airmobile).

Napoleon divided his cavalry into a screening force of light cavalry that covered the army's advance, and a reserve of heavy cavalry that led the attack.

The Chinese employed cavalry during the **Korean War** (1950–53), not to great effect, and maintained several horse divisions as late as 1976.

The **Germanic invaders** of the Roman Empire during AD 3rd–5th c probably used both saddle and stirrups; their cavalry was also much more effective than that of the Roman defenders.

The **Macedonians** Philip II and Alexander the Great were the first to use cavalry as a principal attack force (4th c BC) against the Greeks and Persians.

The **Mongols** demonstrated the value of a highly mobile cavalry, but in medieval Europe (as both horse and rider became more heavily armoured) the advantage of manoeuvrability was lost.

CELTS

Celtic society was based on clans and blood ties, with powerful princes and prosperous, outward-looking settlements, often established on well-defended hilltops.

Celts were skilled **metalworkers** in gold and bronze, fashioning exquisite torques and bracelets, hammered, embossed or set with coral and amber as symbols of princely power.

Domesticated **horses** first appeared in Celtic Gaul (now France) during the Bronze Age, and Caesar tells of the great passion the Gauls bore for their horses.

Druids, elite priests, were versed in mathematics and in the movements of the stars. They controlled access to the spirit world by complex and secret rites.

In AD 61 **Boudicca**, Celtic Queen of the Iceni in Britain, rebelled against the Romans and sacked Colchester and London before her rebellion was suppressed.

Of the ancient **Celtic languages**, only Breton, Welsh and Gaelic survive. Many place names, including London, still show their Celtic roots.

The Celts in southern Europe **traded** briskly with Mediterranean peoples, bartering salt, furs and gold for wine, oil, mirrors and luxury items of pottery.

The ancestors of the **Celts'** were already living in southern Europe during the late Iron Age and Bronze Age, in about the 8th c BC. This time was contemporary with classical antiquity.

CHEMISTRY

Ancient civilisations were familiar with many **chemical processes** such as extracting metals from their ores and the making of alloys.

As part of their search for the philosopher's stone **alchemists** in the 17th c endeavoured to turn base metals to gold, and through many of their techniques modern chemistry was born.

Chemistry looks at the composition of matter and the changes that happen under certain situations. All matter is either solid, liquid or gas and is composed of perpetually moving molecules.

Henry Cavendish discovered the composition of water and John Dalton gave us **atomic theory**, which gave a relative weight to the atoms for each element.

Much of the work in the 20th c has been in the field of **biochemistry**, such as in 1913 when Leonor Michaelis and M. Menten developed a mathematical equation describing the rate of enzyme-catalysed reactions.

▲ *Henry Cavendish, who discovered the composition of water*

The doctrine of **four elements** was demolished in the 18th c through the works of Joseph Black, Antoine Lavoisier and Joseph Priestley who discovered the presence of oxygen in the air.

The **periodic system** of classification was developed by John Newlands in 1863 and established by Dmitri Mendeleyev in 1869, classifying elements by their atomic masses.

CHEROKEE

For the Cherokee, the **Medicine Wheel** symbolised the individual journey. It included the four cardinal directions and four sacred colours.

The **Cherokee** are a Native American people of the Hokan-Siouan geographical linguistic group.

The Cherokee functioned with a **written constitution** and an elected, republican government after 1827. Their leader Sequoyah developed their written language.

The Cherokee Heritage Center **living museum** in Tahlequah, Oklahoma has tribal elders demonstrating basket weaving and displays of native grass and other plants.

The Cherokee possessed an **advanced agricultural culture**, but after 1750 smallpox halved their numbers. In 1838, they were removed to Oklahoma.

CHEYENNE

The **Cheyenne** are a Native American people of the Algonquin-Wakashan geographical linguistic group.

In the 18th-c lodge-dwelling Cheyenne acquired horses (c. 1760) and became nomadic. Resistance to whites led to Gen. George Custer's defeat at **Little Big Horn (1876)**.

After their **1877 surrender**, the US government moved the Cheyenne to Oklahoma and then to Montana. More than 3,000 live on reservations today.

The Cheyenne of the US Plains enjoyed **friendly relations** with whites until gold was discovered on their tribal lands in Colorado.

The Cheyenne **treasured a sacred bundle** holding: headgear made from a buffalo cow's skin and hair; two arrows for hunting; and two for war.

CHICKASAW

The **Chickasaw** are a Native American people of the Hokan-Siouan geographical linguistic group.

Chickasaw males wore panther, deer, bear, beaver and otter skins in winter. Warriors **shaved both sides** of their head leaving a central crest.

The Chickasaw lived in northern Mississippi. After 1834 they were removed to reservations in Oklahoma.

The Chickasaw Nation Dance Troupe perform **traditional community dances** and serve as ambassadors for the active Chickasaw Nation.

The Chickasaw, like many North American Indian tribes, have a legend of a **great flood**.

CHILE

Chile (capital: Santiago) is a ribbon-like republic on the Pacific coast of South America, with an area of 756,626 sq km/292,135 sq mi.

Chile exports copper, iron, manganese, zinc, silver, gold and petroleum and natural gas. Nitrates (from bird droppings) have been superseded by artificial fertilisers.

Conquered by Pedro de Valdivia in 1541, **Chile** declared its independence of Spain in 1810 but did not gain its freedom until Feb. 1818.

Copper, of which **Chile** has a quarter of the world's reserves, has accounted for more than 75% of Chile's foreign earnings in recent years.

▼ *The Villarica volcano in Chile.*

The **Great Wall of China**, built in the 3rd c BC, extends about 2,414 km/1,500 mi from the Yellow Sea into central Asia and is the only man-made object visible from the Moon.

The **population of China** is 1,149,667,000, comprising 91.96% Chinese and relatively small numbers of Chuang, Manchu, Hui, Miao, Uighur, Yi, Tuchia, Mongolian and Korean.

The **population of Chile** is 13,173,000 (est. 1991), comprising 91.6% mestizo, 6.8% Indian and 1.6% European. More than 80% are Roman Catholic, 6.1% Protestant and 0.2% Jewish.

CHINA

China (capital: Beijing) is the world's largest country, with an area of 9,572,900 sq km/3,696,100 sq mi.

China exports textiles, rubber and metal products, light-industrial goods, foodstuffs, mineral fuels, machinery and transport equipment.

In 1912 the Manchu dynasty was overthrown and **China** became a republic. In 1949 Mao Tse-tung established a people's republic, admitted to the UN in 1971.

CHINESE DYNASTIES

As well as a personal name, **Chinese emperors** often had a 'temple name' and an 'era name', both of which could be changed every year.

During the **Han** dynasty (202 BC–AD 220), Chinese technology was far ahead of the rest of the world, with the invention of paper, gunpowder, iron weapons and water clocks.

Over 6,000 life-size terracotta figures and horses were made for the tomb of Emperor **Ch'in Shi-huangdi** of the Qin Dynasty in 210 BC. The burial mound was discovered in 1974.

▲*The Great Wall of China.*

The Chinese emperor Ch'in Shi-huangdi, from whose first name comes the name 'China' that we use today, had the **Great Wall of China** built.

The last Chinese dynasty was that of the **Manchu**, or Ch'ing. The last emperor, Pu-yi, was overthrown in the 1911 revolution, but the Japanese made him ruler of Manchukuo (1931–45).

The **Ming** dynasty (1368–1644) is famous for the excellence of its rich, colourful porcelain. The celebrated abstract blue-on-white patterns developed into the willow pattern so in demand in Europe.

The very first Chinese emperor was Fu Hsi, whose birth was said to have occurred in the 29th c BC. He, Shen Nung and Huang-ti are known as the **Three Sovereigns**.

Archaic tripod vessel from the Shang dynasty of China. ▶

There were around 20 major Chinese dynasties. The first dynasty for which there is historical material is the Shang (18th–12th c BC).

CHLOROPHYLL

Bacteriochlorophyll is a pigment found in some photosynthetic bacteria, identified in 1940 by C. S. French and others.

Chlorophyll (from Greek meaning 'green' and 'leaf') is the substance that gives leaves their colour and is necessary for photosynthesis.

Chlorophyllase is an enzyme found in leaves. C. Weast (1940) found that the chlorophyllase content of spinach varied with the season and variety.

Chlorophyllides are oxides of chloro-phyll, formed when leaves are allowed to stand in an alcoholic solvent at a steady temperature.

J. B. Conant (1931) showed that **allomerisation** is a slow oxidation process whereby chlorophyll under-goes certain changes on standing, particularly in a solution of alcohol.

Porphyrins (from the Greek word for purple) are various compounds from which others, notably chlorophyll, were first synthesised by H. Fischer in 1940.

The **spectra** of chlorophyll solutions in various solvents were studied by D. G. Harris (1943). The colours are most vividly seen in solutions of ether.

CHOCTAW

The **Choctaw** are a Native American people of the Hokan-Siouan geographical linguistic group.

The Choctaw lived in central and southern Mississippi where they were **excellent farmers**. They were removed to an Oklahoma reservation in 1832.

Choctaw music expresses the value they place on living in harmony with nature.

The Choctaw have led **civilised, peaceful lives** in spite of official and individual resistance. Several have become members of the US Congress and attained prominence in public life.

As citizens of Oklahoma, the Choctaw tribe **endures in strong numbers** in spite of poverty and abuse by the whites.

CHRISTIANITY

Jesus Christ (the Messiah, or 'anointed one') was born in Palestine about 6 BC and is believed by his followers to be the Son of God.

If historical importance is assessed by impact on numbers of people, perhaps no event in human history is as important as the **birth of Jesus Christ**.

Jesus's followers saw him crucified and yet believed he later rose from the dead, and believed that they too, being **baptised**, would conquer death.

After Jesus himself, **St Paul** is the most important figure in the history of Christianity for his missionary work and his interpretation of Jesus's teachings.

The **Twelve Apostles** were Simon Peter and his brother Andrew, James and his brother John, Philip, Bartholomew, Matthew, Thomas, James, Simon, Jude, and Judas Iscariot.

Judas Iscariot betrayed Jesus to the authorities with a kiss. After he killed himself in remorse his place as a disciple was taken by Matthias.

Christianity promises eternal life and forgiveness from sin, and this, with its message of equality before a loving God, has made it the **world's largest religion**.

A fish is a **Christian symbol** because the letters of its Greek name *ichthus* form an acronym of Greek words for Jesus Christ, Son of God, Saviour.

There are two broad groupings of Christians: **Episcopalians**, who recognise a hierarchy of priests and bishops, and non-Episcopalians, who do not.

The central faiths of Christianity are contained in a **Creed** or statement of belief, especially the 'Apostles' Creed' and the 'Nicene Creed'; one is usually recited during church services.

The most important Christian festival is **Easter**, celebrating Jesus's resurrection. The date changes each year according to a calculation connected with the full moon.

There are approx. 1500 m. Christians worldwide, of which about half are **Roman Catholics**, about 55 m. are Anglicans, the rest are members of other Protestant churches.

CHURCHES

Antonio Sangallo the Younger's Church of **Santo Spirito** (1538–44) in Sassia illustrated the new idea of a single-aisle church flanked by shallow chapels leading to a large high-altar chapel in the wide apse.

Giacomo Vignola's Church of **Il Gesu**, begun in Rome in 1568, shows the full development of the Baroque style. It is a large, single-aisled church, with truncated transept arms and a large dome over the crossing, leading to the altar.

In the US neo-classicism found impressive expression in Benjamin Latrobe's **Roman Catholic Cathedral of Baltimore** (1804–18), a shallow-domed Latin cross plan with segmental barrel-vaulting of the nave and side aisles.

Le Corbusier's stunningly original pilgrim church of **Notre Dame du Haut** (1950–55) in Ronchamp, France, is an example of the architect's handcrafted buildings.

St Peter's Basilica, the premier church of Roman Catholic Christendom, is named after Christ's disciple Peter. The building history (1546–1784) involved architects Bramante, Michelangelo, Giacomo della Porta, Carlo Maderno, Bernini and Marchionni.

The Church of **Hagia Sophia**, in Istanbul, for nearly 1,000 years the most important church of the Byzantine Empire, was completed in 5 years (AD 532–37), designed by the scholars Anthemius of Tralles and Isidorus of Miletus

The word **church** (from the Greek *kyriakon doma*, 'the Lord's House') first described the building that housed the worshippers and later referred to the entire Christian community.

CINEMA

Friese-Greene showed the first celluloid film and patented a movie camera (1888). **Edison** invented 35-mm film (1889); using perforated film, he developed his Kinetograph camera and Kinetoscope viewer (1890–94).

In 1900 attempts to synchronise film and disc were made by **Gaumont**, leading later to the Vitaphone system (US). **Méliès** made the first film *Le Voyage dans la lune* (1900).

In 1918–19 the German Tri-Ergon **sound system** was developed, leading to sound being recorded on film photographically; photography with sound was also developed by Lee De Forest (Phonofilm system, US).

In 1997–98 the release of both James Cameron's *Titanic* and Roland Emmerich's *Godzilla* set new technical standards in live action with computer-generated special effects.

◀ *Audrey Hepburn.*

Le Prince produced the first series of images on perforated film and **Edison**, having developed the phonograph, began developing a motion-picture recording and reproducing device to accompany recorded sound (1887).

Pathé introduced the Berliner gramophone, using discs in synchronisation with film, but lack of amplification made the performances ineffective (1896). **Edison** tried to improve this with banks of phonographs (1899).

The first sound film (Phonofilm) was demonstrated (1923). *Don Juan* (a silent film with synchronised music score) was released (1926). *The Jazz Singer*, the first major sound film starring Al Jolson, was released (1927).

The **Lumière brothers** projected (to a paying audience) film of an oncoming train arriving at a station: some of the audience fled in terror (1895).

The Praxinoscope (1877) was developed as a projector of successive images on screen (France, 1879). **Marey** (French physiologist) developed various types of camera for recording human and animal movements (1878–95).

The stroboscope, zoetrope and thaumatrope were invented to show moving images (1826–34). **Muybridge** (English photographer) demonstrated movement of horses' legs by using 24 cameras (1877).

CIVIL WAR

Afghanistan was a monarchy from 1747–1973, when the country was proclaimed a republic; the republic dissolved in 1992 as the country erupted in civil war.

Angola became independent in 1975. Two governments took power; one formed by the MPLA in Luanda, the other by UNITA and FNLA in Huambo. The ensuing civil war assumed international overtones.

▼ *Peacekeeping troops in Afghanistan.*

In the aftermath of the Franco-German War, left-wing rebels formed the Commune in Paris. This insurrection was brutally suppressed by government troops in May 1871; more than 20,000 **Communards** were killed or summarily executed.

The **American Civil War** (1861–65) was fought to preserve the Union against the slave-owning Southern States that formed the Confederacy. It raged for four bitter years.

The **English Civil War**, which started in 1642, consisted of three campaigns: the first, between Charles I and Parliament (1642–46); the second, when the Scots fought Parliament (1648); and the third, mainly in the West Country (1649–51).

The **Huguenots** (French Protestants) were persecuted in the reigns of Charles IX and Henri II, and they made reprisals upon the Roman Catholics. Between 1562–98 eight bitter wars were fought between Roman Catholics and Protestants.

The **Irish Civil War** was fought in 1922–23, between the forces of the Irish Free State led by Michael Collins and those who opposed the Anglo-Irish Treaty, led by Eamonn de Valera.

The **Lebanese Civil War** (1975) completely divided Beirut. The city was dominated by factionalism, with Sunnis, Shi'ites, Druze, Palestinians, Maronites and Falangists all controlling territory.

The **Spanish Civil War** began in 1936 as a right-wing military revolt led by Franco and ended with the defeat of the Republicans in 1939.

The Soviet Union erupted into a civil war that lasted from 1918–20. The Bolsheviks began the '**Red terror**' campaign against the poorly organised Whites and Allied interventional forces who were defeated by the Red Army.

CLASSICAL ART

All 4th-c Greek **murals**, including those of the great Apelles, have perished. Their influence, however, may probably be seen in the illusionistic (giving an illusion of reality) landscapes and architectural scenes depicted on the walls of Roman houses in Pompeii and Herculaneum in AD 1st c.

Almost all the mural painting created during the early Classical period has been lost. It includes the work of the painter **Polygnotus**, whose murals in the *Lesche* or assembly hall in Delphi were described by Pliny the Elder.

During the Renaissance in the 15th and 16th c the Greek tradition in art was revived and developed: **realism**, a sense of proportion and Greek architectural and design motifs began to appear in European art.

The **Early Classical Period** (*c.* 475–448 BC) began after the Greek victory over Persia; the need to repair the devastation caused by the Persian invasion generated great activity in both architecture and sculpture, particularly in Athens.

The **Late Classical Period** (*c.* 400–323 BC) had fewer architectural projects when Athens was defeated in the Peloponnesian War, but a new, detailed characterisation of figures typified the visual arts.

The major periods of Greek art can be divided into the **Archaic** (late 8th c–480 BC), Classical (480–323 BC) and Hellenistic (323–27 BC).

The **Middle Classical Period** (*c.* 448–400 BC) was characterised by 'mature classicism' developed during the second half of the 5th c BC, especially under the patronage of the Athenian statesman Pericles.

The term **'Classical'** denotes the art and aesthetics created by the ancient Greeks and Romans and may be used to characterise any style or period of creative work distinguished by 'classical' qualities, including conscious restraint in the handling of themes.

▲ *Classical Greek vase.*

CLIMATE

A study in New Zealand classified climate on the basis of human **psychological response**. Each climate was assessed for its favourability rating, taking into account sun, temperature, dryness and lack of wind.

By combining the two main elements of climate – temperature and precipitation – scientists have identified 11 **basic climates**. A climatic boundary may alter from year to year because of fluctuating conditions.

Climate describes general average weather conditions, for example tropical or tundra. Weather describes short-term conditions. Thus, a semi-arid region may sometimes experience a few days' rainy weather.

In 1915 Dr Ellsworth Huntington, an American geographer, published *Civilization and Climate*, postulating that climate exerted control over human activity. He even suggested that **climatic changes** explained the downfall of the Inca and Roman empires.

In 1918 the Russian meteorologist Vladimir Köppen published a climate classification based on mean temperature and precipitation and recognising five main groups based on vegetation types. The **Köppen classification** is still in use.

No **climate classification** is entirely satisfactory because of the reliance on averages. Factors contributing to a classification include temperature, precipitation, sunshine, wind, humidity and amount of cloud.

W. H. Terjung (US) identified two climate indices: a **comfort index** and a wind-effect index. He noted that, for example, people feel uncomfortable if high humidity at high temperatures prevents perspiration.

◀ *Floods in Bangladesh.*

CLOUDS

A **mackerel sky** precedes a warm front. The cloud, broken into long, thin, parallel masses, is called cirrus (Latin for 'curl') or cirrocumulus, and it forms a thin layer at 6,000–12,000 m/30,000–40,000 ft.

Clouds form when air temperature is cooled sufficiently for the air to become saturated with water vapour. When the air cannot hold any more water as vapour, the water condenses into droplets.

Cumulus clouds consist of rounded heaps with a horizontal base. They usually appear in good weather and form when rising air cools. Winds above the condensation level may boost their height.

If there were no clouds, most of the heat radiated from the earth's surface would be lost to space, but clouds and water vapour absorb **heat**, which they re-radiate, largely back to earth.

In moist conditions over the sea, rain can form from cloud over 900 m/3,000 ft in about 40 minutes. Over continents, a thicker **cloud layer** is needed and the rain takes one to two hours to form.

There are two main types of cloud, the **convectional** and the layer cloud. Convectional clouds form as rising air cools. Layer clouds, often a monotonous grey, form as water-bearing air slowly lifts over large areas.

Water vapour condenses around nuclei, such as dust or salt particles. The resulting **cloud droplets** are also minute. Their growth depends on the speed of conversion of water vapour to liquid form.

COAL

Burning coal can produce **combustion gases** as hot as 2,500°C/4,500°F, but few materials can withstand such heat forces so power plants limit steam temperatures to 540°C/1,000°F.

▲ *Welsh coal mines.*

Coal cinders were found amongst **Roman** ruins in England which suggest that the Romans were familiar with its use before AD 400.

References to coal mining in Europe appear in writings of the 13th c. It was used on a limited scale until the 18th c. when methods developed using coke in **blast furnaces** and forges.

The incomplete burning in coal conversion produces some carcinogenic compounds. The process also produces sulphur and nitrogen oxides which react with atmospheric moisture making sulphuric and nitric acids (**acid rain**).

The main chemical reactions that contribute to **heat release** from coal are oxidation reactions, which convert the constituent elements of coal into their respective oxides.

The most common use of coal is in **combustion**, where heat is generated to produce steam, which in turn powers turbines to produce electricity.

COINS

Coins are graded on a scale ranging upward as follows: poor, good, very good, fine, very fine, extremely fine, uncirculated and 'proof'. A proof coin

has been specially struck for collectors.

In the US (1979) a small 13-sided **dollar coin**, bearing the head of Susan B. Anthony, was issued for general circulation. It failed because the government refused to withdraw the dollar note.

Numismatics is the collecting and the study of coins and related forms of money, such as paper currency and tokens.

One estimate puts the number of people (**numismatists**) in the US who collect coins, bills, tokens and medals and decorations at around 20 m.; worldwide, the figure is likely to be four or five times as large.

The **metal content** of coins has varied greatly over time. Gold, silver and copper, along with such lesser metals as zinc, have all been used in coins minted for general circulation.

The systematic collecting of coins for their rarity or historical significance began during the Renaissance, when wealthy admirers of the Ancient Greek and Roman civilisations made **collections** of coins from those eras.

The **value** of collections of older coins usually increases with time and many coins of even fairly recent vintage are now worth more than their face value because of their gold or silver content alone.

COLD WAR

In 1949 the western allies formed the **North Atlantic Treaty Organisation** (NATO), designed as a military counterweight to the Soviet forces in Europe.

In 1955, a new round of Soviet-American confrontations ensued, all the riskier because now both sides possessed nuclear weapons. 'Brinkmanship', a term coined by John Foster Dulles, peaked in 1962 with the **Cuban Missile Crisis**.

In May 1948, USSR authorities severed all land-access routes to Berlin; only the success of the **Berlin Airlift** in supplying West Berlin, permitted the West to resist the pressure.

The Cold War initially centred on the use of USSR military forces to install **Communist governments** in Eastern Europe. The US government insisted upon the right of self-determination.

Soldier and citizen in South Vietnam. ▶

The expression 'cold war' was coined by the American journalist, Herbert Bayard Swope, in 1947. It describes the **strategic struggle** between the West and the USSR.

The first phase of the cold war culminated in the **North Korean invasion of South Korea** in 1950, resulting in western involvement in a land war in Asia.

The **Nuclear Test Ban Treaty of 1963** was a turning point in the cold war. Both US and USSR leaders wanted to end a struggle that increased the danger of global annihilation.

The US strategy was called '**containment**', a term first used by George Kennan in arguing that Soviet expansionism might be contained by a strategy of responding to Soviet pressures.

The USSR considered US objections to their actions a betrayal of wartime understandings and placed Eastern Europe behind a military and political barrier known as the **Iron Curtain**.

With the rise to power of Mikhail Gorbachev in 1985, policies of domestic reform and **reconciliation** with the West led to the self-imposed end of the Soviet system.

COLOMBIA

Colombia (capital: Bogota) is located in the north-western corner of South America, with an area of 1,141,748 sq km/440,831 sq mi.

Colombia exports petroleum, coffee, textiles, fruit, flowers, iron and steel, mainly to the US, Germany and the Netherlands.

Largely as a result of the **illegal narcotics industry** the major cause of death is gunshot wounds – twice as likely as a heart attack (the chief natural cause).

The first permanent European settlement in America, **Colombia** was known as New Granada until 1861. Independence was declared in 1813 and secured in 1819.

The **population of Colombia** is 33,613,000 (est. 1991), comprising 58% mestizo, 20% white, 14% mulatto, 4% black, 3% mixed black and Indian and 1% Amerindian.

COLONIALISM

Colonies have been founded by religious groups fleeing **persecution** (e.g. Pilgrims in Massachusetts) or organised

▲ *The Battle of Bunker Hill in the American Revolution.*

by groups of merchants or businessmen (e.g. British, Dutch and French East India Companies).

European colonialism from the 15th to the 19th c was usually associated with economic aims; it was linked with the **imperialism** of the new nation states and governed by the economic policies of mercantilism.

In southern Africa in the 18th c **Dutch colonists** drove the Khoikhoi and San back toward the desert, but were not able to prevent the more numerous Bantus from occupying much of what is now the Republic of South Africa.

Some colonies have been established by the migration of settlers from the colonising country, as in the **British colonies** in North America, Australia and New Zealand.

The **American Revolution** ended British rule in what is now the US. Revolts in Latin America established the independence of most of that area by 1825, but Spain continued to hold Cuba, Puerto Rico and the Philippines until 1898.

COLOUR

A person can see in **dim light**, but cannot distinguish colours. Colours only appear in brighter light. This is due to the cones at the back of the eye, which see colour, only working in bright light.

Impressionist painters laid great emphasis on the use of colour. ▶

A surface looks red because it absorbs light from the blue end of the spectrum and reflects light at the red end. **Absorption** is due to molecular structure of material and applied dyes.

Colour is the quality or wavelength of light that is emitted or reflected from an object. Various colours correspond to different wavelengths.

Colour-blindness is a hereditary defect of vision which cuts down the ability to distinguish certain colours, often red and green. It is sex-linked affecting approx. 5% of men and only 1% of women.

Colours are **classified** by the way they vary in brightness, hue and saturation (the extent to which they are mixed with white).

From long to short **wavelengths** (approx. 700 to 400 nm) the colours are red, orange, yellow, green, blue, indigo and violet.

It was originally thought that **splitting light** actually produced colours instead of the fact that it was separating into already existing colours.

COMANCHE

Comanche acquired **horses early in the 18th c**, afterwards dominating south-west Texas and Oklahoma and warring against the Spanish and Apache.

Comanche religious practices focused on **direct appeal** to various supernatural powers without whose assistance success in life was impossible. There were few group rituals.

Comanche warrior horsemen **killed more whites** in proportion to their own numbers than any other American Indian tribe.

In modern times, less than 4,000 Comanches remain, living **mainly in Oklahoma**.

The **Comanche** are a Native American people of the Aztec-Tanoan geographical linguistic group.

COMETS

A **comet** is a small, icy body orbiting the Sun, usually on a highly elliptical path. It consists of a central nucleus a few km across and consists mostly of ice mixed with dust.

▲ The comet Hale Bopp.

As a **comet** approaches the Sun its nucleus heats up, releasing gas and dust which form a tenuous coma, up to 100,000 km/60,000 mi wide.

Most comets swing around the Sun, return to distant space and are not seen again; some however have their orbits altered by the gravitational pull of planets and reappear every 200 years or so (**periodic comets**).

Of the 800 or so comets whose orbs have been calculated, approx. 160 are periodic. The shortest period belongs to **Encke's comet** which orbits the Sun every 3.3 years.

The brightest periodic comet, and best known, is **Halley's comet**, named after Edmund Halley who predicted its return. It was observed in 1758 and returned 1986.

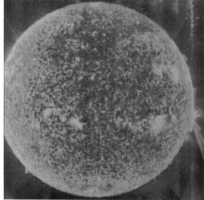

Comets are thought to have been formed at the beginning of the Solar System. Bns of them reside in a halo, the **Oort cloud**, beyond Pluto.

The **comet's tails** are formed by gas and dust streaming away from its coma; these may extend for millions of km.

▲ The Sun.

COMICS

Best-selling **British comics** of all time are, in order: *Beano, Comic Cuts, Dandy, Eagle, Film Fun, Illustrated Chips, Mickey Mouse Weekly, Radio Fun, Rainbow* and *School Friend*.

Comic strips are a popular art form dating from the 1890s, when they were introduced into the Sunday colour supplements of American newspapers as a means of promoting readership.

For 43 years (1930–73) Murat Bernard ('Chic') Young produced the world's most widely syndicated comic strip, **'Blondie'**, which between 1938 and 1951 inspired more than a dozen movies.

George Herriman's **'Krazy Kat'** (1911), a comic drama of love and rejection in the manner of a surreal *commedia dell'arte*, proved a hit with intellectuals because of its wit and advanced style.

In the 1930s comic strips such as 'Tarzan', 'Terry and the Pirates' and 'Prince Valiant', along with 'Buck Rogers' and 'Flash Gordon' created an appetite for further adventure heroes: **'Superman'**, 'Batman' and 'Wonder Woman'.

James Swinnerton's cartoon strip **'The Little Bears and Tigers'** run by the *San Francisco Examiner* (1892), was the first newspaper comic strip. The first successful comic series was Richard Outcault's 'Down in Hogan's Alley' (1895).

The **'Teenage Mutant Ninja Turtles'** began their existence in 1983 as the crude heroes of an underground, adult comic. Its success guaranteed profitable films and animated cartoons for the next generation.

The children in Charles Schulz's still-popular **'Peanuts'**, begun in 1950, spoke to the aspirations and frustrations of adults through the actions of children and spawned a series of animated films, the latest in 1998.

The pointed political satire in Garry Trudeau's popular '**Doonesbury**' (begun 1970) won a Pulitzer Prize for its creator in 1975.

COMMONWEALTH

England was declared a **Commonwealth** on 30 Jan. 1649 after the execution of Charles I (1600–49). Oliver Cromwell (1599–1658) became Lord Protector of the Commonwealth on 16 Dec. 1653.

In 1949, when India became a republic, the modern **British Commonwealth** was born, with the British monarch (then George VI, 1895–1952) becoming a symbol rather than a legal entity.

In 1998, with Elizabeth II (b. 1926) as formal head of the **Commonwealth's 54 member states**, 16 accept the Queen as head of state, 33 are republics and five have their own monarchs.

The British Commonwealth (originally **Commonwealth of Nations**) was formed (1931) by those countries within the British Empire that recognised allegiance to the British monarch, George V (1865–1936).

The 1971 meeting formulating the Singapore Declaration of Commonwealth Principles was the first to be termed a **Commonwealth Heads of Government Meeting**, reflecting the republican status of many new members.

The Commonwealth Heads of Government Meeting (CHOGM) in Harare (20 Oct. 1991) resulted in the **Harare Declaration**, a major restatement and updating of Commonwealth principles.

The **Commonwealth Secretariat**, headed since Oct. 1989 by Sec.-Gen. Chief Emeka Anyaoko of Nigeria and based in London, comprises staff from member countries who pay the Secretariat's costs.

COMMONWEALTH GAMES

Between 1970 and 1994 four Olympic champions monopolised the **Commonwealth 100 m title**. Don Quarrie (Jamaica), Allan Wells (Scotland), Ben Johnson (Canada) and Linford Christie (England) won the seven golds in that period.

Canadian swimmer Graham Smith holds the record for **most gold medals at one Games**. At the Edmonton Games in 1978 he won six golds.

Daley Thompson (England) won the decathlon title at three successive games: 1978 (world record), 1982 and 1986.

English fencer Bill Hoskyns (1958–70) and Australian swimmer Michael Wenden (1966–74) share the **record of nine gold medals**.

The **Commonwealth Games** are open to member nations of the British Commmonwealth. Originally called the Empire Games until 1970, they were first held in Canada in 1930. They are nicknamed 'the Friendly Games'.

Whilst representing Canada **Lennox Lewis**, subsequently WBC world heavyweight champion, won the super-heavy-weight boxing gold medal in 1986 at Edinburgh.

◀ *Queen Elizabeth opening the Commonwealth Games.*

COMMUNISM

Exiled (1929) in the power struggle following Lenin's death (1924), **Leon Trotsky** (1879–1940), who believed in world revolution, was assassinated in Mexico on Stalin's orders.

In 1848 the word 'communism' acquired new meaning when used as a synonym for socialism by Karl Marx (1818–83) and Friedrich Engels (1820–95) in their *Communist Manifesto*.

Joseph Stalin (1879–1953) became Soviet Communist Party leader (1922), eliminating all opposition in the Great Purge (1936–38), but was denounced after his death by Khrushchev.

One of the few communist leaders to survive the USSR's demise, **Fidel Castro** (b. 1927; PM 1959; Pres: 1976) led the 1959 revolution that overthrew Cuban dictator Fulgencio Batista (1901–73).

Soviet Communism by 1917 was a blend of 19th-c European Marxism, traditional Russian revolutionism and the organisational, revolutionary ideas of Bolshevik leader Vladimir Ilyich Lenin (1870–1924).

Soviet leader (1985–91), **Mikhail Gorbachev** (b. 1931) introduced liberal reforms and communication with the West (*perestroika* and *glasnost*) but was ousted by Boris Yeltsin (1991) during the Soviet collapse.

Stalin's successor in 1953 (Soviet premier 1958–64), **Nikita Khrushchev** (1894–1971) initiated de-stalinisation, leading to revolts in Poland and Hungary (1956), and was ousted by Brezhnev and Kosygin.

The **People's Republic of China** (est. 1949, first leader: Mao Zedong) is run by the Marxist-Leninist-Maoist Chinese Communist Party (CCP). Jiang Zemin has been leader since 1993.

COMPOSERS

Franz Joseph Haydn (1732–1809), Mozart and Beethoven's teacher, major exponent of the classical sonata form and first great master of the string quartet, wrote over 100 symphonies and choral music.

Igor Stravinsky (1882–1971), Russian composer, later adopting French (1934) and US (1945) nationality, wrote music for Diaghilev's ballets (*The Rite of Spring*, 1913), later using serial techniques (*Canticum Sacrum*, 1955).

Influenced by Haydn, **Wolfgang Amadeus Mozart** (1756–91) composed prolifically from childhood (27 piano concertos, 23 string quartets, 35 violin sonatas, over 50 symphonies). Operas include *Don Giovanni*. Mozart's music marks Classicism's pinnacle.

Johann Sebastian Bach (1685–1750), master of counterpoint, epitomises Baroque polyphonic style with a prodigious output: orchestral, keyboard, choral, chamber and sacred music (200 church cantatas, oratorios and passions).

Ludwig van Beethoven (1770–1827) spanned Classicism's transition to Romanticism. Haydn's pupil and a virtuoso pianist, by 1792 he was deaf, but plunged into composition of his great symphonies, piano sonatas and string quartets.

Only 31 when he died, **Franz Schubert** (1797–1825) was a prodigious composer; his 10 symphonies (including the 'Unfinished'), piano music and 600 *lieder* combined Romantic expression with pure melody.

Robert Schumann (1810–56), German Romantic composer, brought the ability to convey mood and emotion to new heights. His compositions include four symphonies, piano music, sonatas and song cycles.

COMPUTERS

A **computer virus** is a portion of computer code designed to insert itself into an existing computer program, alter or destroy data and copy itself into other programs in the same computer or into programs in other computers.

The main breakthrough in computing came in 1946 when J. Mauchly and P. Eckert (US) built the high-speed electronic digital computer known as the **ENIAC** (Electronic Numerical Integrator and Computer).

◄ *Ludwig van Beethoven.*

Designed to handle business data, **UNIVAC I** (Universal Automatic Computer), Eckert and Mauchly's later computer, financed by Remington Rand Inc. in 1950, found many uses in commerce and effectively started the computer boom.

During the 1970s many companies, some new to the computer field, introduced programmable **minicomputers** supplied with software packages. The size-reduction trend continued with the introduction of personal computers.

In 1949 **EDVAC** (Electronic Discrete Variable Computer) was invented by John Von Neumann; it was the first to use binary arithmetic and to store its operating instructions internally.

In computers, the unit of **memory** is the byte, which can hold one character of text. A kilobyte (kB) is 1,024 bytes, a megabyte (MB) is 1,024 kB and a gigabyte (GB) is 1,024 MB.

The core of a computer is its central processing unit (CPU) which executes individual program instructions and controls the operation of the other parts, it is usually referred to as the **processor**.

Intel launched the first **microprocessor**, the Intel 4004, in 1971. This was a complete CPU contained on a single integrated circuit or chip.

Since their introduction in the 1940s **computers** have become an integral part of the modern world. Besides systems found in government sites, industries, offices and homes, microcomputers are embedded in a multitude of everyday locations (e.g. cars, telephones, VCRs and kitchen appliances).

The computer was **conceived** by Charles Babbage in 1835 but never went beyond design stage. Thomas Flowers built Colossus, the first electronic computer, with Alan Turing in 1943.

The electronics engineer Stephen Wozniak (b. 1950), together with Steve Jobs (b. 1955), built a revolutionary microcomputer that formed the basis of the **Apple Computer Company** and helped create the enormous personal computer industry of the 1980s.

The **IBM** System/360 was launched in 1964 and was the first compatible family of computers. Since then IBM have become the standard for PC design.

The memory capacity of early **PCs** was often as small as 16 kB, but by the mid-1990s typical PCs were equipped with 4–16 MB of memory. This can often be expanded to as much as 128 MB or even to several GB in a workstation.

William (Bill) Henry Gates (b. 1955) is a leader in the US computer industry and founder of **Microsoft**, the first micro-computer software company. In 1980 he created Microsoft Disk Operating System or MS-DOS and later applications, most notably Windows.

CONQUESTS

Alexander the Great's conquests freed the West from the menace of Persian rule and spread **Greek civilisation** and culture into Asia and Egypt.

From the end of the Roman Empire until the 15th c, Arabs, Mongols, Franks, Vikings, Christian Crusaders and Turks all crossed vast areas searching for **new lands** to conquer.

In AD 406 the Vandals, the Suebi, and the Alamanni invaded Gaul (France) and Spain. In AD 455 several **Germanic tribes**, led by the Ostrogoths, conquered Italy.

In the 7th c, Islam succeeded in uniting the many tribes of Arabia. **Arab armies** conquered lands from the

Indus River in the east to Spain in the west.

Persia already numbered among its conquests the Greek cities of **Ionia** in Asia Minor. The Persian Wars began when some of these cities revolted in 499 BC.

The Spanish conquest by Francisco de Montejo, whose house still stands on the central plaza in the capital of Merida, completed the downfall of the **Mayan civilisation** in 1542.

William's conquest in 1066 for ever changed the **course of English history**. In political terms his victory brought the country into closer contact with Western Europe.

CONSERVATION

Conservation is the philosophy and policy of managing the environment to assure adequate supplies of natural resources for future, as well as present, generations.

Conservationists aim to ensure the **preservation** of genetic diversity and to assure that utilisation of species and ecosystems, such as forests and grazing lands, is sustainable.

Conservationists recognise that human activities profoundly change the face of the earth and can irreparably damage or destroy the natural resources on which human well being and survival depend.

Increasingly conservation concerns are being incorporated into economic development plans. At the UN-sponsored 1992 **Earth Summit** in Rio de Janeiro, the largest congregation of world leaders in history agreed on the broad principles that must guide environmental policies.

Renewable resources are those which, under proper management, regenerate and even improve their resource values, but which when misused can be depleted or lost entirely. They include plants, animals, soils and inland waters.

Rainforests are a main focus for conservation groups. ▲

The first goal of conservation is the **maintenance** of essential ecological processes (global cycles of nitrogen, carbon dioxide and water; localised regeneration of soil; recycling of nutrients; and cleansing of waters and air) and life-support systems (agricultural systems, water systems and forests).

The UN Conference on the Human Environment, held in Sweden in 1972, firmly established conservation of **natural resources** as an important concern of governments throughout the world.

Unrenewable resources are minerals and fossil and nuclear fuels, which are present on the earth in fixed amounts and, once used, do not regenerate. Elements of the environment, such as oceans, tidal lands and the air, are also being recognised as natural unrenewable resources.

CONSTELLATIONS

A **constellation** is one of 88 areas into which the sky is divided for the purposes of identifying and naming celestial objects.

Orion is one of the most prominent constellations in the equatorial region of the sky. It contains the bright stars Betelgeuse and Rigel, as well as a row of three distinctive stars which make up Orion's Belt.

The constellation of **Pisces** in the northern hemisphere contains the vernal equinox, the point at which the Sun's path around the sky crosses the celestial equator. This happens each year around 21 Mar.

The **constellations** used today come form a list of 48 compiled by the Ancient Greeks, who took some from

▲ *Signs of the zodiac are derived from the constellations.*

the Babylonians. The 88 of today were adopted by the International Astronomical Union in 1930.

The first constellations were simple patterns of stars in which early civilisations saw gods, heroes and sacred beasts. Some of them gave rise to **astrological signs**.

The **Scorpius** constellation between Sagittarius and Libra has a red supergiant star Antares in its centre. It has the strongest X-ray source in the sky, Scorpius X-1.

The **Virgo** constellation is the second largest in the sky and contains the nearest large cluster of galaxies to us, 50 m. light years away. It also contains the nearest quasar, 3C 273.

COPENHAGEN

Copenhagen (literally 'merchant harbour') was only a fishing village until 1167 when Axel Hvide erected a castle around which the merchant community developed.

Copenhagen was the site of a naval battle on 21 Mar. 1801 between the Royal Navy and the combined fleets of Denmark, Russia, Prussia and Sweden.

Copenhagen, the capital of Denmark, lies on low ground on the east side of the island of Zealand at the southern end of the Sound.

Copenhagen, though not primarily a manufacturing city, is renowned for fine porcelain from the KPM factory (est. 1755), and hand-wrought silver.

The **population of Copenhagen** is 1,343,916 (est. 1988), including the municipalities of Frederiksberg and Gentofte, part of the greater metropolitan area.

CREE

The **Cree** are a Native American people of the Algonquin-Wakashan geographical linguistic group.

Cree mythology was based on the spirits of the hunt. Their religion was rooted in **ancestor relationships**. They believed in an earth spirit, mother of animals.

In modern times the Cree tribe are one of **Canada's largest** and also live in Montana in the US.

Creek

In **feuds with rival tribes**, the Cree saw horses and captives as symbols of glory and of social achievement.

The Cree occupied lands in the **Canadian forests** and **US Plains** and worked closely with fur traders.

CREEK

A confederacy of **50 bands** made up the Creek, settled mainly in Georgia and Alabama. They rebelled (1813–14) but were subdued by Andrew Jackson.

The Creek adopted farming and ranching techniques from the whites. The **modern capital** of the Creek Nation is Okmulgee, Oklahoma.

The **Creek** are a Native American people of the Hokan-Siouan geographical linguistic group.

The Creek **held land in common** and governed themselves democratically.

The Creek maintained a **sacred fire** in a central plaza which was rekindled annually at the Green Corn Festival.

▲ *England cricketer Ian Botham.*

CRICKET

The **first women's Test match** was played between Australia and England at Brisbane, 28–31 Dec. 1934, and the first World Cup was in 1973, two years before the men's version.

The **highest number of wickets** taken by a

bowler in an English first-class season is 304 by Alfred 'Tich' Freeman of Kent and England in 1928.

The **most dismissals by a wicket-keeper** in a Test match is ten, all caught, by Bob Taylor of England v India at Bombay between 15 and 19 Feb. 1980.

The **most runs scored** by an individual in Test cricket is 11,174 by Allan Border of Australia between 1978 and 1994.

The **oldest man to play Test cricket** was England's Wilfred Rhodes who was aged 52 years and 165 days when England played the West Indies at Kingston, Jamaica on 12 Apr. 1930.

The West Indies' Brian Lara rattled up the **highest individual Test innings** score when he clocked up 375 against England in Antigua between 16 and 18 Apr. 1994.

CRISES

Although Lithuania was allowed multi-party elections (1989), troops were sent to **Azerbaijan during civil war with Armenia** (1990) and Gorbachev opposed Baltic independence (1990).

Cuban leader Fidel Castro. ▶

Boris Yeltsin, popularly elected Russian Republic president, banned Communist Party cells in the RSFSR (Jun. 1991). A hardline **communist coup** temporarily removed Gorbachev from power (Aug. 1991).

Castro refused to admit UN observers to Cuba, resenting exclusion from the Kennedy–Khrushchev exchanges, but by Nov. 1962 the US Defence Dept accepted that **the Soviet missiles in Cuba** had been dismantled.

Civil war between federal and republic armies of former Yugoslavia, including '**ethnic cleansing**', continued well into the 1990s despite international **sanctions** and calls for ceasefires.

In Russia, efforts to form a Union of Sovereign States failed (Nov. 1991). Gorbachev resigned. With the Commonwealth of Independent States created, the Soviet parliament **voted the USSR out of existence** (Dec.).

Gorbachev imposed **sanctions** on Lithuania after Vytautas Landsbergis' UDI (1990). A referendum to preserve the USSR as a federation of republics was approved, though **boycotted** by six republics (1991).

In 1973, in protest against Israel's expansion beyond 1967 ceasefire lines, OPEC's Arab member-states **drastically cut oil supplies**, raising crude oil prices by 200 per cent over three months.

In 1989 reformist Croation Ante Markovic became PM of Yugoslavia;

29 died in **ethnic riots** in Kosovo and a state of emergency was declared. Inflation rose by 490%.

In **Yugoslavia** (1988–89) with economic difficulties, 1,800 strikes, 250 per cent inflation, 20 per cent unemployment and ethnic unrest in Montenegro and Vojvodina, Branko Mikulic's government resigned.

Increasingly since the death of Marshal Tito (1892–1980), there had been **unrest in Yugoslavia**; to curb this, use of the army was threatened (1987).

On 16 Oct. 1962 aerial photos convinced Pres. Kennedy that the Soviets had installed **ballistic missiles** with nuclear warheads in Cuba, capable of reaching any US city.

On 22 Oct. 1962 Pres. Kennedy announced that the US Navy would impose a **blockade on Cuba** and formally requested that Khrushchev remove all missiles from the island. On 26 Oct. 1962 the Russians

offered to withdraw their weapons from Cuba if NATO missiles were removed from Turkey. The US rejected the condition. Consequently there was a definite **risk of nuclear war**.

On 28 Oct. 1962 Khrushchev agreed to order **withdrawal of Soviet missiles from Cuba** under UN supervision provided the US lifted the naval blockade and promised not to invade Cuba.

In the former Yugoslavia, Serbia and Croatia established multi-party systems (1990); Slovenia, Croatia, Bosnia-Herzegovina and Macedonia declared **independence** (1991–92); and Serbia and Montenegro became FRY (the Federal Republic of Yugoslavia, 1992).

The steep increase in oil prices in 1973 had vast repercussions, causing **world recession**, making some Arab states extremely rich but attacking the economies of developed and developing countries.

The **power of OPEC** (Organization of Petroleum Exporting Countries) in the 1970s was demonstrated by its ability to increase oil prices from $3 a barrel (1973) to $30 a barrel (1980).

The **US naval blockade of Cuba**

ended 20 Nov. 1962, the Soviets pledging to withdraw all bombers and rocket personnel from Cuba within a month. Kennedy's firmness in the crisis enhanced his prestige.

Though restored to power, Gorbachev's position was undermined by **Yeltsin's dismantling all existing communist structures** (Jul. 1991). With Latvia, Lithuania and Estonia's independence, the remaining Soviet republics seceded from the USSR (Sept. 1991 onwards).

With **nationalist challenges** in Kazakhstan, the Baltic republics, Armenia and Azerbaijan (1988); nationalist riots in Georgia (1989); and **Eastern Europe**'s communist regimes **overthrown** (1989), the USSR was in crisis.

CROATIA

A medieval duchy, later absorbed by Hungary (1102–1918), **Croatia** formed part of Yugoslavia. A separate state (1941–45), it again became independent in 1991.

Croatia (capital: Zagreb) lies on the north-east Adriatic, bordered by Slovenia, Bosnia and Serbia, and has an area of 56,538 sq km/21,829 sq mi.

◀ *Israel's capital Jerusalem.*

Croatia **exports** machinery and transport equipment, manufactured goods, chemicals and food products, mainly to Italy, Germany, Austria and France.

Croatia takes its name from the Croats (Chrobati, Hrvati), a Slav tribe which invaded Illyria and Dalmatia in 640.

The **population of Croatia** is 4,763,941 (est. 1991), comprising 94% Croat, 4% Serb and 2% Bosnian, predominantly Roman Catholic in religion.

CROW

In modern times the Crow **live in Montana** where tourism, ranching, and mineral leases provide a tribal income.

The **Crow** are a Native American people of the Hokan-Siouan geographical linguistic group.

The Crow believed the design they painted on their **buffalo-hide shields**, which came to them in a vision, would protect them in battle.

The Crow were a **hunting tribe** of the Plains who also cultivated tobacco.

The highly complex social system of the Crow stressed **care of children**.

CUBISM

Cubism was a movement in modern art, especially painting, that was primarily concerned with abstract forms rather than lifelike representation. It began in Paris *c.* 1908, reached its height by 1914 and developed further in the 1920s.

Cubism was a **revolt** against the sentimental and realistic traditional painting of the late 19th and early 20th c and against the emphasis on light and colour effects and the lack of form characteristic of Impressionism.

In **synthetic cubism**, an object is viewed from different angles, not simultaneously visible in life, which are arranged into a unified composition.

The **doctrines of the Cubist school** follow the dictum of the French Post-Impressionist Paul Cézanne, 'Everything in nature takes its form from the sphere, the cone and the cylinder'.

The first Cubist painting is considered to be *Les Demoiselles d'Avignon* (1907) by Picasso; his masterly draughtsmanship, visual intelligence and immense originality made him the master of the movement.

The leaders of the **cubist school** were the Spaniard Pablo Picasso and Frenchman Georges Braque; other notable Cubist painters were the Frenchmen Albert Gleizes, Robert Delaunay, Fernand Leger and Francis Picabia.

To avoid simple, naturalistic and emotional effects the early, or analytical, Cubists used mainly restrained greys, browns, greens and yellows and often executed their works in **monochrome**.

CURRENCIES

Paper money was first invented by the Chinese and introduced between AD 812 and 970; by this time it was in general circulation throughout Imperial China.

The **golden muhur**, minted in Agra in 1613 during the reign of Nur-ud-din Muhammad Jahangir, weighs nearly 12 kg/13.12 lb and is 20.3 cm/7.9 in wide. Only 100 were struck.

The **highest–value British** ever issued were for £1,000. They were introduced in 1755 and withdrawn in 1945. 100 of them have never been surrendered.

▲ *Nature Morte aux Pigeon* by *Picasso.*

The **lowest-value banknote** ever issued was the one-sen (one hundredth of a rupiah) Indonesian note. It had a value of over 300,000 to the pound in 1993.

The **oldest coin** is said to be an electrum stater of King Gyges of Lydia (now Turkey), believed to be dated *c.* 630 BC.

The **oldest surviving banknote** printed by the Bank of England is one for £555 and dated 1699. It measures 11.4 x 19.1 cm/4.5 x 7.5 in.

The **US Treasury Mint** on Independence Mall, Philadelphia has an annual production of 12 bn coins. The Graebner Press can mint coins at a rate of 42,000 per hour.

CYCLING

Beryl Burton was the **greatest British female cyclist**, winning the British all-round time championship 25 times in succession from 1959 to 1983.

Four men, Jacques Anquetil, Eddy Merckx, Bernard Hinault and Miguel Indurain share the record of **most Tour de France victories** with five each.

In an attempt to boost the circulation of his struggling newspaper *L'Auto*, proprietor Henri Desgrange instigated the **Tour de France** in 1903, cycling's most prestigious event.

Koichi Nakano (Japan) holds the record for **most world championship victories** in one event. He won the professional sprint title 10 times in succession from 1977 to 1986.

The **men's one-hour speed record** is held by Tony Rominger (Switzerland)

who covered 55.291 km/34.363 miles at Bordeaux on 6 Nov. 1994.

The **most successful cyclist overall** in the Tour de France has been Eddy Merckx (Belgium) with 35 stage victories between 1978 and 1986.

CYCLONES

Centres of **low air pressure** are called cyclones or depressions or lows. Centres of high pressure are called anticyclones or highs.

In some parts of the world hurricanes are called typhoons or **cyclones**. In Queensland, Australia, people call them willy-willies.

CYPRUS

Conquered by Assyrians, Egyptians, Persians, Macedonians, Romans, Byzantines, Crusaders and Turks, **Cyprus** became a British colony in 1914 and won independence in 1960.

Cyprus (capital: Nicosia) lies in the eastern Mediterranean, 71 km/44 mi south of Turkey, and has an area of 9,251 sq km/3,572 sq mi.

Czechoslovakia receives independence, 1992. ▶

Cyprus derives its name from the Greek word for copper, alluding to the fact that the island was the principal source of this metal during the Bronze Age.

Cyprus exports clothing, potatoes, wines, citrus fruit, cattle and footwear, mainly to the Arab countries, UK and Turkey.

The **population of Cyprus** is 747,600 (est. 1991), of which 574,000 are Greeks who live in the southern two-thirds, while the rest live in the so-called Turkish Republic of Northern Cyprus.

CZECH REPUBLIC

Formerly part of Czechoslovakia, the **Czech Republic** under Vaclav Havel became a separate independent state on 31 Dec. 1992 when the federation was dissolved.

In 1516 silver from Joachimsthal (now Jachymov) in the **Czech Republic** was converted into large coins known as thalers. From this comes the dollar now in universal use.

The **Czech Republic (capital: Prague)** lies in central Europe, bordered by Slovakia, Hungary, Austria, Germany and Poland, with an area of 78,864 sq km/39,450 sq mi.

The **Czech Republic exports** machinery and transport equipment, consumer goods, chemicals and mineral fuels, mainly to Germany, Austria, Hungary and Slovakia.

The **population of the Czech Republic** is 10,298,731 (est. 1992) comprising 81% Czech, 13% Moravian and 6% German and Hungarian.

DANCE

Busby Berkeley (b. William Berkeley Enos, 1895–1976) transformed the Hollywood musical with his unique flair for kaleidoscopic choreography, notably in *Forty-Second Street* (1933).

Fred Astaire (b. Frederick Austerlitz, 1899–1987) starred, acted, sang, choreographed and danced his way though such immortal Hollywood musicals as

Top Hat (1935), *Easter Parade* (1948) and *Funny Face* (1957).

Gene Kelly (b. Eugene Curran, 1912–96), dancer, singer, choreographer, actor and director, starred in such MGM musicals as *On the Town* (1949), *An American in Paris* (1951) and *Singin' in the Rain* (1952).

Popular dance forms this century have included: foxtrot, quickstep, tango, animal (Turkey Trot, Bunny Hug), Charleston, Latin American (cha-cha-cha, samba), jitterbug, jive, twist, frug, disco and break dancing.

The nine dances of modern world championships in **ballroom dancing** are: waltz, foxtrot, tango, quickstep, samba, rumba, cha-cha-cha, paso doble and the Viennese waltz.

DELHI

Delhi produces textiles, cotton, machinery, transport equipment and electrical goods. It is also a centre for silver filigree work, jewellery and embroidery.

The capital of the Mogul empire in India, **Delhi** dates from *c.* 1050 when Anangapala built the Red Fort. It became the capital of British India in 1912.

The signing of the Warsaw Pact. ▶

▲ *The Golden Temple in India.*

The **population of Delhi** is 8,375,188 (1991 census), with a further 294,149 in New Delhi. The combined population in 1941 was only 521,849.

While the old city of **Delhi** is noted for its splendid mosques and Mogul palaces, the new city, designed by Sir Edwin Lutyens, is noted for the Parliament and government buildings.

DEMOCRACY

In 1989–91 the Eastern European and Soviet republics rejected communist control by the **Warsaw Pact and Soviet Union**, opting to a greater or lesser extent for Western democracy.

The **Internet** global on-line computer network (1984) is, arguably and potentially, the world's greatest modern democratic institution: anyone may transmit or receive information via e-mail or the World Wide Web.

The **Republic of India**, created 1947, population 952,969,000 (est. 1996), first PM Jawaharlal Nehru (1947–64, b. 1889), is the world's largest modern democracy.

The **State of Israel**, created 1948, population 5,481,000 (est. 1996), first PM David Ben-Gurion (1948–53, 1955–63, b. 1886) is a Western-style democracy surrounded by Arab states.

The **United States of America**, created 1776, population 265,455,000 (est. 1996), first Pres. George Washington (1789–96, b. 1732) is the most powerful modern Western democracy.

DENMARK

Denmark (capital: Copenhagen) is located at the mouth of the Baltic Sea in north-western Europe, with an area of 43,093 sq km/16,638 sq mi.

Denmark exports machinery and instruments, agricultural products (butter, pigs, pork), chemicals, drugs, textiles and clothing, mainly within Scandinavia and to Germany.

In 1917 **Denmark** sold three islands in the West Indies (St Thomas, St John and St Croix) to the US for $25 m. This part of the Virgin Islands had been Danish since the 17th c.

In the 11th c **Denmark** ruled an empire stretching from Ireland to Sweden, but the kingdom in its present form dates from 1814.

The **population of Denmark** is 5,146,000 (est. 1991), comprising 97.2% Danish, 0.5% Turkish, 0.4% other Scandinavian and 0.2% British. Over 90% are Lutheran, the rest mainly Roman Catholic.

DESERTS

A distinctive type of extremely **dry west-coast desert** is found in western Africa (Sahara and Namib) and America (Sonora and Atacama). Coastal fog and unusually large amounts of fish are characteristic.

Although the world's **highest shade temperatures** have been recorded in deserts – 58°C/136°F at Al'Aziziyah, Libya – plants can grow if there is enough moisture for them to transpire (lose water through leaves).

▼ *The Sahara Desert.*

Deserts associated with clear skies and burning sun occur where there is **high atmospheric pressure** and stable air, generally in middle latitudes, not in the atmospherically unstable equatorial zone.

Every year more than 60,000 sq km/23,000 sq mi of soil turns to **desert**. This is equivalent to half the area of England. Similarly, each year over 200,000 sq km/70,000 sq mi of land becomes unsuitable for crops.

In 1910 Albrecht Penck formulated the first scientific definition of **dry deserts**: areas bounded by a line along which evaporation equals precipitation. The definition has since been refined.

Remoteness from the sea accentuates the dryness of the **continental interior deserts** of central Asia. Below-freezing winter temperatures and scorching summer temperatures of more than 57°C/100°F are common.

The largest desert is the **Sahara**, North Africa. Its maximum east–west extent is 5,150 km/3,200 mi. Its north–south extent varies from 1,280 km/800 mi to 2,250 km/1,400 mi. Its area is about 9,269,000 sq km/3,579,000 sq mi.

Benito Mussolini ▶

DICTATORS

Benito Mussolini (1883–1945) was the founder of Italian fascism and premier (dictator) of Italy, 1922–43. In 1936 he concluded an agreement with Germany that eventually resulted in Italy's disastrous participation in World War II.

Dictator of Paraguay for 35 years, **Alfredo Stroessner** (b. 1912) became commander in chief of the armed forces in 1951. After toppling the government of Federico Chavez in a coup in 1954, Stroessner was elected president.

IL MATTINO ILLUSTRATO

Ferdinand Marcos (1917–89) was president of the Philippines (1965–86). His dictatorial rule was ended in 1986 when Corazon Aquino, the widow of the assassinated opposition leader Benigno S. Aquino, Jr, was elected president.

Gen. Francisco Franco led the nationalist forces in the Spanish Civil War (1936–39) and ruled Spain as dictator until his death in 1975.

German dictator **Adolf Hitler** (1889–1945), founder of the Third Reich, came to power in 1933. His aggressive expansionism precipitated World War II, which culminated in the defeat of Germany and Hitler's suicide in 1945.

Joseph Stalin (1879–1953), dictator of the USSR after the death of Lenin, led his country to victory in World War II. Although he brought the Soviet Union to world-power status, he imposed upon it one of the most ruthless regimes in history.

Juan Manuel de Rosas (1793–1877), twice governor of Buenos Aires (1829–32 and 1835–52), ruled Argentina as dictator during his second term of office.

Panamanian dictator **Manuel Noriega** (b. 1934) became commander of Panama's defence forces in 1983 and subsequently installed and deposed presidents. In 1988 he was indicted for drug trafficking, racketeering and money laundering.

DINOSAURS

Brachiosaurus, one of the largest dinosaurs, lived from 140 to 165 m. years ago. Much larger than the modern African elephant, this dinosaur measured about 21 m/70 ft long and 12 m/40 ft high.

Dinosaur (from the Greek for 'terrible lizard') is the name given to various kinds of large extinct reptiles of the Mesozoic Era (230–65 m. years ago), when they were the dominant land animals on earth.

Dinosaurs ranged in weight from 2–3 kg/4–6 lbs (*Compsognathus*) and up to 73 tonnes/160,000 lbs (*Brachiosaurus*). Most dinosaurs weighed more than 500 kg/1100 lbs; most were **herbivores**, but

◄ *Dinosaurs are believed to be ancient reptiles.*

some *Saurischians* were carnivorous.

Dinosaurs were traditionally assumed to have been **reptilian**, cold-blooded and ectothermic (dependent on external heat sources). In recent years evidence indicates that dinosaurs may have had warm blood, comparable to that of birds and mammals.

The dinosaur order ***Ornithischia*** is divided into four or five suborders: the bipedal ornithopods, the plated stegosaurs, the armoured ankylosaurs and the horned dinosaurs or ceratopsians.

The dinosaur order ***Saurischia*** includes two different and perhaps distantly related kinds of dinosaurs: the carnivores (suborder *Theropoda*) and the huge herbivores and their ancestors (suborder *Sauropodomorpha*).

▼ *Dinosaur fossils.*

The first recorded **dinosaur remains** found consisted of a few teeth and bones and were discovered (1822) by an English doctor, Gideon Mantell, who named them *Iguanodon* ('iguana tooth'). Other fossils were found by Rev. William Buckland, who called them *Megalosaurus* ('great lizard').

The **Tyrannosaurus** was a meat-eating dinosaur that lived about 70 m. years ago. The fiercest and last of the now-extinct carnivorous dinosaurs, it was 15 m/50 ft long and 5.5 m/18 ft high and had dozens of sharp, flesh-tearing teeth that were up to 20 cm/8 in long.

Triceratops, a herbivorous ceratopsid dinosaur of the late Cretaceous Period, was about 6 m/20 ft long and probably weighed about 7 tonnes. *Ceratopsids* were the last group of dinosaurs to become extinct.

DISEASES

Body systems can also be affected by disease. The immune system, which forms antibodies against foreign agents such as bacteria, can manufacture antibodies that attack the body itself (an **auto-immune** condition).

Disease is the abnormal state or functioning of all or part of an organism. In humans diseases are categorised as acute or severe and short-term, chronic or long-term, and recurrent or periodic.

Diseases may arise from internal causes, such as **hereditary disorders**, which are transmitted by the genes and chromosomes of one or both parents.

Each organ system is subject to particular diseases. The circulatory system is subject to **heart diseases** such as valve damage from atherosclerosis, which narrows the blood vessels.

External agents that cause diseases include such chemical and physical agents as **radiation**, which causes aplastic anaemia; irritants, which cause such occupational diseases as black lung; drugs; poisons; and injury.

Infectious diseases are caused by such external agents as bacteria, viruses and parasitic worms and are transmitted by humans, animals, insects or substances.

The musculoskeletal system can be weakened by many diseases, including osteogenesis imperfect, which is the presence of weak, brittle bones. **Tumours** or abnormal growths may affect any organ or organ system.

DRUGS

A **side-effect** may be defined as any result of a drug's actions other than that for which the drug is therapeutically intended. The most common side-effects are those involving the nervous system and the intestinal tract.

Drugs are substances given to humans or animals for the treatment, prevention or diagnosis of illness. They are used to relieve pain or other suffering and to improve and control abnormal conditions of the mind and body.

Drugs can be administered in a number of ways, including through the skin, **injections**, intestinally (e.g. a suppository) and tissue linings (e.g. nasal passages).

Drugs generally act at the **cellular level**. They influence the way in which the body's cellular machinery performs, either stimulating or slowing it. Drug molecules eventually reach the body's many tissues, where they exert action.

During the 1940s and '50s many drugs were developed and used to treat diseases that had previously been untreatable. **Anti-cancer drugs** and steroids came into clinical use in the late 1940s.

Humans have used drugs in various forms since prehistoric times. Primitive humans ate **plants** such as mushrooms, which had physiological effects. The Romans and Ancient Greeks used various plants and waters therapeutically.

In the 18th c, scurvy was effectively treated with citrus fruit and physicians discovered that **digitalis**, derived from foxgloves, could be used to treat heart disease.

DUBLIN

Dublin exports agricultural produce, textiles, biscuits, glass, cigarettes, whiskey and stout. It also has iron foundries and shipyards.

Dublin is situated at the head of a bay of the Irish Sea, to which it gives its name. The name Dublin signifies 'black pool'.

Shopping centre in Dublin. ▶

First recorded in AD 291, **Dublin** was converted to Christianity by St Patrick *c.* AD 450. The Anglo-Normans ousted the Danes in 1171.

The General Post Office, **Dublin** was the scene of fierce fighting in May 1916 when Padraig Pearse proclaimed the Irish Republic from its steps.

The **population of Dublin** was 502,749 (1986 census); the vast major-ity were Roman Catholic but there were small Anglican, Presbyterian and Jewish communities.

EARLY INVENTIONS

A Sumerian pictograph (*c.* 3500 BC), shows a sledge equipped with **wheels**. Wheeled transport probably developed from the use of logs for rollers.

Archimedes, b. *c.* 290–280 BC in Greece, is credited with inventing the **Archimedes screw**, a device for rais-ing water and used to remove it from ships' holds.

Around the middle of the 4th millen-nium BC, the use of copper metallurgy, with **cast tools and weapons**, was a factor leading to urbanisation in Mesopotamia.

During the 2nd millennium BC the use of true bronze, an **alloy** of copper and tin, greatly increased. The tin deposits in Cornwall, Britain, were much used.

It was not until *c.* 7000 BC that Neolithic man acquired reliable **fire-making** techniques, using either drills, saws or flint struck against pyrites.

The **aeolipile** was a steam turbine invented in AD 1st century by Hero of Alexandria and described in his *Pneumatica*. It is the first known device to transform steam into rotary motion.

The first use of **fire** was thought to be by Peking Man (approx. 500000 BC). However, evidence uncovered in Kenya (1981) and South Africa (1988) suggests the earliest controlled use of fire was about 1,420,000 years ago.

EARLY MEASUREMENTS

Although the Chinese Emperor Huang Ti (2634 BC) is said to have invented a south-pointing chariot, the first mariner's **compass** was devised by the Arabs in the 11th c.

Measurement theory dates back to the 4th c BC, when a theory of magni-tudes was developed by the Greek mathematicians Eudoxus and Thaeatetus. It was included in Euclid's *Elements*.

One of the earliest weight measures was the **Babylonian mina**. Its actual weight is unsure as of two surviving examples one weighs 640 g/1.4 lbs, the other 978 g/2.15 lbs.

The **armillary sphere**, the oldest known astronomical instrument, was essentially a skeletal celestial globe whose rings represented the great circles of the heavens; it was known in ancient China.

The **equal–arm balance** was invented by the ancient Egyptians *c.* 5000 BC. In the earliest types, the beam was supported at the centre, the pans hung from the ends by cords.

The Greeks were familiar with the armillary sphere. They modified it to produce the **astrolabe**, which could tell the time, or measure the length of day or night. It could also measure solar and lunar altitudes.

The most widespread unit of linear measurement in the ancient world was probably the **Egyptian**

cubit (3000 BC). It was based on the length of the arm from elbow to extended fingertips.

EARTH

A complete **orbit** of the Earth around the Sun takes 365 days 5 hr 48 min 46 sec. It travels at an average speed of 30 kps/18.5 mps.

The crust and top layer of the mantle form about 12 moving plates, some of which carry the **continents**. The plates are in constant motion known as tectonic drift.

The Earth is 4.6 bn years old and was formed, along with the rest of the solar system, by consolidation of interstellar dust. **Life began** 3.5 bn years ago.

The Earth is made up of **three concentric layers** the core (made up of iron and nickel), the mantle and the crust (made of solid rock).

The Earth is the **third planet** from the Sun. It is almost spherical but flattened slightly at the poles, and 70% of its surface is covered with water.

The Earth's **plane of orbit** to the Sun is inclined at an angle of 23.5° which gives us changing seasons. Each day lasts 23 hr 56 min 4.1 sec.

The mean distance from the **Earth to the Sun** is 149,500,000 km/92,860,000 mi. Its circumference is 40,070 km/24,900 mi with an equatorial diameter of 12,756 km/7,923 mi.

EARTHQUAKES

An **earthquake** is a shaking of the Earth's surface resulting from a build-up of stresses in rocks.

In 1987 a Californian earthquake was **successfully predicted** by measurement of underground pressure waves. Prediction also uses water levels, animal behaviour and gas changes from crust seepage.

Most **earthquakes** occur along faults (fractures or breaks) in the Earth's crust. Plate tectonic movements (two plates moving past each other) cause most of them.

The majority of earthquakes happen beneath the sea. Their scale is measured on the **Richter scale** named after US seismologist Charles Richter.

The point where an earthquake originates is called the **seismic focus**. The

The Rocky Mountains in Canada. ▶

point on the Earth's surface directly above this is called the epicentre.

The **San Francisco earthquake** and fire of 18 Apr. 1906 caused the deaths of around 700 people, obliterated 500 city blocks and caused $500 m. of damage.

The **strongest earthquake** ever recorded occurred in 1920 in Gansu, China and measured 8.6 on the Richter scale. No other earthquake so far has reached more than 8.3.

▲ *Pollution from factories is a major cause of environmental concern.*

ECOLOGY

A Friends of the Earth campaign (1972) to persuade consumers not to buy **fur coats** of tiger, leopard and cheetah skins led to a ban on the sale of these goods.

According to the ***Global 2000 Report*** (1982), efforts then under way to preserve the environment were too little, and 'An era of unprecedented global cooperation and commitment is essential'.

Although Kublai Khan was reportedly keen to protect the plant and animal life of his Mongol Empire, in modern times Switzerland has the longest tradition of **conservation**: it set up the first game preserve in 1542.

◄ *Tropical rainforest in Costa Rica.*

CFCs are chemicals used as coolants in refrigerators and in spray cans to expel other gases. They damage the ozone layer (a kind of oxygen), which protects the earth against harmful rays from the sun.

Ecology is not only the study of the environment but also a campaign to conserve it. Proponents argue that a flourishing **environment** is the precondition of a prosperous, healthy society.

In industrialised countries power stations, vehicles, factories and homes burn fossil fuels (coal, oil, gas). The most harmful products of this process are sulphur dioxide and nitrogen oxide, which cause **acid rain**.

In northern China erosion is destroying the soil where forests were cleared long ago to make way for farming. To save the situation, the Chinese are planting a **green 'Great Wall'** of trees.

Minimum distances for **dumping wastes** off the coast of the UK are: treated rubbish, 15.55 km/3 nau. mi; treated sewage, 20.73 km/4 nau. mi; poisons, untreated rubbish and untreated sewage, 62.16km/12 nau. mi; and oil, 155.4 km/30 nau. mi.

Parts of **Antarctica** are now infested with rats, brought in by ship, and strange grasses are growing wild. A disease common to poultry may have infected the emperor penguin.

The Italian scientist Aurelio Peccei described the '**green movement**', which began in the 1970s, as a 'popular army' acting like antibodies 'to restore normal conditions in a diseased biological organism'.

There are 1,500 m. ha/3,700 m. ac of **farm land** in the world, but erosion is destroying 1 m. ha/2.5 m. ac per year.

▼ *Containers are often made of recyclable materials.*

ECONOMICS

Balance of payments is the relationship between the amount of money a country spends abroad and the income it receives from other countries.

Economies of scale cause average costs to be lower in larger scale operations that smaller ones: doubling output does not mean a doubling of costs.

Fiscal policy is government policy towards its raising of revenue and its level of public spending. Taxes represent a withdrawal that funds public spending.

Gross National Product (GNP) is a term in economics used to describe in monetary value the total annual flow of goods and services in the economy of a nation.

Monetary policy is government policy regarding growth of the money supply, interest rates and the availability of credit.

National Debt is the sum total of governmental financial obligations, the result of a state's borrowing from its population, from foreign governments or from international institutions.

EDINBURGH

Edinburgh is dominated by its castle, high on a rock overlooking the city. At the end of the Royal Mile stands the Royal Palace of Holyrood.

A Pictish and later Roman stronghold, the castle rock was fortified by Edwin, King of Northumbria in AD 617. **Edinburgh** derives its name from 'Edwin's burgh'.

Edinburgh was formerly a centre of printing and publishing. Today its **main industries** are paper, whisky, machinery and electronics.

Edinburgh, the county seat of Midlothian and the **capital of Scotland**, stands on a cluster of hills and valleys south of the Forth estuary.

The **population of Edinburgh** is 433,000 (est. 1991), about the same as it was at the 1931 census and less than its peak of 469,448 in 1941.

Edinburgh Castle. ▶

EDUCATION

Ancient **Hebrew education** centred on the study of the Torah. Scholars known as scribes and later as rabbis taught the Jews in the synagogues, although responsibility for the education of children fell to parents.

During the 17th c several theorists emerged who were to exert a continuing influence on **education**. Among them were Francis Bacon, John Amos Comenius and John Locke.

In 18th-c England Andrew Bell and Joseph Lancaster helped bring about an elementary school system. Bell developed a **systematic monitorial system**, which Lancaster modified, whereby children taught other children in the classroom.

In all countries education systems change in response to society's economic, political and social needs and ambitions. Developing countries are concentrating on eradicating **illiteracy** and providing economic and technological training.

In Ancient Rome boys were given a **general education** that included the study of literature, linguistics, astronomy, geometry, music, logic, history and philosophy; girls received only an elementary education.

In Egypt and Sumer (3rd millennium BC) young people were selected to serve as priests, clerics, builders and political rulers and were taught writing, mathematics, astronomy, architecture and government in **temple schools**.

The **Protestant Reformation**, led by Martin Luther and John Calvin, began in 1517. Both believed that it was important for all Christians to read the Bible. They urged the state to help establish an educational system.

Up to *c.* 600 BC, formal education in China was available only to rulers and nobles. By 400 BC education, conducted in private homes, followed four schools of thought: **Confucianism**, Taoism, Mohism and Legalism.

EDUCATIONAL PSYCHOLOGY

Behaviourism (the behaviourist approach to educational psychology), which originated with the work of Edward L. Thorndike and John B. Watson and culminated in that of B. F. Skinner, focuses on the control of behaviour through reinforcement.

During the early 19th c Johann Heinrich Pestalozzi refined and applied Jean Jacques Rousseau's naturalistic, child-centred approach to education and was acclaimed for developing a **psychology of education**.

Educational psychology began to emerge as an applied speciality within psychology during the late 19th c when James McKeen Cattell and Hermann Ebbinghaus laid the foundation of **educational measurement**.

Educational psychology emerged as a distinct discipline in the early 1900s. However, the **origins** of educational psychology can be traced to ancient Greek philosophers.

Educational psychology, a field of study that investigates problems of teaching and learning, shares some of the characteristics of cognitive psychology and behaviourism.

Humanistic educational psychology, which emphasises the human attributes of thoughts and feelings, emerged as a reaction to the reductionist and mechanistic views of behaviourism.

The precursor to the **developmental approach** to educational psychology, Jean Plaget, revolutionised the study of children with his observations of four stages of intellectual development.

The **psychoanalytic approach** to educational psychology is based primarily on the writings of Sigmund Freud, and focuses on the role of emotion in influencing what is learned.

◀ *Study of the Jewish Torah.*

EGYPT

Among the antiquities of **Egypt** the great Pyramid of Cheops at Giza (2900 BC) is the only survivor of the Wonders of the Ancient World.

Egypt (capital: Cairo) occupies the north-eastern corner of Africa, bordering Libya, Sudan and Israel, and has an area of 997,739 sq km/385,229 sq mi.

Egypt exports cotton (both raw and yarn), textiles and petroleum, mainly to Italy, Romania, UK, Japan, France, Russia and Germany.

The overthrow of King Farouk in Jul. 1952 led to the establishment of the republic of **Egypt**. Under Colonel Nasser there was a brief union with Syria and the Yemen.

The **population of Egypt** is 54,609,000 (est. 1991), comprising 99.8% Egyptian of whom 90% are Sunni Muslin and 10% Christian.

ELECTRICITY

Belgian scientist Zenobe Théophile Gramme first demonstrated that electric power could be transmitted efficiently from place to place by overhead **conductors** in 1873.

In 1808 Sir **Humphry Davy** demonstrated that electricity could provide light or heat by separating two charcoal electrodes that were carrying a current and thus drawing an arc.

Michael Faraday showed how a magnetic field induces an electromotive force in a moving conductor in 1831. This led to the development of the **dynamo**, the electric motor and the transformer.

Proper study of electricity began late 16th c, when William Gilbert investigated the relation of static electricity and magnetism. Benjamin Franklin proved the electrical nature of **lightning** in 1752 using kites.

The Greeks discovered **static electricity** by realising that amber, rubbed with fur, attracted light objects such as feathers: the word 'electric' comes from the Greek *elektron*, meaning amber.

In 1964 **IBM** consolidated its position in the marketplace with the introduction of the enormously successful System/360, the first compatible family of computers.

In 1971 Marcian Hoff, Jr, an engineer at the Intel Corporation, located in Silicon Valley, invented the **microprocessor**, and another stage in the development of the computer began.

In 1975 a group in Silicon Valley led by Steve Jobs and Steve Wozniak decided that computer responses needed to be made more 'user-friendly', and founded the **Apple** company.

In the 1980s the microprocessor industry was creating new **integrated circuits** many times faster than any that came previously. By the early 1990s, the power of the IBM 360 could be bought for about $100.

The **Leyden jar**, invented in 1745 by Pieter van Musschenbroek, was the first device that could store large amounts of electric charge.

Thomas Edison invented both the incandescent lamp in 1879 and constructed the first central **power station** and distribution system in New York in 1881.

ELECTRONICS

First produced by the Digital Equipment Corporation in 1963, **minicomputers** were also later produced by Data General. Digital's compact machines could be installed almost anywhere.

► *Apple's revolutionary new iMac.*

The **Eckert-Mauchly Computer Corporation** was the US's first computer company. It embarked upon a highly innovative project, the development of a general-purpose computer system.

The **first widely used personal computer** was introduced in 1975 by Microinstrumentation and Telemetry Systems (MITS). Called the Altair 8800, it used an Intel microprocessor.

EMPLOYMENT

At its **seasonal high point** (Jan. and Feb.) unemployment in the US between 1976 and 1996 was typically 20% higher than at the seasonal low (Oct.).

Before 1990 **female labour-force participation rates** ranged from 38% in Germany to 55% in Sweden. Most countries have some form of equal employment or protective legislation.

By early 1992 Japan's **unemployment rate** was still low (just over 2%) despite an economic slowdown, but the rate was approaching 10% in the UK.

During the latter part of the 18th c in Great Britain children, five and six years of age, worked from 13–16 hours a day in **cotton mills**.

The **highest recorded unemployment rate** in the UK stood at 22.8% on 23 Jan. 1933. This amounted to nearly 3 m., the highest pre-World War II total.

The **lowest unemployment rate** in the UK accounted for a mere 0.9% (185,000) in Jul. 1955. In Switzerland in 1973 only 81 people were unemployed from a population of 6.6 m.

When the barber's assistants **strike** ended in Jan. 1961, the strikers, based in Copenhagen, Denmark had been in dispute for 33 years.

ENDANGERED SPECIES

A ban was placed on ivory trading in 1989 when the **African elephant** was declared endangered by the United Nation's Convention on International Trade in Endangered Species.

In 1973, 80 nations that originally participated in the **Convention on International Trade** in Endangered Species of Wild Flora and Fauna in Washington, DC, agreed to halt imports of endangered species.

Many species have also been hunted to the point of **extinction** for their furs, hides or feathers. These include the big cats, crocodiles, caimans, quetzal birds, eastern grey kangaroos, egrets and birds of paradise.

National refuges exist in Africa, protecting such game as elephants and lions and also lesser-known, rare species of animals; such refuges have also been established in India, Australia, Europe and numerous other regions worldwide.

▼ *The endangered African elephant.*

Populations of the **giant sea turtle**, fur seal and unique bird species of the Galapagos Islands have been protected under the Charles Darwin Foundation for the Galapagos Islands, established (1959) with the support of UNESCO and the International Union for the Conservation of Native and Natural Resources.

Species of **salamanders** in New England are dying out because the ponds in which they breed and the moist soil in which they must live are watered by acid rain, water that combines with pollutants in the air to form acids and other corrosive compounds.

The International Whaling Commission (IWC) was formed in 1946 to regulate whaling, revive endangered species and establish 'sustainable **whale** populations' on a global basis.

ENERGY

Energy can be converted from one form to another in many ways. Usable mechanical or **electrical energy** is, for instance, produced by many kinds of devices such as generators or batteries.

Energy is the capacity for doing work. It can exist in froms such as potential, kinetic, thermal, electrical, chemical and nuclear.

Galileo in the 17th c recognised that when a weight is lifted, the force applied multiplied by the distance through which that force must be applied remains constant.

Heat was identified as a form of energy by Hermann von Helmholtz of Germany and James Prescott Joule of England during the 1840s.

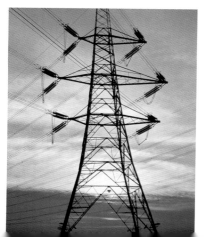

Potential energy can be converted into motion energy (**kinetic energy**), and then again to electrical energy; for example, water behind a dam may flow through turbines which then turn electric generators.

Potential energy is stored energy. It depends upon the relative position of various parts of a system, for example, a coiled spring has more potential energy than one at rest.

The kinetic energy produced by molecules in a solid, liquid or gas is known as its **thermal energy**. Liquids expand when thermal energy increases; this is how thermometers work.

ENGINEERING

By 1945 **diesel power** was forming 7% of freight and 10% of passenger traffic; by 1952, for the first time, diesel units exceeded steam locomotives.

Constant improvements in **airframe design and engines** made military aviation a dominant feature of warfare by 1945, and commercial aviation had aircraft capable of transatlantic travel by the same year.

In 1990 the **Institute of Electrical and Electronic Engineers**, the most

▲ Henry Ford introduced the assembly line to car manufacture.

important professional society, had a membership of 275,000, most of the engineers in the field.

Large dams rank among the greatest engineering feats. The **Itaipu Dam** completed in 1982 on the Parana River between Brazil and Paraguay, generating 12,600 MW, is the largest power complex on earth.

Motor-vehicle manufacturing grew to an enormous scale, especially after the adoption of **mass production** with Henry Ford's moving assembly line (1913).

Nuclear energy has been used successfully in large warships. Commercially, nuclear energy is being used in several countries to generate electric power.

The fundamental principles underlying the operation of **the maser and laser** were established by Albert Einstein long before these devices were successfully demonstrated.

ENVIRONMENT

Environmental movements are social movements that are concerned with the protection of natural surroundings from overuse and degradation by humans. They are a post-Industrial Revolution phenomenon primarily initiated in the US and Europe.

Greenpeace is an international environmental organisation founded in 1969 by a group of Canadian environmentalists. It advocates direct, non-violent action to halt threats to the environment.

Efforts have been made to create environmentally friendly packaging. ▶

In Europe 20th c-environmentalist sentiment took political form with the formation of the **'Green' party** in Germany and of 'green' movements throughout the continent.

Since 1955, at least 70,000 new **chemicals** have been released into the environment.

Pollutants may cause primary **damage**, with direct identifiable impact on the environment, or secondary damage, in the form of disturbances in the delicate balance of the biological food web that are detectable only over long time periods.

Population pressures now exacerbate most serious environmental problems, among them shrinking forests, expanding deserts, dwindling clean water supplies, mountains of waste and the blanket of greenhouse gases.

The American biologist and educator **Paul Ralph Ehrlich** (b. 1932) is a major proponent of the theory that the survival of humans depends on their realisation that the Earth's natural resources are unrenewable and too limited to support the increasing population.

The principles of **ecology** are useful in many aspects of the related fields of conservation, wildlife management, forestry, agriculture and pollution control.

The publication of **Silent Spring** by Rachel Carson in 1962 marked the beginning of the modern environmental movement. Carson wrote about the dangers of such recently developed agricultural chemicals as DDT, sending warnings about the risks of technologies producing artificial pesticides and other new chemical products.

Today, reflecting an increasing understanding of ecology (the science of the interrelationships between living things and their **environment**) the use of the term 'conservation' has been extended to consider the environment as a whole.

EQUATOR

Equatorial currents, predominantly controlled by the winds, flow near the equator in the Atlantic, Pacific and Indian oceans.

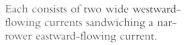

Each consists of two wide westward-flowing currents sandwiching a narrower eastward-flowing current.

The area close to the **equator** is almost directly beneath the sun in the sky, at all times of year. Constantly rising heated air brings moisture in from north and south and causes rains.

The earth's **equator** is like a giant greenhouse, where plants grow in profusion. The annual rainfall can be as much as 2,000 mm/80 in and the high temperatures (26–28°C/79–82.5°F) vary little.

The **equator** is the great circle around the earth that is equidistant from the geographic poles and lies in a plane perpendicular to the earth's axis.

The **geographic equator** divides the earth into northern and southern hemispheres and forms the imaginary line from which latitude is reckoned; it is the line of 0° latitude.

The surface of the earth and anything on it at the equator are moving eastwards at a speed of 1,670 kph/1,040 mph because of the **earth's spin** on its axis.

ESKIMO

Many modern Eskimo continue to inhabit their ancestral lands and to follow a **largely traditional existence.**

The Eskimo build their **social organisation** around whale, seal and caribou hunting.

The Eskimo's arctic environment has produced **inventive measures** like ice igloos for shelter, the kayak and special footwear for snow.

▼ *Native Greenlanders.*

The Eskimo, one of the world's most **widely distributed people**, have never exceeded a population of 60,000. They live from south-east Alaska to Greenland.

The **Eskimo**, or Inuit, are a Native American people of the Eskimo-Aleut linguistic group.

ETHIOPIA

Africa's oldest independent country, **Ethiopia** was allegedly founded by Menelik I, son of Solomon and the Queen of Sheba, in the 4th c BC.

Ethiopia (capital: Addis Ababa) lies in north-east Africa, bordering the Sudan, Eritrea, Somalia and Kenya, with an area of 1,223,500 sq km/472,400 sq mi.

Ethiopia exports coffee, hides, live animals, petroleum products, pulses and oilseeds, mainly to Germany, the US, Italy, Russia and Saudi Arabia.

Ethiopia emerged from medieval isolation under Menelik II (1883–1913). Occupied by Italy (1936–41), it later became a socialist republic (1976).

The **population of Ethiopia** is 51,617,000 (est. 1991), comprising 37.7% Amhara, 35.5% Galla, 8.6% Tigrinya, 3.3% Gurage, 2.4% Sidamo, 1.9% Tigre, 1.8% Afar, 1.7% Somali and 4.6% other.

EUROPE

Because of its many bays, inlets, peninsulas and islands, Europe has the longest **coastline** of any continent.

Europe has an **area** of about 10,498,000 sq km/4,052,000 sq mi. It covers 2% of the world's total surface area and 6.7% of total land area.

Europe stretches from the Atlantic shoreline to the Ural mountains. In the north are the mountains of Scotland and Norway, about 400 m. years old, while the south is edged by newer fold mountains.

In the zoogeographical classification, Europe, northern Asia and North Africa belong to the **Palearctic Realm**.

◄ *Life in Ethiopia.*

Mt El'brus, Russia, is the **highest** point in Europe, 5,642 m/18,510 ft, and the Caspian Sea its **lowest point**, 28 m/92 ft.

EUROPEAN UNION

The European Union, known as the European Community until 1993, is a political and economic alliance established in 1952 with the creation of the **European Coal and Steel Community (ECSC)**.

Association agreements, providing for free trade within ten years and the possibility of full membership of the EC, were signed with the Czech Republic, Hungary, Poland (1991), Romania, Bulgaria and Slovakia (1992).

At an ECSC Foreign Ministers' meeting (1955), Paul-Henri Spaak (Belgium) proposed an economic association based upon free trade and joint social and financial policies, forming the **basis of the EEC**.

The EC was renamed **European Union** (EU) in 1993. East Germany (GDR) was incorporated on German reunification (1990) and Austria, Finland and Sweden joined in 1995.

Estonia and Latvia applied for full **membership of the EU** (1995) and the European Commission agreed to entry talks with Poland, the Czech Republic, Hungary, Slovenia and Cyprus (1997).

Pres. Charles de Gaulle (France) used **right of veto** to stop UK attempts (Macmillan government, 1961) to join the EEC, blocking Britain's application (1963) after long negotiations by Edward Heath.

▲ *Vineyards in Spain.*

Pres. de Gaulle (France) again prevented UK entry to the EEC when Harold Wilson's government applied (1967). After de Gaulle's resignation (1969), tension within the EEC eased, clearing the path for Britain's entry.

The **European Atomic Energy Commission** (Euratom) was incorporated into the EC (1957). More countries joined: the UK, Denmark and the Irish Republic (1973), Greece (1981), Spain and Portugal (1986).

The **European Economic Community** (EEC, popularly known as the Common Market) was incorporated into the EC in 1957 with the same members as the ECSC.

EXPLORATION

Capt. James Cook (UK), made the first European discovery of Hawaii; he landed at Waimea in Jan. 1778. On returning in 1779, he was killed during an affray with Hawaiians at Kealakekua Bay.

Christopher Columbus, the Genoese explorer, made four voyages to the New World. The first two were: 1492 to San Salvador, Cuba and Haiti, and 1493–96 to Guadeloupe, Montserrat, Antigua, Puerto Rico and Jamaica.

Christopher Columbus's third voyage was in 1498 to Trinidad and the South American mainland, and his fourth in 1502–04 to Honduras and Nicaragua.

English explorer and buccaneer **Francis Drake** was sponsored by Elizabeth I for an expedition to the Pacific, sailing round the world in the *Golden Hind*, 1577–80.

Robert Scott (**Scott of the Antarctic**) commanded two Antarctic expeditions. In 1912 he reached the South Pole just after Norwegian Amundsen but on returning he was caught in a blizzard and died with his colleagues.

The first recorded sighting of **Australia** by Europeans was in 1606

◄ *Nineteenth-century naval expedition to the Arctic.*

when the Dutch ship *Duyfken* commanded by Willem Jansz saw the West coast of Cape York.

Venetian **Marco Polo** travelled overland to China in 1271–75 and served Emperor Kublai Khan. His writings (1296–98) were the primary source of information about the Far East until the 19th c.

EXPRESSIONISM

Expressionism, in the visual, literary and performing arts, was a movement or tendency that strove to express subjective feelings and emotions rather than to depict reality or nature objectively.

In 1905, a group of expressionist artists in Dresden (Germany) started **Die Brucke** ('The Bridge'), developing Fauve ideas and led by Ernst Ludwig Kirchner (1880–1938). They broke up in 1913.

In Expressionism the artist tried to present an **emotional experience** in its most compelling form. The artist was not concerned with reality as it appears but with its inner nature and with the emotions aroused by the subject.

In Munich *Der Blaue Reiter* ('The Blue Rider') Expressionist group was

set up in 1911 by Wassily Kandinsky (1866–1944), who painted the first abstract painting.

The **Expressionist movement** developed during the late 19th and early 20th c as a reaction against the academic standards that had prevailed in Europe since the Renaissance (1300–1600), particularly in French and German art academies.

The first definitive revolt against Impressionism was made in 1906 by artists derisively known as *Les Fauves* ('the savages'). Leaders of **Fauvism** were Matisse, Braque, Dufy and Vlaminck.

Painting by Expressionist Wassily Kandinsky. ▶

FAMINES

A recent **theory** suggests that famine arises when one group in a society loses its opportunity to exchange its labour or possessions for food.

Drought-induced famine caused around 1.5 m. deaths in **Ethiopia** (1971–73). In the mid-1980s severe food shortages threatened the health and lives of 150 m. in drought-stricken sub-Saharan Africa.

Famine can have natural or political **causes**. Natural causes include drought, heavy rain and flooding, unseasonable cold weather, typhoons, vermin and insect infestation and plant disease.

Famine is a severe shortage of food which causes widespread and persistent hunger and a substantially increased death rate.

Recorded famine in **India** dates from the 14th c and continues in the 20th. Famine in the Deccan, India (1702–04), reportedly caused the deaths of about 2 m. people.

Since 1700 **Asia** has been one of the main famine regions of the world. Many famines have been due to over-population and tend to occur in drought- and flood-prone areas with low agricultural production.

The **earliest recorded famines** date from the 4th millennium BC and occurred in Ancient Egypt and the Middle East. These were often due to the natural environment's hostility to intensive agriculture.

FARMING METHODS

Agricultural production began to rise after the Middle Ages with the enclosure of land, **crop rotation** and the use of the 'grass-break' to depress weeds and build up soil fertility.

Giant **kelp** has been cultivated in open water off California. It grows 60–90 cm/2–3 ft per day and makes excellent feed for such livestock as goats and sheep.

◀ *Famine in the Third World.*

In **agroforestry** (a form of multiple cropping) tree cultivation is combined with crops and/or livestock, partially or sequentially, to produce both food and a tree product.

Multiple cropping is a very ancient method of farming still in use. In Nigeria in 1984, a study showed 156 different types of crop mixtures involving two to six crops.

Organic farmers use no factory-made chemicals, whether fertilisers, pesticides, herbicides or yield-enhancing drugs for animals. There are about 10,000 organic farmers in Europe.

Terraces are a means of cultivating sloping land. Bench-type terraces are a series of steps, each supported by a rock wall or firm mound. Broad-based terraces are low mounds of earth along a contour.

Where rainfall is sparse and irrigation is impossible, a method of **dry-farming** is sometimes adopted. Two years' rainfall is allowed to soak into the soil before sowing can take place.

FASHION

After the Revolution French women's costume moved towards simplicity and freedom with the *robe en chemise* (virtually undergarments), pioneered by Mmes Récamier and Tallien (1790–1800).

Countering the crinoline fashion, Mrs Amelia Bloomer (Amelia Jenks, 1818–94, US women's-rights campaigner) introduced **bloomers** (1849), a knee-length skirt with loose trousers gathered at the ankles.

Desire to accentuate the wasp-waist led (c. 1550) to the **Spanish farthingale** (underskirt distended by graduated whalebone hoops, producing a bell-shaped substructure), introduced to England when Philip II married Mary Tudor.

In the 1670s the *Fontanges* headdress, a towering wired structure of starched lace, named after a mistress of Lous XIV, was introduced into the French court.

In the 18th c men wore **wigs**. The Ramillies (after Marlborough's defeat of the French, 1706) had the hair dragged back into a pig-tail, held in place by two black ribbon bows.

In the Romantic period (1815–50), **men's neckwear** was elevated to an art form, H. Le Blanc's *The Art of Tying the Cravat* (1828) being the definitive work.

Mary Quant (b. 1934), British fashion designer, revolutionised women's clothing and make-up in the 'swinging London' of the 1960s with her Chelsea boutique, Bazaar.

FBI

Agents of the US FBI are stationed in **more than 60 field offices** across the nation and are qualified in law, accounting or auditing.

The FBI investigates violations of US domestic law not specifically assigned to other agencies and is primarily concerned with **internal security**.

The FBI is part of the US **Department of Justice** and reports to the Attorney-General.

The US **Federal Bureau of Investigations** (FBI) was formed in 1908 and became a powerful government agency under the directorship of J. Edgar Hoover (1924–72).

FESTIVALS

A rock-music festival, the **Woodstock** Music and Art Fair was held in 1969, on a farm near Woodstock, New York. Attracted by the presence of the most famous rock-music bands, a huge crowd of perhaps 500,000 fans camped in a meadow for 3 days.

Famous for its opera productions, the **Glyndebourne Festival** in England was inaugurated in 1934 by John Christie and Audrey Mildmay. This renowned summer festival began on a high artistic level with a production of Mozart's *The Marriage of Figaro*.

Founded in 1948 by the English composer Benjamin Britten and the tenor Peter Pears, the **Aldeburgh Festival** of Music and the Arts (Suffolk) is one of Europe's most important summer music venues.

The annual musical celebration initially known as the **Newport Jazz Festival** has for more than 25 years attracted the foremost jazz artists. The first festival (1954) included performers such as Ella Fitzgerald, Dizzy Gillespie and Stan Kenton.

The annual **Salzburg Festival**, held during the summer in Salzburg, Austria, presents a variety of symphonic and stage works. The international Mozarteum was founded (1870)

as an educational institution for musicians in honour of Mozart.

The **Cannes Film Festival** (begun 1946), the most famous of international film competitions, is held in the French resort, Cannes. Its main award is the Golden Palm (*Palme d'or*), given by the jury to the best film.

The **Festival of the Two Worlds** was begun in Spoleto, Italy, in 1958 by the composer Gian Carlo Menotti. Since 1977 the festival has been literally 'of two worlds' because of the establishment of the Spoleto Festival, US.

The **Ravinia Festival** is the oldest summer festival of the performing arts in the US. Ravinia Park opened in 1904 as an amusement park and presented many performing-arts events, including fully staged operas with international stars.

Jazz star Louis Armstrong. ▶

FINLAND

Finland (capital: Helsinki) is the second most northerly country in Europe, bordering Norway, Sweden and Russia, with an area of 338,145 sq km/130,559 sq mi.

Finland exports metal products and machinery, paper, wood products and furniture, glassware and ceramics mainly to Germany, France and the US.

Formerly a Russian grand duchy, **Finland** became an independent republic in Dec. 1917, shortly after the Bolshevik Revolution.

The country names of **Finland** (Swedish for 'fen-land') or *Suomi* (Finnish for 'swamp') allude to the fact that 47% of the land area is swamp and 11% lakes.

The **population of Finland** is 5 m. (est. 1991), almost 100% Finnish but divided linguistically into 94% Finnish and 6% Swedish speaking.

FISH

About 1,500 species of **Carp** are known from the rivers and lakes of Africa, Asia, Europe and North America. Some attain a weight of 45 kg/100 lb.

Eels are fish with the body form of, but no relationship to, a serpent and lack ventral fins. Adapted to both salt and fresh water, they can even spend time out of water.

Fish are vertebrate animals that live in water, swimming by fins and breathing by gills. Their vital organs are in the lower part of the front, while the back and tail provide propulsion.

Houndfish, sometimes called needle-fish or silver gars, are slender, elongate

marine species, common in all warm seas. They have large eyes and jaws lengthened to form a beak.

The **Angelfish** (*Angelichthys ciliaris*) has a deep, compressed body covered by small, rough scales, bright colours and a small mouth. It lives in coral reefs of the West Indies.

The **Herring** and its relations, the trout and salmon, are the oldest and most primitive group of modern true bony fish, recorded at the end of the Mesozoic period.

The **Piranha** (*Serrasalmus*) is a fresh-water fish of South America. Though only 25 cm/10 in long, it is more dangerous than a shark, its powerful jaws being equipped with razor teeth.

FLOODS

A **flash flood** is a sudden, unexpected torrent of muddy and turbulent water rushing down a canyon or gulch. It is unusual, brief and mostly the result of summer thunderstorms in mountains.

A **flood** is a high-water stage where water overflows its natural or artificial banks on to normally dry land, such as a river inundating its flood plain.

Flood control along the **Mississippi** River dates to the foundation of New Orleans in 1717 by the French, who built a small levee to shelter the new city.

Floods are **measured** for height, peak discharge, area inundated and volume of flow. These figures are used to help construction of bridges and dams, and in the prediction and control of floods.

Heavy rains and centuries of human neglect were the cause of the River Arno overflowing and flooding **Florence**, Italy (4 Nov. 1966). 149 people drowned and over 100,000 were trapped in their homes.

▲ *Floods in Bangladesh.*

Often **excessive rainfall** in a short time is responsible for floods as in the floods of Paris (1658 and 1910) and of Rome (1530 and 1557).

Some **floods** are **beneficial** – the regular spring floods of the Nile River were originally depended upon to provide moisture and soil enrichment for the fertile flood plains of its delta.

FLOWERS

Flowers are the blossom of any plant, including trees and shrubs, although it is specifically applied to the phanerogams or flowering plants.

The **Chrysanthemum** is the national flower of Japan, where it can be traced back centuries. It was introduced to Europe in 1789 by Pierre Louis Blancard.

The **Foxglove** comprises some 25 species of biennial and perennial plants in Europe and western Asia. It is the chief source of digitalis, used to treat heart disease.

The **Poppy** comprises about 140 species, including *Papaver somniferum* cultivated in Asia and South America for its milky juice yielding opium.

The **Rafflesia** of Malaysia, named after Sir Stamford Raffles (1781–1826), has the world's largest flower, 0.5 m/19 in in diameter. It smells like decaying flesh.

The **Rose** is the flower of erect or climbing shrubs. Apart from the wild species of the temperate zone, there are countless cultivated varieties.

The **Tulip** is a bulbous plant of the lily family. They grow wild in Turkey,

The World Health Organisation (WHO) recommends a minimum daily adult **calorie consumption** of 2,600 per head and full protein consumption of 65g per head.

whence they were brought to Holland, triggering off a boom in 1637, with 2,600 guilders paid for a single root.

FOOD AND NUTRITION

Although the population of England and Wales soared from 9 m. in 1800 to 32 m. in 1900, **food shortages** did not occur because of improved farming technology, higher crop yields and increased trade.

The **'Great Hunger'** of 1845–50 in Ireland killed 1 m. people, nearly one-eighth of the population, when a fungal disease caused the failure of the potato crop, the staple food of many.

The UK and Japan are the world's largest **food importers** but the UK has tried to reduce imports, which represented 67% of its food requirements in 1914. By 1992 the proportion was 43.5%.

There are many different varieties of **potato**. The McDonald's fast-food chain uses only the Russet Burbank variety, which has the right dimensions and texture for their French fries.

FOOD CHAINS

Agriculture is the starting point in the **food chain**. It indirectly creates millions of jobs in related activities such as food manufacturing and retailing. It also contributes to economic output and land development.

Animals that eat plants directly, e.g. caterpillars and deer, are herbivores. Meat eaters, or carnivores, eat plants indirectly by preying on herbivores. Humans are **omnivores**, eating both plants and meat.

At each level in the food chain, some of the **energy in plants** is transferred out of the system. The longer the food chain, the greater are the energy losses.

In a **forest food chain**, caterpillars eat tree leaves, small birds eat caterpillars, hawks may prey on small birds. When the hawks die, insects feed on their bodies: their waste goes into the soil, where it feeds trees...

Malnutrition and hunger may result from poor **food distribution**, which depends on global issues such as financial markets and international politics, as well as on transport and storage.

The clearing of rainforest destroys a vast and complex **ecosystem**, with serious consequences for food production and climate, not only locally but worldwide.

FOODS

Apples, the fruit of the genus *Malus*, are the most widely cultivated tree fruit. They were eaten by the earliest Europeans, varieties being recognised more than 2,000 years ago.

Chocolate is the food made by combining the roasted ground kernel of the cacao bean with sugar and cocoa butter, the fat released when the bean is ground. In 1728 Swedish botanist Karl Linnaeus classified the cacao plant as the 'food of the gods'.

Eating **bananas** is mentioned in early Greek, Latin and Arab writings. Alexander the Great saw bananas on an expedition to India. After the discovery of America, they were brought from the Canary Islands to the New World.

Ice cream is a popular frozen food made from varying mixtures of cream and milk, sweeteners, flavourings and air; it was popularised in Italy. The first ice cream factory was built (1851) by Baltimore milk dealer Jacob Fussell.

Maple syrup is made from the 'sweetwater' sap of North American maple trees. The syrup has been made in Canada and the US since the first colonial settlers learned the art from the Indians. Today the Canadian province of Quebec produces some 11.4 m. litres/3 m. gal yearly.

Pasta, a large family of shaped, dried wheat pastes, is a basic staple in many countries. According to legend, Marco Polo brought a pasta recipe with him in 1295 from China. Pasta quickly became a major element in the Italian diet and its use spread throughout Europe. Today it is one of the most popular foods in the world.

Pasta, the food made from dough of durum wheat flour, water and egg, has been used in Italian cooking since the early Middle Ages.

Rapid societal changes in 20th-c Europe and, especially, the US (such as the growth of automobile transportation or travel and leisure time and of urban business and industry) created a demand for **fast food** and self-service operations.

Rice has been cultivated since prehistoric times in the East; it derived from grass *Oryza sativa* and was probably native to India and south-east Asia.

The **Irish Potato Famine** of 1845–50 was the worst famine to occur in Europe in the 19th c. The crop failed in successive years, caused by late blight fungus that destroys the tubers of the potato plant.

The **potato** was under cultivation in South America when the Spaniards found it in 1524. Sir Walter Raleigh is said to have brought the potato to England in 1585, but John Hawkins (1565) and Francis Drake (1580) preceded him.

The **tomato**, fruit of the cultivated varieties of *Lycopersicon esculentum*, a plant of the nightshade family (Solanaceae) was introduced to Europe by the Spanish in the early 16th c.

White **potatoes** are edible tubers that grow at the end of underground stems of the plant *Solanum tuberosum*. In the US annual per-capita consumption is 19 kg/42 lb fresh potatoes and 13 kg/30 lb processed potatoes, such as frozen french fries.

Yoghurt is a fermented, slightly acidic food product made from milk. The introduction of fruit yoghurt during the 1940s revolutionised the market and until recently yoghurt sales increased by 20% or so every year.

FOOTBALL

The Football Association introduced a knockout competition in 1872 – the first in football history. Wanderers won the initial **FA Cup** by defeating Royal Engineers 1-0 at Kennington Oval before 2,000 spectators.

The world's **first professional League competition** was formed in England in 1888 when 12 northern and midland clubs agreed to form the Football League.

The **highest scorer in a World Cup Final** tournament is Just Fontaine of France who scored 13 goals in 1958 in Sweden.

Peterborough United hold the record for **most goals scored in an English season**. In their debut season in the Football League they scored 134 goals in 46 matches, 1960–61.

Peter Shilton is the only player to appear in **1,000 League matches**. Between 1966 and 1996, including cup and representative matches, he made a total of 1,390 first-class appearances.

William Ralph 'Dixie' Dean

◄ *Manchester United footballers Solksjaar, Beckham and Giggs.*

scored a **record 60 League goals** for champions Everton in the 1927–28 season – international and cup goals brought his total to 82.

FORESTS

In the coniferous forests of Pacific North America grow redwoods and **sequoias**, respectively the world's tallest and bulkiest trees. One sequoia, the General Sherman tree, may be 4,000 years old.

Most **deciduous trees** shed their thin, delicate leaves in winter. They are also recognisable by their rounded crowns, supported by low boles (the part of the trunk beneath the lowest branches).

One of the largest and most impressive forest areas in the US is preserved in **Great Smoky National Park**, Tennessee. Here grow 130 different native trees, a greater number than in Europe.

Rainfall determines the existence of forests. In temperate latitudes this must be at least 36 cm/14 in a year. Another requirement is three successive months with minimum temperatures above 6°C/43°F.

The **forests of eastern North America** were once inhabited by wild turkeys, black bears, woodland bison, deer, mountain lions, martens and wolves. Native Americans such as the Iroquois cut clearings for dwellings and cultivation.

Vast stands of larch, cedar, birch, pitch pine and alder stretch across the Siberian taiga. The climate in these **boreal (northern) forests** is generally unsuitable for agriculture.

Tropical rainforest. ▶

FOSSILS

Entire or partial bodies of organisms are called **body fossils**. Marks left in rock by the activities of organisms are called trace fossils and include artefacts, burrows, faeces, tracks and trails. Fossils measured in mm are called microfossils and those in cm are called megafossils.

Fossils are remains of prehistoric organisms. Preserved by burial under many layers of sedimentary material, they are a record of the history of life beginning approx. 3.5 bn years ago, the study of which is called paleontology.

Some of the most spectacular fossils of the Cretaceous Period, including fish, marine reptiles, pterodactyls and birds, have come from the Smoky Hill Chalk, near Hays, Kansas. Remarkable Eocene lake fauna have been uncovered in the **Green River Formation**, Wyoming.

The Earth's sedimentary strata are initially layers of muds and sands, each covering an older stratum and being covered, in turn, by a younger one. The fossils in each stratum can be arranged in time (**law of superposition**).

The **fossil record** contains a history of the evolution of life on Earth and provides geologists with a chronology. It also contains much information about the geographical and ecological changes that have occurred in the course of geologic time.

The fossilised skull of **Steinheim man** (actually a woman) was found (1933) in a gravel pit at Steinheim, Germany. Animal bones found in the deposit with the skull suggest that the fossil dates from more than 200,000 years ago.

FRANCE

Economic instability in **France** and the Algerian conflict brought Charles De Gaulle back to power in 1958, a new constitution giving the president greater power.

France (capital: Paris) lies in western Europe between Spain, Italy, Germany and Belgium, with an area of 543,955 sq km/210,026 sq mi.

▲ *Dinosaur fossils.*

France exports machinery, agricultural products, textiles and transport equipment including cars, mainly to Germany, Italy, the UK, Belgium, the US, Netherlands and Spain.

The best-known landmark in **France** is the Eiffel Tower, erected for the Paris Exhibition of 1889. Constructed by Gustave Eiffel (1832–1923), it was meant to last 20 years.

The **population of France** is 56,942,000 (est. 1991), comprising 90% French, 1.5% Algerian, 1.4% Portuguese, 0.8% Moroccan, 0.6% Spanish, 0.6% Italian and 4.5% other.

FRUIT

Fruit is the ripened fertilised ovary of a flowering plant, together with its contents. They range from dry grain, legumes, nuts and capsules to fleshy pomes and berries.

The **Fig** is the fruit of *Ficus carica*, indigenous to Turkey

▲ *The Eiffel Tower in Paris.*

and northern India but now widely cultivated for consumption fresh or dried.

The **Grapefruit** or Pomelo is the fruit of *Citrus paradisi*, believed to have originated in Jamaica where it was recorded by John Lunan (1814) as a mutation of the Shaddock.

The **Pineapple** (*Ananas comosus*) produces a cluster of flowers which consolidate to form a single fleshy fruit. Christopher Columbus found them on Guadeloupe in 1493.

The **Plum** is the fruit of *Prunus domestica*, originating in the Caucasus but now widespread. It is a drupe (like the peach and cherry), with a stone in the centre.

The **Raspberry** is the juicy red fruit of a bush (genus *Rubus*), mentioned by Pliny (AD 23–79) as growing on Mt Ida, Greece but now widespread.

FUNGI

Fungi are a large group of plants devoid of chlorophyll and reproduced by spores. They are found all over the world and at least 10,000 species are known.

The **Cep** (*Boletus edulis*), distinguished by its brown bun-like top, is the most sought-after edible fungus. It stands up to 25 cm/10 in tall, with a cap 20 cm/8 in in diameter.

The **Chanterelle** (*Cantharellus cibarius*) is a small funnel-shaped fungus growing to a height of 75 mm/3 in. Its bright yellow colour and apricot smell identify it.

The **Devil's Bolete** (*Boletus satanas*), similar in shape and size to the Cep, has a grey-white cap and red trunk. It is poisonous, producing hallucination or vomiting.

The **Field Mushroom** (*Agaricus campestris*) is the most commonly eaten wild mushroom and should not be confused with the Yellow Stainer or Death Cap whose colours are slightly different.

The **Giant Puffball** (*Langermannia gigantea*) attains a diameter of 80 cm/32 in. White when young and edible, it turns dark brown with age.

The **Truffle** (*Tuber melanosporum*) is an underground fungus which is traditionally located by pigs. It is highly prized as a flavouring in French cuisine.

FURNITURE

After the Romans it was not until the 14th and 15th c that there was a major revival of **furniture making**, with new types of cupboards, boxes with compartments and desks.

An important 19th c change was the separation of those who made furniture from those who sold it. After the mid-19th c the **showroom** gained popularity.

Ancient furniture examples are rare, but from pictures we know that craftsmen in China, India, Egypt, Mesopotamia, Greece and Rome made beds, tables, chairs, boxes, stools, chests etc., from natural wood.

Chair finishing was seldom done by cabinet-makers and specialists in the 19th c made this French polishing the standard method of finishing furniture.

Chair making was at first closely associated with woodturning, but by the 18th c turned legs were replaced by shaped legs of the cabriole type.

Charles Rennie Mackintosh (1868–1928), designer of the Glasgow School of Art (1897–99), was a pioneer of modern design, his furniture characterised by emphatic rectilinear patterns.

Directoire furniture is transitional between the restrained Classicism of Louis XVI (c. 1760–89) and the heavier Empire style (1804–1840s), with gradual loss of delicacy and increasing use of Roman motifs.

During the **Italian Renaissance** (1400–1500) sumptuous furniture, such as the highly decorated *cassone* (marriage chest), was executed at the bidding of the Medici and other patrons.

In the reign of **Louis XVI** (c. 1760–89) Röntgen and Reisner developed restraint and delicacy, accentuated by their preference for Classical furniture (**late Rococo**).

▲ *George III giltwood chairs by Thomas Chippendale.*

Modern methods of furniture construction are largely based on the availability of man-made materials such as plywood, laminated board, chipboard and hardboard instead of natural solid wood.

Post-modern furniture design, ironically revamping past styles, led by Venturi, appeared in *Studio Alchymia* (1979) and *Memphis* (1981), *avant-garde* groups developed from Italian radical design in the late 1960s.

The designs of Meissonier, goldsmith to **Louis XV**, fostered **Rococo** (1735–65) which is non-classical, curvilinear and fantasticated. Other celebrated furniture-makers were the Caffieris and Oeben.

The Egyptians used **veneers** for coffins and the Romans used them for decorative purposes. Bronze was also used in Roman tables, stools and couch frames.

Thomas Chippendale (*c.* 1718–79), furniture designer, set up his workshop in London. Influenced by Louis XVI, Chinese, Gothic and neo-Classical styles, he worked mainly in mahogany.

GALAXIES

A **galaxy** is a collection of billions of stars held together by gravity. Three types have been defined: spiral, barred spiral and elliptical.

Barred spirals are spiral galaxies that have a straight bar of stars across their centre, from the ends of which the spiral

◀ *The constellation Orion.*

arms emerge. The arms contain gas and dust which are forming new stars.

Elliptical galaxies contain old stars and very little gas; they may be formed by merging spiral galaxies and are the biggest, containing maybe a trillion stars.

Our own galaxy, the **Milky Way**, is about 100,000 light years in diameter and contains at least 100 bn stars.

Spiral galaxies, like the Milky Way, are flattened in shape with a central bulge of old stars surrounded by a disc of younger stars, arranged in spiral arms.

The **Local Group** contains about 30 galaxies; the two largest are the Milky Way and Andromeda. Galaxies do not expand with the expanding Universe.

The Milky Way is a member of a small cluster, the **Local Group**. The Sun lies in one of its spiral arms, about 25,000 light years from the centre.

GALLERIES

Designed by Italian architect Gae Aulenti and opened to the public in Dec. 1986, the **Musee d'Orsay** in Paris is a museum dedicated to 19th- and early 20th-c French art.

The Guggenheim Museum in New York. ▶

The **Art Institute of Chicago** evolved from the Chicago Academy of Design, established in 1866. It was incorporated as the Chicago Academy of Fine Arts in 1879 and assumed its present name in 1882.

The Centre National d'Art et de Culture Georges Pompidou is a museum for art and culture located in the **Beaubourg** district of Paris. Pres. Pompidou conceived (1969) the idea for Beaubourg, as the centre is also known. It was completed in 1978.

The **Courtauld Institute of Art**, established (1931) in London by Samuel Courtauld, contains the collection of the University of London, which is composed chiefly of Impressionist and Post-impressionist paintings.

The **Museum of Modern Art** (MOMA), perhaps the world's most comprehensive collection of modern art, was founded (1929) by prominent New York art collectors for the purpose of acquiring and exhibiting the best modern works of art.

The **National Gallery** in London ranks among the greatest galleries in the world and contains works representing the major periods of European painting. The gallery was founded (1824) with paintings from the J. J. Angerstein Collection.

The **Prado** Museum in Madrid, which houses one of the world's most important collections of Western European painting and Classical art, was begun during the reign (1759–88) of King Charles III and inaugurated in 1819.

The sculpture museum **Glyptothek** in Munich was built (1816–30) by the Bavarian king Maximilian I. The gallery was designed to house the pedimental sculpture from the temple of Aphaia at Aegina, Greece (*c.* 490 BC).

The **Tate Gallery** in London, originally known as the National Gallery of British Art, was opened in Jul. 1897. Originally conceived by Sir Henry Tate (1819–99) as a showplace for contemporary British art, the Tate gradually evolved into a more broadly based art gallery and museum.

GAMBIA

In 1588 English slavers purchased land at the mouth of the **Gambia** River, establishing Britain's first African colony, which gained its independence on 24 Apr. 1970.

The **Gambia (capital: Banjul)** lies along 320 km/200 mi of the Gambia River, entirely surrounded by Senegal, with an area of 10,689 sq km/4,127 sq mi.

The **Gambia exports** fish and peanut meal, mainly to the UK and the EU countries. Some 40% of its trade is unofficial, smuggling with neighbouring Senegal.

◄ *The Gambia.*

The **Gambia** river, passed by Hanno the Carthaginian in his voyage along the west African coast *c.* 500 BC, was believed by Arab geographers to be a mouth of the Nile.

The **population of the Gambia** is 883,000 (est. 1991), comprising 40.4% Malinke, 18.7% Fulani, 14.6% Wolof, 10.3% Dyola, 8.2% Soninke and 7.8% other.

GAMBLING

Gambling is the wagering of money or other valuables on the outcome of a game or other event. There is no historical period or culture to which gambling is unknown.

Las Vegas, a city in south-eastern Nevada, is, because of its gambling casinos, a world-famous resort. Income from luxury hotels, gambling casinos and other entertainment used by approximately 15 m. tourists a year forms the base of the city's economy.

Once associated with organised crime and outlawed almost everywhere in the US, the **slot machine** is today among the most ubiquitous of gambling devices. The machines date from the late 19th c and were popular through the 1930s.

Poker, originally a card game for unprincipled gamblers only, is now played for amusement or stakes at home or exclusively for stakes in gambling establishments. There are two basic forms of the game: draw, or closed, poker and stud, or open, poker.

Roulette is a game in which one or more players gamble against the bank or house, playing on a rectangular table in the centre of which is a wheel whose perimeter is non-consecutively numbered 1–36 and zero and double zero.

Horse racing, one of the most popular sports for gamblers. ▶

Today the UK appears to have the most liberal **gambling laws**, but legal gambling can be found in many other places, including the Czech Republic, Ghana, France, Macao, Monaco, Puerto Rico and Scandinavia.

Wagering on the outcome of **horse races** has been an integral part of the appeal of the sport since prehistory and today is the sole reason horse racing has survived as a major professional sport.

GAS

In the **US natural gas** first came from a shallow well in New York, in 1821. Distributed through a small-bore lead pipe, it was used for lighting and cooking.

Natural gas is often found in association with crude oil. Often it is the pressure of natural gas exerted upon the subterranean **oil** reservoir that forces oil up to the surface.

Natural gas was first discovered in Europe (UK, 1659) but did not come into wide use. The main fuel for illuminating streets and houses from 1790 was gas from **carbonised coal**.

The complete combustion of gas is relatively free of soot, carbon monoxide and the nitrogen oxides usually formed by burning fossil fuels. This makes it **environmentally safer**.

The **earliest discoveries of natural gas** seeps were made in Iran between 6000 and 2000 BC. Gas seeps, ignited by lightning, formed the 'eternal fires' of the fire-worshipping Ancient Persians.

The first known **well** drilled for natural gas was in China in 211 BC (depth of 150 m/500 ft). The wells were drilled with bamboo poles and primitive percussion bits.

Up to 1960 associated gas was considered a nuisance **by-product of oil** production by most of the world. The gas was separated from the crude oil stream and eliminated by flaring.

▲ *Gas from carbonised coal was used for lighting in the nineteenth century*

GEMS

Antwerp and Amsterdam have been leading **diamond-cutting** centres for over three centuries. Since World War II, Tel Aviv and New York City have also become important centres.

Colourless zircon, sapphire and quartz are natural gemstones that might easily be mistaken for diamond, a common target for mimicry because of its normally high value.

Crystallographers today continue to use X-ray diffraction to understand crystal structures. Diffraction experiments are greatly aided by the use of computer-controlled diffractometers and powerful data-analysis software.

Diamond-studded rotary bits are used to drill oil wells and bore tunnels in solid rock. Much low-grade diamond is crushed to dust and used as abrasive powder.

European **emeralds** were discovered in 1830 near Sverdlovsk, in Russia's Ural Mountains. They have been produced artificially by using a process developed by Carroll Chatham in the 1930s.

Fewer than 20% of the diamonds mined each year are suitable for use as gems. Most are sold at monthly 'sights' through the **Diamond Trading Company** in London.

Synthetic sapphires, produced by the Verneuil flame-fusion process since 1902, are used for abrasion-resistant applications such as thread guides, phonograph needles, watch bearings and machinists' dies.

GENETICS

A **genetically engineered gene** was used for the first time in a human in 1990. The four-year-old girl (US) was suffering from a rare enzyme deficiency (ADA) which cripples the immune system.

Developments in genetic engineering led to the synthesis of an **artificial growth hormone** by Howard Goodman and Baxter in 1979 at the University of California.

Genetic fingerprinting was devised by Alec Jeffreys in 1985. It uses isolated DNA from a sample as small as one cell as a unique fingerprint for each individual.

Har Gobind Khorana and his colleagues constructed the first **artificial gene** to function naturally when inserted into a bacteria cell and kicked off genetic engineering in 1976.

In 1993 Michael Smith (Canada) developed the technique for splicing foreign **genetic segments** into an organism's DNA in order to modify the proteins produced and was awarded the Nobel Prize.

The grandfather of genetics was Gregor **Mendel** who pioneered the study of inheritance with his pea experiments; the work was ignored at the time (1866) but rediscovered in 1900.

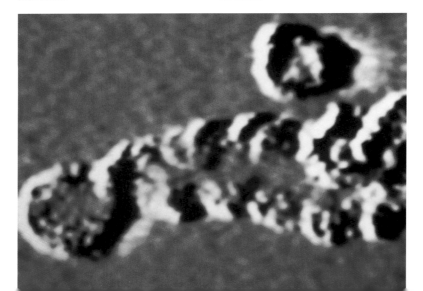

The major project of the moment is the international **Human Genome Project**, which is currently mapping the entire genetic code of all 23 human chromosomes.

GENEVA CONVENTION

A 1988 conviction of a war criminal was overturned by the Israeli Supreme Court. John Demjanjuk had been accused of being the concentration camp guard nicknamed '**Ivan the Terrible**'.

At the end of World War II the victorious Allied countries established an international military tribunal at **Nuremberg**, in order to investigate the possibility of war crimes perpetrated by surviving Axis leaders.

Hermann Goering (1893–1946), Nazi leader, Minister of Aviation, pres. of Reichstag, chief of Secret Police and field marshal; **sentenced to death** for war crimes Sept. 1946; he committed suicide in Oct.

In 1992, under the Geneva Convention, the UN voted to establish a war-crimes commission to investigate reports of '**ethnic cleansing**' and other atrocities in Bosnia-Herzegovina.

◀ *A DNA strand showing a double helix.*

It became clear that the Allies intended to punish those guilty of war crimes. In Oct. 1943 the **United Nations War Crimes Commission** was formed in London.

Jean Henri Dunant's efforts led to the organisation of the first **Red Cross** societies in 1864. He was co-winner of the first Nobel Peace Prize in 1901.

Other conventions were added in 1899, 1907 and 1929, covering the treatment of **prisoners of war**. Four more conventions in 1949 codified the laws of war.

The **Geneva convention** 'for the amelioration of the condition of the wounded and sick of armed forces in the field' was signed in Geneva, Switzerland, in Aug. 1864.

The **Helsinki Accords** declared inviolable the frontiers of all the signatory nations and pledged the signatories to respect 'freedom of thought, conscience, religion, or belief'.

War crimes, as defined by the Allied powers after World War II, included: (1) crimes against peace; (2) violations of the customs of war; (3) **crimes against humanity**.

GEOLOGY

A **diamond** is pure carbon, made into a crystal by great heat and pressure inside the earth and brought to the surface by volcanic action. It is the hardest mineral on earth.

Anaximander, a 7th c BC Greek, proposed that **fossils** were the remains of real animals and plants. In the 16th c Leonardo da Vinci went further, claiming that these forms had once been buried on sea bottoms.

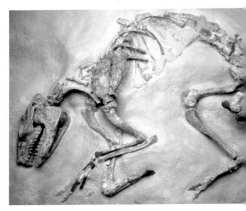

▲ *Fossil of a herbivore from the Tertiary Period.*

Coal is formed in swamps from dead plants covered in mud, which, over some 250 m. years, turn to rock. A coal seam 3 m/10 ft thick may be formed from 60 m/200 ft of rotting plants.

De Re Metallica (1556) by the German Georg Bauer, known as Agricola, was the first attempt to classify **minerals** not by their supposed magical properties but by their physical forms.

Folds are made in beds of rocks by earth movements. Strata that have been folded upwards make an anticline. When rocks are folded downwards they make a syncline.

The earliest rock in Britain is probably the **felspar** of Sutherland, Scotland. It is 2,450 m. years old. Fossilised plant life 1,000 m. years old has been found in slate in Leicestershire.

The first scientist to grasp the meaning of **erosion** was James Hutton, a Scottish physician. His *Theory of the Earth* (1795) argued that present landscapes had taken hundreds of thousands of years to form.

The top 16 km/10 mi of the **earth's crust** is composed of different strata or layers, many containing fossils. Below these are rafts of granite floating on a plastic layer called basalt.

GERMANY

After World War I **Germany** was beset by inflation; by Nov. 1923 the value of the mark had fallen so far that it required 10 bn to post a letter.

Germany (capital: Berlin) lies in north-central Europe, bordered by France, the Low Countries, Austria, Switzerland, the Czech Republic and Poland, with an area of 356,957 sq km/137,822 sq mi.

Germany exports iron, steel, textiles, machinery, transport equipment, electronic goods, chemicals, pharmaceuticals and medical equipment.

On 3 Oct. 1990 **Germany** was reunified, when the German Democratic Republic, West Berlin and the German Federal Republic came together for the first time since 1945.

The **population of Germany** is 79,096,000 (est. 1991), comprising 94.4% German, 1.9% Turkish, 0.7% Yugoslav, 0.7% Italian and 2.3% other.

GHANA

Ghana (capital: Accra) lies on the west coast of Africa between the Ivory Coast and Togo, with an area of 238,533 sq km/92,098 sq mi.

Ghana exports cocoa, palm oil, coffee, gold, manganese, industrial diamonds and timber, mainly to the UK, Netherlands, Japan, the US, Russia and Germany.

The monetary unit of **Ghana**, the *cedi*, comes from a local word denoting the cowrie shells formerly used as money by the coastal tribes.

The **population of Ghana** is 15,509,000 (est. 1991), comprising 52.4% Akan, 15.8% Mossi, 11.9% Ewe, 7.8% Ga-Adangme, 3.3% Gurma, 1.3% Yoruba and 7.5% other.

The republic of **Ghana**, comprising the Gold Coast and British Togoland, attained independence on 6 Mar. 1956, the first Negro-African colony to do so.

◄ *Boris Becker, one of Germany's leading sportsmen.*

GLACIERS

A **glaciated landscape** has such distinctive features as heaped moraines of sand and gravel, scratched boulders, U-shaped valleys, ice-gouged mountain ravines and amphitheatre-like hollows.

A glacier's edges keep freezing to the rocky walls of the mountain hollow where it begins and breaking loose again. This plucking action eventually turns the hollow into a large, rounded half-bowl called a **cirque**, corrie or cwm.

A valley glacier ends at a terminus, or **snout**, where the ice melts, usually as fast as it arrives. If the temperature increases, the ice melts faster and the glacier retreats.

In 1837 a young Swiss zoologist, Louis Agassiz, presented his idea that **glaciers** have not always been as at present but have shrunk from the great ice sheets of the past. At first no one believed him.

In 1936–37 the **Black Rapids Glacier**, Alaska, was moving some 30m/100 ft per day, the fastest advance ever recorded for a glacier. This was probably because of heavy snowfalls in previous years.

The fastest-moving large glacier is the **Columbia Glacier**, Alaska, US. It flows between Anchorage and Valdez at an average rate of 20 m/65 ft per day.

The world's longest glacier is the **Lambert Glacier** in Australian Antarctic Territory. At its widest, it is 64 km/40 mi, and with its seaward extension, the Amery Ice Shelf, at least 700 km/400 mi long.

◄ *A glacier in Alaska, US.*

GLASSWARE

Bohemia had a large number of factories taking up Venetian innovations in the 16th c. **Bohemian glass** again achieved a high reputation in the 19th c.

Georg Schwanhardt, founder of the **Nuremberg school of engravers**, was taught by Caspar Lehmann (gem cutter to Rudolf II, who first applied this art to glass engraving in 1605).

Glass vessel manufacture reached high standards in Egypt (18th dynasty, *c.* 1490 BC) and at Tell el-Amarna, palace of Akhenaton (*c.* 1379–1362 BC).

Glass-making was the first **American** industry after the Spanish conquest, with glass being made at Puebla, Mexico (1535). Wistar opened his glasshouse in New Jersey (1739); Stiegel his in Pennsylvania (1763).

Louis Comfort Tiffany (1848–1933), US, outstanding exponent of Art Nouveau, created distinctive glass vases and lamps in sumptuous forms and iridescent colour (from 1881).

Medieval **Venetian glassmakers** made clear, colourless glass (*cristallo*), austerely simple by the early 16th c, but more elaborate by the early 17th c (e.g. *vetro de trina*, vessels with lacy white patterns).

Stained glass originated in medieval times. By the mid-12th c incidents in Jesus's life were commonly depicted (notably in cathedrals such as Canterbury, Lincoln, Chartres, Cologne and Rouen).

The **earliest glass objects** are beads (Egypt, *c.* 2500 BC). A green glass rod at Eshnunna, Babylonia goes back to 2600 BC; blue glass at Eridu to 2200 BC.

The most famous example of Roman era cameo glass engraving (grinding through an opaque, white layer to darker ground) is the **Portland vase** (British Museum), made in Augustus's reign (27 BC–AD 14).

◀ *Lamp by Louis Comfort Tiffany.*

GLOBAL WARMING

▲ *Man-made emissions contribute to global warming.*

The '**greenhouse effect**' ('global warming' in environmental science), is a popular term for the effect that certain gases of the Earth's lower atmosphere have on surface temperatures.

A drier **climate**, the result of global warming, would increase pressure on water supplies, encourage the spread of pests like cockroaches and extend the reach of deadly tropical diseases such as malaria and yellow fever.

Carbon dioxide (CO_2) is the most important greenhouse gas – and is produced by all plants. It also comes from burning fossil fuels, like coal and oil, chiefly for electricity and cars.

Even a limited rise in Earth's average surface **temperature** might lead to at least partial melting of the polar ice caps and hence a major rise in sea level, along with other severe environmental disturbances.

It is thought that CO_2 concentrations in the atmosphere have increased by nearly a third since the Industrial Revolution. Other greenhouse gases include **methane** (produced by sewage and rotting processes) and CFCs (Chlorofluorocarbons).

Normally the gases in the planet's atmosphere act like the glass in a greenhouse, making the planet habitable. As we add to these gases with our own emissions we are increasing the 'double-glazing' effect of this process, and accelerating **global warming**.

The 10 **warmest years** in the last 130 all occurred in the last 2 decades of the twentieth century; at least 3 of these were recorded in the 1990s.

GOLF

Golf was banned in Scotland in 1457 as it distracted men from archery training. Scottish monarchs James IV and Mary later encouraged its popularity.

Jack Nicklaus is, arguably, **the most successful golfer** of all time having won 18 major tournaments between 1962 and 1986.

The acknowledged ruling body of golf is the **Royal & Ancient** based at St Andrews. The R&A's predecessors played their first round on the famous links on 14 May 1754.

The **lowest four round total** for a Major tournament is 267, shot by Greg Norman (Australia) when he won the British Open at Sandwich in 1993.

The Ryder Cup, brainchild of American businessman Samuel Ryder, was introduced in 1927. Originally contested by the US and the UK, Europe have faced the US since 1979.

The six victories of Englishman Harry Vardon in the **British Open** make him the most successful competitor in the tournament's history. He was also runner-up four times.

◀ *Jack Nicklaus.*

GOVERNMENT ECONOMICS

Government instability, endemic corruption and wide swings in economic policy make the **Third World's economic prospects** seem even less auspicious for the new millenium.

In Dec. 1968 Rafael Caldera Rodríguez won a narrow election victory in Venezuela. The government eliminated guerrilla activities. Economically, he pursued a policy of **nationalising foreign enterprises**.

▲ *Mexico City.*

Recent **economic achievements** in Mexico result from a reduction in the number of enterprises owned by the government, from 1,155 in 1982 to 210 by the mid-1990s.

Since 1984 successive New Zealand governments have pursued economic policies that have transformed a strongly regulated welfare state into an **open-market economy**.

The **Gross National Product per capita** is a way of measuring how rich a country is; Lichtenstein is the highest at $54,607 and Mozambique the lowest at $60.

The term **laissez-faire** ('let things alone') in economics is the policy of domestic non-intervention by government in individual or industrial monetary affairs.

United Nations Conference on Trade and Development (UNC-TAD) is a permanent arm of the United Nations General Assembly.

The conference, established in Dec. 1964, promotes world trade among countries.

GOVERNMENTS

China's ultimate government authority is the National People's Congress (NPC), but its controlling force is the Chinese Communist Party (CCP), ruled by the elected **Politburo**.

Each of China's provinces, regions and municipalities has an elected local **people's government** with policy-making power in defined areas.

France has a **two-chamber legislature** (comprising a national assembly of 577 elected deputies and a senate of 321 indirectly elected members) with executive govern-

ment shared between the president (Jacques Chirac, 1995) and PM (Lionel Jospin, 1997).

Germany's federal parliamentary democracy is built around a **two-chamber legislature** comprising a directly elected 662-member lower house (*Bundestag*) and indirectly elected 69-member upper house (*Bundesrat*).

Germany's government (reunified since 1990, Pres.: Roman Herzog, 1994; Chancellor: Helmut Kohl, 1990) is based on the West German constitution with a system built around 16 *Länder* (federal states).

The **People's Republic of China** (PM: Li Peng from 1987) is divided into 22 provinces, five autonomous regions and three municipalities (Biejing, Shanghai and Tianjin).

The **Russian Federation**, formerly (until 1991) the Russian Soviet Federal Socialist Republic (head of state: Boris Yeltsin), includes 16 autonomous republics; it functions as an emergent democracy within the Commonwealth of Independent States (CIS).

The United States of America (US, 42nd Pres.: Bill Clinton, 1993), a **liberal democracy**, is a federal republic comprising 50 states and the District of Columbia.

US government is separated into branches working by a system of checks and balances: executive (headed by the president); legislative (Congress and the Senate) and judicial (headed by the Supreme Court).

GREAT DEPRESSION

Before Franklin D. Roosevelt's 1932 election, US slang contained '**Hooverisms**' mocking Pres. Herbert Hoover's handling of the Great Depression. A 'Hoover Flag' was an empty pocket.

During the Great Depression Franklin D. Roosevelt's economic philosophy, known as '**pump priming**', called for government spending to stimulate the economy.

During the Great Depression in the US (1930s) devastating drought struck New Mexico, Texas, Oklahoma, Kansas and Colorado, an area known as the **Dust Bowl**.

During the Great Depression US First Lady **Eleanor Roosevelt** worked to ensure her husband's policies addressed the needs of women and minorities.

◀ *Bill Clinton, 42nd US president.*

During the Great Depression, 15,000 World War I veterans Marched on Washington, DC (1932) seeking payment of monies owed them in 1945. Troops forcibly removed the **Bonus Army**.

During the Great Depression, Pres. Franklin D. Roosevelt gave radio addresses called '**Fireside Chats**' to apprise the public of the progress of his programmes.

Franklin D. Roosevelt, elected US president in 1932, implemented the **New Deal**, a programme of government spending and public works to combat the Great Depression.

The **Great Depression** in the US was precipitated by the 29 Oct. 1929 stock-market crash when the index plunged 43 points.

HAGUE, THE

The Hague began as a hunting lodge of the Count of Holland in the 13th c. The Dutch name *Gravenhage* means 'count's lodge'.

The Hague is a residential and administrative centre and has played a major role in international diplomacy, notably the **Peace Conferences** of 1899 and 1907.

The Hague, chief city of South Holland and administrative capital of the Netherlands, lies near the North Sea coast at the junction of rail and waterway systems.

The International Court of Arbitration was established in 1899 at **The Hague**, and has its seat at the Peace Palace, erected in 1913.

▼ *The Royal Palace at the Hague.*

The **population of The Hague** is 441,506 (est. 1990), a drop from its pre-war peak (1939) of 495,518.

HEATING

Apart from the Greeks and Romans most cultures relied upon **direct-heating** methods. Wood was the earliest fuel used, though in China, Japan and the Mediterranean charcoal was used because it produced less smoke.

Central heating returned in the 19th c. The use of steam provided a new way to heat sites. **Coal-fired boilers** delivered hot steam to rooms by means of standing radiators.

Central heating, invented in Greece, was widely used in the Romans' hypocaust system: mosaic tile floors had air spaces beneath which fires were lit; the resulting hot gases warmed the floors from beneath.

Enclosed **stoves** for heating were first used in China c. 600 BC and eventually spread through Russia into northern Europe then to America, where Benjamin Franklin invented the Franklin stove in 1744.

Roman villas used 'hypocaust' heating systems. ▶

Steam heating predominated in North America because of very cold winters. The advantages of hot water, which has a lower surface temperature and milder effect than steam, began to be recognised c. 1830.

The **chimney**, originally just a hole in the centre of the roof and later rising directly from the fireplace, appeared in Europe by the 13th c.

The common form of modern heating is known as **central heating**. Here energy is converted to heat, but not within the room. The resulting heat is conveyed to the site by air, water or steam for example.

HELICOPTERS

A helicopter achieves both lift and propulsion by means of a **rotor** on top of the fuselage. It can take off and land vertically, move in any direction, or remain stationary in the air.

In the US there are about 13,000 helicopters in use in the military, primarily employed by the US Army, and about 8,000 are in **commercial use**.

It was not until 1935 that a **coaxial helicopter** constructed by Louis Breguet and Rene Dorand in France achieved flights of sustained duration.

Leonardo da Vinci is generally credited with sketching and describing a **helicopter** in 1483. But the invention of the gasoline engine supplied the lightweight power source required by a helicopter.

The **first successful lift-off** and short helicopter flight took place in 1907. Ukrainian-American engineer Igor Sikorsky built the first practical single-rotor craft in the US 1939.

The **maximum speed** of a conventional helicopter is limited to about 400 kph/250 mph because the lift depends on the relative velocity of the air past the rotor blades.

The Spanish engineer Juan de la Cierva designed the first successful **autogiro** (1923) by hinging the rotor blades so that they could rise and fall freely in response to variations.

HELSINKI

Helsinki is beautifully laid out with wide streets and large parks. Eliel Saarinen designed many of the modern buildings, notably the railway station.

Helsinki is situated on the north side of the Gulf of Finland and consists of two ports, separated by a promontory and protected by a group of small islands.

Helsinki manufactures iron and steel, metal goods, foodstuffs, luxury goods and printed matter. It is also an important shipbuilding centre.

Little more than a village in 1810, **Helsinki** developed rapidly in the 19th c as the capital of the grand-duchy and, from 1918, the republic of Finland.

The **population of Helsinki** is 492,240 (est. 1991), although the greater metropolitan area numbers 826,664, mainly Finnish speaking but with a large Swedish community.

HERBS

A **Herb** is any plant whose stem or stalk dies entirely and does not have a permanent woody stem. It is used to describe those plants used for flavouring, perfume or medicinal purposes.

Coriander (*Coriandrum sativum*) is an umbelliferous plant native to southern Europe. Its seeds are used in cooking and also in medicine as an aromatic and carminative.

Marjoram is an aromatic herb, indigenous to Europe and Asia. The leaves of *Majorana hortensis* are used, either green or dried, for cooking purposes.

Parsley (*Petroselinum hortense*) is a hardy biennial herb, the leaves of which are used for garnishing and flavouring. The Hamburg variety is also grown for its fleshy root.

Peppermint (*Mentha peperita*) is a perennial herb with stalked leaves and spiky flowers. It is cultivated for its essential oils, used in medicine and cookery.

Spearmint (*Mentha spicata*), growing wild in the UK or cultivated, is commonly used in cooking. It has smooth sessile leaves and tapering flower-spikes.

The **Saffron Crocus** (*Crocus sativus*) originated at Corycus in Cilicia. A single corm, smuggled by a 13th c pilgrim into England, led to its cultivation at Saffron Walden.

HINDUISM

Hinduism is one of the world's oldest religions, with its wellspring the great Indus Valley Civilisation of 5,000 years ago, and today numbers over 700 million faithful.

Hindus teach that the cycle of reincarnation (**samsara**) may be escaped by the gaining of spiritual knowledge through meditation, or by performing good works.

Male Hindus should pass through four stages (**ashrama**) in life, first a student, then a householder, next a thinker and last a wandering holy man or *sanyasin*.

The **Bhagavad Gita**, the Song of the Lord, is the greatest statement of *bhakti* (warm devotion) in Hinduism, and tells of the god Krishna and Prince Arjuna.

The four **Vedas** are the oldest of Hinduism's sacred books, and the *Rig Veda* is the most sacred. The *Upanishads* contain the philosophy known as the *Vedanta*.

The great myths of the Hindu religion were written down in the **Ramayana** and the *Mahabharata c.* 300 BC, and describe how order and chaos alternate throughout history.

The **Hindu pantheon** contains hundreds of gods and goddesses, including Krishna, often portrayed as a cowherd, and the terrifying Kali, with her garland of skulls.

HOBBIES

Birdwatching combines the joy of discovery with scientific curiosity and aesthetic appreciation. Binoculars, a field guide for identification and patience are necessary, and telescopes and a camera are useful. With feeding stations, a bird bath and plants to entice birds, birdwatching can be a backyard vocation.

▲ *Raising tropical fish is a popular hobby.*

During the 1930s an interest in paper folding (**origami**) emerged in Spain and South America, perhaps stimulated by the Spanish writer Miguel de Unamuno, who espoused it as a hobby and invented several original folded forms. In the US and UK origami also enjoyed a vogue as a pastime.

Embroidery may be one of the world's oldest crafts, although it has taken on 'hobby' status since its decline in the 19th c. Important stitches include tent stitch, feather, chain, cross-stitch, satin, herringbone, ladder, blanket and Gobelin.

Knitting is the making of fabric by using special needles to interlace yarn in a series of loops or stitches. Ancient Egyptians were among the first to knit and today hand-knitting is a popular hobby around the world.

Raising **aquarium fish** is believed to be among the most popular hobbies in the US, with many millions of households possessing aquariums. In the past most tropical fish were imported, with South America, especially the Amazon basin and Guyana, supplying the greatest number.

Spelunking is the amateur pursuit of speleology, the exploration and study of caves, as a hobby or sport. It is a popular recreation among both adults and children in parts of the world where there are caves.

The popularity of **mathematics** as a hobby today is due in part to Martin Gardner (b. 1914, US), the author of a widely read column and publisher of numerous puzzle collections.

HOCKEY

Heiner Dopp of West Germany has made the **most international appearances** – 286, between 1975 and 1986.

India held the **men's Olympic hockey title** from 1928 to 1960 when they were defeated 1-0 by Pakistan in the final.

The **biggest margin of victory in men's international hockey** came when India defeated the US 24-1 at the Los Angeles Olympics in 1932.

The **European Club Champions Cup** was inaugurated, officially, in 1971 and German club Uhlenhorst Mülheim won the trophy nine consecutive times from 1988–96.

The **highest score in a women's hockey international** was England's 23-0 victory over France at Merton, south London on 3 Feb. 1923.

The **most prolific scorer in men's international hockey** is Paul Litjens of the Netherlands who scored 267 goals in 177 matches.

HOLOCAUST

3 m. Polish Jews were subjected to a **Blitzpogrom** of murder and rape. Reinhard Heydrich issued a ghetto decree fencing in the Jews into the ghettoes of Warsaw and Lvov.

◄ *A survivor of the Holocaust.*

Between 1933 and 1938 the Nazis boycotted Jewish businesses, established quotas in Germany's professions and schools and forbade intermarriage between **Jews and Gentiles** (Nuremberg Laws, 1935).

By the end of World War II 6 m. Jews had been systematically **murdered** by the Nazis and a creative religious and secular community destroyed.

Dachau was the first Nazi concentration camp (1933). By the time the camp was liberated in 1945 more than 200,000 people had been detained, and 70,000 were killed or starved to death.

Four *Einsatzgruppen* ('strike squads') were deployed against Soviet Jews. The worst atrocity was committed at the **Babi Yar** ravine, Kiev; 33,771 Jews were machine-gunned on 29–30 Sept. 1941.

In 1942 Reinhard Heydrich chaired the Wannsee Conference on the **Final Solution** of the Jewish Question. Jews would account for 60% of those exterminated in concentration camps.

In **Buchenwald** (opened 1937) inmates were used as guinea-pigs for doctors experimenting with amputations, lethal germs and poisons. By the time it was liberated (1945) 50,000 people had been murdered.

Jewish inmates destroyed Sobibor and Treblinka. However, two-thirds of Europe's Jews had been murdered, more than in **Pogroms** ('race riots') during the previous 1,800 years.

Methods of killing at **Auschwitz** (1–3 m. killed) and other camps included cyanide gas or carbon monoxide gas, electrocution, phenol injections, flame-throwers and hand grenades.

Simon Wiesenthal, an Austrian Jew, lost 89 family members in the Holocaust. Wiesenthal located 1,000 Nazi **war criminals** including Adolf Eichmann, the administrator of the death camps.

HOLY ROMAN EMPIRE

Charlemagne, first ruler of the Holy Roman Empire, chose Aachen as the site of his palace because of its hot springs, where he loved to bathe.

From 1273 the Holy Roman Empire was dominated by the Habsburg family. **Francis II** (1768–1835), the last emperor, dissolved the Holy Roman Empire in 1806 and thereafter ruled as Emperor of Austria.

Napoleon Bonaparte's victories in Europe, particularly at Austerlitz on 2 Dec. 1805, led to the dissolution of the Holy Roman Empire and the rise of Austria as an independent power.

▲ *Napoleon Bonaparte.*

Pope Leo III crowned Charlemagne the first emperor on 25 Dec. 800, the papacy wishing to maintain the ancient Roman traditions of European unity.

The **Holy Roman Empire** is the term used to describe the loose political entity based mainly on German and north Italian states between 800 and 1806.

HOME FRONT

British citizens were encouraged to 'dig for victory' and new allotments were allocated regularly. By Jun. 1940 vegetables were growing in the Tower of London moat.

Daily life in the UK was subject to government restriction to ensure that resources were equally allocated. In Jun. 1941 **clothes rationing** began and by Nov. 1941 a points rationing system had been introduced.

In 1939 British men between the ages of 18 and 41 were conscripted. By 1941 the upper age limit was raised to 51 and for the first time unmarried women between the ages of 19 and 30 were conscripted. All British women up to 50 had to register for **war work**.

In 1941 it was necessary to set up a National Fire Service (**NFS**) in the UK. By 1943 almost 2 m. volunteers had joined civil defence organisations: ARP, fire, ambulance and police services.

In May 1940 British volunteers jointed **Home Guard** units (a term first used by Churchill in Jul. 1940) and by 1943 more than 2 m. men had joined this 'Dad's Army'. These were to be the last line of defence against Hitler.

In Sept. 1939 ration books were issued in the UK, every British adult carried a grey-blue identity card, **gas masks** were distributed and British children were evacuated to the countryside.

Women in the Air Transport Auxiliary (**ATA**) ferried aircraft from factories to airfields. The famous pilot Amy Johnson (1909–41) was killed off the Thames Estuary ferrying a Spitfire.

HORSE RACING

Eclipse is recognised as the **greatest British racehorse**, having an un-beaten career of 18 races between May 1769 and Oct. 1770.

Gordon Richards is the **most successful jockey in British racing** history. He rode a total of 4,870 winners between 1921 and 1954.

If you'd like to send a birthday card to your favourite race-horse, make sure he or she receives it on 1 Jan., the **official 'birthday' of all UK racehorses**!

British jockey Lester Piggot. ▶

Lester Piggott has ridden more **British classic winners** than any other jockey, a total of 30 between 1954 and 1992.

The **Epsom Derby** was inaugurated in 1780. The prestigious race for three-year-old colts and fillies was named in honour of Lord Derby, the leading racing figure of the day.

The **most successful jockey of all time** is the legendary Bill Shoemaker (US) who rode 8,833 winners between 1948 and 1990.

The **US Triple Crown** comprises the Kentucky Derby, Preakness Stakes and Belmont Stakes for three-year-olds. Eleven horses have won the Triple Crown, last of which was Affirmed in 1978.

▼ *Fields of tulips – a popular sight in Holland*

HORTICULTURE

Floriculture is that branch of horticulture concerned with the cultivation of flowers, including the breeding of new varieties.

Horticulture, derived from Latin *hortus* (garden) and *cultura* (cultivation) is that division of agriculture which relates to fruit, vegetables, flowers and ornamental plants.

Olericulture is the branch of horticulture concerned with the cultivation of vegetables of all kinds, for salads or cooking.

Ornamental horticulture is concerned with the cultivation of plants for their aesthetic or decorative value and includes annual and perennial plants, shrubs, vines and trees.

Pomology is that branch of horticulture concerned with the cultivation of fruit bushes and trees. It is a hybrid word, from Latin *pomum* (fruit) and Greek *logos* (word).

The **propagation of plants** is carried out either by planting seeds or by vegetative means, using a portion of the plant, leaves, stem or roots.

Vegetables are defined on the basis of their use as food. They are grouped according to the part of the plant used, from the tuber (potato) to the leaf (lettuce).

HOUSING

A lack of adequate housing is one of **Mexico**'s most serious problems. Although sub-standard housing is more visible in urban areas, living conditions are probably worse in rural areas.

Building societies (UK), that lend money for house purchases, originated in 1781. In the US the equivalent is called a *savings and loan association* and the first was founded in 1831.

Despite an increase in the number of single-family homes built, **Japan** has serious housing shortages in metropolitan areas. This is due to high urban-population concentrations, with land prices and housing costs that far exceed average.

In the UK 14 m. were **homeowners** in 1986. In 1980 legislation was passed for council tenants to buy their homes and nearly 1 m. were sold by 1986.

In the UK, under the Housing (**Homeless** Persons) Act of 1977, local authorities have a statutory obligation in certain circumstances to find housing for homeless families.

The agricultural revolution, *c.* 10,000 BC, gave a major boost to **building**

▲ *Mexico City, where housing is a major problem.*

construction. People no longer travelled in search of game but stayed in one place to tend their fields and made permanent dwellings.

The trend for **high-rise buildings** began in Chicago in the early 1880s due to high land costs. Architect-engineer William Le Baron Jenney built the 10-storey, all-metal structured Home Insurance Company Building (1885).

HUMAN EVOLUTION

About 35 m. years ago appeared the first evidence of primitive monkey-like primates. The largest and best known of these, *Propliopithecus*, was about the size of a cat and is believed to be in the ancestral line of apes and humans.

After more than 20 years of observation and experiment, Charles Darwin presented a statement of his theory of evolution through natural selection (1858). The following year Darwin published his full theory in **On the Origin of Species**.

As well as favouring the evolution of the brain, the early development of technology and culture also affected the evolution of the teeth and jaws. By about 1.6 m. years ago, these trends had produced

a mentally and physically advanced population called **Homo erectus**.

By 250,000 years ago humans had become sufficiently advanced to be assigned as *Homo sapiens*. Until about 40,000 years ago, they were not identical to modern humans, retaining many ancestral features recalling *Homo erectus*.

Charles Darwin (1809–82), a British naturalist, formulated a theory of evolution based on natural selection, which had a profound effect on the scientific and theological beliefs of his time. This theory was presented in *On the Origin of Species* (1859) and *The Descent of Man* (1871).

British naturalist Charles Darwin. ▶

Climatic fluctuation in the **Pleis-tocene Era** was probably an important factor in human evolution, opening up new territory for colonisation by creating dry-land bridges. Rapid changes and rigorous climates provided the environmental challenge to spur physical and cultural adaptation.

For many years anthropologists assumed that the origin of **hominids** as a group separate from apes must have occurred in Europe between 14 and 10 m. years ago. Most anthropologists now believe that the split occurred much later and in Africa.

Fossil evidence indicates that the earliest true humans (members of the genus *Homo*) appeared close to the end of the Pliocene Epoch, 2–3 m. years ago. Most of human evolution therefore occurred during the Pleistocene Epoch (2.5 m. years ago to present).

From deposits dating from 2 m. years ago have emerged the first direct evidence of behaviour that decisively separates the species *Homo* from other animals; for example, regular use of stone tools and other artefacts.

Pierre Louis Moreau de Maupertuis (1698–1759) was perhaps the first to propose a general theory of **evolution**. He concluded that hereditary material, consisting of particles, was transmitted from parents to offspring.

The earliest humans are known as *Homo habilis*. Physically, they were much like *Australopithecus*, apart from the larger size of their brains. Most *Homo habilis* fossils have been discovered in East Africa. They are often found with simple tools.

The human species is a member of the mammalian order **Primates**. It is related, in descending order of closeness, to apes, monkeys, tarsiers and lemurs.

Thomas Robert Malthus (1766–1834), an English clergyman, through his work *An Essay on the Principle of Population* (1798), had a great influence in directing naturalists towards a theory of natural selection.

HUMAN RIGHTS

Ancient Greek and Roman thought recognised the existence of immutable, **natural laws** to which individuals might appeal in defiance of unjust state laws.

Humanitarian law principles governing the rules of war developed extensively from the writings of Hugo Grotius (17th c) through the **Hague Conference** (1899 and 1907) to the Geneva Convention (1949) and its two Additional Protocols (1977).

International and regional bodies have established forums for the examination and adjudication of **human-rights violations**, including the European Commission of Human Rights and the Inter-American Commission on Human Rights of the Organisation of American States.

Key international human-rights declarations include: **Universal Declaration of Human Rights** (United Nations General Assembly, 1948), International Covenant on Civil and Political Rights (1976) and the International Covenant on Economic, Social and Cultural Rights (1976).

The **Helsinki Accords** (1975) were embodied in a 'declaration of policy intent' by the US, Canada, USSR and 32 European countries. They pledged to respect human rights, including 'freedom of thought, conscience, religion or belief'.

The **United Nations** (UN) is a general international organisation established at the end of World War II (1945) to promote international peace and security. It replaced the League of Nations, which was founded after World War I.

▼ *Martin Luther King fought for rights for black Americans.*

Treatment that is condemned by **human-rights organisations** includes: extrajudicial execution; disappearance; kidnapping; torture; arbitrary detention or exile; discrimination; and violation of the rights to due process, free expression, free association, free movement and peaceable assembly.

HUNGARY

From Mar. 1920 **Hungary** was a kingdom without a king, ruled by an admiral (Nicholas Horthy) without a navy. Technically he was regent, but the monarchy was never restored.

Hungary (capital: Budapest) lies in central Europe, bordered by Romania, Serbia, Croatia, Austria and Slovakia, with an area of 93,033 sq km/35,920 sq mi.

Hungary exports semi-finished products, raw and basic materials, machinery and transport equipment, food and agricultural products and industrial consumer goods.

The **population of Hungary** is 10,326,000 (est. 1991), comprising 96.6% Magyar, 1.6% German, 1.1% Slovak and 0.7% other. 64.1% are Roman Catholic and 23.3% Protestant.

The Soviet Army liberated **Hungary** in 1945 and helped establish a communist regime which was abolished on 23 Oct. 1989.

HURRICANES

A **hurricane** in the US in 1965 did $1,419,000 worth of damage. Agriculture suffers in severe weather; to a lesser extent, so can the power, transport and building industries.

A hurricane, also called a typhoon or tropical cyclone, is an extreme form of low-pressure **air cell**. It brings torrential rain and extremely strong winds.

◄ *Budapest, the capital of Hungary.*

During World War II the practice began of giving hurricanes girls' **names** for easy identification. The names are given in alphabetical order following the dates of the hurricanes.

Every year some 11 hurricanes sweep across the US from one of their breeding grounds in the **Atlantic**. They are characterised by very strong rotating winds, which may reach 240–320 kph/150–220 mph.

Hurricane 'Diane', which struck the east coast of the US in the mid-1950s, was the first to cause more than a billion dollars' worth of damage.

Hurricanes are found only over large ocean areas with a surface temperature above 27°C/81°F, and rarely form within five degrees either side of the **equator**.

Hurricanes form from pre-existing disturbances within the **trade winds**, when a core of warm air (the eye) exists, accompanied by an anticyclone in the upper atmosphere.

In 1876 a hurricane moved inland over the Ganges Delta area of Bengal, India. The accompanying **storm tide**

engulfed the coastal area and islands. More than 100,000 people drowned.

The **eye of a hurricane** is its centre. Dry air descends into this calm, very low-pressure area. High-level winds and cirrus clouds spiral outwards from the centre.

HYDROLOGY

Applications of hydrology include development of irrigation systems, flood and erosion control, waste-water disposal, pollution abatement, preservation of fish and wildlife, hydroelectricity generation and recreational use of water.

▲ *Hurricanes and tornadoes are characterised by strong rotating winds.*

Hydrology is the study of the waters of the earth, including their occurrence and distribution and the relationship between water and its environment.

It is estimated that earth holds 1,360 m. cu km/525 m. cu mi of **water**. Of this, just over 97.2% lies in the oceans.

Some rocks allow little or no water to pass through: these are called impermeable rocks, or aquicludes. Others store considerable amounts of water and act as major sources of water supply: these are **aquifers**.

The '**hydrologic cycle**' describes the system in which waters of the sea evaporate, condense within the atmosphere, fall back to earth as precipitation and finally flow in rivers back to the sea.

Water is the most abundant substance on earth and the principal constituent of all living things. Water in the atmosphere also plays a major role in maintaining a habitable environment.

When sunlight is reflected from a drop of water it splits into all the colours of the spectrum, each reflected at a different angle. A mass of raindrops may appear as a band of colours, a **rainbow**.

ICE

An **icebreaker** is a ship with a strong hull and big engine, used to clear a passage through pack-ice for other ships. Its sloping bow lets the ship ride up over the ice and smash it.

Changes in the sun's heat output may have caused the **Little Ice Age** that occurred in the later 17th c. The River Thames used to freeze so hard in winter that Frost Fairs were held on it.

Falling ice crystals may partly melt before they reach the ground, forming **sleet**.

Part of the sun's radiation is reflected back into space from earth. The amount reflected, the **albedo**, depends on the nature of the surface.

Polar ice reflects about 90% of the sunlight that falls on it. It thus retains

ICELAND

Formerly a Danish dependency, **Iceland** became an independent republic on 17 Jun. 1944 while Denmark was under German occupation.

Iceland (capital: Reykjavik) is an island in the North Atlantic between Greenland and the UK, with an area of 102,819 sq km/39,699 sq mi.

Iceland boasts the world's oldest democratic parliament, the *Althing* having been in continuous existence since 930.

little warmth and so the ice caps do not melt.

The **Baltic Sea** froze between Sweden and the Danish island of Sjaelland in 1924. People could walk across the ice from Sweden to Denmark.

The **greatest thickness of ice** known was recorded by radio ech soundings over Antarctica 440 km/270 mi from the Wilkes Land coast. The ice was 4.28 km/2 mi 704 yd thick.

Iceland exports fish (frozen, salted or fresh), lobsters, shrimps and scallops, mainly to the UK, Germany, US, France, Japan and Denmark.

The **population of Iceland** is 258,000 (est. 1991), comprising 96.5% Icelanders. Danes, Swedes, Americans and Germans make up the rest.

▲ *Glacier in Alaska.*

IMPRESSIONISM

Painters who began as Impressionists developed other techniques, which started new movements in art. French painters Georges Seurat and Paul Signac painted canvases with small dots of colour in an application known as **pointillism**.

French Impressionism influenced artists throughout the world, including the Americans **J. A. M. Whistler**, Mary Cassatt and John Singer Sargent, English Walter Sickert, Italian Giovanni Segantini and Spanish Joaqu'n Sorolla.

Impressionism was a movement in painting that developed in late 19th-c France in reaction to the formalism and sentimentality that characterised academic art. The movement marks the beginning of the modern period in art.

Rejecting the standards of the *Academie des Beaux-Arts*, the **Impressionists** preferred to paint outdoors, choosing landscapes and street scenes, as well as figures from everyday life.

The direct precursors of Impressionism were the English landscape painters John Constable and **J. M. W. Turner** and the French Barbizon school: Monet and Pissaro were most influenced by these artists.

The foremost Impressionists included **Edgar Degas**, Claude Monet, Edouard Manet, Berthe Morisot, Camille Pissarro, Pierre Auguste Renoir and Alfred Sisley.

The Impressionists achieved effects of naturalness and immediacy by placing short **brush-strokes** of colour side by side, juxtaposing primary colours and achieving a greater brilliance of colour.

The Impressionists developed individual styles and as a group benefited from their common experiments in colour. **Monet** alone was doctrinaire in applying what had become Impressionist theory.

The Impressionists' primary object was to achieve a sponta-

◀ *The Impressionist artist Monet by Edouard Manet.*

neous, undetailed rendering of the world through careful representation of the effect of **natural light** on objects.

INCAS

At its height the **Inca Empire** stretched 4,000 km/2,500 mi north–south and 800 km/500 mi east–west. Population estimates vary from 3.5 m. to 16 m.

Communication in the Inca Empire was by river and a network of stone-paved roads. Relays of trained runners (horses and wheels were unknown) kept authorities in touch.

The attraction for the conquistadors was gold and silver, but the Incas' real gifts to the world were maize and **potatoes**, which the Incas had learned to freeze-dry.

The fabulous Inca citadel of **Machu Picchu** remained hidden high in the Andes peaks until American Hiram Bingham revealed it to the world in 1911.

The **Spanish conquistadors** of 1531 were assumed by the Incas to be returning gods. Unopposed, these 180 soldiers extinguished over 300 years of Inca Civilisation.

INDIA

India (capital: New Delhi) is a triangular peninsula jutting south from Asia, with an area of 3,166,414 sq km/ 1,222,559 sq mi.

India became an independent dominion on 14 Aug. 1947, and a federal republic within the Commonwealth on 26 Jan. 1950.

▲ *Hindu is one of India's central faiths.*

India exports pearls, precious stones and jewellery, machinery, transport equipment, iron and steel, electrical equipment, paper and paper products.

The **population of India** is 871,158,000 (est. 1991), comprising 82.4% Hindu, 11.35% Muslim, 2.43% Christian, 1.97% Sikh, 0.71% Buddhist, 0.48% Jain and 0.01% Zoroastrian.

Under Mahatma Gandhi (1869–1948) a policy of non-violent non-co-operation began in Jul. 1920 which led eventually to **India** achieving independence.

INDIA, EARLY

Alexander the Great (356–323 BC), King of Macedonia, conquered the north of India in 326 BC. One of the results of this was a lingering Greek influence on the art of India.

In 1498 the Portuguese explorer **Vasco da Gama** arrived in Calicut on the Malabar Coast and established a monopoly on Indian maritime trade, not broken until the 17th c.

Indian **writing** first appeared in the 4th c BC, and can probably be traced back to the Phoenician alphabet. By the 3rd c BC Indians were already skilled grammarians.

The **Taj Mahal**, a white marble mausoleum, was built by Shah Jehan near Agra, India, in memory of his wife. It took more than 20 years to complete.

The **Veda**, the collection of sacred writings of about 1200 BC, depict the emergence of the great socio-religious system of Hinduism.

INDONESIA

Formerly the Dutch East Indies, **Indonesia** declared independence on 17 Aug. 1945,

▲ *Alexander the Great in battle.*

INDUSTRIAL REVOLUTION

'Robber Baron' was the popular term for 19th-c American industrialists who amassed terrific wealth through monopolistic tactics.

finally achieving it in Dec. 1949 after a four-year campaign by the Dutch to regain control.

Indonesia (capital: Jakarta) is the world's largest archipelago extending 4,827 km/3,000 mi along the equator, with an area of 1,919,317 sq km/741,052 sq mi.

Indonesia exports crude petroleum, natural gas, plywood, garments, tin, copra and rubber, mainly to Japan, the US and Singapore.

Most famous of the Buddhist temples of **Indonesia** is Borobudur, built in the 8th c with elaborate murals and carvings depicting the life of Siddharta Gautama Buddha.

The **population of Indonesia** is 181,451,000 (est. 1991), comprising 40.1% Javanese, 15.3% Sundanese, 12% Bahasa Indonesian, 4.8% Madurese and 27.8% other.

▲ *The Indonesian capital Jakarta.*

In the 1880s and 1890s a **second Industrial Revolution** transformed post-Civil War US society, driving the gross national product to $37 bn (1900).

On the Continent, Belgium, rich in iron and coal, was first to embark on industrialisation in the 1820s and by the 1830s the **French Industrial Revolution** had begun.

Organised labour groups like the Knights of Labor (1869) and American Federation of Labor (1886) formed in the US due to the second Industrial Revolution.

The first Industrial Revolution occurred in the UK at the end of the 18th c and profoundly altered Britain's **economy** and society. Labour was transferred from the production of primary products to the production of manufactured goods.

The historical term '**Industrial Revolution**' can be applied to specific countries and periods of the past, but the process known as 'industrialisation' is still going on, particularly in developing countries.

The Industrial Revolution, which began in Britain in the 18th c, spread to the rest of western Europe and North America during the 19th c. The pattern of diffusion was quite uniform, beginning with **textiles**, coal and iron.

The **influx of immigrants** to the US during the 19th c fueled the Industrial Revolution. Immigration numbers jumped from 352,569 in 1869 to 1,514,816 in 1884.

The main defining feature of the Industrial Revolution was a dramatic increase in production per capita that was made possible by the mechanisation of manufacturing and other processes carried out in **factories**.

The main social impact of the Industrial Revolution was that it changed an agrarian into an **urban industrial society**, with cities worldwide becoming centres for industry.

The Soviet Industrial Revolution (pre-World War I and post-1930s) involved **state investment** in plant, machinery and heavy industrial goods and a restriction on consumption of consumer goods.

The US federal government established its **first regulatory agency** in 1887, the Interstate Commerce Commission, in response to rising 19th-c industrialism.

The US's first 'big' business was the **railways** that expanded after the Civil War to connect the coasts by 1869.

Urbanisation and industrialisation went hand in hand in 19th-c America. In 1880 20% of Americans lived in cities; 51% did so in 1920.

INDUSTRY

By the 1980s there were 6 **zaibatsu** ('financial cliques') with 650 member companies between them, employing 6% of the workforce and controlling more than 2% of the world economy.

Electronics and automated controls are now applied extensively throughout industry, particularly in steel mills, oil refineries, coal mines and chemical plants.

In 1988 the **number of people employed** in the manufacturing industry in the US dropped below 5 m. for the first time since the 19th c, largely due to closures and former overmanning.

Major trends in industrial activity 1960–90 were the growth of electronic, robotic and microelectronic technologies and the expansion of the offshore oil industry.

The **Fortune 500** defines an industrial corporation as one that derives at least 50% of its revenue from manufacturing or mining.

The period after World War II has been marked by the development of shipbuilding and motor manufacture in the **low-cost countries**, such as Japan, Korea and Taiwan.

The products of **hi-tech industries** have low bulk but high value; Silicon Valley in the US and Silicon Glen in Scotland are two areas with high industry concentrations.

INDY CAR RACING

Although Grand Prix and **Indy Car Racing** are perceived as two separate and, to some extent, conflicting motor sports, the Indianapolis race was part of the Formula One calendar until 1960, although it was not eligible for championship points.

Anthony Joseph Foyt, Jr is the first man to have won the Indianapolis 500 four times and the only driver to have achieved a hat-trick of wins at the Indy 500, Daytona 500 and Le Mans 24 Hours. He qualified for a record 35 consecutive Indy 500s and won 67 Indy Car races.

CART's **PPG Indy Car World Series** is a 16-race championship run on superspeedways like Indianapolis; short 1.6 km/1 mi ovals such as Milwaukee; permanent road courses like Road America, Wisconsin; and temporary street circuits like Long Beach, California.

Nigel Mansell burst on to the Indy Car scene on 21 Mar. 1993, becoming the first ever Indy Car rookie to take pole position and victory on his race debut. Mansell's team for the 1993 season was the Newman Haas team's Lola–Chevrolet T9300.

Ford GT40, winning the 1968 Le Mans. ▲

The Indianapolis 500 – consisting of 200 laps on a 4.02-km/2.5-mi oval track totalling 805 km/500 mi – is sanctioned by the US Auto Club (**USAC**). Traditionally the Indy 500 has been the crown jewel of the American national championship.

The qualifying procedure for the Indianapolis 500 is different from that used in most motor races. There are 33 grid positions up for grabs: a **qualification run** consists of four consecutive timed laps at speed and drivers are dispatched individually.

The winner of the original Indianapolis 500 in 1911, **Ray Harroun**, managed to average a speed of 120.04 kph/74.602 mph during the race.

INFLATION

By mid-1923 the German currency, the **mark**, was losing value so fast that prices changed by the minute. Workers demanded pay every day, spending it before it decreased.

Chronic inflation is characterised by high price increases, with annual rates of 10–30% in some industrial nations and even 100% or more in a few developing countries.

▲ *The caterpillar – a member of the Lepidoptera family.*

Economists have identified the 16th–early 17th c in Europe as a period of **long-term inflation**; the average annual rate of 1–2% was modest by modern standards.

Inflation and deflation are terms used to describe, respectively, a decline or an increase in the value of money in relation to the goods and services it will buy.

The **hyperinflation** in Germany following World War I caused the currency in circulation to expand more than 7 bn times and prices to jump 10 bn times during a 16-month period before Nov. 1923.

The **impact of inflation** on individuals depends on many variables. People with relatively fixed incomes, particularly those in low-income groups, suffer during accelerating inflation.

Widespread price declines have become rare and inflation is now the **dominant variable**: affecting public and private economic planning, and linked to wars, poor harvests and political upheavals.

INSECTS

Insects are those members of the phylum Arthropoda in which the body is divided into three parts: the head, the thorax and the abdomen. They usually have six legs.

The order **Coleoptera** consists of 154 families and 250,000 species (about half of all recorded insects), encompassing all kinds of beetles, characterised by hard shells.

The order **Lepidoptera** consists of 190 families and 150,000 species. They include moths and butterflies which go through caterpillar and chrysalis stages.

The order **Odonata** consists of 17 families and 4,500 species. They include dragonflies, large insects with long slender bodies and membranous narrow wings.

The order of **Diptera** consists of 138 families and 73,000 species. It includes two-winged flies such as gnats, mosquitoes, midges, horseflies and houseflies.

The order of **Hymenoptera** consists of 118,000 species and includes ants, bees, sawflies and wasps. They are distinguished by intelligent behaviour and organisation.

The order **Orthoptera** consists of 7 families and 21,000 species. They include cockroaches, grasshoppers and crickets, with leathery forewings and hard shells.

INSURANCE

An **Act of God** is any occurrence not caused by human intervention or negligence, such as lightning or floods. Most insurance policies do not provide compensation for these.

Following the Piper Alpha oil field disaster in Jul. 1988, some $836 m. were paid out in compensation; the biggest-ever **marine insurance** loss.

Lloyd's, popularly known as **Lloyd's of London**, is an association of approximately 300 insurance syndicates, each of which comprises many individual underwriters. They suffered huge losses in the early 1990s.

Metropolitan Life Insurance, New York has **the highest volume of insurance** in the world. On 1994 figures this stood at $1,240.7 bn.

The American insurance group, the **Blue Cross and Blue Shield Association**, has 65.8 m. members and pays out $62 bn in hospital benefits per year.

The **earliest known type of life insurance** was the burial benefits that Greek and Roman religious societies provided for their members.

The **first life-insurance company in North America** was founded in 1759 in Philadelphia. It was named the Corporation for the Relief of Poor and Distressed Presbyterian Ministers and of the Poor and Distressed Widows and Children of Presbyterian Ministers.

INTERIOR DESIGN

A. W. N. Pugin (1812–52) equated good design with high moral standards. **The Victorian Gothic revival** was inspired by his interiors for the Houses of Parliament (1836–37).

Architect-designer **Victor Horta** (1861–1947), leader of the **Art Nouveau movement**, pioneered Modernism in Belgium (notably Maison du Peuple building, 1896–99), designing every detail down to flower-shaped light-fittings.

Bauhaus design (founder **Walter Gropius**, Germany, 1919) bonded design with industrial technique; its style was strictly economical, impersonal and geometric, refining line and shape from close study of materials.

Charleston Farmhouse, the Bloomsbury Group's country retreat (1913), was designed by Omega Workshops (Roger Fry, art critic; Duncan Grant and Vanessa Bell, artists), painting furniture and printing Matisse-inspired textiles.

Post-modern interior design, spearheaded in the US by Robert Venturi and inspired by mass culture, self-consciously manipulated past styles. The post-modern Memphis group (1981), led by Sottsass, included Bellini and Columbo.

▼ *Tapestries were once popular interior decorations.*

The **Aesthetic movement** (late 1860s–70s), inspired by William Morris and Japanese design and epitomised by Whistler's Peacock Room (painted turquoise and gold for Leyland, 1876-77), had great influence in America.

William Morris (1834–96, Arts and Crafts founder) and the **Pre-Raphaelite Brotherhood** decorated the Red House (1859–60), designing, hand-crafting and matching interior to exterior. Morris & Co (1861) pioneered interior design.

INTERNET

The Internet originated in a US Department of Defence program called **ARPANET** (Advanced Research Projects Agency Network), established in 1969 to provide a secure communications network for organisations engaged in defence-related research.

The Internet is a **global on-line network** connecting many computers and based on a common addressing system and communications protocol called TCP/IP (Tranmission Control Protocol/Internet Protocol).

From the **Internet**'s beginnings in 1983, it was estimated by 1994 to have over 40 m. users on 11,000 networks in 70 countries. In 1998, approx. 1 m. new users were joining per month.

Networked games, networked business transactions and virtual museums are among **applications** being developed that both extend the use of the network and test the limits of its expanding technology.

NSF (the National Science Foundation) maintains the network, but Internet protocol development is governed by the Internet Architecture Board and the **InterNIC** (Internet Network Information Centre).

Originally, the Internet's uses were electronic mail (e-mail), file transfer and newsgroups. The **World Wide Web**, giving navigation to Internet sites through a browser, expanded rapidly in the 1990s and is now its main component.

Researchers and academics in other fields used ARPANET and the National Science Foundation. This created a similar network, called **NSFNet**, that took over the TCP/IP technology and established a new netweork capable of handling far greater traffic.

INTOXICANTS

Alcoholic beverages were used in primitive societies. They had important nutritional value. They were the best medicine available for some illnesses and especially for relieving pain, and for intoxication at festivals.

Cannabis was used in central Asia and China as early as 3000 BC. Its introduction to Europe was by way of Africa. It was used as a folk medicine prior to the 1900s.

Heroin, Diacetylmorphine, was first developed from morphine by the Bayer Company, Germany (1898). Originally used as a narcotic analgesic, its undesirable side effects soon outweighed its value as a painkiller.

Sumerian records from the time of Mesopotamia (5000–4000 BC) refer to the narcotic and sleep-inducing qualities of the poppy, and medicinal reference to **opium** is contained in Assyrian medical tablets.

The Incas knew about the ability of **cocaine** to produce euphoria and hallucinations; the Germans first extracted it from the coca plant in the 19th c when it was used as a local anesthetic.

The **Opium Wars** were waged in 1840 and 1855 by the UK against China to enforce the opening of Chinese ports to trade in opium.

When Christopher Columbus discovered the Americas, he found **tobacco** smoked by the natives. The American Indians believed it had medicinal properties, which was the main reason for its introduction to Europe in 1556.

INVENTORS

Alexander Graham Bell (1847–1922) invented the telephone (1876) as a spin-off from his main researches on deafness. Later he invented the hearing aid and the iron lung, and pioneered aviation in Canada.

American organic chemist **Wallace Hume Carothers** (1896–1937) was the inventor of nylon, the first successful synthetic fibre, which has become as familiar to the world as the natural materials that it often replaces.

An electrical engineer who invented the thermionic valve, **Sir John Ambrose Fleming** (1849–1945) also contributed to the science of photometry. His work with the thermionic valve (1904–05) was important to the development of radio.

Benjamin Franklin (1706–90), an American scientist, inventor (discoverer of electricity) and writer, figured prominently in the governmental organisation of the emerging US.

British inventor **Sir Clive Marles Sinclair** (b. 1940) has pioneered in the field of microelectronics, producing such items as a 340-g/12-oz hand-held personal computer and a pocket-sized television set.

French inventor **Joseph Marie Jacquard** (1752–1834) built the first successful loom for weaving patterned fabrics. This loom, which used a system of punched cards to produce a pattern, was a forerunner of the computer.

George Westinghouse (1846–1914) was an American inventor and industrialist who during his lifetime obtained approx. 400 patents, including that on the air brake and railway signalling equipment.

S.F.B.Morse.

▲ *Samuel Morse, inventor of the Morse Code.*

Hungarian-born American inventor **Peter Carl Goldmark** (1906–77) invented the long-playing phonograph record and a number of important electronic devices.

James Watt (1736–1819) was a Scottish engineer and inventor who played an important part in the development of the steam engine as a practical power source.

Samuel F. B. Morse (1791–1872), an American inventor and artist, developed the electric telegraph and the signalling code that bears his name. He established the first US telegraph link in 1844.

The English engineer and inventor **Richard Trevithick** (1771–1833) built the first high-pressure steam engine and the first steam-powered carriage to transport passengers (1801) and invented a steam threshing machine.

The German physical chemist and inventor **Hermann Walther Nernst** (1864–1941) was awarded the Nobel Prize for chemistry in 1920, for his discovery (1906) of the third law of thermodynamics.

The inventor **Charles Francis Jenkins** (1867–1934) pioneered the early development of cinematography and television. He invented the phantascope, one of the earliest successful motion-picture projectors.

Thomas Alva Edison (1847–1931) was one of the most prolific American inventors of the 19th c. His many inventions included the first practical incandescent lamp, the phonograph and the movie projector.

INVERTEBRATES

Hairworms (*Gordiacea*) are a group of elongate, thread-like, unsegmented worms found in fresh water. They range up to 1 m/3ft 3 in in length but are never thicker than whipcord.

Larva is the name given to the sexually immature stage of an animal, such as the tadpole or caterpillar, when this is free-living but distinct from the adult form.

Invertebrates are all those animals which do not possess a backbone. They include insects, snails and worms and the larval stage of other animals.

Ribbon Worms (*Nemertinea*) are characterised by a soft extensible body without segmentation. Most are flat and ribbon-like and may grow to 4 m/13 ft in length.

The **Slug** (*Arion ater*) is related to the land snail but lacks a shell. Its eyes and tactile organs are on tentacles. It feeds on decayed vegetation and dead animals.

The unsegmented **Roundworms** (*Nematoda*) range in size from 0.25 mm to 1 m/3ft 3 in in length. Many are parasitic and include the plague of fiery serpents (Numbers 21:6-9).

Worms (*Vermes*) include all forms of worm-like invertebrates and include blindworms, flatworms, flukes, earthworms, tapeworms and leeches.

IRAN

Formerly the Persian Empire, **Iran** adopted its present name in 1935, on the 10th anniversary of the seizure of power by Riza Khan Pahlavi.

Iran (capital: Tehran) lies between the Caspian Sea and the Persian Gulf in south-western Asia, with an area of 1,638,057 sq km/632,457 sq mi.

Iran exports petroleum and petroleum products, carpets, fruit, nuts and hides, mainly to Japan, the Netherlands, India, Germany, Romania and Turkey.

Iran was a powerful empire under Cyrus the Great (600–529 BC), extending from the Indus to the Nile, before falling to Alexander the Great in 328 BC.

The **population of Iran** is 57,050,000 (est. 1991), comprising 45.6% Persian, 16.8% Azerbaijani, 9.1% Kurdish, 5.3% Gilaki, 4.3% Luri, 3.6% Mazandarani, 2.3% Baluchi, 2.2% Arab and 10.8% other.

IRAQ

Iraq (capital: Baghdad) is located in the Near East, bordered by Kuwait, Iran, Turkey, Syria, Jordan and Saudi Arabia, with an area of 435,052 sq km/167,975 sq mi.

Iraq, the reputed site of the Garden of Eden, was the location of several ancient empires – Sumerian, Assyrian and Babylonian.

▼ *Iraqi president Saddam Hussein with UN Sec.Gen. Kofi Annan.*

More than 99% of **Iraq's exports** consist of crude oil and petroleum products, the rest being foodstuffs, mainly going to the US, Brazil, Turkey, Japan and the Netherlands.

The Mesopotamia of biblical times, **Iraq** became an Islamic republic in Jul. 1958 when King Faisal was murdered and the monarchy overthrown.

The **population of Iraq** is 18,317,000 (est. 1991), comprising 77.1% Arab, 19% Kurdish, 1.4% Turkmen, 0.8% Persian, 0.8% Assyrian and 0.9% other.

IRELAND

Colonised by England in 1171, **Ireland** became a Free State on 6 Dec. 1921 and an independent republic on 18 Apr. 1949.

Ireland (capital: Dublin) occupies four-fifths of the island of the same name, with an area of 70,285 sq km/27,137 sq mi.

Ireland exports machinery and transport equipment, foodstuffs, chemicals, beverages and tobacco, mainly to the UK, Germany, France and US.

The **population of Ireland** is 3,494,000 (est. 1991), a drop of 50,000 since the 1986 census. 93% are Roman Catholic, 2.8% Anglican, 0.4% Presbyterian and 3.7% other faiths.

IRON AGE

By 1000 BC iron objects and the knowledge of **iron metallurgy** had spread throughout the Near East and the Mediterranean and westward into Europe. This development marked the end of the Near Eastern Bronze Age.

In about 500 BC the technique of forging iron tools and jewellery was introduced in Europe. The Celtic migration (450 BC), commonly named the **La Tene** phase of Celtic culture,

◀ *Ireland's capital, Dublin.*

marked the division between the Early and Late Iron Age.

Occasional objects of **smelted iron** are known from as early as 3000 BC in the ancient Near East and predynastic Egypt, but these objects were inferior in hardness to comparable objects produced in bronze.

The beginning of the European Iron Age varied, depending upon available sources of raw materials. Outside of Greece, the earliest use of iron in Europe occurred c. 800–750 BC in the late **Urnfield Culture** of central Europe and northern Italy.

The **Iron Age** marks the period of the development of technology, when the working of iron came into general use, replacing bronze as the basic material for implements and weapons.

Hallstatt (a town in Austria) gave its name to the earliest phases of the Celtic Iron Age and to the last phases of the preceding Urnfield Culture of the Bronze Age; it was the first Iron-Age site recognised by archeologists.

True iron metallurgy began among the **Hittites** in eastern

Anatolia between 1900 and 1400 BC. The art of iron smelting was perfected by the time of the fall of the Hittite Empire (c. 1200 BC).

IRRIGATION

About 10% of total cultivated land depends on irrigation. Another 20% is potentially irrigable. **Irrigable land** is limited by the constraints of landforms, soil and water supply.

In **Israel** irrigated agriculture has developed extremely rapidly since the 1950s, bringing much desert land under cultivation; 65% of its arable land is irrigated. In Egypt all arable land is irrigated.

In Zimbabwe irrigated winter cereals have provided a stable habitat for the **leafhopper** virus, which normally lives on seasonal grasses. It is now a serious cause of disease in irrigated maize.

Crop irrigation in Cuba. ▶

Irrigation tends to increase salt content in the soil. In the Punjab, India 15% of land brought under cultivation in the 19th c by large irrigation schemes was no longer cultivable by 1960 because of **salinisation**.

Many early eastern Mediterranean civilisations developed on the basis of **irrigation agriculture**. Water was lifted by hand or simple implements and applied directly to fields or open channels.

Soil salinity affects the type and yield of crops grown under irrigation. Citrus fruits, almonds, avocados, grapes and many deciduous trees are extremely salt-sensitive.

The 'green revolution' denotes the huge rise in food production in some countries where high-yielding varieties and high fertiliser use have boosted yields of wheat, maize and rice.

The two main sources of **water supply** for irrigation are surface water, which is limited in arid and semi-arid areas, and groundwater, the use of which is determined by depth and location.

ISLAM

Allah is the Islamic name for the One True God. The word is singular, has no plural, and is not associated with masculine, feminine or neuter characteristics.

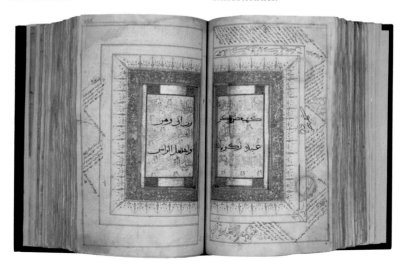

Before Muhammad there were other prophets, including Noah, Abraham, Moses and Jesus. **Muslims** believe that Muhammad was sent by Allah to complete divine religious law.

Islam is one of the world's three great **monotheistic faiths** (Christianity and Judaism are the others); all three spring from the same roots.

The code of conduct for Muslims, based upon the *Qur'an* and *Sunnah*, is known as the **Shari'ah**. Because this is Allah's law, it is immutable.

The prophet **Muhammad** was born in Mecca in AD 570. His followers believe that Allah sent messages to the people on earth through him.

The *Sunnah*, the practices of Muhammad's life, are recorded by his companions in the *Hadith*, which is a major source of Islamic law.

The two main branches of Islam are the *Shi'ah* and the *Sunni*. All Muslims face Mecca in prayer and follow the teaching of Muhammad.

There are approximately 1,000 m. Muslims worldwide and Islam's emphasis on the equality of all people has been a factor in its long reach.

◄ *The Qur'an is the Islamic Holy Book.*

ISLANDS

According to legend, the principal god sent his children to find the best place to found the **Inca dynasty**. They chose the Isla del Sol in Lake Titicaca, which lies between Bolivia and Peru.

Apart from the Australian mainland (usually accorded the status of a continent), the **largest island** is Greenland. Its area is about 2,175,000 sq km/840,000 sq mi.

Indonesia is the world's **greatest archipelago**. It forms a 5,600-km/3,500-mi crescent of more than 17,000 islands.

Rockall, 307 km/191 mi west of the Western Isles, is the **remotest British islet**. The rock, 21 m/70 ft high and 25 m/83 ft wide, has attracted bungyjumpers but few other visitors.

Submarine volcanic activity beginning in Jun. 1995 created the **world's newest island**, in Tonga, Pacific Ocean. It now covers about 5 ha/12 ac with a maximum height of 40 m/131 ft.

The **largest inland island** is the Ilha do Bananal, Brazil. Covering 20,000 sq km/7,700 sq mi, it is entirely surrounded by rivers.

ISRAEL

Formerly the Turkish province of Palestine but mandated to Britain by the League of Nations in 1920, **Israel** declared independence in May 1948.

Israel (capital: Jerusalem) lies at the eastern end of the Mediterranean between Lebanon, Syria, Jordan and Egypt, with an area of 20,700 sq km/7,992 sq mi.

Israel exports machinery, diamonds, chemicals, textiles, foodstuffs, beverages, tobacco, rubber and plastic, mainly to the US, Japan, UK, Germany, Belgium and France.

Israel spends 14% of its gross national product on defence, almost three times the world average. Military service is compulsory for both sexes.

▲ *Israel's capital Jerusalem.*

The **population of Israel** is 4,821,000 (est. 1991), comprising 81.8% Jewish and 18.2% Arab (mainly Sunni Muslim, Christian or Druze).

ITALY

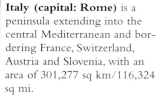

Italy (capital: Rome) is a peninsula extending into the central Mediterranean and bordering France, Switzerland, Austria and Slovenia, with an area of 301,277 sq km/116,324 sq mi.

Italy exports machinery, cars, tractors, construction equipment, chemicals, textiles, clothing and footwear, foodstuffs and live animals, mainly to Germany, France and the UK.

Italy was the centre of the Roman Empire which stretched from Scotland to the Danube, from North Africa to India, but collapsed in AD 476.

The kingdom of **Italy**, unified in 1860, became a republic in 1946 on the abdication of King Umberto.

The **population of Italy** is 57,590,000 (est. 1991), comprising 94.1% Italian, 2.7% Sardinian, 1.3% Rhaetian and 1.9% other.

Jakarta, capital of Indonesia. ▶

JAKARTA

Jakarta is situated on the north-west coast of Java facing the Java Sea and takes its name from the River Jakarta draining the level, swampy ground on which it was built.

Jakarta has oil refineries, natural gas and petro-chemical plants and factories producing a wide range of manufactured goods, textiles, plywood and rubber.

Jakarta, formerly Batavia, was **founded by Pieter Both** in 1610, as a trading post for the Dutch East India Company. It reverted to the local name in 1949.

The picturesque **old town**, with its Javanese, Chinese and Arab quarters, vies with the modern capital whose grandiose buildings date from the 1970s.

The **population of Jakarta** is 7,829,000 (1990 census), an almost 20-fold increase since the census of 1930 when it stood at 435,184.

JAMAICA

A tropical country, which has never seen snow, **Jamaica** sent a bobsleigh team to the 1998 Winter Olympic Games at Nagano, Japan.

Jamaica (capital: Kingston) is situated in the Caribbean south of Cuba and has an area of 10,991 sq km/4,244 sq mi.

Jamaica exports aluminium, bauxite, raw sugar, garments, bananas, rum and coffee, mainly to the UK, Canada, the Netherlands and US.

Jamaica was discovered by **Christopher Columbus** on 3 May 1494, settled by Spain in 1509 and captured by the British in 1655. It attained independence on 6 Aug. 1962.

The **population of Jamaica** is 2,420,000 (est. 1991), comprising 76.3% black, 15.1% Afro-European, 3.4% East Indian, 3.2% white and 2% other.

JAPAN

According to legend, the empire of **Japan** was founded in 660 BC. Under the Emperor Mutsohito (1867–1912), westernisation rapidly transformed the country from 1868 onwards.

Japan (capital: Tokyo) is an archipelago off the north-east coast of Asia, with an area of 377,835 sq km/ 145,883 sq mi.

Japan exports motor vehicles, office equipment, chemicals, plastics, iron and steel, scientific and optical equipment, electronics, power generators and textiles.

Japan first came into contact with the west in 1542 but fear of Christian missionaries led to the exclusion of all foreigners from 1639 until 1854.

The Dome of the Rock in Jerusalem. ▶

The **population of Japan** is 123,920,000 (est. 1991), comprising 99.2% Japanese, 0.6% Korean and 0.2% Chinese and other. 40% are Shintoist, 38.3% Buddhist, 3.9% Christian and 18.3% other faiths.

JERUSALEM

Jerusalem is the seat of the Israeli government and is an important commercial centre, rather than a manufacturing town, though it has light industries, notably jewellery and handcrafts.

Jerusalem stands on a rocky plateau projecting southwards from the main line of the Judaean hills. In the east the Kidron valley separates the ridge from the Mount of Olives.

Jerusalem was settled by Semites about 2500 BC. The present city was founded *c.* 1000 BC by King David who bought land from the Jebusites to build his temple.

The **population of Jerusalem** is 504,100 (est. 1990), mainly Jewish but including about 150,000 Palestinian Arabs in the Old City and south-east suburbs.

The principal city of the Jewish and Christian faiths and third holiest city of Islam, **Jerusalem** is noted for its many mosques, synagogues and churches.

JUDAISM

According to Orthodox Jewish law, a Jew is one born of a Jewish moth-er. Jewish children have **lessons** on the Hebrew language, dietary laws and the teach-ings of the Bible.

Early Rabbinical interpretations of the *Torah* were collected in the *Mishnah*, which together with its attendant com-mentary the *Gemara*, forms the **Talmud**.

Food is **kosher**, meaning 'permitted', when it conforms to Jewish dietary laws. Only certain animals are allowed, and they must be slaughtered accord-ing to strict law.

Judaism is the oldest of the world's three great monotheistic religions, and is the parent of Christianity, Islam and many other faiths.

▲ *Jewish boy being taught the* **Torah**.

Moses was the Jewish leader to whom God revealed his teachings, including the **Ten Commandments**, which were given to Moses on Mt Sinai *c.* 1200 BC.

The Jewish calendar is lunar, so the timing of festivals is flexible. **Rosh Hashana** is the New Year, a two-day festival which begins a period of reflection.

233

The sacred Jewish text, the *Torah*, is a handwritten scroll mounted on carved spindles. It is usually read using a silver hand-shaped pointer.

The stone tablets on which the Ten Commandments were written were kept in a chest, or **Ark of the Covenant**, in the temple built by Solomon in the 10th c BC.

JUPITER

Jupiter has a **mass** of more than twice that of all the planets combined; 318 times that of the Earth's mass.

Jupiter has a strong **magnetic field** that gives rise to a large surrounding magnetic 'shell' or magnetosphere, from which bursts of radio waves are detected.

Jupiter has at least 16 **moons**. The four largest, Io, Europa, Ganymede and Callisto are the Galilean satellites discovered in 1610 by Galileo.

Jupiter is the **fifth planet** from the Sun and is the largest in the solar system with an equatorial diameter of 142,800 km/88,700 mi.

Jupiter takes 11.86 years to **orbit** the Sun at an average distance of 778 m. km/484 m. mi. It is largely composed of hydrogen and helium.

Jupiter's main feature is the **Great Red Spot**: a cloud of rising gases, revolving anticlockwise, its colour caused by red phosphorus. It is 14,000 km/8,500 mi wide and 30,000 km/20,000 mi long.

Jupiter's **visible surface** consists of clouds of white ammonia crystals stretched out into belts by its rotation speed of 9 hr 51 min, the fastest of all the planets.

KINGS OF ENGLAND

Canute (1016–35), son of Danish King Svein Fork-Beard, became King of England after defeating Edmund Ironside. He brought firm government and security from external threat.

Edward the Confessor (1042–66) founded Westminster Abbey, where all subsequent coronations have been held. The controversy over his successor paved the way for the Norman Conquest.

William II, Rufus (1087–1100), son of William the Conqueror, extorted money ruthlessly from his barons and the church. He was killed by an arrow while hunting in the New Forest.

Richard I (1189–99) spent most of his reign away from England fighting the Third Crusade, where his bravery earned him the nickname 'Lionheart'.

Henry V (1413–22) proved himself a brave soldier and an excellent king. He destroyed the French army on the field of Agincourt, France in 1415.

Richard III (1483–85) has always been suspected of having murdered his nephews, the Princes in the Tower. He met his death at the Battle of Bosworth (1485).

Henry VII (1485–1509) brought prosperity and stability to his realm after 100 years of unrest. He financed exploration of the Canadian seaboard and encouraged trade with Europe.

Henry VIII (1509–1547) is remembered for his six wives, but he achieved greater prosperity and ensured future national security by founding a permanent navy.

The reign of **James I** (James VI of Scotland) (1603–1625) is noted for religious strife. Roman Catholics hatched the Gunpowder Plot, while the Puritan Mayflower pilgrims left for America.

▲ *Windsor Castle, home to the kings of England.*

George III (1760–1820) presided over the loss of the American colonies. He suffered repeated attacks of insanity, now believed to be the result of the disease porphyria, and became permanently ill in 1811.

Edward VII (1901–10), son of Queen Victoria, proved a huge success despite his mother's misgivings and his well-earned reputation for gambling and debauchery as a young man.

George VI (1936–52) became king when his brother Edward VIII abdicated. By remaining in London and 'taking it' during World War II he restored prestige to the monarchy.

KUWAIT

In 1899, fearing Turkish encroachment, Sheikh Mubarak placed **Kuwait** under British protection. Britain ended the protectorate on 19 Jun. 1961.

Kuwait (capital: Kuwait City) lies on the Arabian peninsula at the head of the Persian Gulf, bordering Saudi Arabia and Iraq, with an area of 17,818 sq km/6,880 sq mi.

Kuwait exports crude petroleum and petroleum products mainly to Japan, the Netherlands, US, Pakistan, Singapore, India, Italy, Denmark and Taiwan.

The liberation of **Kuwait** on 27 Feb. 1991 ended a seven-month occupation by Iraq, during which four-fifths of the population were murdered or fled into exile.

The **population of Kuwait** is 2,142,000 (est. 1991), comprising 51.6% Kuwaiti Arab, 45.3% non-Kuwaiti Arab and 3.1% Asian.

LAKES

Lake Baikal is the world's **oldest lake**, dating back almost 25 m. years. It has the greatest volume of any freshwater lake, containing some 20% of the world's freshwater supply.

◄ *Kuwaiti soldiers.*

Lake Baikal, Russia, is the world's seventh largest as well as the **deepest lake**. At its deepest point, the bed is 1,637 m/5,371 ft below the surface. The water is extremely clear, allowing visibility down to 40 m/131 ft.

Lake Superior, one of the North American Great Lakes, has a total surface area of 82,350 sq km/31,800 sq mi, and is the world's largest freshwater lake.

Lake Titicaca is the world's highest navigable lake, its surface being 3,180 m/10,433 ft above sea level. Some local people live on floating rafts built from papyrus called *totora*.

Loch Ness, alleged home of a 'monster' nicknamed Nessie, is the UK's deepest, longest and most capacious lake. Nearly 39 km/24 mi long, it reaches a depth of 240 m/788 ft.

On an island off Western Australia is a glistening, pastel, icing-sugar-pink lake, **Lake Hillier**. It was first mapped in 1802 by Matthew Flinders. No one knows why it is pink.

Sir Walter Raleigh, on landing in 1595, was the first European to hear about the **Trinidad Pitch Lake**. The 44-ha/109-ac lake probably constitutes the world's largest deposit of pitch.

The largest known **underground lake** was discovered in Drachenhauchloch cave near Grootfontein, Namibia, in 1986. Its surface area is 2.61 ha/6.45 ac. At its surface it is 66 m/217 ft underground.

The world's only freshwater seal lives in **Lake Baikal**, Siberia, the world's deepest lake. The seals probably travelled upriver during the last Ice Age. In winter they chew holes in the ice to breathe.

When Mt Mazama, Oregon, erupted nearly 7,000 years ago, it blew away about 1,000 m/3,300 ft of its top. The rest collapsed into a hole, which filled with water, to make **Crater Lake**.

◄ *View across Loch Ness.*

LAND SPEED RECORDS

Frenchman **Léon Serpollet**'s land speed record (3 Apr. 1902) of 120.79 kph/75.06 mph with his steam car *Oeuf des Pâques* was a remarkable achievement that wrested the advantage away from the electric car.

In 1927 at Pendine **Sir Malcolm Campbell** reached 281.439 kph/174.883 mph. In Feb. 1928, with *Bluebird* much modified, he claimed 333.054 kph/206.956 mph.

In 1965, **Craig Breedlove** became the first man to hit 965 kph/600 mph, with his fifth record, at 966.54 kph/600.601 mph, in *Spirit of America*.

In Jul. 1964 **Donald Campbell** finally succeeded in breaking the official land speed record, with a speed of 648.708 kph/403.1 mph on Lake Eyre in the Australian outback.

On 17 Jul. 1903 the Belgian racing driver **Arthur Duray** took a specially streamlined car to a speed meeting on the Nieuport road just outside Ostend and there he raised the land speed record to 134.32 kph/83.47 mph.

On 23 Oct. 1970 **Gary Gabelich** recorded 1,009.492 kph/627.287 mph and the record was his at 1,001.639 kph/622.407 mph, the first time anyone had broken the 1,000 kph barrier.

On 27 Aug. 1938 **George Eyston** increased his own record to 556.01 kph/345.50 mph before John Cobb retaliated with 563.57 kph/350.20 mph on 15 Sept. Less than 24 hours later, Eyston regained the honours with a speed of 575.32 kph/357.50 mph.

The land speed record was officially inaugurated on 18 Dec. 1898, when the Frenchman **Count Gaston de Chasseloup-Laubat** drove his Jeantaud electric car through an officially timed flying km at a speed of 63.15 kph/39.24 mph.

▼ *Solar-powered land speed car.*

◀ *The Qur'an is written in the Arabic language.*

LANGUAGES

A **pidgin** is a reduced and rudimentary variety of speech arising in a situation of limited social interaction between groups not sharing a common language. It combines vocabulary and grammatical features from different languages.

Anthropological linguistics is the study of natural human languages, whether written or unwritten, contemporary or historical, as an intrinsic part of the general study of human culture and society.

Extinct languages are not limited to ancient times: Dalmatian, a Romance language died (1898) when Anthony Udina, the last known native speaker, was killed in a mine explosion; Cornish became extinct when Dolly Pentreath died (Mousehole, Britain, 1777).

Historical linguistics examines the changes that languages undergo. It makes use of descriptive linguistics, which analyses languages at a specific stage and draws on sociolinguistics and on psycholinguistics.

Over 2,000 separate languages were spoken by **Native-American** peoples at the time of European contact. Approximately 1,400 of these existed in South America and roughly 200 were spoken in the territory constituting present-day California.

Somewhere between 3,000 and 8,000 **distinct languages** are spoken in the world at present. The discrepancy in count is attributable to such factors as differing definitions of language versus dialect.

LASERS

A continuous visible beam from a laser using a gas, such as helium-neon, provides a nearly ideal **straight line**. It can therefore be used for alignment in large construction such as laying pipelines.

A gallium-arsenide chip produced by IBM in 1989 contains **tiny lasers** in cylinder form, roughly one-tenth of the thickness of a human hair.

A vertically directed **laser radar** in an aeroplane can serve as a fast, high-resolution device for mapping fine details, such as the shape of the roof of a house.

Albert Einstein recognised the existence of **stimulated emission** in 1917, but it could not be used until the 1950s when US physicists Charles Townes and A. Schawlow showed how to construct such a device using optical light.

Any substance where the majority of its atoms can be put into an excited energy state can be used as laser material. **Uses** include communications, cutting, welding and surgery.

Laser (light amplification by stimulated emission of radiation) is a device for producing a narrow beam of light, capable of crossing large distances without dispersion and of being focused to high power densities.

The **first laser** was constructed in 1960 by Theodore Maiman; it used a rod of ruby. Since then many types of laser have been built.

Scientist Albert Einstein. ▶

LAW

A **franchise**, in law, is a right granted by a government or sold by a business that allows the recipient to carry on commercial activity under protected conditions.

Contract law determines which contracts are enforceable in court and defines what must be done to comply with contractually established obligations.

During the Middle Ages the economic ideas of the Roman Catholic Church were expressed in the **canon law**, which condemned usury and regarded commerce as inferior to agriculture.

In the US there are three principal ways **of organising a business**; sole proprietorship, partnerships or corporations. In the UK there are also private and public limited companies.

Since the 4th c, ecclesiastical and civil legislation has frequently regulated work on **Sunday**. In the US laws limiting business activity and amusements are known as blue laws.

The **Law of the Twelve Tables** was the earliest code of Roman law. It was formalised in 451–450 BC and called *decemvirs*, inscribed on tablets of bronze or wood.

The oldest written code of law came from the Mesopotamian legal system, 2100 BC; the 285 provisions of **the Code of Hammurabi** controlled commerce, family, criminal and civil law.

LIBRARIES

Adopting the Chinese papermaking skills **Muslim scholars** created and reproduced thousands of books. A library in Cordoba, Spain had over 400,000 books in the 10th c.

Scholar and diplomat Sir Thomas Bodley established the library at the **University of Oxford** by ensuring the delivery of copies of all books published in the UK.

The first Egyptian library was founded by Rameses II. ▲

The **Bibliotheque Nationale de France** in Paris houses a staggering 10 m. books and 350,000 bound manuscripts. It was founded in 1367 by Charles V.

The **British Library**, dating from 1753, houses over 18 m. books, 33 m. patents, 2 m. maps, 8 m. stamps, 600,000 newspaper volumes, 1 m. records and millions of manuscripts.

The first Egyptian library was founded by Rameses II in 1250 BC. It contained over 20,000 **papyrus scrolls**. Many of these survive to this day.

The **first public library** in Britain was established by David Drummond at Innerpeffray, Perthshire in 1691. Other early public libraries were founded by Allan Ramsay at Leadhills (1741) and Robert Riddell at Monklands (1788).

The library of **Alexandria** was established in the 3rd c BC and was at the centre of learning for the Hellenistic world. At its height it contained over 700,000 scrolls.

The **Library of Congress**, Washington, DC, was established in 1800. Despite two fires, it boasts 28 m. books in 470 languages.

The Sumerians established the oldest libraries: depositories of thousands of **clay tablets**. The libraries were destroyed by earthquakes and fires. The cuneiform script used was not deciphered until the 19th c.

LIGHT

A **light second** is the unit of length equal to the distance travelled by light in one second. It is equal to $2.997925 \times (10)8$ m$/9.835592 \times (10)8$ ft.

A **light year** is the distance travelled by a beam of light in a vacuum in one year, approx. 9.46 trillion (million, million) km/5.88 trillion mi.

In 1666, **Newton** first discovered that sunlight is composed of light of differ-

▲ *Isaac Newton.*

ent colours and that it could be split into its components by dispersion.

Light is considered to display both particle and wave properties. The **fundamental particle**, or quantum, of light is called the photon.

Light is **electromagnetic waves** that exist in the visible range from about 400 nm in the extreme violet to 770 nm in the extreme red.

The **speed of light** in a vacuum is approx. 300,000 kps/186,000 mps; it is a universal constant denoted by c.

Ultraviolet light is electromagnetic radiation invisible to the human eye, of wavelengths 4–400 nm. It is extremely powerful causing sunburn and causing the formation of Vitamin D in the skin.

LIGHTING

An **electric–discharge lamp** was first demonstrated in 1860 to the Royal Society of London. It produced a brilliant white light by the discharge of high voltages through carbon dioxide at low pressure.

Coal gas was first used for lighting by William Murdock at home in Cornwall (1792). In 1798 Matthew Boulton allowed him to experiment in lighting at his workplace and it was soon adopted nationwide.

Modern **fluorescent lights** work by mercury atoms in the lamp being excited by electric discharge; the ultraviolet light emitted by the mercury atoms is transformed into visible light by a phosphor.

Thomas Edison, inventor of the light bulb. ▶

Most gas lights were provided by a fishtail jet of burning gas, but with competition from electric lighting the quality of gas lighting was improved by the invention of the **gas mantle**.

The idea of the filament lamp (**light bulb**) was that a thin conductor could be made incandescent by an electric current if it were sealed in a vacuum to stop it burning out.

The **light bulb** was first demonstrated by Joseph Swan (UK, 1878) and Thomas Edison (US, 1879). Both experimented with various materials for the filament and both chose carbon.

The **modern light bulb** is a thin glass bulb filled with an inert mixture of nitrogen and argon gas; the filament is made of fine tungsten wire.

LISBON

A Roman and later Moorish city, **Lisbon** was under Spanish rule 1580–1640. It was destroyed by an earthquake in 1755 and rebuilt along modern lines.

Lisbon exports textiles, clothing, machinery, electrical goods, wine, olive oil, cork, sardines and fruit. It is also the centre of Portuguese tourism.

Lisbon, capital of Portugal, lies on a range of hills on the right bank of the River Tagus near its entrance to the Atlantic Ocean.

The name of **Lisbon** is a modification of the ancient form *Olisipo*, also written *Ulyssipo*, from belief in the myth that it was founded by Ulysses.

The **population of Lisbon** is 830,500 (1988 census), compared with 594,390 (1930) and 709,179 (1940).

LITERACY

After 1000 literacy slowly began to spread through Europe. After the Reformation, Protestant countries encouraged people to read the Bible. By 1700 Europe's **literacy rate** ranged from 30–40%; by 1850, 50–55%; and by 1930, 90%.

In 1979 two-thirds of the world's population were literate including probably one-half functionally literate. It is uncertain whether the development of electronic and **computer technology** will increase or diminish the spread of literacy.

Literacy first arose in the ancient Near East. About 3100 BC, the Sumerians developed or perhaps borrowed a system for representing speech, not ideas, as in earlier systems, by means of a set of **standardised visual symbols**.

Literacy is the ability to read and write. The level of ability has been defined in many ways. UNESCO classifies it as understanding and producing simple statements on everyday life.

Several nations (including the USSR, Cuba, Mexico, China and Argentina), which at the beginning of the 20th c had illiteracy rates of 70% or higher, have since 1945 greatly reduced or nearly **eliminated illiteracy**.

The development of the **Greek alphabet** during the 9th–8th c BC dramatically increased literacy. This alphabet consisted of a small, easily mastered set of symbols for representing all sounds of the Greek language.

The Germans who conquered Rome during AD 5th c were **illiterate** and attached little value to literacy. Literacy was largely eradicated: by the year 1000, probably only 1 or 2% of Europe's population was literate.

◄ *The River Tagus in Lisbon.*

LITERARY FIGURES

Charles Dickens (1812–70), who is regarded as one of the greatest English writers, portrayed the grim life of an increasingly industrialised Victorian England in novels such as *Oliver Twist* (1837), *Hard Times* (1854) and *Great Expectations* (1860–61).

Elizabeth Barrett (1806–61) was an English poet who married Robert Browning. At 20 she published her first volume of poetry, *An Essay on Mind, with Other Poems* (1826). Her finest work is probably *Sonnets from the Portuguese* (1850).

Fyodor Dostoyevsky (1821–81), a Russian novelist, probed the complexities of the human heart in his masterpieces *Crime and Punishment* (1866) and *The Brothers Karamazov* (1888).

Henrik Ibsen (1828–1906), a 19th-c Norwegian playwright, profoundly influenced the development of modern drama. Notable works include *A Doll's House* (1879) and *The Wild Duck* (1884).

Henry James (1843–1916), an American writer, is regarded as one of the most influential figures in the development of the modern novel. Great works include: *The Portrait of a Lady* (1882), *The Wings of the Dove* (1902) and *The Ambassadors* (1903).

Herodotus was a Greek writer of the 5th c BC who wrote the first Western, historical work; a 'history' in the conventional sense of the term. He is therefore known as the 'father of history'.

Jane Austen (1775–1817) wrote six novels about provincial middle-class society that are regarded as classics of English literature, including *Pride and Prejudice*, *Emma*, *Mansfield Park* and *Sense and Sensibility*.

Kawabata Yasunari (1899–1972) was one of the greatest modern Japanese novelists and the first of his countrymen to receive the Nobel Prize for Literature (1968). Works include: *The Dancing Girl of Izu* (1926) and *The Old Capital* (1962).

Lord Byron (1788–1824), an English poet, influenced Romantic literature with his flamboyant lifestyle and his poetry. Notable works include: *Don Juan* (1819–24) and *Childe Harold's Pilgrimage* (1812).

Lucius Annaeus Seneca (c. 4 BC–AD 65) was one of the most broadly

William Shakespeare and other Elizabethan dramatists. ▶

influential philosophical writers in the Stoic tradition. He wrote 12 works entitled *Moral Essays*, 124 so-called *Moral Letters* and several poetic tragedies.

Samuel Beckett (1906–89), an Irish playwright and novelist, wrote most of his works in French and translated many of them into English himself. A Nobel laureate in 1969, Beckett is best known for *Waiting for Godot* (1952).

Sir Walter Scott (1771–1832), one of the most famous authors of the early 19th c, introduced the historical novel to English literature. *Waverley* (1814) and *Ivanhoe* (1820) are among the best known of Scott's work.

The Irish author **James Joyce** (1882–1941) was a seminal influence on the development of the 20th-c novel; his novel *Ulysses* (1922) is regarded as his masterpiece.

The most accomplished verse satirist in the English language, **Alexander Pope** (1688–1744), was the pre-eminent poet of the Augustan age. Notable works include: the *Pastorals* (1709), *An Essay on Criticism* (1711) and *The Rape of the Lock* (1712).

William Shakespeare (1564–1616) was the foremost dramatist and poet of Elizabethan England and is considered by many the most gifted literary figure of all time. His work comprises 36 plays, 154 sonnets and 2 narrative poems.

LITERARY GENRES

A systematic study of **folk tales**, deriving from folklore and mythology, was made by Jacob Grimm (1812–22). Many survive today as fairy tales, e.g. *Sleeping Beauty*.

After Poe, Doyle's Sherlock Holmes (1879–*c.* 1900s) became the archetypal **fictional detective**. In the 20th c the genre has split into many sub-genres, e.g. police prodecurals.

Aristophanes wrote the earliest **satires**, ridiculing human pretensions, exposing human evils. Roman poets Juvenal and Horace wrote *Satires*. Voltaire, Swift and Pope (17th–18th c) developed the genre.

Carroll, Potter, Kingsley and Barrie created a late 19th-c golden age of illustrated **children's literature.** Early 20th-c writers included Grahame and Milne. Modern writers include Dahl.

Fantasy fiction in the 20th c thrived after Tolkien's *The Lord of the Rings* (1954–55). The genre tends to be pseudo-medieval in subject matter and form.

Horror, a fiction and film genre, aims to scare, usually attempting catharsis. Early exponents were Shelley (*Frankenstein*, 1818), Poe, Stoker and Lovecraft. Modern writers include Stephen King.

Romances, tales combining love and adventure, became popular in France (1200), later in England (Chaucer and Arthurian romance). Modern writers of romantic novels include Barbara Cartland.

Science fiction has its roots in the works of Mary Shelley (*Frankenstein*, 1818). Early practitioners were Verne and Wells, creating a variety of 20th-c sub-genres, e.g. cybperpunk.

◄ *Sherlock Holmes.*

The earliest known **children's literature** is *Goody Two Shoes* (Goldsmith, 1765). Fairy tales were collected (Perrault, France), written (Andersen, Denmark) and adapted (the Grimms, Germany).

The earliest work of **detective fiction** was Poe's *Murders in the Rue Morgue* (1845), which became a model for the solving of crimes by deduction from a series of clues.

The **thriller** genre originated in the novels of Dickens, Wilkie Collins and Edgar Allen Poe (19th c), spawning a variety of sub-genres this century (techno-thriller, psychological thriller).

LIVESTOCK

Artificial insemination techniques have been used in animal breeding since the 1960s. In **embryo transfer** (ET), eggs are harvested from prime cows, fertilised in test tubes and implanted into another animal.

Bovine spongiform encephalopathy (**BSE**) is a disease of cattle that is causing great concern. It may be transmissible to humans. Its incubation period is many years and there is no test for its presence in live animals.

Livestock farming is a wasteful means of producing food. In the early 1980s, 72% of grain consumed in developed countries was fed to animals, compared with only 13% in the developing world.

Livestock farming is energy-inefficient but yields profitable products. Many people in the developed world can afford these. As incomes rise people tend to consume more animal than plant products.

Some livestock are sold at **auctions**, conducted by auctioneers who earn a commission from the seller. Some farmers sell direct to slaughterhouses and meat-packing plants instead.

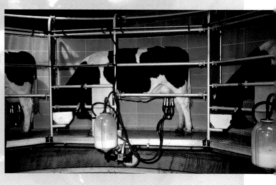

▲ *The disease BSE is found in cattle bred on farms.*

The so-called **'factory farm'** was pioneered by the broiler industry in the US, superseding the 'luxury roaster' production after World War II. Batteries accommodating 1,000 laying birds could be readily mechanised.

When choosing livestock, farmers look for characteristics of **animal reproduction**, in particular breeding frequency, offspring per litter, gestation period and lifespan.

LONDON

In 1381 the Peasants' Revolt ended dramatically in **London** when the mayor, Sir William Walworth, stabbed the rebel leader Wat Tyler, as alluded to in the dagger on the civic arms.

London has a vast range of manufacturing industries, from chemicals to computers. It is also a world leader in insurance, banking and financial services.

London is situated on the River Thames, at the head of its estuary. The greater metropolitan area covers 1,579 sq km/610 sq mi.

The **population of London** is 6,757,900 (1991 census), a substantial drop on the pre-war figure of 8,700,000 (est. 1938).

The Roman Londinium, **London** was founded by Cunobelin about AD 5, sacked by Boudicca in AD 61 and rebuilt. It emerged from the Dark Ages in 604 as the see of Bishop Mellitus.

LUXEMBOURG

Luxembourg (capital: Luxembourg Ville) is situated in north-western Europe between Germany, Belgium and France, with an area of 2,586 sq km/999 sq mi.

Luxembourg exports metal products, machinery, transport equipment, rubber and plastics, textiles, chemicals, foodstuffs, beverages and tobacco.

The county of **Luxembourg** was founded in AD 963 by Sigefroi, a descendant of Charlemagne, and was made a grand duchy by the Congress of Vienna (1815).

The **official language** of

Harrods is one of London's most famous landmarks ▶

Luxembourg since 1939 is *Letzeburgesch*, based on Teutonic origins with Celtic, Roman and French borrowings.

The **population of Luxembourg** is 385,317 (1991 census), comprising 72.5 Luxembourger, 9% Portuguese, 5.4% Italian, 3.4% French, 2.5% Belgian, 2.4% German and 4.8% other.

MADRID

During the Spanish Civil War **Madrid** withstood a Nationalist siege from Nov. 1936 until 29 Mar. 1939 when it surrendered to Franco.

Madrid is located on a plateau on the left bank of the **River Manzanares**, a tributary of the Jarama which flows south into the Tagus.

▼ *The Royal Palace in Madrid.*

The **industries of Madrid** include tanning and leather goods, glass, porcelain, paper, iron and copper foundries, transport and machinery.

The *Majrit* of the 10th c-Arab chronicles, Madrid was taken from the Moors in 1083 by Alfonso VI and became **capital of Spain** in 1560.

The **population of Madrid** is 3,120,732 (1991 census), a 10-fold increase since 1877 and three times what it was in 1940.

MAGNETISM

A free-spinning, magnetised needle points to magnetic north on a **compass dial**. There are two forms of compass; the simple magnetic version which has been used since the 12th c and the gyrocompass developed in the 20th c.

American electrical engineer and inventor **Nikola Tesla** (1866–1943) was one of the pioneers of electrical power. Amongst his many inventions are the high-frequency coil (1890) and the Tesla coil (1891); both have immense applications in radio communications.

Karl Gauss and Hans Oersted discovered the properties of **magnets** in the 19th c, including the fact that like poles repel and unlike poles attract.

Magnetic tape was first used in sound recording in 1947 and made overdubbing possible. Two-track tape was introduced in the 1950s and four-track in the 1960s.

Magnetism is extremely important to modern science, with applications in dynamos, electrical motors, particle accelerators in nuclear research, memory stores for computers and tape recorders.

Substances differ in the amount they can be **magnetised** by an external field (susceptibility). Materials that can be strongly magnetised are said to be ferromagnetic and include iron, cobalt and nickel.

The **Chinese** had known of the concept of magnetism since 2400 BC, but it was not until the 12th c that Peregrinius experimented in the West. He inspired the work of William Gilbert who wrote an influential book in the 16th c.

MALAYSIA

Malaysia (capital: Kuala Lumpur) is located in south-east Asia, bordering Thailand and Indonesia, with an area of 330,442 sq km/127,584 sq mi.

Malaysia exports thermionic valves and tubes, crude petroleum, timber, palm oil, rubber and natural gas, mainly to Singapore, UK, Taiwan and Australia.

▼ *Malaysian capital Kuala Lumpur.*

Malaysia includes Sarawak, ceded to an adventurer, James Brooke, by the Sultan of Brunei in 1842. The so-called '**white rajahs**' ruled until 1 Jun. 1946.

On 16 Sept. 1963 Malaysia, comprising the former Straits Settlements and the federated and unfederated Malay states, became an independent member of **the Commonwealth**.

The **population of Malaysia** is 18,239,000 (est. 1991), comprising 61.4% Malay, 30% Chinese, 8.1% Indian. 53% are Muslim, 17.3% Buddhist, 7% Hindu and 6.4% Christian.

MAMMALS

Mammalia is a term coined by Carl Linnaeus of Sweden in 1758 to cover that class of animals in which the young are brought forth alive and nourished with milk from their mothers' breasts.

Sirenia is an order of aquatic placental mammals, consisting of the manatees or sea cows, and dugongs. The name was given in allusion to their resemblance to mermaids or sirens.

The **Aardvark** or Earth Pig (*Orycteropus afer*) of South Africa is the direct descendant of the primitive ungulates. It has an elongated snout with a long prehensile tongue.

The **Cetaceans** are mammals who dwell in the sea, divided into the toothed whales (sperm whales and dolphins) and those in which teeth are replaced by baleen.

The **Mole** (*Talpa europea*) is a small soft-furred mammal with minute eyes and broad, strong forelimbs moved forward under the neck to facilitate digging through earth for food.

Volplaning Mammals are those whose limbs and bodies have been adapted to leap from trees and glide. They include the colugos and flying foxes.

Raccoon, native North American mammal. ▶

MAN-MADE DISASTERS

167 crew died when a fire swept the *Piper Alpha* oil production platform in the North Sea in Jul. 1988. This was the worst disaster of its type.

188 people were killed when the Theatre Royal, Exeter burned down in 1887. In 1212, London Bridge caught **fire** at both ends trapping and killing 3,000 people.

A Russian military helicopter was shot down by Georgian separatists in 1992. The **helicopter crashed** killing the crew and 61 refugees near Lata.

During 11–12 May 1941, nearly 1,500 people were killed by German bombers in the London area. This death toll was the highest figure during the '**Blitz**'.

Sikh terrorists murdered 329 airline passengers and crew when their bomb exploded on an Air India Boeing 747 off the coast of south-west Ireland in 1985.

The highest death toll for a **civilian airline disaster** occurred off Tenerife when a KLM–Pan Am Boeing 747 crashed killing 583 people in 1977.

When the USSR accidentally **vented plutonium** at Kyshtym in 1957, 30 small communities were wiped out with an estimated death toll of over 8,000.

MARRIAGE

Although **monogamy**, the marriage of one man and one woman, is the rule in Western society, many other cultures allow polygamy, plural marriage. Many African and Asian men practise polygyny (multiple wives).

Arranged marriages are predominant primarily in societies that place great importance on property inheritance, on links between lineages or religion, or in which elders think that young people are unable to make sound choices.

In 1995 the US **divorce** rate was 4.9 per 1,000 people (over twice that of England and Wales).

◄ *Diana, Princess of Wales, who divorced the heir to the British throne.*

MARS

Mars is slightly pear shaped with a low, level northern hemisphere. US planetary probes from the *Mariner* series photographed the cratered volcanic and wind-blown southern hemisphere, 1964–71.

Mars is the **fourth planet** from the Sun, is reddish in colour and is named after the Roman god of war. It is half as far away again from the Sun as Earth at 228 m. km/142 m. mi.

Mars' thin atmosphere mainly comprises carbon dioxide with traces of nitrogen and argon. The ice caps are frozen water and carbon dioxide.

In most societies of the world, **husband and wife** live together, either with or near the natal families of one or the other or else in a new household more or less independent of their families.

In traditional societies in many parts of the world, notably among the tribal peoples of Africa, the wedding occurs as a stage in a series of payments known as **bride price** or bridewealth (less commonly, in payments of groomwealth).

Marriages are either arranged between families (usually with some right of veto by the bride or groom) or are begun through a **courtship** in which the partners have found one another.

Not until the Middle Ages, when much church usage was codified as **canon law**, did marriage become associated with legal codes in the Western world.

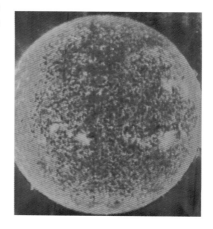

Mars is the fourth planet from the Sun. ▲

Olympus Mons is the largest known volcano in the solar system with a base 600 km/375 mi wide and a height of 24 km/15 mi.

The 1985 discovery of a vast **frozen-water** area has made the colonisation of Mars a distinct possibility by the middle of the 21st c.

The **Martian day** is called a Sol and is 24.6 Earth hours; there are 687 days in the Martian year. The planet has two small satellites, Phobos and Deimos.

Valles Marineris, a gigantic equatorial rift on Mars' surface, is 4,000 km/2,500 mi long and was caused by the separation of tectonic plates.

MARTIAL ARTS

Developed by Master Morihei Uyeshiba, **aikido** is based on Japanese warrior arts called Bujutsu. The techniques provide defence against an attack by one or several opponents.

Judo was synthesised from several jujitsu methods by Jigoro Kano, a late-19th-c Japanese educator and sports enthusiast. Originally it had two forms, self-defence and physical conditioning.

Jujitsu is a generic term referring to many styles, some jujitsu favour hitting and kicking and cannot be distinguished from karate; other styles bear a striking resemblance to judo.

Karate is used as a generic term for many styles of hand-and-foot fighting methods developed in Asia, particularly the Japanese forms. Hundreds of styles exist using similar techniques.

Kendo is derived from Japanese sword fighting. Players use a *shinai* (a bamboo sword bound with leather); for training and practice a *bokken* (wooden sword) is used.

Kung fu is the earlier, Chinese form of martial arts, mainly using hand-and-foot blows. Technical skills are demonstrated in a series of fluid, dance-like movements called *kata*.

Tae kwon do is the Korean form of martial arts, emphasising kicking to a greater degree. In some styles, contests and tournaments are the favoured training method.

MATHEMATICS

Alan Turing (1912–54) pioneered computer theory and applications in electronic computing. He proposed that a device, known as the Turing Machine, could read commands and data from a tape. This was the basis of modern computer technology.

During the 17th-c Johann Kepler, Descartes and Newton developed **calculation**, algebra and geometry. Pascal and Fermat developed probability.

Euclid worked at the Museum of Alexandria. In addition to his studies in astronomy and music, he wrote a 13-book set *Elements* which detailed geometry, areas and the theory of numbers.

Our present **decimal numerals** are based on an Indo-Arabic system that reached Europe about *c.* AD 100 from Arab mathematicians of the Middle East such as Khwarizmi.

Pythagoras (6th c BC) is credited with the theory of numbers in musical intervals and several mathematical theories, the measurement of squares and right-angled triangles.

The earliest records of mathematics date back to the **Babylonians** *c.* 3000 BC. Their counting system was based on the number 60.

We have **Archimedes** to thank for levers, screws and catapults; all practical applications of his mathematical theories. He also discovered the principle of water displacement whilst having a bath.

MAYA

Chichen Itza was a vast Mayan religious and civic centre, consisting of temples, courts and terraces on a 27-ac site.

In the Mayan **philosophy** and world view, time and space, the physical and supernatural worlds, are one single continuous reality.

The Maya built huge stepped stone **pyramids** as temples and administrative centres, brightly painted and decorated with carvings and mosaics, all without the use of metal tools.

The Maya developed a highly complex and accurate **calendar**, linking a ritual cycle of 260 days with a solar year of 365 days, each connected to specific patron deities.

The Maya were skilled potters, and produced fine **ornamental work** using copper, gold, silver and jade. They domesticated dogs and turkeys, but did not use the wheel.

The **Maya**, Amerindian people of Central America, emerged over 1,500 years, peaking between AD 300–900 then declining before the Spanish arrival in the 16th c.

The Mayan **writing** system is only partly deciphered, despite the discovery of many detailed inscriptions and paintings on *stela*, or stone slabs.

MEDIA

During World War II and until 1958 newsprint rationing prevented market forces from killing off the weaker papers. Polarisation into **'quality' and 'tabloid' newspapers** followed.

Mechanical devices were used at the **first practical demonstration of television**, given by Scottish electrical engineer John Logie Baird in Jan. 1926. Cathode-ray tubes were used experimentally from 1934.

Robert Maxwell was a publishing and newspaper proprietor who owned the *Daily Mirror* and the *New York Daily News*. He died owing some $3.9 bn.

◀ *Mayan temple.*

▲ *Media magnate Rupert Murdoch.*

Rupert Murdoch is a **media magnate** with worldwide interests. He owns the *Sun*, *News of the World*, *The Times*, 50% of 20th Century Fox and 50% of BSkyB.

The 1930s saw the rise of the **photojournalism** magazines such as *Life*. US pulp magazines were breeding grounds for writers such as Raymond Chandler and Isaac Asimov.

The world's **first public television service** was started from the BBC station at Alexandra Palace in Nov. 1936. In 1990 the average viewing time per person in the UK was 25.5 hours each week.

There were nine evening papers in the London area at the end of the 19th c, and by 1920 50% of British adults read daily **newspapers**.

The discovery of DNA was one of the greatest advances in medical science in history. ▶

MEDICAL SCIENCE

Although *in vitro* **fertilisation** or the test-tube concept had been used in animal breeding for some years, the first human child was born by this method in 1978. Patrick Steptoe and R.G. Edwards successfully reimplanted fertilised eggs in a woman from Oldham, UK.

An early theory stated that the body had four fluids or **humours**. These were blood, phlegm, choler (yellow bile) and melancholy (black bile). These were said to determine a person's temperament, and physical and mental abilities.

Edward Jenner (1749–1823), an English surgeon, discovered the **smallpox** vaccination. The availability of the vaccine spread rapidly and the death rate from smallpox plunged.

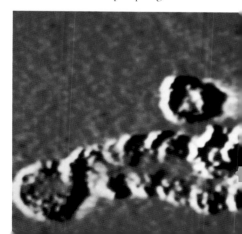

In 1928 Fleming discovered **penicillin**, but it was Howard Florey and Ernst Chain who managed to isolate it and produce sufficient quantities to make commercial production possible.

In 1981, the first cases of **AIDS** (Adavanced Immune Deficiency Syndrome) were noted amongst gay and drug-using communities of the US. The disease has claimed thousands of lives including the celebrities Rock Hudson, Liberace, Freddie Mercury, Rudolf Nureyev and Arthur Ashe.

Mary Stopes (1880–1958) was one of the first advocates of **birth control**. Working against immense opposition she greatly influenced the church and society's views on birth control.

Pasteur (1822–95) proved that micro-organisms cause fermentation and disease. He was the first to use vaccines for rabies, anthrax and cholera. He also saved the beer, wine and silk industries with his applications.

MEDIEVAL ART

During the last quarter of the 10th c Trier became the principal centre for production of **illuminated manuscripts**; from here emerged the leading artist of the century, the Gregory Master, who created illuminations unequalled in the early Middle Ages.

During the medieval period **art patronage**, although still mainly concerned with religious imagery, burgeoned in many small courts of Europe, and under this influence art became more stylised, delicate and refined.

Main **schools of art** in medieval times include early Christian and Byzantine (330–1453), Migration (252–900), Romanesque (10th c), Gothic (12th and 13th c), Gothic Classicism (13th c) and International Gothic (15th c).

The 500 years between the fall of the Roman Empire and the establishment of Charlemagne's new Holy Roman Empire (800) are known as the Dark Ages and its art that of the **Migration Period**. The best-known statements on the relationship between medieval art and worship come from members of the Cistercian order in the 12th c, particularly by St Bernard in his *Apologia* (1127) against artistic adornment.

The principal **art centres** of the early Holy Roman Empire were key bishoprics such as Mainz, Speyer and Bamberg; ancient cultural crossroads of

the Rhineland such as Cologne and Trier; and monastic centres such as Echternach and Reichenau.

The term 'Ottonian' defines the art and architecture produced (c. 950–1050) in Germany under the Saxon rulers of the Holy Roman Empire, the first three of whom were named Otto.

Under the unifying force of the Latin Church, a new civilisation spread across Europe which during the 10th c produced a style in art called Romanesque and in England, **Norman**.

MERCURY

In 1974 the US space probe *Mariner 10* discovered that Mercury's surface is cratered by meteorite impacts. It has no known moons.

Mercury contains an iron **core** which takes up three-quarters of the planet's diameter. This produces a magnetic field 1% the strength of the Earth's.

Mercury is the **closest planet** to the Sun, at an average distance of 58 m. km/36 m. mi. It was named after the Roman messenger of the gods.

Medieval manuscript depicting the Hundred Years' War. ▲

Mercury **orbits** the Sun every 88 days and spins on its axis every 59 days. It's atmosphere shows traces of argon and helium.

Mercury's diameter is 4,880 km/3,030 mi, just over a third the size of the Earth, and it's mass is 0.056 of the Earth's.

Mercury's largest feature is the **Caloris Basin**, 1,440 km/870 mi wide. It also has cliffs hundreds of km long and over 4 km/2.5 mi high.

The sunward side of Mercury reaches a **surface temperature** of over 400°C/752°F, but on the 'night' side it falls to -170°C/-274°F.

MEXICO

Maximilian, brother of the Austrian emperor, reigned as Emperor of **Mexico**, 1864–65. Captured by supporters of Juarez, he was executed by firing squad on 19 Jun. 1865.

Mexico (capital: Mexico City) is located in North America, between the US and Guatemala, with an area of 1,967,138 sq km/759,516 sq mi.

Mexico exports crude petroleum, metal products, machinery, transport equipment, electrical goods and food-stuffs, mainly to the US, Japan, Spain and France.

The **population of Mexico** is 83,151,000, comprising 55% mestizo, 29% Amerindian, 15% white, 0.5% black and 0.5% other. Almost 93% are Roman Catholic and 3.3% Protestant.

The site of the Aztec Empire, Mexico was conquered by **Hernán Cortés** in 1519–21. It declared its independence of Spain in 1810 and achieved it in 1821.

MEXICO CITY

Mexico City is situated on the drained bed of a lake at an altitude of 2,600 m/7,800 ft, amid the barren mountain ranges of the Sierra Madre.

Mexico City's chief landmark is the great cathedral on the site of an Aztec temple. The foundations were laid in 1573 but the building not completed until 1811.

The advent of cheap hydro-electric power has transformed **Mexico City** into a major centre for light industries of all kinds, cotton, paper and cigars being the chief products.

The Aztecs founded the lake-city of Tenochtitlan in 1325. **Mexico City** was the capital of Cuauhtemoc, executed by the Spaniards in 1519.

The **population of Mexico City** is 8,236,960 (1990 census), although it has been estimated that a further 343,000 people occupying shacks were not counted.

MICROCHIPS

In 1968 Noyce and colleague Gordon Moore founded Intel Corp.; in two years they devised the 1103 memory chip of silicon and **polysilicon**, to replace the less efficient ceramic cores used to store data in computers.

In 1971 Intel introduced the micro-processor that combined on one silicon chip the circuitry for both information storage and information processing. Intel soon became the leading producer of **microprocessor** chips.

Microchips are produced on a single crystal of a semiconducting material, usually **silicon**. They often measure only 5 mm/0.2 in sq and 1 mm/0.04 in thick.

Robert Noyce was the US engineer and co-inventor (1959) of the integrated circuit, a system of interconnected transistors on a single silicon **microchip**.

The first **optical microchip**, using light instead of electricity, was developed in 1988 and a year later water-scale silicon chips, able to store 200 m. characters, were launched.

The world's largest chip producer Intel officially introduced the **Pentium** processor in 1993. Using a technology referred to as submicron, it consisted of 3.1 m. transistors, double those of the 486 processor.

Very fine gold or copper wiring, as thin as 30 micrometres, is used to carry electric current to and from the pads along a **microchip** to other components on a circuit board.

MICROWAVES

Although microwaves were **first produced** and studied in 1886 by Heinrich Hertz their practical application had to wait for the invention of suitable generators, such as the klystron and magnetron.

Microwaves are **electromagnetic waves** that have a wavelength in the range of 0.3–30 cm/0.1–12 in or 300–300,000 MHz (between radio waves and infrared radiation).

Microwaves are the main carriers of high-speed telegraph data between stations on Earth and **satellites** and space probes. A system of satellites about 36,000 km/22,370 mi above Earth are used for television, telephone and fax communications.

Microwaves play a large role in heating and **cooking** food. They are absorbed by water and fat in foodstuffs and produce heat from the inside, reducing cooking time significantly.

Radar beams consist of short microwave pulses.

You can determine the distance of an aeroplane or ship by measuring the time it takes a pulse to travel to the object and be reflected back to the radar dish antenna.

The **heating** effect of microwaves destroys living tissue when the temperature exceeds 43°C/109°F. Exposure to intense microwaves in excess of 20 milliwatts of power per sq cm of body surface is harmful.

Various types of **microwave generators** and amplifiers have been developed; for example vacuum-tube devices, klystron and magnetron. Klystrons are employed as amplifiers in radio relay, whilst magnetrons are used for radar and microwave ovens.

MILITARY

Adolf Hitler (1889–1945) German dictator: 'In starting and waging a war **it is not right that matters**, but victory.' *Mein Kampf* , Ch. 14.

Benjamin Franklin (1706–90), US scientist and statesman: 'There **never was a good war** or a bad peace.' Remark on signing the Declaration of Independence, 4 Jul. 1776.

Douglas Macarthur (1880–1964), US general: '**I shall return.**' Message

(11 Mar. 1942) on leaving for Australia from Corregidor, which he had been defending against the Japanese.

Earl Kitchener (1850-1916), field marshal: '**I don't mind your being killed**, but I object to your being taken prisoner.' To the Prince of Wales when he asked to go to the Front, 18 Dec. 1914.

Prince Otto von Bismark: 'If there is ever **another war in Europe**, it will come out of some damned silly thing in the Balkans.' (Speech, Reichstag, 15 Mar. 1884).

Otto von Bismarck. ▶

Gen. Douglas Haig (1861–1928): 'Every position must be held **to the last man**: there must be no retirement.' Order to the British Army, 12 Apr. 1918.

Karl von Clausewitz (1780–1831), Prussian general and military theorist: 'War is nothing but a continuation of **foreign policy by other means**.'

FitzRoy Raglan (1788–1855) field marshal: '**Don't carry away that arm** until I have taken off my ring.' After his arm had been amputated at Waterloo (1815).

Ulysses Grant (1822–85), US general, later president: 'No terms except **unconditional and immediate surrender** can be accepted.' To opposing commander during siege of Fort Donelson, 1862.

Woodrow Wilson (1856-1925), US president: 'The war we have just been through is not to be compared with the war we would have to face **next time**.'

MINERALS

After the airborne **magnetometer** was developed to detect submarines in World War II, various airborne geophysical techniques were developed for mineral exploration.

Minerals comprise the vast majority of the material of the earth. Aside from air, water and organic matter, the only non-minerals in the earth are molten rocks.

Modern industrial civilisation is based primarily **upon raw materials** produced from various types of ore deposits; machines are fabricated from metals, and agriculture depends on chemical fertilisers.

Since 1950 modern techniques, such as atomic absorption and radiation counting, have become increasingly popular for **assaying metals**. Historically, most metals were assayed by wet gravimetric methods.

The chemical analysis of minerals advanced importantly with the invention of the **electron microprobe** by R. Castaing in 1949.

The major **development in mineralogy** in the 20th c has been the creation of minerals, reproducing the phases present during the formation of natural minerals.

Within the past century national power has become synonymous with industrial power. The growth of industrial power has always begun with the **national possession of mineral resources**.

MINING

After 1900 diesel locomotives were used to haul ores underground and the **Leyner water drill**, invented in 1907, reduced the dust caused by drilling.

Current mine operations in the UK produce 3.6 bn tonnes of waste yearly. The **Environmental Protection Agency** has issued regulations regarding the containment and processing of many of the wastes.

In **coal mines** after 1900 mechanical cutters at the face forced the introduction of conveyor belts to carry the material away more rapidly.

In the US an estimated 558,000 **abandoned mines** have left at least 809,000 ha/2 m. ac of private and public land covered with mine wastes.

The **US mines** and processes iron, gold, silver, copper and lead. It also produces minerals used in industry, primarily stone, clays, phosphate rock, sand, gravel, salt, boron and soda ash.

Worldwide, **hydraulic cement** is the leading mineral commodity by weight. Others include iron ore, peat and salt. Leading mineral producers include South Africa, Australia, China, Zambia and the US.

MONEY

A **function of money** is to serve as a standard of value or unit of account, so that economic values in terms of money can be measured.

In **colonial America** merchants kept their financial records in British pounds, but most of the medium of exchange they received consisted of Spanish coins.

In early **medieval Europe** the money economy went into a decline and barter re-emerged. During the 9th c, however, the European economy started to become monetary again.

Money market funds are investment trusts that pool the money of many individuals to buy high-yield, short-term debt instruments such as US

treasury bills, bank-issued certificates, or corporate IOUs.

Primitive societies did not use money for everyday trade, but only for certain ceremonial and public transfers such as tribute, bride price and blood money.

The heyday of the **gold standard** was between 1870 and 1914, when the English pound dominated international trade and prices remained fairly stable.

Without **money** a complex, modern economy (based on the division of labour) and the consequent widespread exchange of goods and services, would be impossible.

MOON

On the Moon's sunlit side **temperatures** reach 110°C/230°F but during the two week lunar night it drops to -170°C/-274°F. The Moon has no atmosphere or water.

Rocks brought back by US astronauts show the Moon to be 4.6 bn years old, the same as Earth. It was possibly **formed** from debris when another celestial body struck Earth.

The largest scars on the Moon's surface are filled with dark lava to produce the lowland plains known as seas or maria. These dark patches give the appearance of a '**man-in-the-Moon**'.

The **Moon's composition** is rocky and it has a scarred surface from meteorite impact. Some craters are 240 km/150 mi across. The young craters are surrounded by bright rays of ejected rock.

MOROCCO

Morocco (capital: Rabat) lies in north-western Africa, bordered by Algeria and the Sahara, with an area of 458,730 sq km/177,117 sq mi.

Morocco exports citrus fruits, foodstuffs, phosphates and canned fish, mainly to France, Spain, Germany and India.

Morocco was partitioned into French and Spanish spheres of influence in 1912, but was reunited as an independent kingdom under Muhammed V on 2 Mar. 1956.

▲ *Walking on the Moon's surface.*

The Moon is a **natural satellite** of Earth. It is 3,476 km/2,160 mi in diameter and has a mass 0.012 (approx. one-eightieth) that of Earth.

The Moon is illuminated by sunlight and **cycles** through phases of shadow waxing from new (dark) to full and waning back to new every 29.53 days (synodic month).

The **Moon orbits** the Earth in a west to east direction every 27.32 days (a sidereal month). Its average distance from Earth is 384,400 km/238,855 mi, and its gravity is one-sixth that of Earth.

98.7% of Moroccans are of the Muslim faith. ▶

The 'isle of the west' of Arab geographers and the Barbary of Europeans, **Morocco** is the remnant of an Arab Empire which covered north-west Africa and Spain in the 7th c.

The **population of Morocco** is 25,721,000 (est. 1991), comprising 99.5% Arab-Berber and 0.5% other. 98.7% are Sunni Muslim and 1.1% Christian.

MOSCOW

Moscow accounts for more than 12% of Russia's industrial output, all branches from heavy engineering to electronics being represented.

Moscow is situated on both banks of the navigable Moskva River, a tributary of the Oka. It is at the hub of Russia's rail, road and canal systems.

Moscow was founded in 1156 by Georgy Dolgoruki, Prince of Rostov. It became the capital of Russia under Ivan I (1328–41).

The best-known landmark in **Moscow** is the Kremlin, a walled citadel containing palaces, cathedrals, museums and government offices.

The **population of Moscow** is 8,801,500 (est. 1991), twice as large as its nearest rival St Petersburg.

MOTOR RACING

In 1966 **Jack Brabham** (Australia) became the first driver to win the Formula 1 championship in a car that he had manufactured and designed himself.

▼ *The start of the 1998 British Grand Prix at Silverstone.*

Italian Giuseppe Farina became the **first Formula 1 Drivers' champion** in 1950. He piloted his Alfa Romeo to win three of the six Grands Prix.

The **first Grand Prix** was held in France, near Le Mans in 1906. The winner was Hungarian Francois Szisz in a Renault at an average speed of 117.93 kph/73.3 mph.

The **Indianapolis 500** was inaugurated in 1911. The race forms part of the Memorial Day celebrations at the end of May and is constested over 200 laps of the 4.02-km/2.5-mi circuit.

The **most successful Formula 1 Grand Prix driver** is Alain Prost (France) who recorded 51 victories from his 199 races from 1980–93.

When **John Surtees** (UK) won the Drivers' championship in 1964 he became the first world champion on four and two wheels having been world 500cc motorcycle champion.

MOTORCYCLES

About 1900 **steel chain** was first used to replace leather belts for power transmission. Roc, a British company, introduced a friction clutch and four-speed transmission in 1904.

Disc brakes, only recently considered standard equipment on automobiles and motorcycles, were employed on the motorcycles built by the Imperial Company of Great Britain as early as 1901.

Following World War II there were a large number of **motorcycle manufacturers**. The major manufacturers remaining are the US's Harley-Davidson, and Japan's Honda, Kawasaki, Suzuki, and Yamaha.

Overhead cams and valves, fuel injection, multi-gear transmissions, shaft drive and telescopic suspension all appeared as **motorcycle developments** prior to 1918.

The Hildebrand brothers of Munich called their design a **Motorad**. With their assistant, Alois Wolfmuller, they produced the Hildebrand- Wolfmuller, the first commercially practical motorcycle.

The history of the motorcycle parallels the developing technologies of the late 19th c. Some of the earliest motorcycle experiments involved fitting **steam engines** to modified bicycles.

The men most often credited with laying the groundwork for modern motorcycles are Nikolaus A. Otto, who developed the concept of a **four-stroke engine**, and Gottlieb Daimler.

MOUNTAINS

Early mountaineers included Bonifacio Rotario, a knight of Asti, who climbed the Alpine peaks of Rochemelon in 1358, and Antoine de Ville, a French noble, who climbed Mt Aiguille in 1492, the year that Columbus discovered the New World.

Measured from their base, the mountain chains of the **mid-ocean ridges** that run along the floors of most major oceans rise to an average height of 1,800 m/6,000 ft.

Mountain animals must be mobile. In winter some migrate to a lower level, some hibernate and others shelter in rocks or under snow. Characteristic animals are the agile wild sheep and goats.

Mountain building, or **orogenesis**, occurs as a result of the movement of the Earth's crustal plates. Volcanic, fold and block mountains are the main types.

Mountains have traditionally been places of mystery and **myth**. East Africans believe that God dwells on

Ancient mummified bodies have been recovered from the Egyptian pyramids. ▶

the snow-capped peak of Mt Kenya. Mt Olympus, to the Ancient Greeks, was the home of the gods. And on Mt Sinai Moses received the tablets bearing the Ten Commandments.

The air temperature falls more than half a degree C for every 100 m/330 ft higher up a mountain. This is called the **lapse rate**. Each temperature belt contains different plants and animals.

The first ascent of the **Matterhorn** (1865), led by Edward Whymper, ended in tragedy. On the descent, four of the party of seven plunged to their deaths when a rope broke.

The Himalaya–Karakoram **range** contains 96% of the 109 peaks in the world that are at least 7,315 m/24,000 ft high. The longest range is the Andes, 7,600 km/4,700 mi long.

The **Nepal Himalaya** includes Mt Everest (8,848 m/29,028 ft), the world's highest mountain, on the Nepal-Tibet border, and at least 22 other summits in excess of 7,625 m/25,000 ft.

The peaks of **Yosemite** valley, California, are fairly low (Half Dome 2,699

m/8,852 ft) but offer challenging climbs on compact, glacier-polished granite. The valley is perhaps the world's most important rock-climbing centre.

MUMMIES

A **mummy** is an embalmed body dating from Ancient Egyptian times. The word is derived through Arabic from the Persian *mumiai* ('pitch'), because Egyptian mummies of the late period were often coated with black resin.

Animals and birds sacred to various deities were also mummified and buried in special cemeteries in Egypt, the most famous being the catacombs of the sacred bulls, known as the Serapeum, at **Saqqara**.

As early as the 4th dynasty (Egypt, *c.* 2600 BC) internal organs were sometimes embalmed separately and put in four vessels known as **Canopic jars**.

By the 5th dynasty (Egypt, *c.* 2350 BC) the bandaged body was coated with a layer of plaster, coloured light green and the facial features were represented in paint like a **mask**.

The Ancient Egyptians placed great stress on the preservation of the human body after death because they believed that the **spirit** of the deceased returned to it when visiting the tomb.

The process of **mummification** consisted of extracting the brain through the nose; removing the lungs and the abdominal organs; placing the body in natron and finally wrapping the body in many layers of bandages.

The **Guggenheim Museum** was established in New York by Solomon R. Guggenheim. The museum opened to the public in 1939. In 1959 it moved to its present building, designed by Frank Lloyd Wright.

The **Louvre** in Paris, one the world's great art museums, houses many works of fundamental importance in Western cultures, including Leonardo da Vinci's *Mona Lisa*. Originally a royal fortress and palace built (12th c) for Philip II.

MUSEUMS

The **British Museum** (London) houses outstanding collections of antiquities and ethnographic art from around the world. The first institution of its kind, the British Museum was founded (1753) with a collection by Sir Hans Sloane (1660–1753).

▲ *The Guggenheim Museum, designed by Frank Lloyd Wright.*

The **Metropolitan Museum of Art**, New York, founded in 1870, is the largest art museum in the Western world. Its collections span 5,000 years of art history and cover almost every area of world art.

The **Royal Ontario Museum** (Toronto) is the largest and most diversified museum complex in Canada. It was established in 1912 as a loose federation of five museums dedicated, respectively, to archeology, geology, mineralogy, paleontology and zoology.

The **Victoria and Albert** (V&A) Museum in London, one of the world's foremost museums of fine and applied arts, was opened by King Edward VII on 26 Jun. 1909.

MUSICAL INSTRUMENTS

Classical **violinists** include: Corelli (1653–1713, first great violinist), Paganini, Stern, Heifetz and Kennedy (who helped popularise classical violin). Jazz violinists include: Grappelli and Ponty.

Great classical **pianists** include: Liszt (concert artist at the age of 12 in 1823), Gould (Bach's keyboard music), Ashkenazy and Horowitz; great jazz pianists include: Evans, Peterson, Powell and Tatum.

Monteverdi, Bach, Purcell and Handel all composed for the trumpet (17th–18th c). Famous **trumpeters** include: (classical) Wilbraham and Marsalis; (jazz) Armstrong, Beiderbecke, Brown, Gillespie, Terry, Baker, Davis and Marsalis.

The **pianoforte** ('quiet-loud') stringed keyboard instrument spanning seven octaves, invented by Cristofori (Italy, c. 1704–09), was first played in public by Dibdin (1767) and J. C. Bach (1768).

The **trumpet**, small high-register brass wind instrument (which, pre-19th c, had no valves and was restricted to harmonies), is mentioned in the Bible and Homer. Trumpets were found in Tutankhamen's tomb (reigned 1358–1353 BC).

The **violin**, four-stringed, is the smallest, highest pitched of the violins that replaced the viol family (16th–18th c). Greatest makers were Antonio Stradivari (1644–1737) and his sons (Cremona).

MUSICAL PERIODS

Baroque (*c.* 1600 from Monteverdi's establishing opera to J. S. Bach's death, 1750) was built on a continuo (one chordal, one bass instrument, both playing from the bassline) to generate essentially improvised accompaniment.

In the **Renaissance** (*c.* 1450–1600), with perspective entering music, Dufay added a bass part. Polyphony's increasing complexity (*ars nova*, the new art), led to polyphonic mass, motet, chanson and madrigal, reaching its apex with Palestrina.

In the **Romantic** period (*c.* 1800–1900) Romantic literature and nationalism influenced a more emotionally expressive music, from Weber and Schumann early in the century to Stravinsky's and Bartok's anti-Romanticism.

The **Classical** period (*c.* 1760–*c.* 1800), though overlapping with Rococo (*c.* 1730–1780), introduced the sonata form, which was developed by Haydn, Mozart and Beethoven.

The **Medieval** period (*c.* 590–1450) introduced Gregorian plainchant (6th–7th c), *organum* (two-part plainchant singing, 12th–13th c) and the beginnings of polyphony.

The **Rococo** period (*c.* 1730–1780) refers to the light, diverting 'galant' or homophonic style of composers such as Telemann, the sons of Bach and the early Haydn and Mozart.

MUSICAL STYLES

Folk music is a body of traditional music originally transmitted orally, e.g. social-protest folk ballads of Guthrie (US, 1912–67); and British folk songs, collected by Child (19th c), Sharp (1907), then revived by MacColl and Seeger (1950s).

Jazz is polyphonic music, originally syncopated and rhythmically dynamic, characterised by solo virtuoso improvisation, which developed in the US (1900s). Its most influential musicians have been Armstrong, Ellington, Parker, Coltrane and Davis.

◄ *Classical composer Ludwig van Beethoven.*

▲ *Jazz musician Louis Armstrong.*

Pop is a general label for post-1940s commercial music, powered by the record industry, crystallising in the rock 'n' roll era and periodically revitalised, prototypically by Presley (mid-1950s), The Beatles (1963–70) and Abba (1974–81).

Rock 'n' roll, pop music created out of the fusion between R&B and C&W, based on electric guitar and drums in the mid-1950s, became, with its greatest exponent Elvis Presley, the expression of teenage rebellion.

Rock (mid–late 1960s) extended rock 'n' roll's 1950s 12-bar blueprint into denser, more complex, initially blues-based, improvisatory and lyrical forms. Prototypical bands were The Rolling Stones (from 1968), Cream, The Grateful Dead, The Doors.

Technology (audio cassettes, videos, 1970s; CDs, satellite TV (MTV), film-record synergy, 1980s; Internet, 1990s) and record-industry multinational monopolisation **globalised pop phenomena** (Michael Jackson, 1983–87; The Spice Girls, 1996–98).

World (or roots) music is any music whose regional character has not been destroyed, for example the West African *mbalax* of Youssou N'Dour (Senegal, b. 1959).

MYTHOLOGY

Finn MacCumhal, in Irish heroic and romantic tales, organised an Irish army (AD 3rd c) becoming Fingal in epic verses by James MacPherson (1736–96) which influenced the Romantics.

In Greek mythology Zeus came to **Leda** (wife of Tyndareus, mother of Clytemnestra) as a swan, becoming the father of her other children, Helen of Troy and twins Castor and Pollux.

▲ *Indonesian mythological god.*

Mahabharata, Sanskrit epic in 18 books and 90,000 stanzas (probably composed 300 BC), forms with the *Ramayana* the two great Hindu epics, containing the *Bhagavad-Gita* in the sixth book.

Mythology, the imaginative traditions concerning gods and other supernatural beings and the study of these myths, is closely interwoven with legend (as in the case of Santa Claus or St Nicholas, AD 4th c).

The story of **St George** (patron saint of England) rescuing a woman by slaying a dragon, derives from the 6th-c Perseus legend; the cult was introduced into western Europe by the Crusaders.

Thor, in Teutonic mythology, was one of the greatest gods (of yeomen, peasants and thunder), possessing the hammer *Miölnir* (thunderbolt), which returned to his hand like a boomerang.

NASA

NASA is an acronym for National Aeronautics and Space Administration. This US government agency was founded in 1958 for space flight and aeronautical research.

▲ *Launch of a NASA space shuttle.*

During the 1960s NASA turned its attention to a programme that featured a permanent manned space station and a reusable Earth-to-orbit craft which culminated in the **space shuttle**.

In 1995 NASA and Russia prepared to start building an **international space station** that could cost a total of $100 bn by the year 2012.

In the early 1990s NASA launched the $1.5 bn **Hubble Space Telescope**, which gave disappointment when scientists discovered problems with its primary mirror after launch.

NASA was downsized on 19 May 1995 when Administrator Daniel Goldin announced a cut of 3,560 civil service jobs and up to 25,300 contractor jobs, 30% of the NASA workforce, by the year 2000.

NASA's **headquarters** are in Washington, DC and its main installation is at the Kennedy Space Centre (the launch site is on Merritt Island near Cape Canaveral, Florida).

The **Kennedy Space Centre** is dominated by the Vehicle Assembly Building (160m/525 ft tall) and is used for the assembly of Saturn rockets and space shuttles.

NATIONAL HOLIDAYS

14 Jul., **Bastille Day**, has been set aside since 1880 as the French national holiday. As with the American Independence Day (Fourth of July), the holiday is celebrated with the setting off of fireworks and with parades and other festivities.

In Canada, **Thanksgiving Day**, first observed in Nov. 1879, is officially celebrated on the second Monday in Oct. and is a national holiday.

In China the most important annual holiday marks the arrival of the lunar **new year**; the observation involves gift-giving and also religious ceremony.

Labor Day is a holiday set aside to celebrate and honour working people. Inaugurated in 1882 by the Knights of Labor, it is now a legal holiday observed on the first Monday in Sept. in the US, Puerto Rico and Canada.

Martin Luther King (1929–68), the impressive American peacemaker, who was felled by an assassin's bullet, had, in 1983, his birthday marked as a national holiday (15 Jan.) in the US.

Martin Luther King ▶

Thanksgiving is an annual holiday celebrated in the US on the fourth Thursday in Nov. It originated in three days of prayer and feasting by the Plymouth colonists in 1621.

NATIVE AMERICAN PEOPLES

Algonquin-Wakashan is the geographical language designation for Native Americans of the Eastern Woodland zone including Cree, Arapaho, Blackfoot, Cheyenne and Ojibwa.

Aztec-Tanoan is the geographical language designation for Native Americans ranging from British Columbia to the US Pacific north-west and south-west with some groups in Newfoundland and Florida.

Eskimo–Aleut is the geographical language designation for Native Americans in Alaska and Canada as well as Greenland, Siberia and the Aleutian Islands.

Hokan-Siouan is the geographical language designation for Native Americans widely scattered across the US from the Atlantic coastline to the Pacific in California.

Na-dené is the geographical language designation for Native Americans in south-east Alaska, the Canadian North-western Territories, the US Pacific north-west and south-west.

Native American peoples are classified by **geographic language groups**: Algonquin-Wakashan, Aztec-Tanoan, Eskimo-Aleut, Hokan-Siouan, Na-dené and Penutian. Language diversity makes linguistic designation impossible.

Penutian is the geographical language designation for Native Americans in the south-west and Pacific north-west with some isolated groups in British Columbia.

NAVAHO

Assimilated with the Shoshone and Yuma, the Navaho remained **a distinct social group**. They became pastoral (17th c) but raided in New Mexico until 1863–64.

The matrilineal Navaho are famous for **outstanding metalwork**, especially in silver, and for their exquisite weaving.

The Navaho thought that the **correct performance** of certain rituals would restore harmony, avert disaster or cure illness.

The **Navaho** are a Native American people of the Na-dené geographical linguistic group.

The Navaho were granted a reservation in 1868 that now covers 16 m. ac in Arizona, New Mexico and Utah. They are **the US's largest tribe.**

NAVIES

The **Battle of Midway** was a decisive US naval victory over Japan in Jun.

1942 off Midway Island, north-west of Hawaii. The victory was the turning point of the Pacific war.

Elizabeth I encouraged Drake, Frobisher, Hawkins, Raleigh and other navigators to enlarge the empire. By mounting heavy guns low on a ship's side, the '**broadside**' was created.

Henry VIII raised a force that included a number of battleships, such as the **Mary Rose**, and created the long-enduring administrative machinery of the Admiralty.

In the 5th c BC naval power was an important factor in the struggle for supremacy in the **Mediterranean**, particularly in the defeat of Persia by Greece at Salamis in 480 BC.

The 1962 **Cuban missile crisis** demonstrated the USSR's weakness at sea and led to its rapid development and expansion under Adm. Sergei Gorshkov.

The **Battle of Jutland** was between British and German naval forces. Its outcome was indecisive, but the German fleet remained in port for the rest of the war.

The British **Royal Navy** under Nelson won a victory over the French at Trafalgar, which ensured British naval supremacy for the rest of the 19th c.

The first **permanent naval organisation** was established by the Roman Empire to safeguard trade routes from pirates and to eliminate the threat of rival sea powers.

The Soviet fleets (based in the Arctic, Baltic, Mediterranean and Pacific) continued their **expansion** in the 1980s, rivalling the combined NATO fleets.

The **US navy** grew out of the coastal colonies' need to protect their harbours during the American War of Independence. The hero of the period was John Paul Jones.

When the **Cold War** ended the Black Sea fleet was split between Russia and the Ukraine, and the Baltic ports were lost to the independent states.

NAVIGATION

An Egyptian temple decoration *c.* 1600 BC shows a ship where a member of the crew is measuring the **depth of the water** with a long pole.

In 1731 the **octant** (an early form of the sextant) was demonstrated independently by John Hadley of England and Thomas Godfrey of Philadelphia. It was used to measure altitudes.

On 3 Aug. 1492 **Christopher Columbus** sailed from Spain. From the Canaries he sailed westward as he thought Japan was on the same latitude. Actually he landed on the Bahama island Guanahaní (now Watling Island), which he called San Salvador.

The forerunners of **lighthouses** were beacon fires on hilltops, referred to in the *Iliad* and the *Odyssey* (8th c BC). The first man-made lighthouse was the renowned Pharos of Alexandria.

The **portolan chart** was a navigational chart of the European Middle Ages (1300–1500). The earliest dated chart was produced in Genoa by Petrus Vesconte (1311).

Viking sailors took soundings with a lead weight on a line, hauling in the line and measuring it by arm span. The word **fathom**, 1.8 m/6 ft comes from the Old Norse *fathmr* ('outstretched arms').

NAZISM

Alfred Rosenberg's (1893–1946) book **The Myth of the 20th Century** (1930) supplied Hitler with the spurious philosophical and scientific basis for the Nazi doctines.

Eugenics is the study of methods to improve inherited human characteristics. It is directed chiefly at discouraging reproduction among those considered unfit, an inherent Nazi doctrine.

Hitler looked toward the conquest of the Slavic peoples of eastern Europe and the USSR to provide the additional **Lebensraum**, or 'living space', that he believed the German people needed.

In the early days Hitler used the **Brownshirts** commanded by Ernst Roehm as bodyguards and for breaking up rival political meetings. They were later absorbed into the SS.

Kristallnacht ('the night of broken glass') occurred on the night of 9–10 Nov. 1938. Nazi storm troopers burned 267 synagogues and arrested 20,000 people.

Leni Riefenstahl was the maker of the powerful Nuremberg Rally film, *Triumph des Willens* (**Triumph of the Will**, 1935); it was the most effective visual propaganda for Nazism.

Nationalsozialistische Deutsche Arbeiterpartei (**National Socialist German Workers' Party**) was formed from the German Workers' Party (founded 1919) and led by Adolf Hitler, 1921–45.

Schutz-Staffel 'protective squadron' was a Nazi elite corps established 1925. Under Himmler its 500,000 included the *Waffen-SS* (armed SS); it was condemned as an illegal organisation at the Nuremberg Trials.

To Hitler the Germans were the highest species of humanity on the Earth – **Aryans** – 'nature's favourite child, the strongest in courage and industry'.

With the outbreak of war in 1939, Hitler began to implement his **final solution** of the Jewish question: the extermination of Jews in all countries conquered by his armies.

NEPTUNE

Neptune has a diameter of 48,600 km/30,200 mi and a **mass** 17.2 times that of Earth. Its rotation period is 16 hr 7 min.

Neptune is a giant gas planet consisting of hydrogen, helium and methane. The methane in its atmosphere absorbs red light, making it appear **blue**.

Neptune is believed to have a central rocky **core** covered by a layer of ice. It has three faint rings and has eight known moons.

Neptune is the **eighth planet** in average distance from the Sun. It orbits every 164.8 years at an average distance of 4,497 bn km/2.794 bn mi.

Neptune was **located** in 1846 by German astronomers J. G. Galle and H. d'Arrest after English astronomer J. Adams and French mathematician U. Leverrier predicted its existence from disturbances in the movement of Uranus.

Six of **Neptune's moons** were discovered by the *Voyager 2* probe, of which Proteus (diameter 415 km/260 mi) is larger than Nereid (300 km/200 mi). Two (Triton and Nereid) are visible from Earth.

When **Voyager 2** passed Neptune in Aug. 1989 various cloud features were noticed, including an Earth-sized oval storm cloud, the Great Dark Spot, similar to Jupiter's Great Red Spot.

NETHERLANDS

▲ *Tulip fields in the Netherlands.*

About a quarter of the **total land area** of the Netherlands lies below sea level and is protected from encroachment of the sea by a system of dykes.

▼ *The Hague, capital of the Netherlands.*

Successively a part of the Carolingian, Burgundian and Habsburg empires, the **Netherlands** revolted against Spain in 1588. The present kingdom dates from 1831.

The **Netherlands (capital: The Hague)** are situated in north-western Europe, bordering Belgium and Germany, with an area of 41,863 sq km/16,163 sq mi.

The **Netherlands export** machinery and transport equipment, foodstuffs, beverages and tobacco, chemicals, mineral fuels, metal products and textiles.

The **population of the Netherlands** is 15,048,000 (est. 1991), comprising 95.8% Dutch, 1.2% Turkish, 0.9% Moroccan, 0.3% German and 1.8% other.

NEW ZEALAND

Discovered by Abel Tasman in 1642 and charted by James Cook in 1769, **New Zealand** became a British colony in 1840 and a dominion in 1907.

New Zealand (capital: Wellington) consists of two main islands in the South Pacific, with an area of 270,534 sq km/104,454 sq mi.

New Zealand exports wool, meat, dairy products, basic manufactured goods, minerals, chemicals and plastics, mainly to Australia, Japan and the UK.

The national symbol of **New Zealand** is the kiwi, the world's oddest bird. It lays an egg a quarter its own weight, is covered with hair and digs with its long, curved bill.

The **population of New Zealand** is 3,432,000 (est. 1991), comprising 82.2% European, 9.2% Maori, 2.9% Polynesian and 5.7% other.

NIGERIA

Nigeria (capital: Lagos) lies on the Gulf of Guinea between Benin and Cameroon, with an area of 923,768 sq km/356,669 sq mi.

Nigeria exports crude petroleum, palm kernels, cocoa beans, rubber and cashew nuts, mainly to the US, Spain, Germany, France and Canada.

Nigeria was formed in 1914 by the union of the British colony of Lagos and the Protectorates of Northern and Southern Nigeria. It became a republic on 1 Oct. 1963.

On 30 May 1967 the eastern region of **Nigeria** broke away to form the republic of Biafra but after a brutal war was reincorporated on 15 Jan. 1970.

The **population of Nigeria** is 123,779,000 (est. 1991), comprising 21.3% Hausa 21.3% Yoruba, 18% Ibo, 11.2% Fulani, 5.6% Ibibio, 4.2% Kanuri, 3.4% Edo and 15% other.

NORTH AMERICA

Climates in North America range from tropical rainforest conditions in Central America through deserts, Continental, Mediterranean and maritime climates to polar and tundra conditions in the north.

North America and Central America together have an **area** of 25,349,000 sq km/9,785,000 sq mi. It occupies 4.7% of the world's total surface area and 16.1% of the total land area.

North America has a classic **continental structure** of a flat core of ancient metamorphic rocks, partly covered by later sedimentary rocks and surrounded by fold mountains.

North America is the **Nearctic Realm** in the zoogeographical classification. Its southern boundary is the Mexican desert.

The **Canadian Shield**, the metamorphic core of North America, contains some of the oldest rocks known. It is partly flooded by Hudson Bay.

The **highest** point in North America is Mt McKinley (also called Denali), Alaska, 6,194 m/20,320 ft; and its **lowest point** is Death Valley, California, US, 86 m/282 ft below sea-level.

The **mountains of western America**, dating from late Carboniferous times onwards, form the isthmus of Central America, connecting North and South America, and have intermittently formed a land bridge to northern Asia.

▼ *The Rocky Mountains, which run through North America and Canada.*

NORWAY

Although a third of Norway lies north of the Arctic Circle, its lengthy coastline is remarkably mild for most of the year, due to the warm **Atlantic currents**.

Formerly joined to Denmark and then Sweden, Norway became an independent kingdom in 1905, electing a Danish prince as **King Haakon VII**.

Norway (capital: Oslo) lies in north-western Europe, bordering Finland and Sweden, with an area of 323,878 sq km/125,050 sq mi.

Norway exports crude petroleum, natural gas, iron and steel, machinery and transport equipment, fish and food products, mainly to the UK, Sweden, Germany and France.

The **population of Norway** is 4,259,000 (est. 1991), comprising 95.7% Norwegians, 0.5% Danes and 3.4% other. 87.9% are Lutheran by religion.

NOVELS

Charles Dickens's **Our Mutual Friend** (1864–65), his last complete novel, gives one of his densest, bleakest and most comprehensive accounts of contemporary mid-19th-c society.

George Eliot's **Middlemarch: A Study of Provincial Life** (1871–72) interweaves the plots of its complex characters against a background of 19th-c social and political upheaval.

Henry James's **The Portrait of a Lady** (1880–81), like many of his major novels, is a complex psychological study of sophisticated European culture's impact on the innocent American.

▼ *The Royal Palace at Oslo, capital of Norway.*

James Joyce's **Ulysses** (1922) uses 'stream of consciousness', linguistic experimentation and parody to describe, in minute detail, one day (16 Jun. 1904) in the life of Dublin Jew, Leopold Bloom.

Leo Tolstoy's masterpiece **War and Peace** (1863–69), chronicling the lives of three noble Russian families during the Napoleonic Wars, combines great moral vision, complex characterisation and imaginative power.

Marcel Proust's **À la Recherche du Temps Perdu** (1913–27), a series of novels, is his immense semi-autobiographical work in which childhood memory is excavated in extraordinary detail.

Miguel de Cervantes's **Don Quixote de la Mancha** (1605–15) is the satirical picaresque romance of a self-styled Spanish knight on chivalrous adventures with his servant Sancho Panza.

NUCLEAR POWER

Data for 1993, released by the International Atomic Energy Agency (IAEA), showed there were 430 **nuclear power units in operation** in 29 countries with a total capacity of 330,651 MW.

In a **gas-cooled reactor** a circulating gas under pressure, often carbon dioxide, removes heat from the core of the reactor. Neutrons are slowed using carbon rods.

Nuclear energy comes from the inner core (nucleus) of an atom as opposed to energy released in chemical processes which comes from the electrons around the nucleus.

Nuclear fission (nuclear power) is achieved by allowing a neutron to strike the nucleus of an atom of fissile material; this splits apart to release other neutrons, releasing energy.

Nuclear fission works by a chain reaction as the newly freed neutrons in turn strike other nuclei if the fissile material is pure (uranium-235 or plutonium-239 are commonly used).

The most widely used reactor is the pressurised-water reactor, which contains a sealed system of pressurised water that is heated to form steam in heat exchangers in an external circuit.

The process of controlling the huge amount of energy released is achieved in a power plant, by absorbing excess neutrons in control rods and slowing their speed.

NUTRITION

Carbohydrates are the most abundant and least expensive food sources of energy. Important dietary carbohydrates are divided into two groups, starches and sugars. These are again broken down into 'refined' and 'unrefined', the latter of which is always healthiest.

Dietary fibre, also known as bulk or roughage, is also an essential element in the diet even though it provides no nutrients. It consists of plant cellulose and other indigestible materials and helps to encourage digestion and the elimination of waste.

Fats, which are widely distributed in nature, are a concentrated food source of energy. Fats are glyceryl esters of fatty acids and yield glycerol and many different fatty acids when broken down by hydrolysis.

Foods can be classified into several groups: milk (and dairy produce), vegetable-fruit, meat and meat substitutes (including vegetarian protein alternatives), bread-cereal (carbohydrates) and other foods.

Minerals, such as calcium, zinc and iron, are essential to life and health. Minerals are a necessary part of all cells and body fluids and enter into many physiological and structural functions.

Nutrients are substances, either naturally occurring or synthesised, that are necessary for maintenance of the normal function of organisms. These include carbohydrates, fats, proteins, vitamins and minerals, water and unknown substances.

Nutrition is the science that interprets the relationship of food to the functioning of a living organism and involves intake of food, digestive processes, the liberation of energy, the elimination of wastes and all processes essential for health.

Proteins are made up of relatively simple organic compounds, the amino acids, which contain nitrogen and sometimes sulphur. Humans and animals build the protein they need for growth and repair of tissues by breaking down the proteins obtained in food.

The world's most prevalent nutritional deficiency is lack of **protein**. This deficiency affects physical growth and mental development, causes emotional and psychological disturbances and reduces resistance to and recovery from diseases.

Vitamins are organic food substances, needed only in minute quantities but essential to enable the normal metabolism of other nutrients to promote growth and maintenance of health. Many act as catalysts or help form catalysts in the body.

OCEANIA

About 30,000 years ago, hunters from south-east Asia **colonised** parts of Melanesia (New Guinea to Fiji). About 3000 BC farmers from Asia followed, pushing eastwards.

Oceania is a name given to the islands of the Pacific Ocean and the East Indies. Sometimes it is taken to include Australia and New Zealand as well.

The **islands of Oceania** vary from volcanic to coral and its climate from equatorial to temperate maritime. Its western zone lies within the hurricane belt.

OCEANOGRAPHY

Jacques Cousteau predicted in 1981 that oceanographic vessels would become rarely used. Instead, drifting **instrumented buoys**, interrogated by space satellites, would provide data, which computers would integrate and analyse.

More than 75% of **marine pollution** comes from sources on land and 33% of it is airborne. Only about 12% comes from ships and boats, accidents or general rubbish.

Oceanographers recognise the role of the oceans in the **regulation of climate**, although even advanced computer models of the coupled atmosphere and ocean have not yet provided the necessary information.

Oceanography is the study of the sea. The British **Challenger expedition** of 1872–76, which sounded and sampled the oceans and their contents, is generally considered to mark the beginning of modern oceanography.

The distribution of **sea surface temperature** can be measured from space or by merchant ships. In the open ocean near the equator it is 30°C or more, decreasing in high latitudes near ice to about -2°C.

The **Gulf Stream** is a warm current, mainly created by wind. It starts in the Gulf of Mexico, changing its name to the North Atlantic Drift, and travels as far as Scotland and Norway.

The oceans are linked by a clockwise flow around the South Pole, called the **Antarctic gyre**, or current wheel. The direction of flow results from the anti-clockwise currents of the Atlantic, Pacific and Indian oceans.

Waves are not a moving piece of water but a shockwave transmitted through water. Wind causes ordinary ocean waves. A wind of 48 kph/30 mph can make waves 4.6 m/15 ft high and 90 m/300 ft long.

OCEANS

Coral reefs are made from accumulations of the protective limy cups of dead coral polyps. Polyps do not grow below 45m/150 ft or in water below 18°C/64°F. Coral reefs therefore occur in the tropics, in shallow, clear water.

In 1855 an American naval officer, Matthew Fontaine Maury, published the first map of an **ocean bed**. In those days ships plumbed the depths using a lead and line. The information thus obtained was sketchy.

In 1960 Dr Jacques Picard and Lt Donald Walsh in the bathyscaphe (submersible) *Trieste* plunged 10.9 km/6.8 mi to settle on the bottom of the **Challenger Deep**, the lowest place on the earth's crust.

The **continental shelf**, the true edge of the continents, is a platform extending from low tide level to about 180 m/600 ft down. Its length varies enormously – 1,200 km/750 mi from Siberia into the Arctic Ocean; almost nothing off Chile.

The **Pacific Ocean** is the world's largest ocean. Its surface area is 166 m. sq km/64 m. sq mi and its average depth is 4,280 m/14,050 ft. The deepest ocean trench is also in the Pacific, having a depth of 11,022 m/36,161 ft.

There is enough **salt** in the oceans to coat the continents 150m/480 ft deep. Most of the salt used in industry and cooking in the West is mined from thick deposits left by evaporation of prehistoric seas.

White tube worms, colourless blind crabs, giant clams and mussels live in darkness at 2,600 m/8,500 ft down, around hot-water jets called '**sea-bed smokers**'. These were discovered only in the late 1970s.

OIL

Offshore **oil rigs** are used to extract oil from the seabed. They are huge structures often containing living quarters for around 300 workers.

Oil is a **fossil fuel** composed of carbon and hydrogen and is insoluble in water. It is found in certain formations of layered rock.

Saudi Arabia is thought to have had the largest original oil endowment of any country; the Al-Ghawar field, discovered in 1948, has proved to be the world's largest, containing 82 bn barrels.

The ancient Sumerians, **Assyrians** and Babylonians used crude oil and asphalt (pitch), collected from large seeps at Tuttul on the Euphrates, for many purposes more than 5,000 years ago.

▲ *An Arabian prince; oil has made the country very wealthy.*

The earliest kind of oil rig was the **fixed-leg platform** which had rigid legs fixed to the seabed. Some were as tall as the Empire State Building.

The **first well**, specifically drilled for oil, was a project by Edwin Drake in Pennsylvania. The well was completed in Aug. 1859.

The largest oil rigs are **floating platforms**. They are anchored to the seabed by cables and chains. Large air tanks below the sea surface keep them stable.

OLYMPIC GAMES

Edward Eagan (US) is the only man to win a **gold medal at both summer and winter Olympics**. He won the light-heavyweight boxing title in 1920 and was a member of the victorious four-man bob-sleigh team in 1932.

Javelin competitor Tessa Sanderson's **Olympic career spanned 20 years** (1976–96), a British record she shares with high jumper Dorothy Tyler (1936–56).

Only five nations have been represented at **all 24 summer Olympic Games**. They are Australia, France, UK, Greece and Switzerland.

The **ancient Olympic Games** were held for over a thousand years until their prohibition in AD 393. Their reintroduction was inspired by Baron Pierre de Coubertin and the first modern games took place in Athens in 1896.

The **Olympic flame** is symbolically carried via a torch from Mount Olympus to the host stadium. Its longest journey took it to Calgary, Canada for the 1988 Winter Games – 18,060 km/11,222 mi.

Two competitors have won **four consecutive individual Olympic titles** in the same event. They are Al Oerter (US) in the discus (1956–68) and Carl Lewis (US) in the long jump (1984–96).

Carl Lewis became one of the greatest ever Olympians. ▶

ORCHESTRAS

From the **late 19th c** composers such as Berlioz, Wagner, Rimsky-Korsakov, Strauss, Mahler and Stravinsky have helped produce orchestras of unprecedented size and tonal resources.

Herbert von Karajan (1908–89), Austrian conductor of the **Berlin Philharmonic Orchestra** (1955–89, est. 1882), is particularly associated with works by Beethoven, Brahms, Mahler and Strauss.

Orchestras began (c. 1700) when polyphony gave way to homophony, with a keyboardist (often the composer) acting as unifying continuo agent. **Carl Theodor**'s court orchestras (Mannheim School, 1742–78) helped develop early symphonies.

The **Hallé Orchestra** (Manchester, 1858) was conducted (1943–68) by Sir John Barbirolli (1899–1970). Under his direction, promoting modern composers' works, it became one of the world's finest orchestras.

The **Orchestre de la Suisse Romande**, founded in Geneva (1918) by Swiss conductor Ernest Ansermet and led by him until 1967, introduced not yet widely accepted works by Debussy, Stravinsky, Bartok and Berg.

The Vienna Philharmonic and **New York Philharmonic** (NYPO) are two of the oldest orchestras, both founded 1842. Leonard Bernstein, composer of *West Side Story*, was NYPO's musical director (1958–70).

◀ *Ludwig van Beethoven.*

ORGANIZATION OF AMERICAN STATES

The **Organization of American States (OAS)** was founded in Bogotá, Colombia (Mar.–Apr. 1948) by a charter signed by representatives of North, Central and South American states.

A regional agency of UN members, the OAS built on foundations established by the International Bureau of American Republics (1890), renamed the **Pan-American Union** (1910).

Canada held OAS observer status from 1972, becoming a full member in 1990. Belize and Guyana were admitted 1991 by which time **OAS membership** had expanded to 35.

In 1997 OAS Sec. Gen. César Gaviria and Pres. Clinton signed the Inter-American Convention against Illicit Arms Trafficking. In 1998 the OAS celebrated its **50th anniversary**.

Latin American states criticised **US dominance of the OAS**, especially anti-communist US resolutions at conferences from 1952 to 1962, culminating in the expulsion of Castro's Cuba.

OAS members unanimously supported Pres. John F. Kennedy (1917–63) in his decision to **blockade Cuba** when Soviet missiles were installed there at the end of 1962.

The **aims and principles of the OAS** (1948) are to promote the joint welfare of nations in the western hemisphere through peaceful settlements of disputes and promotion of economic development.

The **headquarters** of the Organization of American States are in Washington, DC.

The OAS eased tensions between Bolivia and Chile, promoted agreements over the Panama Canal and adopted the Charter of Punta del Este (1961) establishing the **Alliance for Progress**.

The Organization of American States was chartered in 1948 by representatives of 30 North, Central and South American States.

The Organization of American States works to **maintain peace and solidarity** in the western hemisphere and to cultivate social and economic development in Latin America.

OSLO

Formerly Kristiania or Christiania (1624–1925), **Oslo** was founded by Harold Hardrada in 1048, became a bishopric and, from the 14th c, capital of Norway.

Oslo has major shipyards and factories producing woollens, linen, paper, pulp, machinery, bricks and tiles, flour, glass, hardware and chemicals.

Oslo is situated in southern Norway, in a basin surrounded by pine-wooded hills on the Aker River, at the head of Oslo Fjord, 128 km/80 mi from the Skagerrak.

The attractions of **Oslo** include Nansen's ship *Fram*, Akershus fortress and the Frogner Park, decorated with sculptures by Gustav Vigeland (1869–1943).

The **population of Oslo** is 461,127 (est. 1991). Its growth, from 7,500 in 1769 to 275,000 in 1943, resulted from the absorption of surrounding villages.

OTTOMAN EMPIRE

Between 1541 and 1909 the sultan's harem of women was kept hidden in the fabled and mysterious **Seraglio**, or Sublime Porte, in the Topkapi Palace in Istanbul.

By 1400, Ottoman Turks under Sultan Mehmet II had established Islam deep into Europe, and on 29 May 1453, its last day as a Christian city, **Constantinople** fell.

From the 14th–19th c **Janissaries** were the sultan's elite guard. They were Christians converted to Islam, cut off from civil society and forbidden to marry.

In 1571 Don John of Austria, leading a Christian navy, destroyed the Ottoman navy at the **Battle of Lepanto**, the last naval engagement at which the boats used on both sides were galleys. Galleys continued to be used by the Turks until the end of the 18th c.

◀ *The Royal Palace at Oslo.*

One cannon used by the **Ottoman army** at the siege of Constantinople in 1453 needed 100 oxen to pull it and could only be fired seven times a day.

Under **Suleiman the Magnificent** (1494–1566), the Ottoman Empire stretched from coastal north Africa to the Middle East, and into Europe as far as Vienna.

With the **Ottoman Empire** a barrier between Europe and Asia, another way to the East had to be found, and in 1488 a sea route round South Africa was discovered.

OZONE LAYER

The **ozone layer** is a layer of the upper atmosphere lying about 20–25 km/12–15 mi above the Earth's surface. It is named because the unstable form of oxygen called ozone is concentrated in this layer.

CFCs (chlorofluorocarbons) attack the ozone layer and contribute to the greenhouse effect, because the ozone layer protects the growth of ocean phytoplankton.

In Australia, where ozone thinning is particularly serious, there has been a substantial increase in **skin-cancer** rates. Ultraviolet radiation can also damage plants and the plankton on which marine ecosystems depend.

In the mid-1980s atmospheric studies showed that an ozone hole was appearing and then disappearing each Antarctic spring. The hole is believed to result from **human activities** and by the early 1990s it had worsened significantly.

The ozone layer strongly absorbs **ultraviolet radiation** from the Sun. If this radiation reached the Earth's surface at unprotected levels, it would be damaging to all forms of life.

When the ozone layer thinned, a hole as large as continental US opened up over Antarctica. The **health risks** are enormous, with skin cancer and eye cataracts among the problems linked with increased ultraviolet radiation from the sun.

PAKISTAN

▲ *Lahore, in Pakistan.*

Formerly part of British India, **Pakistan** became a separate dominion on 14 Aug. 1947 and a republic in 1956. East Pakistan seceded in 1971 to form Bangladesh.

Pakistan (capital: Islamabad) lies on the north-west side of the Indian subcontinent, between India and Afghanistan, with an area of 796,095 sq km/307,374 sq mi.

Pakistan exports raw cotton, yarn, ready-made garments, leather, rice, synthetic textiles and carpets, mainly to the US, Japan, Germany and the UK.

The name **Pakistan** is an acronym for Punjab, Afghania and Kashmir, plus *stan* 'land'. As *pak* is the Urdu word for 'pure', Pakistan also means 'land of the pure'.

The **population of Pakistan** is 126,400,000 (est. 1991), comprising 48.2% Punjabi, 13.1% Pushtu, 11.8% Sindhi, 9.8% Saraiki, 7.6% Urdu and 9.5% other.

PALACES

About 21 km/13 mi south-west of Paris, in the city of Versailles, stands the largest palace in France: the **Palace of Versailles**. It served as a royal residence for little more than a century (1682–1789).

Buckingham Palace, once the residence of the Duke of Buckingham, was purchased by George III and rebuilt by John Nash before Queen Victoria chose it for her home in 1837. The palace and its 40-ac gardens are now open to the public.

In 1377 Pope Gregory XI took up residence in a home that would swell across the centuries to become a palace. Today the **Vatican Palace** is a collection of buildings of different periods that cover 5.5 h/13½ ac and

Forbidden City, containing the palaces of 24 of the Ming and Ch'ing emperors. They occupy an area of 100 h/250 ac, with more than 9,000 rooms.

St. James's Palace, on the north side of the Mall in London, was the royal residence from the time Whitehall burned down (1698) to the accession of Queen Victoria. It is now set aside for conferences and court functions.

contain more than 1,400 rooms. The most celebrated section of the palace is the Sistine Chapel with magnificent frescoes by Michelangelo.

In Ancient Rome more than 93,000 sq m/1 m. sq ft of the **Palatine Hill** were devoted to splendid residences of such emperors as Augustus, Tiberius and Septimius Severus.

In the 1980s the Sultan of Brunei, Sir Muda Hassanal Bolkiah Muizzaddin Waddaulah, opened his new palace. Named **New Istana**, it contains 1,788 rooms.

On Tiananmen (Gate of Heavenly Peace) Square in the heart of China's capital city, Beijing, stands the

The **Great Kremlin Palace**, built from 1838 to 1849 as a royal residence by Konstantin Thon and once used for sessions of the Supreme Soviet of the Soviet Union is connected to the Armory (Oruzheynaya) Palace, built by the same architect from 1844 to 1851.

The word **palace** derives from the Palatine Hill in Rome, where the emperors built their residences. The first palaces were built for the pharaohs of Ancient Egypt (16th c BC).

▲ *The Vatican Palace in Italy.*

PALEONTOLOGY

The term **paleontology**, derived from the Greek words for 'ancient life', refers to the science that deals with the study of prehistoric life. The main objects of study in this field are fossils.

In studying fossils, paleontologists use principles from both **geology** and biology, making paleontology an amalgamation or meeting point between these sciences.

The discipline of paleontology, which once involved only identification of **macrofossils**, now includes identification of microfossils (for example, *foraminifera* and pollen) and measurement of trace elements in skeletal material.

Baron Georges Cuvier (1769–1832) was a French naturalist and anatomist who made important contributions to comparative anatomy and vertebrate paleontology. Cuvier studied fossils and was the first to classify them.

The American paleontologist **Othniel Charles Marsh** (1831–99) discovered over 1,000 fossil vertebrates, mainly dinosaurs, during his many scientific explorations of the US, and he was a pioneer in the field of vertebrate paleontology.

Paleobotany is the study of the geologic history of the plant kingdom. Traditionally a major branch of paleontology, the study of ancient life, Paleontology is now restricted to animal fossils and paleobotany to plants.

PARAGUAY

Arising from boundary disputes, **Paraguay** fought a disastrous war (1865–70) with its neighbours, losing four-fifths of its population as a result.

Paraguay (capital: Asuncion) is landlocked in South America, bordered by Argentina, Bolivia and Brazil, with an area of 406,752 sq km/157,046 sq mi.

Paraguay exports raw cotton, soybeans, processed meats, timber, perfume oils, coffee and vegetable oil, mainly to Brazil, the Netherlands, Argentina and Switzerland.

Sebastian Cabot explored **Paraguay** in 1526–29 and later it was colonised by the Jesuits. It declared independence in 1811, resisting attempts to merge it with Argentina.

The **population of Paraguay** is 4,397,000 (est. 1991), comprising 90.8% mestizo, 3% Amerindian, 1.7% German and 4.5% other. 96% are Roman Catholic and 2.1% Protestant.

PARANORMAL PHENOMENA

In the UK the **Society for Psychical Research** was founded in 1882 by F. H. Myers and Henry Sidgwick to investigate the claims of the spiritualist movement and other paranormal phenomena.

Paranormal comes from the Greek word *para* meaning 'beyond' and is the study of phenomena not explicable by normal science. The faculty in humans and animals is known as *psi*.

Paranormal phenomena include: mediumship, supposed contact with the spirits of the dead, usually through a medium; precognition, foreknowledge of events; and telekinesis, movement of objects by human mental concentration.

Telepathy was the term coined by English essayist F. Myers (1843–1901) for 'communication of impressions of any kind from one mind to the other, independently of the recognised channels of sense'.

Mysterious corn circles, said to be created by UFOs. ▶

The **spiritualist movement**, a belief in the survival of the human spirit and the communication with these through mediumship, originated in the US in 1848.

The very first chair of **parapsychology** was established at Edinburgh University in 1984 and was endowed to Hungarian author Arthur Koestler.

US escapologist **Harry Houdini** (1874–1926) became fascinated with life after death when his mother died. Before he died he left a message with his wife Rosabel to try and prove that life after death existed.

PARIS

Originally Lutetia, the capital of the Parisii and later a Roman town, **Paris** became the capital of the Franks under Clovis in 508.

Paris developed at a ford on the River Seine, dominated by the Ile de la Cite. It spread gradually to encompass the plain on both banks surrounded by Jurassic heights.

Paris is the political, commercial and industrial centre of France. The city itself specialises in art and luxury goods, most of the heavy industry being in the suburbs.

The cultural gem of Europe, **Paris** boasts more palaces, churches, museums and great public buildings than any other city. The Cathedral of Notre-Dame (1163–1240) is particularly outstanding.

The **population of Paris** is 2,152,423 (1990 census), about the same as in 1881, but that of the greater metropolitan area is 9,060,257.

The Eiffel Tower in Paris. ▶

PARLIAMENT

During the **General Strike** (1926), Baldwin's government's monopoly of information services, which included for the first time broadcasting, prevented any general wave of panic.

In May 1940 Winston Churchill formed a **coalition government**, the beginning of his 'walk with destiny', leading the British to victory in World War II until his defeat in the 1945 general election.

On 29 Nov. 1995, following the Major-Bruton Irish peace initiative, on the eve of the first visit by a US president to Northern Ireland, **Bill Clinton** addressed both Houses of Parliament.

Ramsay MacDonald (1866–1937), leader of Britain's first two Labour governments (1924/1929–31), met the financial crisis of 1931 by forming a predominantly Conservative 'National' **coalition government** (1931–35).

Winston Churchill. ▲

Stanley Baldwin (1867–1947), Conservative PM during the General Strike (4–12 May 1926) recruited special constables (volunteers to run essential services) and used troops to maintain food supplies.

The **Commons debating chamber** was destroyed by incendiary bombs (1941); the chamber was rebuilt by architect Sir Giles Gilbert Scott (1950) to preserve its former character.

The miners, resenting TUC 'betrayal' in calling off the **General Strike** (May 1926), stayed out until Aug. The following year Baldwin's government passed an Act making general strikes illegal.

The miners, who stayed out longest during the General Strike (May–Aug. 1926), challenged Margaret Thatcher's government during the **longest strike in British history** (1984–85).

The **Trades Disputes Act 1927**, outlawing general strikes, was repealed in 1946 by Attlee, the year in which the coal industry was nationalised.

The **TUC** called off the General Strike (1926) after nine days, arguing that the government was better prepared than the unions and accepting a compromise, rejected by the miners.

PETS

Guinea pigs are rodents of the genus *Cavia*. The coat is brown or grey in wild guinea pigs, but the domesticated variety may exhibit a wide range of colours. Guinea pigs are native to South America and were domesticated for food centuries ago in Peru. Guinea pigs are popular pets in North America and Europe.

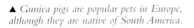

▲ *Guinea pigs are popular pets in Europe, although they are native of South America.*

Only in certain regions such as western Europe and North America are **cats** kept as pets in numbers sufficient to support such large, subsidiary industries as veterinary services, pet foods and novelty products, welfare societies and publications. Elsewhere, cats are tolerated but not regarded as pets.

Hamster is the common name of about 11 species of Old World rodents. Hamsters have stocky bodies; soft, dark or yellowish fur; and short tails. Cheek pouches are used for storing and carrying food. Golden hamsters are frequently kept as pets.

Parrots are easily distinguished by their short, curved beaks; large heads; short necks and feet; and reversed toes. Parrots are intelligent and gregarious birds and in isolation they mimic their human keepers as a form of social behaviour.

The **dog** has been bred for many domestic purposes other than as pets, but dogs are now one of the most popular pets in the world, with over 30 m. registered in the US. Worldwide, more than 340 breeds are registered with kennel clubs.

Tropical fish are small fish that have become popular as pets in aquariums because of their beauty and their interesting behaviour. Most aquarium fishes are in fact from the tropics or warm temperate areas, but the term is also used for some species from cooler waters.

Turtles live much longer than most other animals. Evidence exists of specimens of several species that have lived for 50 years in captivity. The collection of turtles for the pet trade is one of the major threats to most turtles, of which more than 30 species are in danger of extinction.

PHILOSOPHY

An intellectual area that has been intimately involved with philosophy is **religion**. In Ancient Greece some philosophers like Anaxagoras and Socrates scandalised contemporaries by criticising aspects of Greek religion.

As Greek thinkers codified their pictures of the world, they saw that for each science or study there could be a corresponding **philosophy of this science** or study, such as the philosophies of science, art and history.

Contemporary philosophers are inclined to think of philosophy as an activity: an investigation of the fundamental assumptions that govern our ways of understanding and acting in the world.

From about 300 BC to AD 200 the central philosophical concerns shifted to how an individual should conduct his or her life. The **Stoics**, the Sceptics and the Epicureans emphasised the question of how humans should survive in a miserable world.

From Socrates through to 20th-c thinkers such as Bertrand Russell and Jean Paul Sartre, a major element of philosophical enterprise has been devoted to designate what constitutes 'well-being' for humans as individuals and as social beings.

Great Greek philosophers include: Heraclitus (c. 544–483 BC), Parmenides (c. 510–450 BC), Socrates (469–399 BC), Plato (428–347 BC) and Aristotle (384–322 BC).

Greek philosophy was the major formative influence on the later philosophical traditions of Judaism, Islam and Christianity. In all three, Greek theories were employed to clarify and develop basic beliefs of religious traditions.

▲ *Greek philosophy influenced Christianity.*

In **developing philosophies**, early thinkers such as Plato and Aristotle saw that their reflections could be used as a means of criticising and refuting popularly accepted mythological views and the thoughts of their predecessors and contemporaries.

In the late 12th and early 13th c the writings of Aristotle were reintroduced to the West. After some initial resistance Aristotle became the dominant **philosophical authority** and remained so until the Renaissance.

In the late 18th and early 19th c the prevailing philosophers in England and France came to the conclusion that the sciences are, and should be, completely independent of traditional **metaphysical interpretations**.

Indian philosophy is commonly divided into two traditions: Hinduism (Samkhya, Yoga, Vaisheshika, Nyaya, Mimamsa and Vedanta that accept Vedic authority) and the non-orthodox schools (Charvaka, Jainism and Buddhism).

Noteworthy **German philosophers** include Karl Marx (1818–83), Wilhelm Dilthey (1833–1911), Friedrich Nietzsche (1844–1900), Martin Heidegger (1889–1976), Arthur Schopenhauer (1788–1860), Georg Hegel (1770–1831) and Friedrich Wilhelm Schelling (1775–1854).

One of the most basic branches of philosophy is **Epistemology**, the theory of knowledge (*episteme* is Greek for 'knowledge'), which deals with what can be known, how it can be known and how certain the individual can be about it.

◀ *Aristotle, the father of philosophy.*

Philosophy is the oldest form of systematic, scholarly enquiry. The name comes from the Greek *philosophos*, which means 'love of wisdom'.

Philosphy is concerned with **fundamental problems** that arise in every area of human thought and activity and that cannot be resolved by a specific method.

Since the 17th c areas of study that been parted from philosophy and assigned to the **natural sciences** include astronomy, physics, chemistry, geology, biology and psychology.

The first recognised philosopher in China was **Confucius** (541–497 BC), who taught the primacy of the family and the duties incumbent upon its various members, stressing harmony and unity and the self-evident goodness of the ethical life.

The oracles of the **I Ching** began to assume their present written form perhaps as early as the 7th c BC and the book as a whole played an important role throughout the subsequent development of Chinese philosophy.

The **philosopher's tools** are logical and speculative reasoning. In the Western tradition the development of logic is usually traced back to Aristotle, who aimed at constructing valid arguments if premises could be uncovered.

The philosophical traditions of India have their beginnings in reflection on the *Vedas* and specifically in attempts to interpret the *Upanishads*. A wide variety of schools emerged.

The **pre-Socratics** (Pre-Socratic Philosophy, *c.* 600 BC) sought to find fundamental, natural principles that could explain what individuals know and experience about the world around them.

The second important indigenous Chinese tradition is **Taoism**. The teaching of the *Tao Tě Ching*, a work attributed to the semi-legendary Lao-Tzu (6th c BC), is complex and teaches the eternal principle of reality.

◄ *Buddhism is the most widespread of the religions to come out of the East.*

The synthesis of Christianity and Aristotelianism was a major form of **Scholasticism**, which dominated European philosophy into the 17th c. During the Renaissance other forms of ancient philosophy began to be revived and used against the scholastics.

Western philosophy began in Greece, in the Greek settlement of Miletus in Anatolia. The first known philosophers were Thales of Miletus and his students, Anaximander and Anaximenes.

PHOENICIANS

Ancient **Phoenicia** was the narrow strip of land at the eastern end of the Mediterranean, now largely in modern Lebanon.

The **Phoenician alphabet**, which contained only consonants, was borrowed by the Greeks and developed into classical Greek.

The Phoenician Empire thrived from about 2000 BC until **Alexander the Great** sacked its capital, Tyre, in 332 BC and incorporated the country into the Greek world.

The Phoenicians are the first to have obtained the colour purple, known as **Tyrian Purple**, from crushed molluscs. The Phoenicians are also credited with the invention of glass.

The Phoenicians were great **seafaring traders**, establishing trading links throughout Asia, into Africa (where they founded Carthage), Spain and even Britain.

The **Phoenicians**, related to the Canaanites of ancient Palestine, considered themselves to be a single nation, but were in fact a collection of city-kingdoms.

PHOTOGRAPHY

Aristotle noted the principles of *camera obscura* (an apparatus projecting the image of an object); Leonardo da Vinci was the first to connect it with how the eye functions (1505).

Fox Talbot's **calotype** process was patented, 1841 (first multi-copy photography method using a negative-positive process, sensitised with silver iodide). His $\frac{1}{1000}$–second exposure demonstrated **high-speed photography** (1851).

George Eastman produced **flexible negative film** (1884); the Eastman Company (US) produced the Kodak No. 1 camera and roll film, allowing universal hand-held snapshots (1889).

George Eastman of Kodak. ▶

In 1750 Canaletto used a *camera obscura* as a painting aid. Thomas Wedgwood (England, 1790) made **photograms**, placing objects on leather sensitised with silver nitrate.

In 1826 Nicephore Nièpce (1765–1833), French doctor, produced the **world's first photograph** from nature on pewter plates with a *camera obscura* and an 8-hour exposure.

In 1835 Daguerre produced the first **Daguerreotype** camera photograph. Daguerre, awarded an annuity by the French government, gave his process to the world (1839).

In 1947 **Polaroid** b&w instant-process film was invented by Land (US) and **holography**'s principles were demonstrated by Gabor (UK). The **zoom lens** was invented by Voigtlander (Austria, 1959).

In the US (1935) Mannes and Godowsky invented **Kodachrome** transparency film, which produced sharp images and rich colour quality, and **electronic flash** was invented.

Leitz launched the **Leica 35 mm** camera (1924), popular with photo-journalists because it was small, quiet and dependable. Rolleiflex produced the twin-lens reflex camera (1929).

The first **telephoto lens** was produced and Lipmann developed the interference colour-photography process (1891). The Lumière brothers patented the autochrome colour process (1904).

The **single-lens reflex plate camera** was patented by Sutton and the principles of three-colour photography were demonstrated by Maxwell (1861). Gelatin-silver bromide was developed (1871).

US astronauts took photographs on the Moon (1969). **Electronic cameras**, storing pictures on magnetic disc, were introduced (Japan). Kodak introduced PhotoCD, digitally converting pictures for CD storage (1990).

PHOTOSYNTHESIS

Carbon dioxide reduction is the process in photosynthesis whereby sunlight and the hydrogen in water are used to produce carbohydrates as a source of energy.

Diatoms or bacillariophyceae are microscopic unicellular or colonial algae, discovered by O. F. Mueller in 1791. They are responsible for most of the photosynthesis in the ocean.

Photosynthesis is the process whereby green plants harness the energy of sunlight absorbed by chlorophyll to create carbohydrates from carbon dioxide and water.

Chloroplasts are strongly coloured structural units within the plant cell. The green or brown colour in them is due to the chlorophylls and carotenoids they contain.

The **factors governing photosynthesis** are temperature, light intensity, carbon dioxide concentration, water supply, the concentration of pigments and activity of enzymes.

The **products of photosynthesis** may be expressed simply in terms of carbon dioxide plus water plus light produces oxygen and carbohydrates.

PHYSIOLOGY

Anatomy is the structural counterpart and, in a historical sense, the parent of physiology. In turn, the fields of bio-

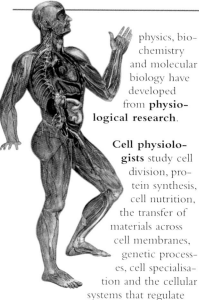

physics, biochemistry and molecular biology have developed from **physiological research**.

Cell physiologists study cell division, protein synthesis, cell nutrition, the transfer of materials across cell membranes, genetic processes, cell specialisation and the cellular systems that regulate these functions.

Experimental physiology dates from the 17th c, when William Harvey described blood circulation. Between 17th and 20th c, such problems as the metabolism, movement, reflexes, feedback control and energy transformation have been researched.

Perhaps the most profound advance in physiological research has been the identification (1944) of the hereditary material deoxyribonucleic acid, known as **DNA**.

The branch of biology dealing with the functions of living organisms and their components is known as **physiology**. It basically describes life processes in terms of physics and chemistry.

PLAGUES

Alexandre Yersin was one of the first to describe the plague bacillus, *Pastuerella pestis* (also called *Yersinia pestis* or *Bacillus pestis*) in 1894.

Bubonic **plague** is characterised by lymph node swelling (buboes); in pneumonic plague the lungs are extensively involved; and in septicemic the bloodstream is so invaded that death ensues before other forms have time to appear.

▼ *A DNA double-helix strand.*

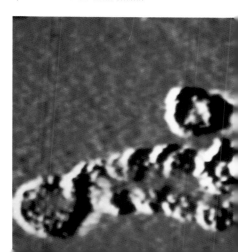

Bubonic plague starts with shivering, vomiting, headache, giddiness, light intolerance, pains and sleeplessness; temperature rises to 40°C/104°F. Most characteristic is the appearance of buboes, usually in the groin and armpits.

In the 14th c the plague was called **Black Death**. It has been calculated that one-quarter of the population of Europe at that time (25 m. people) died from plague during the great epidemic.

Mild infections of plague are bubonic; pneumonic and septicemic plague are invariably severe and fatal unless treated. **Incubation period** is usually 3–6 days but may be as short as 36 hours.

Plague is an infectious fever caused by the bacillus *Pastuerella pestis*, transmitted by the black rat flea. In man plague has three forms: bubonic, pneumonic and septicemic.

The **Great Plague of London** (1664–65) resulted in more than 70,000 deaths in a population estimated at 460,000. An outbreak in Canton and Hong Kong in 1894 left around 100,000 dead.

PLANET X

After its mass was calculated astronomers demonstrated that a body of such mass as Planet X would disturb the **orbits** of the outer planets by amounts incompatible with the observed path.

The planets **Uranus** and Pluto show no detectable irregularities, and so it now seems unlikely that this planet exists at all.

For a while it was thought **Charon** was the tenth planet, but it was then classified as an asteroid and finally as a giant cometary nucleus.

It was shown that if the density and albedo of Planet X had plausible values it would have been **visible** by normal astronomical techniques.

Planet X was a supposed planet of the solar system, 10th in distance from the Sun, surmised on calculations of its effect on the orbit of Halley's comet, Uranus, Neptune and Pluto.

Planet X was calculated to have a **mass** about three times Saturn's and a period of revolution around the Sun of 500 years.

Planet X's existence was proposed in 1972 and assumed to be located in the direction of the constellation **Cassiopeia**.

PLANTS

Cryptogams are plants which have no flowers, and their sexual-reproductive organs are inconspicuous. They include the lowest forms of plant life.

Dicotyledons are plants with two seed leaves. According to Adolf Engler's classification (1892) they embrace 30 orders of *Archichlamydae* and 10 of *Sympetalae*.

Monocotyledons are plants with a single seed leaf, usually parallel-veined. Engler classified 11 orders from *Pandales* (marsh herbs) to *Orchidales* (orchids).

Phanerogams represent the higher plants, including the *Gymnosperms* (seeds not enclosed in an ovary) and *Angiosperms* (male and female organs on the same plant).

The **Bryophyta** are distinguished from the Thallophyta by having multicellular sex organs. They include the *Hepatica* (liverworts) and *Musci* (mosses).

The **Pteridophyta** are the higher cryptogams and include the horsetails and club-mosses as well as the *Filicales* numbering 150 genera and 6,000 species of fern.

The **Thallophyta**, comprising the lowest group of cryptogams, are plants possessing a thallus or plant body which shows no differentiation between roots, stem and leaves.

PLASTICS

Biodegradable plastics, like Biopol (1990), are much in demand. Soil micro-organisms are used to build the plastic in their cells from carbon dioxide and water. Discarded plastic will then break down back to its constituents.

Plastics are polymeric materials that have the capability of being moulded or shaped, usually by applying heat and pressure. They are chiefly derived from petroleum.

Polyurethane polymer is made from the monomer urethane. It is a thermoset plastic and is used in liquid form as a paint or varnish and in foam form in upholstery (highly flammable).

Shape-memory polymers are plastics which can be crumpled or flattened and will resume their original shape when heated. They include transpolyisoprene and polynorbornene.

The property of plasticity, and the combination of other **special properties** such as low density, low electrical conductivity, transparency, and toughness, allows plastics to be made into a huge range of products.

Thermoplastics soften when warmed up then reharden as they cool. Examples are polystyrene, polythene and polyvinyl chloride (PVC, used for floor tiles, shoes etc.).

Thermosets remain rigid once set and do not soften again when warmed. These include Bakelite (used in phones), epoxy resins (paints and varnishes) and polyesters.

PLAYS

Harold Pinter's **The Caretaker** (1960) established his reputation as a leading playwright: in a run-down house three characters attempt to communicate with each other and manifestly fail.

In Arthur Miller's **Death of a Salesman** (1949) the tragedy of sales representative Willy Loman's spiritual disintegration expressed disillusionment in the great American dream.

In Shakespeare's tragedy (1602), **Hamlet** (in agonised indecision about whether to avenge his father's death or kill himself, feigning or genuinely pitched into madness) was literature's first true protagonist.

Samuel Beckett's **Waiting for Godot** (1955), Theatre of the Absurd masterpiece, abandoned conventional structure and development in plot and language: two indecisive tramps wait for help that never comes.

Tennesee Williams's **A Streetcar Named Desire** (1947) explores the gulf between men and women; the longing for innocence, persistence of desire; and brute experience ranged against fragility.

Trapped in small-town society, Hedda, in Henrik Ibsen's **Hedda Gabler** (1891) takes out her spiritual and sexual frustration on everyone around her, including her husband, before committing suicide.

▲ *Shakespeare wrote 36 plays during his lifetime.*

PLUTO

Pluto orbits the Sun every 248.5 years at an average distance of 5.9 bn km/3.6 bn mi. It has an elliptical orbit which sometimes takes it into the orbit of Neptune as in 1979–99.

Pluto's moon, **Charon**, was discovered in 1978 by James Christy. It is approx. 1,200 km/750 mi in diameter, half Pluto's size, making it the largest moon in relation to its parent in the solar system.

Charon orbits about 20,000 km/12,500 mi from Pluto's centre every 6.39 days, the same time it takes Pluto to spin on its axis.

Pluto has a **diameter** of about 2,300 km/1,400 mi and a mass of about 0.002 of that of Earth.

Pluto is **composed** mainly of rock and ice, with frozen methane on its surface, and has a thin atmosphere.

Pluto is the smallest and, usually, **outermost planet** of our solar system. It is named after the Greek god of the underworld.

The **existence** of Pluto was predicted by P. Lowell and located by American Clyde Tombaugh in 1930. It is a planet of low density.

POETRY

American experimental poets, using 'free verse' relying exclusively on metre and rhythm and rejecting rhyme, included: cummings, Eliot, 'HD', Moore, Pound, Stevens and Williams.

Eliot revived interest in the **Metaphysicals**, 17th-c poets (Donne, Herbert, Marvell, Vaughan and Traherne) who shared 'discovery of occult resemblance in things apparently unlike' (Johnson).

Metre is language 'measured' into line-lengths of patterned verse. Accentual metre, used in Anglo-Saxon and pre-Chaucerian poetry, was revived by Hopkins (1844–89), who called it 'sprung rhythm'.

Shakespeare's Sonnets (*c.* 1598–1609), dedicated to 'Mr W. H.' (probably the Earl of Southampton), fall into two sections: 1–126 (to the 'youth' of the sonnets), 127–54 (and to the 'mistress').

Byron, Keats) shared belief in poetry's sacred mission — the 'institutionalisation of the imagination and emergence of the poet's special faculty'.

POLAND

A medieval kingdom stretching from the Baltic to the Black Sea, **Poland** was partitioned among its neighbours. It re-emerged, as a republic, in 1918.

In 1919 the first prime minister of the independent republic of **Poland** was Ignacy Jan Paderewksi (1860–1941), the celebrated concert pianist.

Poland (capital: Warsaw) lies in central Europe on the Baltic, bordered by Lithuania, Belarus, Ukraine, Slovakia, the Czech Republic and Germany, with an area of 92,389 sq km/35,672 sq mi.

Poland exports machinery and transport equipment, iron and steel, chemicals, fuel and power, textiles and clothing, mainly to Russia, Germany, the UK and the Czech Republic.

The **population of Poland** is 38,273,000 (est. 1991), comprising 98.7% Polish, 0.6% Ukrainian and 0.7% other.

▲ *The poet T. S. Eliot.*

T. S. Eliot (1888–1965) caused a sensation with *Prufrock and Other Observations* (1917) with its experimental forms and rhythms, establishing his reputation with the desolate modernity of *The Waste Land* (1922).

Two generations of **Romantics** (Blake, Wordsworth, Coleridge; Shelley,

POLITICAL SYSTEMS

'As with the Christian religion, the worst advertisement for **Socialism** is its adherents.' George Orwell, 1903–50, *The Road to Wigan Pier*, 1937, ch. 11.

'**Communism** is like prohibition, it's a good idea but it won't work.' Will Rogers, 1879–1935, *Weekly Articles* (1981), vol. 3 (first published 1927).

'**Democracy** means governments by the uneducated, while **aristocracy** means governments by the badly educated.' G. K. Chesterton, 1874–1936, *New York Times*, 1 Feb. 1931.

'We started off trying to set up a small **anarchist** community, but people wouldn't obey the rules.' Alan Bennett, b. 1934, *Getting On*, Act I, 1972.

Elected ANC president (1991) after release from prison (1964–90), Nelson Mandela was elected president of South Africa (1994), ending the notorious era of **apartheid** (racial segregation).

Harry S. Truman (1884–1972, 33rd US president, 1945–53) said, 'Wherever you have an efficient government you have a **dictatorship**.' Lecture at Columbia University, 28 Apr. 1959.

Military juntas have perhaps taken place most frequently in African and Latin American countries but also in Europe, as in Turkey (1980), when after an army takeover Bulent Ulusu became PM.

Oswald Spengler (1880–1936) wrote, '**Socialism** is nothing but the capitalism of the lower classes' (1933). Never a Nazi, his bleak view of Western civilisation unfortunately encouraged them.

◄ *ANC president Nelson Mandela.*

POLLUTION

Across Western countries, **asthma** cases among small children are up 80% over the last 20 years, with many experts blaming traffic exhaust fumes for exacerbating the condition.

Burning tobacco is the main source of **indoor pollution** worldwide. Tobacco smoke contains 4,000 chemicals, a number of them known to cause cancer.

Environmental pollution is any discharge of material or energy into water, land or air that causes or may cause short- or long-term damage to the Earth's ecological balance or that lowers the quality of life.

In London, in Dec. 1952, 3,900 deaths in five days were attributed to the high smoke and sulphur-dioxide levels, which caused a **smog**. Smoke can also have an adverse effect on materials and vegetation.

Major sources of **heavy-metals pollution** include mineral and metal processing, manufacturing of inorganic products and large-scale use of coal in power production.

Mexico City has high levels of pollution. ▶

New research shows that **road humps** increase car-exhaust pollution by at least 50% – and worsen petrol consumption, because of the braking and accelerating they encourage.

Oceans also receive all of the pollutants that are fed to them by the rivers of the world. Even when ships are not actively engaged in dumping wastes, they are themselves sources of pollution, most notably the giant tankers that have caused numerous massive oil spills.

Particulate pollution is at its worst at the roadside and the main source is usually the burning of diesel. Estimates of the number of people whose deaths are accelerated by particulates range from 2,000 to 10,000 a year in the UK and 60,000 in the US.

Radiation pollution is any form of radiation that results from human activities. The best-known radiation results from the detonation of nuclear devices and the controlled release of energy by nuclear power generating plants.

Since 1950 it is estimated that humankind has consumed more natural resources – and produced more **pollution** and waste – than in all its previous history.

Smoke has always been the major contributor to the air pollution of cities. Long-term exposure to contaminated air can result in respiratory diseases such as bronchitis and lung cancer. Smoke can also aggravate asthma, bronchitis, emphysema and cardiovascular ailments.

The run-off from animal manures and **silage** is highly damaging when it gets into rivers. Silage effluents are some 200 times more polluting than raw human sewage.

POP ART

Among the leading US Pop Artists are **Roy Lichtenstein**, Claes Oldenburg, James Rosenquist, George Segal, Andy Warhol and Tom Wesselmann. Major British Pop Artists are Peter Blake and Richard Hamilton.

Most prevalent in the US and the UK, **Pop Artists** have appeared in all highly industrialised countries, notably in France, Italy, Japan and Sweden. In the US, Pop Artists have clustered in New York and in California.

Pop Art is indebted to Dada, particularly the collages of **Kurt Schwitters**, the 'readymades' of Marcel Duchamp and the female nudes of Abstract Expressionist Willem de Kooning.

The **images of Pop Art** (shortened from 'popular art') were taken from mass culture. Some artists duplicated beer bottles, soup cans, comic

◀ *210 Coca-Cola Bottles by Pop artist Andy Warhol.*

strips, road signs and similar objects in paintings, collages and sculptures.

The term 'Pop Art' was first used in the 1950s in London by the critic **Lawrence Alloway** to describe works by artists who combined bits and pieces of mass-produced graphic materials to enshrine contemporary cultural values.

POPES

Adrian IV (1154–59) was the only Englishman to hold the office of Pope. The granting of sovereignty over Ireland to Henry II is attributed to him.

Clement VII (1523–34), who refused to sanction Henry VIII's divorce, endured the catastrophic **Sack of Rome** in 1527 and the foundation of the Protestant League.

Gregory I (590–604), after seeing 'angels, not Angles' in a slave market, sent Augustine to England. He introduced Gregorian chant into the liturgy.

Innocent III (1198–1216) asserted papal control over reluctant rulers and states. In 1209 he excommunicated **King John** of England for refusing to accept Stephen

Langton as Archbishop of Canterbury.

John Paul II (1978–), born in Poland, became the first non-Italian Pope in 450 years. He travels widely, often preaching to huge crowds at open-air venues.

Julius II (1503–13) worked to restore papal sovereignty in its ancient territory. A patron of the arts, he commissioned Michelangelo to paint the ceiling of the Sistine Chapel.

Pius VI (1775–99) oversaw the completion of St Peter's Church, Rome. He died a prisoner of the French after his vigorous opposition to the French Revolution.

▲ *Vatican City, the centre of the Roman Catholic faith.*

The first Pope, **St Peter** (AD 42–67) was one of the Twelve Apostles. Tradition holds that he suffered his martyrdom in Rome, possibly by crucifixion.

Urban II (1088–99) inspired the **First Crusade** to the Holy Land in 1095 by his eloquence and passion at the Council of Clermont, France.

PORTUGAL

▲ *The River Tagus in Lisbon.*

An independent kingdom from the 13th c, **Portugal** became a republic on 5 Oct. 1910 when King Manoel II abdicated.

Portugal (capital: Lisbon) is on the western side of the Iberian peninsula, bordering Spain, and has an area of 92,389 sq km/35,672 sq mi.

Portugal exports textiles, clothing, machinery, transport equipment, wines, wood products, cork, footwear and chemicals, mainly to Germany, France, Spain and the UK.

The **population of Portugal** is 10,421,000 (est. 1991), comprising 99% Portuguese, 0.3% Cape Verdean and 0.1% each of Brazilian, Spanish and British.

Under Prince Henry the Navigator (1394–1460), **Portugal** briefly became the world's leading maritime nation, laying claim to half the known world between 1415 and 1550.

POTTERY

Classical Greece reached high standards of vase making and decorating. The two painting techniques were black figure, where the design was in black on red clay, and red figure, with black painting leaving a red relief.

In Europe **tin-glazed ware** was perfected in the 15th–18th c. Italian tin-glazed ware was called *maiolica* and in

French, *faience*. In the Netherlands, they were decorated in Chinese designs and called delft, or delftware.

In the 17th and early 18th c, many potters tried to make hard, translucent **Chinese porcelain**; this was widely imported into Europe, but not made there until *c.* 1707 in Germany.

Islamic cultures developed some **technical achievements** in pottery such as rediscovering the Assyrian technique of tin glaze (9th c) and developing lustre painting (simulating the effect of precious metals).

Josiah **Wedgwood** started his famous factory in Staffordshire, UK, mid-18th c. By 1765 Wedgwood was well known for producing a type of earthenware called creamware that soon replaced tin-glazed ware in popularity.

Porcelain is made by adding feldspar to kaolin and then firing at a high temperature. It was made in China as early as the 9th c, but not by Europeans until the 18th c.

Pottery is one of the oldest and most widespread arts, whereby objects made of clay are hardened with heat. In China pottery has been made since the **Neolithic Period**.

PRAGUE

Inhabited since Paleolithic times, **Prague** emerged in the 10th c as a Slav town. German settlers built the Old Town in the 13th c and the New Town in the 14th c.

Prague is dominated by the 1,000-year-old castle on Hradcany Hill and **St Vitus Cathedral**. Many fine Baroque buildings were added in the 18th c.

Prague is situated on both banks of the **Vltava**, a tributary of the Elbe, facing northward across a fertile plain, with a range of hills to the south.

▲ *A statement of independence in Prague.*

Prague produces foodstuffs, sugar, flour, furniture, glass, leather, heavy machinery, chemicals and electrical goods.

The **population of Prague** is 1,212,010 (1991 census), almost twice the size it was in 1938 when 5% were German. Today it is 99% Czech.

PRE-RAPHAELITE

The Pre-Raphaelites were inspired by medieval and early Renaissance painters up to the time of the Italian painter **Raphael** and influenced by the Nazarenes (1810), who aimed to restore art to medieval purity.

Millais eventually left the Pre-Raphaelites, but other English artists joined, including Edward Coley Burne-Jones and William Morris. The eminent English art critic **John Ruskin** was an ardent supporter of the movement.

The Pre-Raphaelite Brotherhood was established in 1848 by Dante Gabriel Rossetti, John Everett Millais and William Holman Hunt. Other members included William Michael Rossetti, Frederick George Stephens and James Collinson.

The Pre-Raphaelites were a group of 19th-c English painters, poets and critics who reacted against Victorian materialism and the neo-classical conventions of academic art by producing earnest works.

The Pre-Raphaelite painters chose their name because of their belief that Raphael was the source of the academic tradition they abhorred. They felt that art should return to the purer vision of Gothic and Early Renaissance art.

The Pre-Raphaelites looked to the past for **inspiration**, dealing primarily with religious, historical and literary subjects. They painted directly from nature and tried to represent historical events exactly as they might have occurred.

PRINCES

At the Battle of Crécy in 1346 Edward, the **Black Prince** (1330–76), won the three ostrich plumes forming the crest of the Principality of Wales, and the motto *Ich Dien* ('I serve').

Edward VII (1841–1910) was Prince of Wales for most of his life, not acceding to the throne until he was nearly 60. He was related to most of the royal families of Europe.

George IV (1762–1830) was king for only ten years, although he reigned as regent from 1811 while George III was suffering from a mental illness.

Prince Alexander Obolensky (1916–40) came to the UK at the outbreak of the Russian Revolution. After a distinguished career as a Rugby Union player for England he died as a Hurricane pilot in the Battle of Britain in 1940.

Prince Consort was the title conferred upon **Prince Albert** by Queen Victoria in 1857. In terms of precedence it made him first in rank after herself.

Prince Rupert (1619–82), James I's grandson, was a Royalist General during the English Civil War but was defeated by Cromwell at the decisive Battle of Naseby in 1645.

The title **Prince of Wales** was first adopted by David ap Llewelyn in 1244, and in 1301 Edward I conferred it on his eldest son, later to become Edward II.

Two skeletons found in the Tower of London in 1674 are believed to be those of the '**Princes in the Tower**', Edward V (1470–?83) and his brother Richard.

William, Prince of Orange (1533–84), was known as William the Silent. In 1573 he became the leader of the Dutch against the Spanish rule.

▼ *Medieval princes in battle.*

PRINCESSES

Diana, Princess of Wales, (1961–97) married Prince Charles in 1981 but was divorced from him in 1993. She was tragically killed in a road accident in Paris in 1997.

Princess Anne (b. 1950), only daughter of Queen Elizabeth II, was given the title Princess Royal in 1987. An excellent three-day event rider, she represented the UK at the 1976 Olympics.

▼ *Diana, Princess of Wales.*

Princess **Eleanor of Castile** (*c.* 1245–90) married the future Edward I of England in 1254. Edward erected a cross where her funeral cortege stopped, at Charing Cross.

The American film actress Grace Kelly (1929–82), star of such classics as *Rear Window* and *High Society*, became **Princess Grace** when she married Prince Rainier of Monaco in 1956.

The German princess **Anne of Cleves** (1515–57) was married to Henry VIII in 1540 after the death of Jane Seymour, but the marriage was annulled after six months.

PROHIBITION

During national Prohibition of alcohol in the US (1919–33) the gangster **'Scarface' Al Capone** built a $60 m. empire on illegal liquor production.

During the national Prohibition of alcohol in the US (1919–33) producers of illegal liquor were called **bootleggers**.

Establishments selling illegal alcoholic beverages during US Prohibiton (1919–33) were known as **speakeasies**.

Inferior quality illegal liquor produced during the national Prohibition of alcohol in the US (1919–33) was called **bathtub gin**.

The **19th Amendment** to the US Constitution (13 Jan. 1919) prohibited manufacture, sale, transportation, import and export of intoxicating liquors. The Volstead Act implemented the amendment.

The **21st Amendment** to the US Constitution (1933) repealed the 18th (1919) which had implemented the Prohibition of alcohol.

The American **Prohibition** movement to outlaw the manufacture and consumption of alcohol began in the 1840s, culminating in a national law in 1919.

The organisation that most actively championed the national Prohibition of alcoholic beverages in the US was the **Women's Christian Temperance Union** founded in 1873.

QUANTUM PHYSICS

British physicist Paul Dirac worked out a version of **quantum mechanics** which was consistent with Einstein's relativity theories. The existence of the positive electron (positron) was one of his predictions.

Niels Bohr used quantum theory to produce a new model of **atomic structure**, and helped validate the theory by using it to explain the spectrum of light emitted by excited hydrogen atoms.

Quantum electrodynamics is the theory describing the interaction of quarks, the elementary units that make up subatomic particles. It combines quantum theory and relativity to predict physical quantities accurately.

Quantum theory began with the discoveries of **Max Planck** (1900) on radiated energy, and it was he who developed the original theory of the indivisible energy unit, quanta.

▲ *Americans celebrating the end of Prohibition.*

Quantum theory in physics is the theory that energy does not have a continuous range of values; instead it is absorbed or radiated discontinuously in definite, indivisible units called **quanta**.

Quantum theory shows how **atomic particles**, such as electrons, may also be seen to have wave-like properties, as light does.

The theory was extended by the work of **Albert Einstein** to include electromagnetic energy in general, including light. He developed the theory of relative, rather than absolute, character of motion and mass.

QUEENS OF ENGLAND

Elizabeth II (1952–) has seen the British Empire transformed into a Commonwealth of independent nations. She is respected for her grasp of foreign affairs and international politics.

It was during the reign of **Queen Anne** (1702–14) that the parliaments of England and Scotland merged, in 1707.

Mary II (1689–94) reigned jointly with her Dutch husband William of Orange. It was during their reign that the Bank of England was incorporated in 1694.

Matilda (1102–67), the only legitimate child of Henry I, was Queen of England for a few months in 1153 until the throne was seized from her by her cousin Stephen.

Queen Mary (1553–58), daughter of Henry VIII, married Philip II of Spain. Her restoration of Roman Catholicism and subsequent persecution of Protestants earned her the nickname 'Bloody Mary'.

Queen Victoria (1837–1901) became empress of one-fifth of the world's population and two-fifths of its land mass, an empire on which it was said the sun never set.

◄ *Albert Einstein.*

▲ *Queen Elizabeth II of England.*

public steam railway from Stockton to Darlington in 1825.

George Stephenson completed the Liverpool and Manchester railway in 1830. At the same time the **first US-built locomotive** was the *Best Friend of Charleston* in South Carolina.

In the 17th c, **coal mining** in Britain was concentrated in Tyneside and in South Wales. By 1800 each of these areas also had an extensive plateway system using gravity or animal traction for movement.

The **electric train** was first demonstrated in Germany by Werner von Siemens in 1879. The first public electric railway was Volk's Electric Railway along the Brighton seafront, UK.

The first **US transcontinental railway** was built in 1869. It was completed in Promontory, Utah when the Union Pacific and Central Pacific railroads met.

The world's first **underground rail system** was opened in London in 1863. It was powered by steam locomotives but converted to electricity in 1890.

The genius of **Elizabeth I** (1558–1603), second daughter of Henry VIII, lay in her capacity for managing Englishmen. Her fleet defeated the Spanish Armada in 1588.

RAILWAYS

Diesel-electric locomotives appeared in the 1920s. These locomotive units provided up to 5,000 hp, equivalent to all the steam-engine power in the US in 1800.

From Watt's work on the steam engine George Stephenson built the **first**

RAIN

1,870 mm/73 ⅗ in of rain fell on Réunion Island, Indian Ocean, on 15–16 Mar. 1952, a **record for 24 hours**. At this rate, a hectare would receive 3,057 tonnes of rain.

A sprinkling of rain in 1971 broke a 400-year-old **drought** in the Atacama desert, Chile. Cold water currents from the Antarctic cause much fog and cloud but no rain, and mountains bar moist air from the Amazon basin.

Annual mean rainfall on the Pacific coast of Chile between Arica and Antofagasta is less than 0.1 mm/¹⁄₂₅₀ in. This is the **driest place on earth**.

The **amount of rain** that falls each year would be enough to cover the globe with water to an average depth of 1.07 m/3 ft 6 in. Some areas get virtually no rain. Parts of India receive 9–12 m/30–40 ft of rain per year.

The **monsoon** brings torrential rainfall as cool winds move across India in summer. The resulting floods may be devastating but they bring fertility after months of drought.

The record amount of rain in a year, 26,461 mm/1,041 ½ in, fell at Cherrapunji, Meghalaya, India, in 1860–61. The **world's wettest place** on average is in the same state, where 11,873 mm/467 ½ in falls.

There is more **water vapour** in the atmosphere over the Sahara desert than there is over Britain in winter. No rain falls because the warm air can hold more water. Anticyclones above also prevent air from rising and cooling.

▲ *Floods in Bangladesh.*

RAINFORESTS

The upper surface of the rainforest formed by the crowns of trees, the **canopy**, is home to apes, monkeys, birds, snakes, lizards and tree frogs. Some animals never leave the canopy to touch the forest floor.

The most exploited of tropical hardwoods has been **mahogany**. The trees are cut in many areas near water and floated downstream for export or processing.

Nearly a quarter of all **medicines** known in the West have been derived from tropical rainforest plants.

The Environmental Investigation Agency warned (1998) that the world's last 15,000–25,000 **orang-utans** are endangered by logging and farming in their habitat, fertile forested land near rivers, and also by trapping.

Rainforests are found in tropical areas, fairly near to the equator. The **largest rainforest** is the Amazon rainforest. It is bigger than Europe, covering 7 m. sq km/2.7 m. sq mi.

The **rainforests** of the world are in serious danger. Many are being cut down at a frightening rate to clear land for crops or cattle ranching.

The Amazon rainforest contains about 15 times as many different **species of tree** in a given area as would be found in the forests of Europe or North America.

Two main **types of tropical forest** exist: the selvas or equatorial forest, where rainfall is distributed fairly evenly through the year; and the monsoon forest, which has a marked dry season.

Tropical rainforests cover only 8% of the earth's land surface but contain about 50% of all growing wood and 40% of all species of animals and plants.

RECYCLING

Discarded materials contain large quantities of potentially reusable paper, glass, metals and organic material. Intensive campaigns have resulted in increased household participation in waste recycling and much successful recycling has been carried out by **industry**.

New processes of sorting ferrous and non-ferrous metals, paper, glass and plastics have been developed and many communities with recycling programmes now require refuse **separation**.

Recycled **paper**, made by shredding and repulping used paper, is made into newsprint, cardboard boxes, paper bags and other paper products. Processes for recycling paper into copying and computer papers are in development.

Recycling **aluminium** cans saves a huge amount of energy because the raw material is energy-intensive to produce. Some other materials (e.g. products made of mixed plastics and many low grades of paper) are not worth the effort.

Several major types of **plastics** can now be recycled. Plastic foam containers can be used to make such plastic materials as plastic 'lumber', furniture frames and rubbish bins. Certain kinds of plastic soda bottles can be shredded and reformed as a fibre, to be used as fibrefill.

Studies indicate that paper forms more than one-third of the bulk in **city rubbish collections**, with glass, metals and plastics each contributing 7–8%. Many of these products are recyclable. Garden waste (about 20%) and food waste (about 9%) are usually biodegradable.

Waste materials can also be reused in the manufacture of new products. The recovery and reforming of paper, glass and metals are key examples of such recycling.

◄ *Some plastic containers can now be recycled.*

▲ *The Christian festival of Easter celebrates Jesus's rise from the dead.*

RELIGIOUS FESTIVALS

Christmas is perhaps the most widely celebrated festival in the world, marking the birth of Jesus Christ to the Virgin Mary and Joseph the carpenter 2,000 years ago in Bethlehem.

Diwali is the Hindu Festival of Light, marking the New Year, and falls in Oct. Lights are placed in windows to welcome the god Rama home to his kingdom.

Jews celebrate the eight-day festival of **Passover** (*Pesach*) around Apr. It recalls the escape of the Israelites from slavery in Egypt 3,500 years ago.

Some **Sikh festivals** are held on the same day as Hindu festivals, but for Sikhs they commemorate special events in the lives of the Gurus.

The central Christian festival is that of **Easter**, which celebrates the day Jesus Christ rose from the dead, this being the primary belief of the Christian faith.

The Islamic festival of **Ramadan** is a time for daytime fasting as an aid to greater concentration on Allah and the message of the Qur'an.

The most important Jain festival is that of **Pasryushana**, held at the beginning of the monsoon season. For about eight days Jains fast and hold special services.

REPTILES

Snakes are elongate animals without limbs, eyelids or external ears. At least 2,000 species are known worldwide, except for Ireland and New Zealand.

The **American Alligator** (*Alligator mississippiensis*), found in the southern US, grows to a length of 4 m/13 ft, was almost wiped out but is now protected and increasing in numbers.

The **Giant Tortoise** (*Testudo elephantina*) has a shell 1.5 m/4 ft long and weighs up to 300 kg/650 lb. It is found in the Galapagos Islands and Aldabra in the Seychelles.

The **Gila Monster** (*Heloderma suspectum*) of Arizona and New Mexico is the only lizard known to be poisonous. It has a short thick blackish body covered with pink or yellow blotches.

The **Iguana** (*Iguana iguana*) of central America reaches a length of 2 m/6ft 6 in. It haunts trees overhanging water and feeds on leaf shoots and fruit.

The **Komodo Dragon** (*Varanus komodoensis*) of Indonesia is the largest lizard in the world, growing to almost 4 m/12 ft. It feeds on animals including pigs and deer.

The **Tuatara** (*Sphenodon punctatus*) of New Zealand is regarded as a living fossil, being indistinguishable from its Jurassic ancestors.

RETAILING

David Sainsbury, head of the **Sainsbury** retailing family, is reputed to be the richest man in the UK. In 1993, it was estimated that he was worth $2.2 bn.

In 1929 **US department stores** sold more than $4 bn worth of merchandise, an amount equal to 9% of the total retail sales in the US.

In 1990 there were more than 1.5 m. **retail firms in the US** employing more than 19.8 m. people and producing a total sales volume of more than $1.8 trillion.

In the early 1920s independent retailers organised opposition to the competition of chain stores. By 1933, 689 **anti-chain-store bills** had been introduced in 28 states of the US.

The first dry-goods store to become a department store was the **Bon Marché**, established in Paris in 1838. By the 1860s it resembled the modern department store.

Harrods in London's Knightsbridge. ▶

The **Great Atlantic & Pacific Tea Company** increased from 200 to 15,670 outlets, and the J. C. Penney Company stores grew from 14 to 1,459 in just 20 years.

The largest department store in the UK is **Harrods of Knightsbridge**. It has a floor space of 10.5 ha/25 ac, 50 lifts, 36 escalators and employs up to 4,000 staff.

REVOLUTIONS

500,000 are believed to have been killed in Mao's **Cultural Revolution**, which was intended to purify Chinese communism and renew his own political and ideological pre-eminence inside China.

In the **Russian Revolution (Feb. 1917)** the liberal intelligentsia overthrew the Romanov dynasty while the Bolsheviks revived the (Soviet) council state, originally established during the 1905 revolution.

During the **Russian Revolution (Oct. 1917)** Bolshevik workers and sailors under Lenin led a revolt against Kerensky's government in the Winter Palace and took power.

Support for Chairman Mao in China. ▶

Mao–Zedong initiated the Cultural Revolution against the Chinese upper-middle class of bureaucrats, artists and academics, who were killed, imprisoned, humiliated or 'resettled' (1966–69).

The **Manchu dynasty** which ruled China since 1644 was overthrown in a revolt on 10 Oct. 1911 organised by the Kuomintang under Sun Yat-sen.

The **revolutions of 1989** were popular uprisings in many Eastern European countries against communist rule, triggered by Gorbachev's policies of *glasnost*, *perestroika* and other Soviet reforms.

The **Russian Revolution (1905)** was triggered by Tsar Nicholas II's refusal to grant liberal concessions on his accession (1894) together with distress among peasants and industrial workers.

RIVERS

Every year the **Mississippi** deposits on to its delta about 140 m. tonnes of dissolved minerals, 400 m. tonnes of sand and silt and 60 m. tonnes of rock material that has been rolled along the bottom.

In 1869 Maj. John Wesley Powell, a one-armed American naturalist, led an expedition down the **Colorado River** from southern Wyoming to the Grand Canyon, studying the behaviour of the river and the landscape it had created.

It is estimated that the Mississippi River and its tributaries sweep more than 440 m. tonnes of boulders and **sediment** into the sea each year.

Large rivers in their lower course usually occupy broad, shallow valleys. The lower Amazon has a **floodplain** (where the river has overflowed its banks and spread alluvium) nearly 50 km/30 mi wide.

The Arab philosopher and physician Avicenna suggested, nearly 1,000 years ago, that landscapes changed largely as a result of the action of **running water**. His views were ignored until early 16th c.

The Hwang he or **Yellow River** of northern China carries an enormous amount of alluvium (sediment), consisting largely of a fine soil called loess. This is yellowish, hence the river's name.

The Nile, 6,695 km/4,184 mi, and the Amazon, 6,437 km/4,023 mi, are the two **longest rivers** in the world. Measurements of their lengths vary according to the criteria selected.

Where the land is rising, a river may cut a channel right through a mountain range instead of going round

▲ *The River Danube, which runs through Budapest.*

it. A spectacular example is the **Indus River** in the Himalayas, which has cut through 5,200 m/17,000 ft of rock.

William Morris Davis postulated a **cycle of erosion**, which created 'young', 'mature' and 'old' landscapes. The final stage was the peneplain, where a sluggish river winds across barely raised land.

ROCK 'N' ROLL

Chuck Berry (b. 1926), singer-guitarist is a prolific songwriter and founding father of R&B and rock 'n' roll. His characteristic double-string guitar licks and sly, witty, story-telling lyrics (especially the 40-odd songs recorded from the mid to late 1950s) were a huge influence on rock.

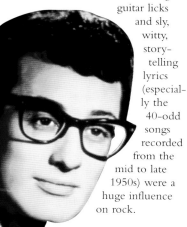

Origination of the term 'rock 'n' roll' is credited to **Alan Freed** (1922–65), radio DJ at WINS (New York, 1954, fired in 1959's payola scandal, though innocent) who cameoed in early rock movies like *Rock Around the Clock* (1956).

Buddy Holly (1936–59), singer, guitarist, songwriter, rock 'n' roll pioneer, who died in a plane crash, had a distinctive C&W-tinged 'hiccuping' vocal style and experimented with recording techniques in classic hits with The Crickets (e.g. *Peggy Sue*, 1957).

Little Richard's no-holds-barred style, howling in wild falsetto and pounding piano, is at the heart of rock 'n' roll. At the height his of success (1957) he quit to become a minister. Ironically, as McCartney's idol, he tried resurrecting his career during Beatlemania (1964), making comebacks ever since.

Elvis Presley (1935–77) was the most influential performer of the era. Following legendary early recordings with Moore and Black for Sun's Sam Phillips (1954–55) he became a nationwide star after Parker became his manager and RCA purchased his Sun contract.

◄ *Original rock 'n' roll icon Buddy Holly.*

ROADS

Asphalt is a mixture of bitumen and stone. In 1824 asphalt blocks were placed on the Champs-Élysées in Paris. The first successful major application was 1858 on the nearby rue Saint-Honoré.

Concrete is a mixture of cement and stone. The first modern concrete roads were produced by Joseph Mitchell who conducted three successful trials in England and Scotland, 1865–66.

The **earliest roads** developed from the paths of prehistoric peoples; construction was concurrent with development of wheeled vehicles, probably in the area between the Caucasus Mountains and the Persian Gulf *c.* 3000 BC.

The **first major road** was the Persian Royal Road, from the Persian Gulf to the Aegean Sea, a distance of 2,857 km/1,775 mi and used *c.* 3500–300 BC.

The initial impetus for renewed **road building** was not the car, whose impact was not felt before 1900, but the bicycle, and road improvement began in many countries during the 1880s and '90s.

The **Romans** recognised the importance of roads in empire building; at the empire's peak it had 85,000 km/53,000 mi of road, from Britain in the north to North Africa in the south.

The world's first **motorway** was built from Cologne to Bonn (1929–32). In 1933 Adolf Hitler began construction of a motorway network, the *Reichsautobahnen* (national motor roads), beginning with the Frankfurt-Darmstadt-Mannheim-Heidelberg Autobahn.

◄ *Example of a Roman road.*

ROMANIA

Romania (capital: Bucharest) lies in south-east Europe on the Black Sea and is bordered by Moldova, Hungary, Serbia and Bulgaria, with an area of 237,500 sq km/91,699 sq mi.

Romania exports machinery and transport equipment, chemicals and mineral fuels, mainly to Russia, Germany, Iran, the Czech Republic and China.

The Danubian principalities of Moldavia and Walachia declared their independence from Turkey in 1877 under the name of **Romania**, becoming a kingdom under Carol I in 1881.

The **population of Romania** is 23,247,000 (est. 1991), comprising 88.1% Romanian, 7.9% Magyar, 1.6% German, 1.1% Gypsy and 1.3% other.

Vlad Tepes the Impaler, 15th c Voivode of Wallachia, was the real-life inspiration for Bram Stoker's *Dracula* and is now a leading tourist attraction in **Romania**.

ROMANTICISM

German Romantic painting was inspired by a conception of nature as a manifestation of the divine (**symbolic landscape**), and the greatest German romantic painter was Caspar David Friedrich (*Polar Sea*, 1824).

In France the formative stage of Romanticism coincided with the **Napoleonic Wars** (1799–1815) and the first French romantic painters found their inspiration in contemporary events.

Outstanding **Romantic water-colourists** included John Robert Cozens and Thomas Girtin, as well as the greatest painters of the age, John Constable and J. M. W. Turner.

Romanticism cannot be identified with a single style, technique, or attitude, but Romantic painting is characterised by a highly imaginative and subjective approach, emotional intensity and a dream-like quality.

Theodore Gericault (*The Raft of Medusa*, 1819) strongly influenced Eugene Delacroix, whose canvases on historical and literary subjects (*The Death of Sardanapalus*, 1827–28), epitomise the notion of Romantic art.

feeling and clear in expression, **Romantic art** strives to express by suggestion states of feeling too intense, mystical or elusive to be clearly defined.

ROME

To some extent the story of Romantic art is found in the accelerating prestige of **landscape painting**, which rose to pre-eminence *c.* 1750–1850.

Rome includes the Vatican City State (109 ac), under the temporal rule of the Pope since 1929 and including St Peter's Basilica.

Toward the middle of the 19th c Romantic painting moved away from the intensity of the original movement. Late Romanticism included the quiet, atmospheric landscapes of the French **Barbizon school** (Corot and Rousseau).

Rome is the administrative and financial centre of Italy, but a wide range of light industries, from film-making to food-processing, are now carried on there.

Rome was built on seven hills on the east bank of the Tiber 28 km/17 mi northeast from its mouth on the Mediterranean Sea, but now spreads over the Latin plain.

While Classical and Neo-classical art is calm and restrained in

▲ *Early Roman coins.*

The **population of Rome** is 2,803,931 (1990 census), more than double the pre-war peak of 1,279,748.

Traditionally **Rome** was founded in 753 BC by Romulus, previously being an Etruscan settlement in 1000 BC. It became the capital of Italy in 1870.

RUGBY

During a football match at Rugby School in Nov. 1823, William Webb Ellis picked up the ball and ran with it. Thus **Rugby Football** was born.

The first player to win **one hundred Rugby international caps** is Philippe Sella (France), who took his total to 111 before his retirement from international rugby in 1995.

The Rugby Football Union (RFU) introduced a knockout competition in 1971–72 sponsored by John Player; Pilkington took over from 1988–89. **Bath** have achieved a record 10 outright wins.

The Rugby Football Union purchased a 12-ac market garden in south-west London for £5,500 with plans to build a new stadium. That's why **Twickenham** is affectionately known as 'the cabbage patch'!

The **Rugby League** was formed in 1895 when the strictly amateur Rugby Union refused players permission to receive payment for loss of wages. The League switched to 13-a-side in 1906.

Wigan have won the Rugby League Challenge Cup a record 16 times, including eight successive victories from 1988 to 1995.

RUSSIA

Formerly the largest republic in the USSR, **Russia** became a separate federation on 1 Jan. 1992 under President Boris Yeltsin.

Lake Ladoga in northern **Russia** is the largest lake in Europe, with an area of 7,200 sq mi. It drains through the River Neva into the Baltic Sea.

Russia (capital: Moscow) extends across northern Europe and Asia, the largest country in the world with an area of 17,075,400 sq km/6,592,800 sq mi.

Russia exports petroleum, natural gas, electricity, chemicals, fertilisers, cereals, wood and paper products, textiles and clothing.

The **population of Russia** is 148,542,700 (est. 1991), comprising 80% Russians and 20% mainly Asiatic peoples.

SAINTS

Antony of Padua (1195–1231) was a charismatic Portuguese preacher who as a monk in Italy reputedly worked miracles. He is invoked to find lost property.

▲ *The martyrdom of St Peter.*

Jude, one of the twelve apostles, is the patron saint of lost causes. He is usually depicted holding an oar and an anchor, perhaps alluding to his early life as a fisherman.

St Christopher is invoked by travellers because he is said to have carried the Christ child on his shoulders across a river ('Christopher' means 'Christ bearer').

St Elmo is the patron saint of sailors, and the bluish electrical discharge seen flickering round a ship's mast before a storm is a sign that the ship is under his protection.

St Patrick (*c.* AD 390–461), the patron saint of Ireland, is said to have explained the Trinity by reference to the shamrock, and to have expelled all snakes from Ireland.

St Peter's name was Simon, but Jesus called him Peter, meaning 'rock', for his steadfast qualities. He is depicted with the keys to the Kingdom of Heaven.

The patron saint of love, **St Valentine**, is associated with birds and with roses. His feast day, 14 Feb., has become a major commercial industry.

SATELLITES

A **satellite** is any small body that orbits a larger one. Artificial satellites are used for scientific, communication, weather-forecasting and military purposes.

At any time there are several thousand **artificial satellites** orbiting some defunct artificial satellites and discarded parts of rockets. They eventually re-enter the Earth's atmosphere.

On re-entry they usually burn up by friction but some, like *Skylab* and *Salyut 7* fall through and hit the Earth's surface.

Many astronomical observations now take place above our atmosphere by satellite. The **IRAS** (Infrared Astronomical Satellite, 1983) made a complete infrared survey of the skies.

Since 1962 satellites have been used to beam TV pictures around the world. In the UK direct broadcasting to people's homes was launched by **Sky** in 1989.

The first artificial satellite launched around the Earth was *Sputnik I* by the USSR, 4 Oct. 1957. It weighed 84 kg/185 lbs and carried only a simple radio transmitter.

The US Global Positioning System uses 24 **Navstar** satellites that enable users, including walkers and motorists, to find their position to within 100 m/328 ft.

SATURN

Saturn has a small **core** of rock and iron, encased in ice with a deep layer of liquid hydrogen above. Like Jupiter its visible surface is made of swirling clouds which are probably frozen ammonia.

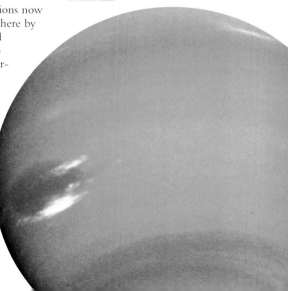

Saturn is the **second largest** planet in the solar system, sixth from the Sun and encircled by equatorial rings, bright and easily visible from Earth.

Saturn orbits the Sun every 29.46 years at an average distance of 1,427,000,000 km/886,700,000 mi. It spins on its axis approx. every 10 hr 14 min.

Saturn's equatorial **diameter** is 120,000 km/75,000 mi, but its polar diameter is 12,000 km/7,450 mi smaller because of its fast rotation and low density (the lowest of any planet).

Saturn's rings are made of small chunks of ice and rock averaging 1 m/3 ft across. *Voyager* showed that these are actually thousands of closely spaced ringlets, like the grooves of a record.

Saturn's rings visible from Earth start at 14,000 km/9,000 mi from the planet's cloud tops, reaching out to about 76,000 km/47,000 mi.

The space probes *Voyager 1* **and** *2* found winds reaching 1,800 kph/1,100 mph, and found more than 20 small moons orbiting Saturn, the largest being Titan.

SAUDI ARABIA

Formerly the heart of a great Arab empire, **Saudi Arabia** was formed in 1932 by Ibn Saud from the Hejaz and Nejd which he had taken from the Turks between 1901 and 1925.

Saudi Arabia (capital: Riyadh) occupies most of the Arabian peninsula, with an area of 2,240,000 sq km/865,000 sq mi.

▼ *An Arabian prince.*

Saudi Arabia contains two of the holiest places in Islam, Mecca, the birthplace of Mohammed (*c.* 569–632), and Medina, whither the prophet fled in 622 and where he is buried.

Saudi Arabia exports crude and refined petroleum and petroleum products and a wide range of manufactured goods.

The **population of Saudi Arabia** is 14,691,000 (est.1991), comprising 82% Saudi, 9.6% Yemeni, 3.4% other Arab and 5% other.

SCHOOL SYSTEMS

After the 1917 revolution, primary and secondary education were made compulsory in the USSR. Today, 10 years of schooling are obligatory, but many students drop out before completing **secondary school**.

British schools, colleges and universities, like those in most European countries, are financed almost entirely by **public funds**, either from the central government in London or from local education authorities.

Formal control of American public schools is held by state government. The powers of **local school boards** are, in all states, derived from state powers by the delegation of state governments.

German education operates on a three-track pattern. After four years (ages 6–10) of compulsory primary school, students either attend a *Gymnasium* (academic secondary school), *Realschule* (general high school) or *Hauptschule* (general school).

In France higher education is free to qualified students. Nearly 1 m. students continue their studies after secondary school in 72 universities and in technological institutes and *grandes écoles*.

In most parts of the UK the old grammar and secondary modern schools have been replaced by **comprehensive secondary schools** that all children in the district attend, a change initiated by the Labour government in 1966.

Nearly all developed countries provide public – **primary education** and require attendance. About three-quarters of the world's 6- to 11-year-old children attend school.

Public education in Canada is the responsibility of the individual provinces. The federal government's role is restricted to providing for the education of children of native peoples and members of the armed forces.

The **British education system** is conventionally described as 'a national system locally administered'. It is a partnership between the central government (the Department of Education) and the 104 local education authorities.

The Spanish school system provides for optional pre-school education and 8 years of **compulsory education** (age 6). Education is free in state-run schools, which offer a primary programme (5 years) and a secondary programme (3 years).

The US has about 5,300 **public school districts**, a number that is dropping as small districts merge. More than 50% of the districts enrol fewer than 1,000 students.

SCIENTIFIC THEORIES

Charles Darwin (1859) assigned the major role in evolutionary change to **natural selection** acting on randomly occurring variations (now known to be by genetic change or mutation).

In 1949 Francis Crick and James Watson began to research the molecular structure of **DNA**. Their theory that the molecule was two strands wrapped around each other in a spiral or helix was proved in the 1950s.

Newton's theory of **gravity** (1684) was that all objects fall to Earth with the same acceleration regardless of mass. At the Earth's surface this force is 9.806 metres per second.

◄ *Charles Darwin invented the 'survival of the fittest' theory.*

Planck's constant (1901) (h) is the energy of one quantum of electromagnetic radiation divided by the frequency of its radiation. In 1912 he extended his quantum theory to all kinds of energy.

The **big-bang theory**, developed by George Gamow in the 1940s, postulates that the universe emerged from a state of extremely high temperature and density. The theory changed the way we understood the universe.

The theory of **relativity** was developed by Albert Einstein. It is the theory of relative, rather than absolute, character of motion and mass and the interdependence of matter, time and space.

The theory of **splitting the atom** was researched in the UK in 1940, but was not achieved until the work of Oppenheimer in 1945. It had far-reaching consequences with the atom bomb and nuclear energy.

SCREEN ACTORS GUILD

The American **Screen Actors Guild** began with clandestine meetings of a group of character actors seeking benefits and better treatment in the 1930s.

The American Screen Actors Guild employs 200 in **20 branches** around the country to serve actors.

The American Screen Actors Guild works to **guarantee a living wage** and a safe, supportive working environment through self-government and collective bargaining with producers.

The American Screen Actors Guild's first home was at the Hollywood Center Building in a one-room second-floor office with room for **just one desk**.

US screen star Humphrey Bogart. ▶

SEAS

During part of the Pleistocene Epoch, the present floor of the **Arafura Sea** was partly above sea level, forming a land bridge between south-east Asia and Australia.

For over 50 m. years the earth's crust has been tearing along the **Red Sea** zone. The sea itself formed 20 m. years ago and is an ocean in the making.

In 1928 Herman Sörgel of Germany proposed **Project Atlantropa**. Dams with hydroelectric power plants would block each end of the Mediterranean; the sea would shrink and much land could be reclaimed.

In 1986 Dutch researchers proved the Weddell Sea off Antarctica to be the world's **clearest sea**. They could see a 30-cm/1-ft white disc at a depth of 80 m/262 ft.

Storms are frequent in the **Baltic Sea** (northern Europe). In Sept. 1994 some 1,000 people were drowned when the ferry *Estonia* sank in a gale off the Finnish coast.

The Dead Sea (Israel/Jordan) contains the world's **saltiest water**. Bacteria are its only form of animal life. The density of the water makes floating easy but swimming impossible.

The **Inland Sea**, Japan, between Honshu and Shikoku and Kyushu islands, is navigable and noted for its fisheries and its numerous picturesque islands.

The **largest sea** in the world is the South China Sea, which covers an area of 2,974,600 sq km/1,148,500 sq mi.

The **Mediterranean Sea**, known to the Romans as *Mare Nostrum* ('our sea'), is almost land-locked but of great economic and political importance. It is a remnant of a vast ancient sea called Tethys.

◀ *The Black Sea in Romania.*

The Mediterranean, Black, Caspian and Aral seas are the remains of the vast **Tethys Ocean** that once separated the supercontinent of Gondwanaland in the south from that of Laurasia in the north.

The **Sea of Marmara** (Marmora) separates the European part of Turkey from the Asian part. It contains several islands on which there are quarries of white marble, the largest being Marmara.

SEISMOLOGY

A **seismograph** records earthquake waves. These pass through different kinds of bedrock, for example shale and basalt, at different speeds. They also change direction passing from one material to another.

Earthquakes happen because rocks that have been under great stress reach breaking point and make sudden jerking movements along faults (cracks in the rocks).

In 1692 an earthquake submerged and shattered **Port Royal** in Jamaica. Divers using airlifts (underwater 'vacuum cleaners') have sucked up thousands of everyday clay, glass and iron objects from the period.

The ancient Indians believed that the world was held up by a giant elephant. When he shook his head he caused an **earthquake**.

The earthquake with the highest **death toll** occurred in the Shaanxi, Shanxi and Henan provinces of China in 1556. It is estimated that 830,000 people died.

The **Kanto earthquake** (Japan) of 1923 caused the most physical damage done by any earthquake. It destroyed about 575,000 houses. A whirlwind swept flames over a wide area.

The place from which earthquake shock waves radiate is called the focus or origin. The point directly above this on the earth's surface is the **epicentre**.

There is a severe earthquake somewhere in the world every two weeks. Most earthquakes happen under the sea. They are measured on the **Kanamori scale.**

SEMINOLE

The **Seminole** are a Native American people of the Hokan-Siouan geographical linguistic group.

Most Seminole relocated to Oklahoma. Those remaining in the Florida swamps were forced to eke out a **living from tourism**.

The Eastern Woodlands Seminole **fled to Florida** where they absorbed remnants of the Apalachee and fought the US until 1842.

The **Stomp Dance** and Green Corn Dance figure prominently in Seminole religious life.

Today **fourteen bands** of Seminole live in Oklahoma with additional tribesmen in Florida.

SHIPBUILDING

By Greek and **Roman times** the rowing galley was powered by as many as three tiers of rowers. To reduce the space taken up by rowers, designers started to rely on sails for initial propulsion.

English engineer Charles Parsons demonstrated the first successful **steam turbine** in 1884. Turbines were more efficient and easier to build than reciprocating steam engines.

Remains of an ancient Egyptian ship. ▶

In the mid-19th c sailing ships reached their peak with the sleek, swift **clipper ship**, but by the end of the century steam power had almost completely replaced sails.

Scottish engineer William Symington developed a **practical steamboat** for towing barges on the Forth and Clyde Canal, Scotland in 1802. In 1807 Robert Fulton successfully demonstrated his steamboat on the Hudson River.

The earliest knowledge of ships comes from Egyptian rock drawings of 6000 BC. These show crescent-shaped **reed boats**; these were rowed, but later sails were added.

The first **all-iron ship** was built in 1818. The hull was formed of iron plates riveted to each other, braced by iron ribs. In 1880 steel began to replace iron.

The **Vikings** used double-ended fighting galleys. These ships had a high bow and stern, a strong hull of clinker construction (overlapping planks), and a single, large, reinforced square sail.

SHIPS

It is probable that the **Phoenician** ships, by 500 BC, were already constructed much as the wooden sailing vessels of later centuries were.

Ocean-going ships vary greatly in size. Fishing vessels may be less than 30 m/100 ft in length; ocean liners and tankers may exceed 300 m/1,000 ft. An average merchantman might be 150 m/500 ft in length.

The **early Egyptians** built their ships by lashing and sewing together small pieces of wood. Such ships could transport great columns of stone, weighing up to 350 tonnes.

The first commercially successful **steamer** was Robert Fulton's *North River Steamboat* of 1807. It is better known today as the *Clermont*, after its home port of Clermont, NY.

The first **ocean-going steamship**, the *Savannah*, crossed the Atlantic to Liverpool in 1819. By the 1840s vessels were crossing the Atlantic entirely by steam power.

The *Great Britain*, built by W. Patterson in 1843, was the first **screw-propelled ship** to cross the Atlantic, and also the first iron-hulled ship to do so. She remained in service until 1886.

The **Suez Canal** opened in 1869, bypassing the long voyage around Africa on routes between Europe and Asia. The Panama Canal, opened in 1914, bypassed the voyage around South America.

SHRUBS

According to Arab tradition **Coffee** was discovered by Kaldi, a goatherd about 850, puzzled at the euphoric antics of his animals after eating some berries.

Lavender (*Lavendula spica*) is a native of the mountains of Spain. It is an evergreen shrub introduced to England in 1568 and grown for its essential oil.

Rosemary (*Rosmarinus officinalis*) is a low shrub, indigenous to the Mediterranean area. It is esteemed for its aromatic qualities and its oil is used in perfume.

Shrubs are low-growing, usually multi-stemmed, woody plants arising at or close to ground level, generally with close-knit foliage.

Tea is a small shrub cultivated in India and the Far East, the dried leaves or leaf-buds being brewed as a drink. It was first mentioned by Kuo P'o in AD 350.

The **Common Laurel** (*Prunus laurocerasus*) is a shrub introduced to Europe from Turkey in 1576 and much prized for its glossy leaves, often used as a flavouring.

Wild Thyme (*Thymus praecox*) is a fragrant shrub forming a dense carpet on grassy banks and sand dunes all over the UK. It contains an essence from which thymol is produced.

SIKHISM

All Sikh men have the surname *Singh* (lion) and all Sikh women the surname *Kaur* (princess). Sikhs must refrain from stimulants and from gambling.

Guru Nanak's poems and writings were collected by Angad, the second Guru, and the first authoritative version of the scriptures, the *Adi Granth*, was completed by the fifth Guru.

Sikh men must wear the five **symbols** of their faith: the *kesh* (uncut hair); *kangha* (comb); *kara* (steel wristband); *kirpan* (miniature sword); and *kach* (shorts).

Sikhs worship at a temple called a *gurdwara*, which means 'door of the guru'. The best-known and most holy is the **Golden Temple** at Amritsar in India.

The founder of Sikhism was **Nanak**, born in the Punjab in 1469. He taught that all religions are the way to the same God and all should be respected.

The Sikh community is referred to as the *Guru Panth* and spiritual guidance is provided by the holy scriptures of the *Guru Granth Sahib*.

Today many Sikhs live outside their native Punjab, the majority in the UK but some in the US, Canada and Africa, where **communities** try to maintain their culture and traditions.

▼ *The Golden Temple at Amritsar.*

SINGAPORE

Founded in 1819 by Stamford Raffles, **Singapore** became one of the Straits Settlements in 1826, a separate crown colony in 1946 and a republic on 9 Aug. 1965.

Regarded as impregnable, the great British military and naval base of **Singapore** fell to the Japanese on 15 Feb. 1942 and was renamed by them *Shonan* ('light of the south').

Singapore exports office equipment, petroleum products, telecommunications equipment, clothing, scientific and optical instruments, industrial machinery and crude rubber.

▲ *The centre of Singapore*

Singapore is an island city, off the southern tip of the Malay peninsula, with an area of 622 sq km/240 sq mi.

The **population of Singapore** is 2,719,000 (est. 1991), comprising 77.7% Chinese, 14.1% Malay, 7.1% Indian and 1.1% other.

SIOUX

After moving to North Dakota (1867), the Sioux under **Sitting Bull and Crazy Horse** resisted white encroachment, slaughtering the 7th Cavalry at Little Big Horn (1876).

Feather headdresses, deerskin clothing, beaded bags and teepee covers depicting the dweller's dreams characterise Sioux culture.

In 1979 the Sioux were awarded **$105 m. for their land**, ending a suit that began in 1923. Today the Sioux are mostly farmers and ranchers.

The **Sioux** are a Native American people of the Hokan-Siouan geographical linguistic group.

The Sioux revered **Bear Butte**, a magma formation near Sturgis, North Dakota.

SNOOKER

In 1985 the **highest British audience for a televised sporting event**, 18.5 m., tuned in to watch Dennis Taylor defeat Steve Davis 18–17 in a gripping World Snooker Championship Final.

Snooker originated in India; the first recorded example was at Jubbulpore in 1875 in a game involving British army officers. The word 'snooker' meant a mild rebuke over a missed shot.

The **fastest 147 maximum break** took just 5 minutes 20 seconds and was achieved by Ronnie O'Sullivan at the 1997 World Professional Championships at the Crucible, Sheffield.

The **women's World Snooker Professional Championship** was first held in 1976 and Alison Fisher (England), with seven titles, has been the most successful competitor.

The **World Snooker Professional Championship** was instituted in 1927 and Joe Davis (England) won the first 16 titles.

The **youngest winner of the World Snooker Professional Championship** is Stephen Hendry (Scotland) who was aged 21 years and 106 days when he won the title in 1990.

SNOW

In Norway, enormous **snow-clearing machines** remove heavy falls of snow. Such machines are too expensive to be economical in the UK, where they would be used perhaps once in 10 years.

Snow and **hail** fall when the air temperature between the cloud and the ground is too low to melt the ice crystals. Snow usually falls from layer clouds, hail from convectional clouds.

Snow is transparent, but reflection from the many sides of its crystals makes it look white. Snow crystals are beautiful, symmetrical hexagons. Snowflakes are collections of partly melted crystals.

Snowfall is usually measured as depth of newly fallen snow. Another measure is the depth of the water that the snow would produce when it melts: 25-30 cm/10-12 in of snow melts to 2.5 cm/1 in of water.

The eruption of Mt St Helens, Washington, US, in 1980 triggered an **avalanche** estimated to contain 2,800 m. cu m/96,000 m. cu ft and to travel at 400 kph/250 mph.

The **greatest snowfall** within 24 hours occurred at Silver Lake, Colorado, US,

when 193 cm/6 ft 4 in was recorded between 14 and 15 Apr. 1921.

SOCIAL CLASSES

A **social class** is a category of people of similar socio-economic status. All societies larger than non-literate tribes are characterised by an unequal distribution of material goods, prestige or honour and power over others.

Aristocracy denotes a group that is superior in wealth, power or intellect. Modern political aristocracies have included the British landed gentry (19th c), French nobility (lost power 1789) and Russian nobility (who clung to power until 1917).

Bourgeoisie ('town dwellers') is a French word originally denoting the class of people between the aristocracy and the peasants. Later, the distinction between the bourgeoisie (employers) and the proletariat (employees) became fundamental to Marxism.

In **caste** systems society is divided into a series of groups recruited by birth: marriage is generally restricted to other members of the same caste, castes are associated with occupational specialisations, and their order is linked to a moral order that dictates codes of behaviour.

In **non-capitalist** or state-socialist societies the upper class comprises the political elite and industrial managers; lower non-manual workers form a middle class; manual workers are below them; and a large peasant population is at the bottom.

Social mobility reflects the movement of groups and individuals up and down the social scale. The extent of social mobility varies in different societies. The caste system, for example, is a 'closed society'.

Sociologists identify four main classes in industrialised societies: an **upper class** of owners, managers and top officials; a middle class of nonmanual white-collar workers; a manual working class; and a lower class of the irregularly employed and rural poor.

SOLAR POWER

A growing application of **solar cells** is in consumer **products**, such as calculators and portable radios. Solar cells used in these devices may utilise indoor artificial light as well as sunlight.

A **solar cell** is an electronic device which converts the energy in light into electrical energy by the process of photovoltaics. There are no chemical reactions and no moving parts.

Charles Fritts constructed the **first true solar cells** (1890s). He coated the semiconductor selenium with an ultra-thin layer of gold. Less than 1% of the absorbed light energy was converted into electrical energy.

In 1989 a concentrator solar cell, one where sunlight is concentrated on to the cell surface by lenses, achieved an **efficiency** of 37% due to the increased intensity of the collected energy.

▲ *Solar-powered car.*

Solar cells can be arranged into large groupings called arrays. These arrays may be composed of many thousands of individual cells, functioning as central electric power stations.

The **silicon solar cell** was developed by Russell Ohl in 1941. In 1954 three other American researchers, G. Pearson, Daryl Chapin and Calvin Fuller, demonstrated a cell capable of a 6% energy-conversion in direct sunlight.

The **solar cell was developed** by French physicist Antoine-César Becquerel in 1839. He discovered the photovoltaic effect while experimenting with solid electrodes in electrolyte solution, finding that voltage developed when light fell upon the electrodes.

SOLAR SYSTEM

If the Sun was basketball size, the closest planet, **Mercury**, would be the size of a mustard seed 15 m/48 ft away from it.

If the Sun was basketball size, the farthest planet, **Pluto**, would be a pinhead 1.6 km/1 mi from the Sun.

The **Earth** on the same scale (Sun as a basketball) would be pea-sized 32 m/100 ft away from the Sun.

The nearest star to our solar system is called **Alpha Centauri**, positioned 4.3 light years away from the Sun.

The **solar system** consists of the Sun and all the bodies orbiting it; the nine planets (Mercury, Venus, Earth, Mars, Jupiter, Saturn, Uranus, Neptune, Pluto), their moons, the asteroids and comets.

The **solar system** is thought to have formed about 4.6 bn years ago from a cloud of gas and dust in space.

The **Sun** contains 99% of the mass of the solar system. The edge is not clearly defined but is marked by the limit of the Sun's gravitational influence (1.5 light years).

SOLOMON ISLANDS

Discovered by Alvaro de Mendana in 1567, the **Solomon Islands** became German and British protectorates in 1885 and 1893. On 7 Jul. 1978 they became an independent Commonwealth member.

The **population of the Solomon Islands** is 328,000 (est. 1991), comprising 94.2% Melanesian, 3.7% Polynesian, 1.4% other Pacific islanders and 0.7% other.

The Solomon Islands. ▶

The **Solomon Islands (capital: Honiara)** are in the south-western Pacific east of New Guinea, with an area of 28,370 sq km/10,954 sq mi.

The **Solomon Islands export** timber, fish products, palm oil, cocoa beans, copra, sea shells and coconut oil, mainly to Japan, the UK, Australia and the Netherlands.

The **Solomon Islands** were the farthest point of the south-west Pacific reached by the Japanese in World War II; the Japanese were checked by US forces in Aug. 1942.

SOUND

All **sound waves** travel in air at a speed that varies with temperature; under normal conditions this is about 330 m/1,070 ft per second.

Sound is heard by the ear by vibration of the **ear drum**, which passes the vibration through to the inner ear and on to the auditory nerves: the three smallest bones in the body are responsible for passing on the vibration.

Sound is the physical sensation received by the air of vibrations caused by pressure variations in the air. It travels in every direction spreading out from the cause as a sphere.

The ability to hear quite **low notes** varies very little with age, but the upper range falls steadily from adolescence onwards.

The **lowest note** audible to the human ear has a frequency of about 20 Hz

(vibrations per second). The highest note is about 15,000 Hz.

The **pitch** of a sound depends on the number of air vibrations per second, but the speed is unaffected by this. The loudness is mostly dependent on the amplitude of air vibration.

The **sound barrier** was the concept that the speed of sound or sonic speed, about 1,220 kph/760 mph at sea level, was a speed limit to flight through the atmosphere. Nowadays planes like Concorde fly at supersonic speed.

SOUTH AFRICA

South Africa (capital: Pretoria) is situated at the southern tip of Africa, bordering Namibia, Botswana and Mozambique, with an area of 1,123,226 sq km/433,680 sq mi.

South Africa exports gold, platinum, precious stones, diamonds, foodstuffs, tobacco, wool and chemicals, mainly to the US, Japan, Italy, Germany and UK.

The discovery of gold at Witwatersrand in 1886 triggered off a gold rush swamping **South Africa** with foreigners whose grievances led to the Boer War.

The **population of South Africa** is 31,394,000 (est. 1991), comprising 23.8% Zulu, 18% North Sotho, 9.7% Xhosa, 7.3% South Sotho, 5.7% Tswana, 11.9% black, 18% white, 10.5% coloured and 3.3% Asian.

The Union of **South Africa**, formed in 1910, became a republic on 31 May 1961 and left the Commonwealth that Oct., but rejoined on 1 Jun. 1994 under Nelson Mandela.

SOUTH AMERICA

Ancient **metamorphic rocks** form the Brazil and Guyanese highlands in northern South America, 610–1,520 m/2,000–5,000 ft above sea level. The Andes, volcanic fold mountains, form the western section of the continent.

In the zoogeographical classification, South America belongs to the **Neotropical Realm**, typified by llamas and anteaters.

South America has an **area** of 17,611,000 sq km/6,798,000 sq mi. It occupies 3.5% of the world's total surface area and 12.1% of the total land area.

South America straddles the equator and extends southwards almost to the Antarctic Circle. The **continental plate** on which it sits continues to South Georgia and the South Sandwich Islands.

▲ *Mixed bathing beach in South Africa.*

The **first settlers** arrived in South America from North and Central America via the Caribbean islands about 20,000 years ago. Europeans arrived at the end of the 15th c.

The **highest** point in South America is Aconcagua, Peru, 6,960 m/22,834 ft; and the **lowest point** is the Valdez peninsula, Chile, 40 m/131 ft below sea level.

There are three main **lowland areas** in South America: the Orinoco River plain, the Amazon Basin and the Pampa-Chaco plain of the south. These contain some gigantic rivers, including the Amazon.

SPACE EXPLORATION

By the 1930s Germany was conducting extensive research on rocket propulsion which led to developing the **V-2 guided missile**. German immigrants worked with US and USSR scientists to develop the ideas further.

In 1976 the **US *Viking* landers** made successful descents to the surface of Mars, where they transmitted detailed colour images of the planet and made *in situ* analyses of soil and atmosphere.

On 4 Oct. 1957 the Soviets launched the first artificial satellite *Sputnik I*, and on 31 Jan. 1958 the US sent up its first Earth satellite, *Explorer I*.

Scientific studies for **space flight** appeared early in the 20th c. Most notable were Konstantin Tsiolkovsky (1903), Robert Goddard (1919) and Hermann Oberth (1923).

The first manned space vehicle was launched on 12 Apr. 1961, when the Soviets launched ***Vostok 1*** carrying cosmonaut Yuri Gagarin.

The Soviet craft ***Luna 1***, launched 2 Jan. 1959, became the first artificial body to escape the gravitational field of the Earth, fly past the Moon, and enter an orbit around the Sun.

The US *Voyager* fly-bys of Jupiter, Saturn and Uranus (1979–86) revealed much new data about these planets, including the revelation of unknown rings around Jupiter.

SPAIN

Spain (capital: Madrid) occupies the greater part of the Iberian peninsula, bordering Portugal and France with an area of 504,783 sq km/194,897 sq mi.

Spain exports transport equipment, agricultural products and machinery, mainly to France, Germany, Italy and the UK. Tourism is one of the largest sources of revenue.

Spain, a republic in 1873–4 and 1931–9, was under the dictatorship of Francisco Franco until his death on 20 Nov. 1975 when the monarchy was restored.

The last Moorish stronghold in **Spain** was destroyed in 1492, the year that Christopher Columbus made his first voyage to America and created the first great world power.

The **population of Spain** is 39,952,000 (est. 1991), comprising 72.3% Spanish, 16.3% Catalan, 8.1% Galician, 2.3% Basque and 1% other.

SPICES

A blend of several spices, **curry** serves as a basic condiment of India and gives its name as well as its flavours to a variety of dishes. Most curries have coriander as a base, with the addition of other spices such as turmeric, fenugreek, cumin, red and black pepper, ginger and cloves.

▼ *The Royal Palace at Madrid in Spain.*

Allspice is the dried, nearly ripe berry of the allspice tree. The name is derived from its flavour, which suggests a mixture of cloves, cinnamon and nutmeg. Allspice is used whole or ground in pickling spices, mincemeat, roast meats and baked goods.

Cloves are the dried buds of a tree that produces abundant clusters of small red flower buds. These are gathered before opening and dried to produce the dark-brown, nail-shaped spice clove. Whole and ground cloves are used as food seasonings.

Spices are made from a plant part that is strongly flavoured and easily stored and processed. Ginseng and horseradish come from the **roots** of the plants; cinnamon, from the bark; cloves, from flower buds; lavender, from the flower; saffron, from flower stigmas; pepper and vanilla, from the fruits; and nutmeg, from the seed.

Spices are the products of tropical and subtropical trees, shrubs or vines and are characterised by highly pungent odours or flavours. Spice seeds – such as caraway, fennel and sesame – are the aromatic fruits and seeds of plants.

The flavour and odour of **vanilla** extract comes partially from a white crystal vanillin, which develops during the curing process. Vanilla is the foremost food flavouring for ice cream, puddings, chocolates, baked goods, syrups, sweets, liqueurs, tobacco and soft drinks.

Whole **mustard** seeds are used as a pickling flavouring and to add pungency to many cooked foods. Powdered dry mustard is a common kitchen spice. Its sharp, hot flavour develops when the powder is moistened.

SPIDERS

The **American Silk Spider** (*Argiope aurantia*) spins an egg cocoon up to 4 km/2.5 mi long. It is deliberately cultivated for its fine thread, used in optical instruments.

The **Black Widow** (*Latrodectus mactans*), found from the southern US to Patagonia, is very poisonous. The female is shiny black with a red spot. The male is smaller with longer legs.

The **Cardinal Spider** is the largest species recorded in England, attaining a size of 75 mm/3 in. It derives its name from having once frightened Cardinal Wolsey (1475–1530).

The **European Aquatic Spider** (*Argyroneta aquatica*), found across southern Europe and Asia, builds her tent under water in the shape of a bell and fills it with air.
The **Funnel Web Spider** (*Agalena naevia*) derives its name from the funnel-shaped web in which it traps its prey. It is found in the southern US.

The **Great Orb-Weaver** (*Nephila madagascariensis*) was cultivated in special gardens in Madagascar in the late 19th c for the fine silk which it produced.

The **Tarantula** (*Lycosa tarantula*) derives its name from Taranto, Italy. It differs from other spiders in that it spins no web but catches its prey by its speed.

SPIRITS

Canadian whiskey is always distilled in the patent still and is always a blend. Most Canadian whiskey is at least 6 years old when sold. Delicate and light bodied, it is often confused with American blended whiskey and thus called **rye**.

Gin is an alcoholic beverage made by distilling fermented mixtures of grains and flavouring the resulting alcohol with juniper berries. The name is derived from the French word *genievre* (juniper).

◄ *Tarantula (**Teraphosa leblondii**)*

Nearly all **Scotch whiskies** are blends. They are usually distilled from barley malt cured with peat, giving the spirit a smoky flavour.

Rum is an alcoholic beverage distilled from sugarcane by-products that are produced when manufacturing sugar. After distilling, the rum is darkened by the addition of caramel and is aged from 5 to 7 years.

Tequila is an alcoholic beverage made of the fermented and distilled sap taken from the base of agave plants, especially those cultivated in Mexico. The liquor, which is usually distilled twice to achieve the desired purity and potency, is colourless and is not aged.

The term 'brandy' refers to the unsweetened, distilled spirit derived from the juice of grapes. Brandy made from other fruits has the name of the fruit attached to it, as in the case of apricot brandy or cherry brandy.

The traditional liquor of Russia and Poland, **vodka** is a colourless, almost tasteless liquid made by distilling a mash of grain, sugar beet, potato or other starchy food material. The name is the Russian diminutive of *voda* ('water').

Whiskey (from Gaelic *uisge beatha*, 'water of life'), like the other distilled spirits, is generally distilled from a fermented or alcohol-containing mash of grains, which may include barley, rye, oats, wheat or corn.

STAMPS

Brazil (1843) was the first country after the UK to issue stamps, nicknamed 'Bull's Eyes' on account of their oval motif.

For many years the 1840 British **stamps** set the pattern for the stamps of other countries: generally about 2.5 cm/1 in in height, slightly less in width and usually printed with a portrait in a single colour.

Included in a **stamp collection** might be pre-stamped envelopes, postal cards, letter sheets such as the current aerogrammes, day-of-issue stamped envelopes (first-day covers), plate blocks and complete panes of stamps as they come from the printer.

Some stamps have been used for small change, substituting for **coins** in wartime shortage: those of tsarist Russia (1915–16) were printed on a thin cardboard and US Civil War issues were encased in transparent mica slipcases, patented by John Gault (1862).

Stamp collections are housed in **albums** that are usually loose-leaf. Stamps are affixed to the page by gummed hinges or are slipped into pochettes or transparent strips that are used primarily for mint stamps (stamps that have never been used).

Stamps are **valued** according to their rarity and condition. Among the world's most valuable stamps is a unique one-cent 1856 British Guiana stamp. Stamps printed with errors are rare and often valuable.

The word **philately**, which was coined by Jules Herpin in 1862 from a combination of Greek words whose sum means 'the love of being tax free' alludes to the fact that, before postage stamps, letters were sent collect.

STARS

A **star** is any massive, self-luminous celestial body of gas that shines by radiant energy generated in its interior. The universe contains trillions, of which few are visible to the unaided eye.

Star surface temperatures range from 2,000°C/3,600°F to above 30,000°C/54,000°F and their corresponding colours range from red to blue to white.

Stars are born from **nebulae** (gas and dust clouds) when they collapse inward under the force of their own gravity. Stars consist mostly of hydrogen and helium gases.

The brightest stars have the largest masses, 100 times that of the Sun, emitting as much light as millions of suns; they live for less than a million years and explode as **supernovae**.

The closest star to the solar system is *Proxima Centauri*, approx. 4.3 light years away from our own star, the Sun.

The faintest stars are called **red dwarfs** and are less than one thousandth of the brightness of the Sun.

The smallest mass possible for a star is 8% that of the Sun, otherwise nuclear reactions do not occur. Objects with less mass than this shine only dimly and are called **brown dwarfs**.

STEAM TRAINS

By the 1850s **British and American locomotives** tended to differ considerably. British engines were shorter, with generally smaller tenders and cabs.

During the prosperous 1920s, 15,000 **new locomotives** were purchased by American railroads, some of the largest being the huge mallet or articulated models.

In 1829 George Stephenson built his successful *Rocket* locomotive. It contributed to the rapid expansion of railroads in the UK and, later, in other countries.

In 1836 Henry Campbell of Philadelphia designed an eight-wheeled engine. It was known as the **American-type locomotive** and was to dominate US locomotive design for half a century.

The first **American-built locomotive** was the *Tom Thumb*, constructed by Peter Cooper. In 1830 this locomotive lost a famous race with a horse-drawn car.

US railways imported more than 100 English locomotives between 1829 and 1841. One of the first was the *Stourbridge Lion*, imported in 1829 by the Delaware & Hudson Railroad.

With improved boiler design, the British engineer Richard Trevithick built a non-condensing **steam-driven carriage** in 1801 and the first steam locomotive in 1803.

STOCKHOLM

Notable buildings of **Stockholm** include the 18th-c Royal Palace, the *Riddarhus* (House of the Nobility), St Nicholas church and the modern Town Hall (1922).

Stockholm was founded in 1255 by Birger Jarl who erected a stockade on an island, hence the name. It became the capital of Sweden in 1523.

Stockholm's industries include iron and steel, shipbuilding, textiles, leather, brewing, tobacco and processed foodstuffs.

Stockholm, known as 'the Venice of the North', is picturesquely located on 13 islands and several peninsulas near the junction of the Baltic Sea and the Gulf of Bothnia.

The **population of Stockholm** is 674,452 (1991 census), about the same as it was in 1945.

▼ *The Old Town in Stockholm.*

STOCKS AND SHARES

The **busiest session on the London Stock Market** occurred on 28 Jan. 1993. A staggering 1.3 bn shares were traded in a single day.

The **Great Depression** caused the Dow Jones average in the US to plunge to an all-time low of 41.22 in 1932. In 1929 it had stood at 381.7.

The **highest value single share** is said to be held in the Moeara Enim Petroleum Corporation. It was valued in Apr. 1992 at a staggering £50,586.

The largest decline in share values in one day occurred on 19 Oct. 1987 (**Black Monday**), a fall of 508 points. Values rose sharply two days later.

The **largest number of investors** attracted to a share issue stands at 5.9 m. The Indian equity fund Mastergain '92 was floated in 1986 by the Unit Trust of India, Bombay.

The **largest-ever flotation** took place in the UK in Dec. 1986. British Gas plc attracted 4.5 m. investors and a record sum of £7.75 bn.

The oldest **stock exchange** was founded in 1602 in Amsterdam. The largest (£1,161 bn) is New York, closely followed by London (£1,045 bn) and Germany (£891 bn).

STONE AGE

In northern Europe and Scandinavia the earliest Neolithic culture was the **Funnel-beaker culture**, named for its characteristic pottery.

Sir John Lubbock recognised (1865) that the Stone Age should be divided into an earlier period (the **Paleolithic**), characterised by the use of chipped stone tools, and a later period (the Neolithic), marked by the introduction of ground and polished stone tools.

The beginning of the Neolithic Period in Britain and Ireland (4000 BC) is

◀ *Rupert Murdoch, plays the world markets to his advantage.*

The Neolithic Period or **New Stone Age** refers to the stage of prehistoric cultural development that followed the Paleolithic and transitional Mesolithic Periods, and preceded the Bronze Age.

The Paleolithic Period or **Old Stone Age**, is the earliest and longest stage of human cultural development, lasting from about 2.5 m. to about 10,000 years ago.

marked by clearance of the forest for agriculture. The earliest monuments are collective tombs: wedge-shaped graves in Ireland (court **cairns**) and earthen long barrows in England.

The earliest Neolithic sites in southeast Europe date from before 6000 BC and are located in areas with the most easily workable soils. Constant settlement on the same location produced the characteristic 'tells' or settlement mounds.

The English archeologist Miles Burkitt ascribed (1920s) to the **Neolithic** four characteristic traits: grinding and polishing stone tools, the practice of agriculture, the domestication of animals and manufacture of pottery.

STRIKES

In Jan. **1946**, 1.5 m. struck in the automotive, electrical, meat and steel industries across the US. During Apr. 1946 John L. Lewis led a strike of 400,000 miners.

In the **General strike** (4–12 May 1926) the Conservative PM Baldwin proclaimed a state of emergency. He organised volunteers to maintain essential services and refused to negotiate with labour leaders.

The experience of the **Solidarity** union in Poland in 1981, led by Lech Walesa, was unusual in its achievement of considerable power before the government clamped down.

The first strike in major league **baseball** history took place in 1972, when players staged a 13-day walkout to demand an increase in pension payments.

The low standard of living in **East Germany** led, in 1953, to strikes in a number of cities. They were put down with the aid of Soviet armed forces.

Trade unions were not legalised until 1871 in the UK; in the US the right to organise trade unions was not guaranteed until the **National Labor Relations Act** of 1935.

When the **Boston police force** went out on **strike** on 9 Sept. 1919 the Governor responded by calling out the National Guard and breaking the strike.

SUN

A **satellite** called *Solar Max* monitors the Sun, sending back data that help scientists understand how the Sun affects the world's climate.

Florida, US, experiences heavy rains but St Petersburg in that state holds the world record for **continuous sunshine**. The Sun shone for 768 consecutive days between 9 Feb. 1967 and 17 Mar. 1969.

Research published in 1998 suggested that periods of global warming had correlated accurately with times of high **sunspot** activity. Hitherto human activity had been thought predominantly responsible.

The annual average of **sunshine** at Yuma, Arizona, US, is 4,055 hours. At that latitude the maximum possible total would be 4,456 hours.

The first **total eclipse of the sun** for which there is firm evidence was at Chu-fu, China, on 17 Jul. 709 BC.

The largest **sunspot** ever recorded was seen in Apr. 1947. Covering about 18,000 m. sq km/7,000 m. sq mi, it was easily visible to the (protected) naked eye.

SURREALISM

In 1925 the first **group exhibition** of Surrealist painting took place in Paris. Among those included were Giorgio de Chirico, Max Ernst, Andre Masson, Joan Miro, Pablo Picasso and Man Ray.

surrealists because he was held to be more interested in commercialising his art than in Surrealist ideas.

The **pre-surrealist** paintings of Giorgio de Chirico, executed before 1919, were of particular influence to certain of the Surrealists, including Max Ernst, Salvador Dalí, Rene Magritte and Yves Tanguy.

Surrealism still exists as a movement in some quarters and its **influence** can be detected in all the major art movements that have come into being since 1945.

Surrealism was a style of art in which imagery is based on fantasy and the world of dreams. It grew out of a French literary movement founded during the 1920s.

The Catalan painter **Salvador Dalí** joined the Surrealist movement in 1930 but was later denounced by most

▲ *Picasso was amongst the first of the Surrealists.*

The term **Surrealist** was coined by Guillaume Apollinaire (1917); the artistic movement came into being only after the French poet Andre Breton published the first Surrealist manifesto, *Manifeste du surrealisme* (1924).

SWEDEN

Modern **Sweden** began in 1523 when Gustavus Vasa expelled the Danes. In the 17th c it was the centre of a great Baltic empire, but declined after defeat at Pultawa in 1709.

Sweden (capital: Stockholm) occupies the eastern part of the Scandinavian peninsula, with an area of 449,964 sq km/172,732 sq mi.

▲ *Sweden's capital, Stockholm.*

Sweden exports machinery and transport equipment, electrical goods, paper products, chemicals, timber, wood pulp, iron and steel.

The king being childless, and there being no suitable heir in **Sweden**, the *Riksdag* elected Jean Bernadotte, one of Napoleon's marshals, who became Charles XIV (1818–44).

The **population of Sweden** is 8,607,000 (est. 1991), comprising 90.8% Swedish, 2.5% Finnish and 6.7% other. 90% belong to the Church of Sweden.

SWITZERLAND

On 1 Aug. 1291 the elders of the cantons of Uri, Unterwalden and Schwyz founded **Switzerland**, whose name comes from the last-named.

Switzerland exports industrial machinery, pharmaceuticals, watches and clocks, electronics and precision instruments. Tourism is also a major industry.

The **population of Switzerland** is 6,820,000 (est. 1991), comprising 65% German, 18.4% French, 9.8% Italian, 1.7% Spanish, 1.5% Yugoslav and 0.8% Romansch.

TAOISM

Both Buddhism and Confucianism have **influenced Tao thought**, and all three religions have co-existed in China in greater harmony than those of most other countries.

Taoism centres on a number of philo-sophical works including the *Tao Tè Ching*, attributed to **Lao Tzu**, who lived in China *c.* 500 BC.

Taoist awareness works in harmony with life's circumstances, and the first step towards understanding the Tao is to think and act spontaneously, without effort.

The **metaphysical absolute of Tao** sustains all things, but serenely, without struggle, beyond the human constructs of good and bad, sickness and health.

The *Tao* is the Way, the ineffable unchanging essence of everything in heaven and earth. To accord with the Way one must be without desires or intentions.

The teachings in the 81 chapters of the *Tao Tè Ching* have been one of the major influences on Chinese thought and culture over the last 2,500 years.

Today there are many different **sects of Taoism**, but all followers seek free-dom (from desire, from mortality and from separation from the Tao).

TAXES

A cross-party movement in the US led to the adoption of the **16th Amendment** to the Constitution in 1913, allowing Congress to impose and collect income taxes.

Alcohol and tobacco may be taxed heavily on the ground that their use is injurious to the health of individuals. Such revenue is often called a 'sin tax'.

In some nations **social welfare** provides economic security for individuals from birth to death; consequently the taxes to account for transfer payments are high.

In the US **poll tax** was tax paid by one wishing to vote; it was repealed in 1964 by the 24th Amendment to the Constitution. A version was introduced to Britain in the 1980s.

Prior to the 20th c taxation was regarded solely as a means to finance the necessary obligations of a government. In the 20th c the **purposes of taxation** have expanded.

The emperor Augustus (27 BC–AD 14) introduced the **property tax and inheritance tax** at the beginning of the imperial period, and later emperors imposed taxes on other products.

The most controversial use of taxes is the redistribution of wealth. The purpose of **income redistribution** is to lessen the inequalities of wealth in society.

TELECOMMUNICATIONS

Alexander Graham Bell pioneered long-distance voice communication in 1876 when he invented the **telephone** as a result of Faraday's discovery of electromagnetism.

Due to Hertz's discoveries using electromagnetic waves, Marconi made a 'wireless' telegraph, the ancestor of radio. He established **wireless** communication between England and France in 1899 and across the Atlantic in 1901.

Integrated Services Digital Network (**ISDN**) is a system that transmits voice and image data on a single transmission line by using digital signals. It began operating in Japan in 1988.

Recent advances include the use of **fibre-optic cables** consisting of fine glass fibres for telephone lines instead of copper. The signals are transmitted on pulses of laser light.

Samuel Morse transmitted the first message along a telegraph line in the US using his **Morse code** system of signals in 1843.

The first **mechanical telecommunications** systems were semaphore, invented by Claude Chappe of France in 1794, and heliograph (using flashes of sunlight).

◀ *Alexander Graham Bell.*

The main method of relaying **long-distance calls** on land is by microwave radio transmission. To achieve transmission across sea communications satellites orbiting the Earth are used.

TELEVISION

Crookes (England) invented the Crookes tube, which produced cathode rays (1878). **Nipkow** (Germany) built a mechanical scanning device, the Nipkow disc (1884).

Braun (Germany) modified the Crookes tube to produce the ancestor of the first TV receiver picture tube (1897). **Rosing** (Russia) experimented with the Nipkow disc and cathode-ray tube, transmitting crude TV pictures (1906).

Experimental **colour-TV transmission** began (US, 1940) and was successfully transmitted (US, 1953). The first **videotape recorder** was produced by Ampex (California, 1956).

Using the system of John Logie Baird (1888–1946), the **BBC began broadcasting** experimental TV programmes (1929) and regular broadcasting from Alexandra Palace (1936).

Zworykin (US) invented the electronic camera tube (iconoscope) (1923). **Baird** (Scotland) demonstrated a workable TV system, using mechanical scanning by Nipkow disc (1926) and colour TV (1928).

TEMPERATURE

In Death Valley, California, US, on each consecutive day from 6 Jul. to 17 Aug. 1917 (43 days), the **maximum temperature** reached 49°C/120°F or more.

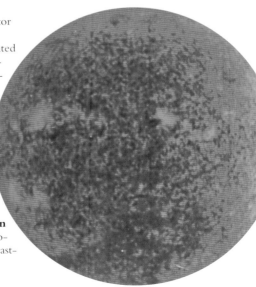

In Verkhoyansk, eastern Russia, the **temperature** has varied between –68°C/–90°F and 37°C/98°F, a record range of 105°C/188°F.

Most **thermometers** work by measuring expansion or contraction of a liquid in a glass tube. Mercury and alcohol are most commonly used, because they neither boil nor freeze at room temperature.

One of the **hottest places** on earth is Dallol, Ethiopia, where the average mean temperature recorded between 1960 and 1966 was 34°C/94°F.

The thermometer, for measuring temperature, was invented in 1592. In weather stations various thermometers may be housed inside a box called a **Stevenson screen**.

TENNIS

Billie Jean King (US) holds the record for **most Wimbledon titles**, winning 20 titles – 6 singles, 10 women's doubles and four mixed doubles.

Boris Becker (Germany) is the **youngest men's Wimbledon singles champion**. He won the title in 1985 aged just 17 years and 227 days.

In 1911 Dorothea Lambert Chambers (UK) won the **most one-sided Wimbledon final** ever played. She defeated Dora Boothby 6-0, 6-0 in just 22 minutes!

Pancho Gonzalez and Charlie Pasarell played the **longest match in Wimbeldon history** in 1969. The match lasted 112 games before 41-year-old Gonzalez won 22-24, 1-6, 16-14, 6-3, 11-9.

Roy Emerson (Australia) has won the **most men's Grand Slam titles**. He won 28 titles – 12 singles and 16 doubles between 1961 and 1967.

◄ *Germany's Boris Becker, the youngest Wimbledon winner.*

US player Dwight F. Davis donated a cup to be contested by national teams in 1900. The most successful nation in **the Davis Cup** has been the US with 31 victories.

TERRORISM

1968 is often considered to be the **starting point** for international terrorism, when protests in the democratic countries helped spawn the international terrorist network; several organisations emerged simultaneously.

A truckload of explosives was detonated by Timothy J. McVeigh in front of the Federal Building in **Oklahoma City** in Apr. 1995, killing 168

people and wounding more than 400 others.

An extremist group called **Black September** emerged within al-Fatah in late 1971. In Sept. 1972 members of the group infiltrated the Olympic Village in Munich, Germany.

Carlos 'the Jackal', the best-known terrorist of the post-Cold War era, was arrested in Sudan in 1994 and handed over to French authorities. He had eluded police around the world for 20 years.

German officials arrested three individuals in Munich as they stepped off a flight from Moscow carrying between 100–300 gm/3.5–10.5 oz of **plutonium 239**. This was the third time.

In 1976 an Israeli airborne commando unit, led by Jonathan Netanyahu, staged a raid on the **Entebbe** airport and rescued 103 hostages hijacked by Palestinian terrorists, seven of whom were killed.

In Mar. 1978 the **Red Brigades** kidnapped and killed Aldo Moro, former Italian prime minister, in Rome. The 12 kidnappers killed all five of Moro's bodyguards.

◄ *Reflections of terrorism in Northern Ireland.*

It has been estimated that more than 550 **terrorist organisations** exist around the world. The tactics they use include murder, kidnapping, arson, bombings, hold-ups, embassy attacks and airplane hijackings.

Ten people were killed and more than 5,500 injured after the deadly nerve gas sarin was released into the Toyko subway system by the religious sect **Aum Shinrikyo**.

The **Irish Republican Army** (IRA), a paramilitary organisation originating in the Republic of Ireland, is committed to terrorist tactics to end British rule in Northern Ireland.

TEXTILES

Egyptian tomb painting shows costumes stamped with orderly, repeated designs (2100 BC). Clay cylinders were used to print border patterns (Peru, 2000 BC). **Tie-dyeing** and batik developed in Mexico, Peru and Java, 1500–1200 BC.

Flax was used along the Nile (ancient Egypt, 5000 BC) to make linen-like fabric. Wool developed on the Euphrates river banks (Mesopotamia, 4000 BC); cotton in India and Peru (3000 BC); and silk in China (2640 BC).

French textile production excelled in style and technique and under Louis XVI (1774–93) design was refined, Classical elements intermingling with earlier floral patterns.

George Leason established the Calico Printing Works (Boston, 1712), the **first US fabric-printing** manufacturer. Over 70 printworks were established in the US during the next 150 years.

The Arts and Crafts movement revived textiles as an applied art; **textile art** began in the late 1950s. Contemporary artists include Toyazaki (Japan), Parsons (UK), DuBois (US), Roos (Netherlands) and Henriksen (Denmark).

◀ *A wool and silk Aubusson tapestry.*

THAILAND

In the 6th c tribes of Thai stock migrated from central Asia into **Thailand**, formerly known as Siam. Under King Taksin (1767–82) the country was consolidated.

Thailand (capital: Bangkok) is situated in south-east Asia, bordering Myanmar, Laos and Malaysia, with an area of 513,115 sq km/198,115 sq mi.

Thailand exports electric equipment, textiles and garments, fish and fish meal, vegetables, precious stones, cereals and rubber.

The native name for **Thailand** is *Maung Thai* (land of the free), alluding to the fact that it is the only country in Asia that has never been conquered.

The **population of Thailand** is 57,150,000 (est. 1991), comprising 79.5% Thai, 12.1% Chinese, 3.7% Malay, 2.7% Khmer and 2% other. Many famines have been due to overpopulation and tend to occur in drought- and flood-prone areas with low agricultural production.

THEATRE

Small enclosed theatres were built in the 16th c in Vincenza, Italy, by Palladio. Burbage opened the first London theatre (Shoreditch, 1576). His son built **Shakespeare's Globe Theatre**.

The Comédie Française (Paris, founded by Louis XIV, 1690, permanently housed 1792) was the first **national theatre**. There are other national theatres in London (1963), Moscow and Vienna.

The rebuilt Shakespeare's Globe Theatre. ▶

THIRD WORLD

In its most general sense, the term 'Third World' refers collectively to more than 100 countries of Africa, Asia and Latin America.

Increasing protectionism in northern markets has shut out some Third World exports, while at the same time, the increased export of some natural resources (e.g. lumber from forests) created rapid **environmental degradation**.

Internationally Third World countries tend to be seen and to identify themselves in opposition to industrialised countries, acting collectively to redress their **subordinate relationship** to older centres of economic and political power.

The accumulation of extensive international debt by many less-developed countries emerged in the 1980s as the intractable 'Third World debt crisis'.

Third World countries tend to have low to modest **life expectancy** and modest to high rates of infant mortality and illiteracy. Governmental instability is common and political opposition and freedom of expression are often restricted.

Third World countries were generally distinguished from those of the **First World** (industrialised free-market economies) and second world (industrialised centrally planned economies).

Third World economies are often dependent on the export of primary products or simple manufactured goods that are highly vulnerable to fluctuations in international prices and to industrialised countries' trade restrictions.

With the rise of **oil** prices in the 1970s, the petroleum-exporting countries emerged as a new group of non-industrial but nonetheless high-income Third World nations.

TIDES

A barrage across the **Rance** estuary in Brittany, built 1961–67, exploits a tidal range of 13.5 m/44 ft to generate electricity. Rising and falling tides spin the blades of 24 reversible turbines.

In the 1930s the US government sponsored a project at Passamaquoddy, on the Bay of Fundy, to consider the possibility of harnessing the tides to create **hydroelectric power**. It proved too costly and was abandoned.

Neap tides, the lowest high tides and the highest low tides, occur when the Sun's pull is at right angles to that of the Moon. They happen at the time of the Moon's first and last quarters.

Resonant tides occur when the tidal waves 'reflected' from the shore meet and reinforce the next ones sweeping in. They happen in the North Sea and the English Channel.

Spring tides are the highest high tides and the lowest low tides. They occur about twice a month when the Sun and Moon line up and jointly exert a pull on the oceans.

The connection between the **Moon** and the tides has been known since classical times. Sir Isaac Newton (1642–1727) was the first to demonstrate an understanding of the forces at work.

The sea generally rises and falls twice in every 24 hrs 50 mins, coinciding with one orbit of the Moon around the earth. The Moon's gravitational pull is the main cause of the **tides**.

The world's highest tides happen where the Atlantic funnels into the long, narrow **Bay of Fundy**, in eastern Canada. The record tidal range recorded was 21.4 m/70 ft.

TIME

From 1986 the term **Greenwich Mean Time** was replaced by UTC, but the Greenwich Meridian (adopted 1884) remains the line from which all longitudes and world time zones are measured.

In Ancient Egypt, **time** during the day was measured by a sun clock (a primitive sundial) and at night by a water clock.

Portable **sundials** were used from the 16th to the 18th c. Watches were invented in 16th c; the first were made in Nuremberg, Germany in 1500. In the 19th c they became cheap enough to be widely used.

The **atomic clock** uses the natural resonance of certain atoms as a regulator controlling the frequency of a quartz –crystal oscillator. They are accurate to within one-millionth of a second per day.

The **clock computerised** at the Greenwich observatory has an accuracy greater than 1 second in 4,000 years.

The measurement of time, the **second**, was formerly based on the Earth's rotation on its axis, but this was

irregular. The second was redefined in 1956 in terms of earth's orbit of the Sun and in 1967 as a radiation pattern of caesium.

Universal time (UT), based on the Earth's actual rotation, was replaced in 1972 by co-ordinated universal time (UTC) which involved the addition, or subtraction, of leap seconds on the last day of Jun. or Dec.

▲ *The Western influences in Tokyo*

TOKYO

A disastrous **earthquake** in Sept. 1923, followed by extensive fires, destroyed a large part of the city. Rebuilding on modern lines was completed by 1930.

Formerly Yedo, **Tokyo** emerged from obscurity in 1457 when Ota Dokwan built a castle there. From 1590 the seat of the Tokugawa shoguns, it became the capital of Japan in 1868.

One of Japan's leading industrial cities, **Tokyo produces** an astonishing range of goods, from heavy engineering to electronics, chemicals, plastics, rubber and foodstuffs.

The **population of Tokyo** is 8,163,127 (1990 census), compared with 6,778,804 in 1940.

Tokyo is located on the banks of the River Sumida, at the head of a bay of the same name on the south-east coast of the island of Honshu.

TOMBS

A **tomb** is a place of burial, in the form of a sarcophagus, crypt, vault or chamber, located either above or below ground. The term 'tomb' also refers to monuments erected over graves to commemorate the dead.

By *c.* 3000 BC the **pyramids** came into use as tomb monuments, the most spectacular being those of the Old Kingdom rulers Khufu, Khafre and Menkaure, at Giza.

Chamber tombs built of boulders or smaller stones were constructed in many parts of prehistoric Europe *c.* 4000–1000 BC. They were often used for collective burials and covered with a mound of earth or piled-up stones.

Considered one of the seven wonders of the world, the tomb of **Halicarnassus** (built *c.* 350 BC) for Mausolus, ruler of Caria), is the origin of the term 'mausoleum', which may be applied to any above-ground funerary monument.

◀ *The pyramids served as tombs for Egyptian pharaohs.*

During the New Kingdom in Egypt (1570–1085 BC), royal dead were often buried in rock-cut tombs excavated deep into the sides of mountains. A notable example is the tomb of **Queen Hatshepsut** at Deir el-Bahri.

In Ancient Egypt the earliest monumental tomb was the **Mastaba** of the predynastic period (*c.* 3500–3100 BC), a rectangular structure with a flat top and either stepped or sloping sides.

Notable Roman tombs include the remarkable **sepulchre** of the baker Eurysaces and his wife, built (*c.* 60 BC) in the shape of an enormous baker's oven, and the marble-sheathed mausoleum of Hadrian.

The most impressive tombs associated with ancient Aegean civilisation are beehive-shaped stone chambers called *tholoi*. The largest and best preserved is the so-called Treasury of Atreus (late 14th c BC), at Mycenae.

TORNADOES

A record number of 148 **tornadoes within 24 hours** was recorded in the southern and midwestern states of the US on 3–4 Apr. 1974.

A **waterspout**, like a tornado, is a narrow, rotating column with an intense vortex. It occurs over the ocean or lakes and water is sucked up into the bottom of the spout. It can cause considerable damage.

The **most destructive tornado** known occurred in Shaturia, Bangladesh, on 26 April 1989. It killed about 1,300 people. The highest speed measured in a tornado is 450 kph/280 mph.

The **updraught of a tornado** can be strong enough to pluck steel bridges from their foundations, trees from the ground, trains from railway lines and people and animals from roads and pavements.

Tornadoes are most frequent in the Mississippi–Missouri valley of the central US, especially Mar.–Jun. They occur elsewhere, for example in the UK, though less often and rarely with such **intensity**.

Tornadoes bring very low **air pressure**. The pressure drop makes the funnel visible. It is also responsible for the destruction of buildings, which may explode because the pressure inside is much greater than outside.

Tornadoes usually cause less damage and **loss of life** than hurricanes, because they travel faster and less far, but almost everything along their path is destroyed.

TOURISM

Ecotourism may well become the prime tourist fad of the 21st c, taking visitors to the wild-animal parks of Africa and the Amazon, the Himalayas and the Antarctic.

In 1991 foreign travellers to the **US** equalled the number of US travellers going abroad for the first time: some 42 m. for each group.

The number of international travellers in 1994 will double to 1 bn by 2010. In the **UK**, **tourism** generates £8 bn a year and accounts for 4% of GDP and 1.5 m. jobs.

The tourist industry is vulnerable to **terrorism** or to shrinking economies: the recession of the late 1980s, the Persian Gulf crisis of 1990–91 and the upsurge of terrorism in Egypt in 1993.

The US averages over $53 bn in **receipts from tourism** per year; at the same time US citizens spend over $40 bn abroad, particularly in Europe.

The **World Tourism Organisation** calculates that France is the most popular tourist destination. In 1997 France was thought to have welcomed over 60 m. tourists.

Harrods is one of London's biggest tourist attractions. ▶

Tourism is the **world's largest industry**. In 1993 tourism employed 100 m. people. It generated more than £200 bn in direct export earnings, excluding transport and domestic tourism.

TOYS

GI Joe was an outstanding action doll of the 1960s, when it became more acceptable for boys to have dolls. His accessories included a rifle, hand grenades and a cartridge belt.

In 1902, the **Teddy Bear** was introduced by Russian-American Morris Michtom and his wife in New York. It had moveable arms, legs and head. The Michtoms obtained Pres. Teddy Roosevelt's permission to use his nickname.

In 1918 the **Raggedy Ann** doll was developed to promote sales of the first book of Raggedy Ann stories. Political cartoonist John

Gruelle's book had 25 sequels and the Raggedy Ann doll grew to become a multi-million-dollar business.

In 1929 the **yo-yo** was introduced to the US by entrepreneur Donald F. Duncan, who had acquired rights to the string-and-spool toy (based on a weapon used by 16th-c Filipino hunters) from Filipino immigrant Pedro Flores.

The **Kewpie doll** had an impish smile, side-turned eyes, topknot and blue wings. Based on a drawing by Rose O'Neill, the Kewpie was so loved from its debut in 1912 that Kewpie clubs still flourish. They were made in bisque, composition and celluloid.

My Little Pony – a line of plastic ponies with doll-like features – was successful with children in the late 1980s and early 1990s. These horses were multicoloured (usually in pinks, purples and reds).

Toys had been almost entirely handcrafted until late in the 18th c, when mass-produced toys began to appear for the first time. Metal rapidly replaced wood in many toys, especially mechanical toys from *c.* 1840.

TRAFFIC

Congestion was severe enough in European cities of the 17th c to require local ordinances prohibiting parking on certain streets and establishing **one-way traffic**.

In the 1970s there were 100 m. cars and lorries in use **world-wide**, by 1990 this had grown to 550 m. 10 m. were in the UK alone.

Nowadays roads in many older cities do not match current needs so **traffic restraint** measures funnel traffic onto certain routes by creating impediments to movement on others. These include speed bumps, barricades to block streets and stop signs.

One-fifth of the space in European and North American cities is taken up by cars. In the UK **congestion** costs about £2–15 bn per year.

Safety is a critical factor in traffic control. In 1988 there were 4,531 deaths from **motor-vehicle accidents** in England and Wales.

There are four basic elements in a **computerised traffic control** system: computer(s), communications devices, traffic signals (and associated equipment) and detectors for sensing vehicles.

Traffic congestion and jams are not a recent problem. In the 1st c BC Julius Caesar banned wheeled traffic from Rome during the daytime.

Traffic control also gives priority to highly occupied passenger vehicles. The most common measures are bus and car pools lanes. Unfortunately the increased congestion for other traffic wastes fuel and increases pollutant emissions.

Ever-increasing numbers of cars are being produced worldwide. ▲

TRAVEL

By Victorian times tourism had become an **industry**, an economic fact quickly exploited by Karl Baedeker and his son, who provided travellers with solidly researched guidebooks in several languages.

In 1991 **foreign travellers** to the US equalled the number of US travellers going abroad for the first time: some 42 m. for each group. (Foreigners who visited the US only for pleasure, however, totalled 13.5 m.)

New tourist attractions emerge constantly. **Ecotourism**, the search for nature in the raw, may well become the prime tourist fad of the 21st c, taking visitors to the great wild-animal parks of Africa and rarely seen regions of the Amazon, the Himalayas and the Antarctic.

The enormous growth in tourism has spurred the increase in **vacation hotels** and in many areas of the world (e.g. the Caribbean or the French and Italian Rivieras) the tourist has become the prime source of income.

The Swiss hotelier Cesar Ritz (1850-1918) established a number of elegant and palatial **hotels** in Paris, London and New York and gave his name to a particular style of conspicuous consumption. He was the founder of the Hotel de Luxe.

The term '**tourism**' refers both to travel undertaken for pleasure and to the modern multimillion-dollar business that caters to the tourist's need for transportation, accommodation, food, entertainment, recreation, health, souvenirs and social contact.

The **tourist industry** is vulnerable to almost instantaneous change when war, terrorism or disease threatens or when economies shrink and vacations are spent at home. Some recent examples are the recession of the late 1980s, the Persian Gulf crisis and the war in Yugoslavia.

▲ *Holidaymakers at the Black Sea.*

Thomas Cook's (1808-92) London-based travel agency was offering, by the 1850s, guided tours of Europe and, a decade later, of the US. Today, his agency is one of the biggest in the world.

TREES

Tree is the name given to woody, perennial, seed-bearing plants which at maturity are at least 7 m/21 ft tall, with a single trunk terminating in a well-defined crown.

The **Giant Sequoia** or Bigtree (*Sequoia gigantea*) is the largest of all trees in bulk and is reputedly the oldest living thing (since 1000 BC). The General Sherman is thought to weigh 2,150 tons.

The **Kauri** (*Agathis australis*) of New Zealand grows to a height of 55 m/180 ft, making it the world's tallest tree. Once extensive, they are now confined to the Waipoua forest.

The **Maple** (genus *Acer*) comprises 115 species of tree in the northern temperate zone. It includes the sugar maple (*Acer saccharum*) of North America.

The **Oak** (genus *Quercus*) comprises about 500 species widely distributed over the northern temperate zones. Oaks played a prominent part in the Druid religion of England.

The **Pine** (genus *Pinus*), comprises about 90 species of evergreen, distinguished by their needle-like leaves growing in tufts. They are a fast-growing source of lumber.

The **Willow** (genus *Salix*), comprising about 170 species, range in height from a few inches to 40 m/120 ft. The flowers are borne in catkins.

A tropical rainforest in Costa Rica. ▶

TRUCKS

By 1920 the **semi-trailer** whose front end rests on the rear portion of the hauling truck tractor was gaining in popularity. The semi-trailer usually has a disc.

By the start (1914) of **World War I**, 300,000 trucks were in use, and by the end (1918) there were more than 1 m.

Early trucks resembled horse-drawn wagons of the 19th c. They lacked roofs, doors and windshields; nothing protected the driver from the elements.

In 1903 the Automobile Club of America staged the first US **commer-cial-vehicle contest** to test the economy, reliability, durability, speed and carrying capacity of the truck.

In the late 1980s there were over 40 m. **trucks registered** in the US. Only about 1 m. were combination tractor-semi-trailers, the standard vehicles used by the trucking industry.

The first tractors powered by diesel engines were built in the early 1930s. **Diesel engines** burned fuel oil instead of gasoline, ranging in power from 125–500 hp.

Trucks **first appeared** in discernible numbers in Great Britain in the 1870s. In 1892 the Frenchman Maurice Le

Blanc introduced steam-powered cartage vehicles for commercial users.

TUNNELS

Channel tunnel trains can travel at speeds of 160 kph/100 mph. Digging began on both sides of the Strait of Dover in 1987–88. Completed in 1991 it officially opened in May 1994.

Earliest tunnels were extensions of cave dwellings. Ancient civilisations used tunnels to carry water. In the 22nd c BC a tunnel for pedestrian traffic was built in Babylonia under the Euphrates river.

In the US, the first **railroad tunnel** was on the Allegheny Portage Railroad. Built 1831–33 it was 214 m/701 ft long and carried canal barges over a summit.

One of the greatest advances in solid-rock excavation was the introduction of **gunpowder** blasting in the 17th c. By then tunnels were being constructed for canals.

Rotherhithe tunnel (1840s) was designed by Marc Brunel and built under the River Thames from Rotherhithe to Wapping, the first subaqueous tunnel. Brunel invented the tunnelling shield to complete it.

The **Channel Tunnel** (Eurotunnel) runs between England and France beneath the English Channel. 50 km/31 mi long, it has three tunnels, two for rail traffic and a central tunnel for services and security.

The first major **canal tunnel** was the Canal du Midi tunnel (Languedoc, France), 157 m/515 ft long, built 1666–81 by Pierre Riquet as part of the first canal linking the Atlantic and the Mediterranean.

TURKEY

Once the heart of the Ottoman Empire, **Turkey** became a republic on 20 Oct. 1923, its present boundaries fixed by the Treaty of Lausanne in that year.

Sultan Mohammed II (or Mehmet II, 1451–81) laid siege to Constantinople and captured it on 20 May 1453. Having gained this foothold, **Turkey** went on to conquer Europe as far as Vienna (1683).

The **population of Turkey** is 58,376,000 (est. 1991), comprising 85.7% Turkish, 10.6% Kurdish, 1.6% Arab and 2.1% other.

Turkey (capital: Ankara) lies in the Near East between the Mediterranean and Black Seas, with an area of 779,452 sq km/300,948 sq mi.

Turkey exports textiles, agricultural products, iron and non-ferrous metals, foodstuffs, leather, hides and chemicals, mainly to Germany, Italy, the US and UK.

UFOs

UFO stands for 'unidentified flying object' and covers any light or object seen in the sky whose identity is unknown. Many sightings turn out to be aircraft, stars, meteors or hoaxes and none have yet been officially proved to be of alien origin.

A series of **radar detections** and sightings near National Airport, Washington, DC in Jul. 1952 led to the setting-up of a panel of eminent scientists by the CIA. Later declassified it said that 90% of reports could easily be dismissed.

In 1948 the US Air Force began maintaining a file of UFO reports called **Project Blue Book**. By 1969 this project had recorded reports of 12,618 sightings or events.

In 1968 the continuing UFO controversy led to **The Condon Report**, sponsored by the US Air Force and conducted by physicist E. Condon. The report covered 59 UFO sightings in detail.

In the mid-1960s, a few scientists such as J. McDonald (meteorologist) and J. Hynek (astronomer) claimed that a small percentage of the most reliable **UFO reports** gave indications of extraterrestrial visitors.

Project Blue Book was terminated in Dec. 1969 after The Condon

Sightings of UFOs often turn out to be meteors or stars. ▲
◄ *Corn circles were initially said to be caused by UFOs.*

Report rejected the hypothesis of any extraterrestrial life, declaring no further investigation was needed. Non-government bodies still keep records of sightings.

The term **flying saucer** was coined in 1947 and has been used ever since. No evidence of life on other planets has been proved; elementary life was found on a Martian meteorite in 1996 but is not yet corroborated.

UNITED KINGDOM

Although the 26 counties of Southern Ireland became the Irish Free State in 1922 the name of the **United Kingdom** was not appropriately amended until 13 May 1927.

The **population of the United Kingdom** is 55,486,800 (1991 census), comprising 94.2% white, 1.4% Indian, 1% West Indian, 0.8% Pakistani, 0.2% African, 0.2% Chinese. 0.2% Bangladeshi and 2% other.

The **United Kingdom** came into being on 1 Jan. 1801 after Acts of the British and Irish parliaments brought about the union of both countries.

The **United Kingdom exports** machinery and transport equipment, chemicals, petroleum, iron and steel, textiles and scientific instruments.

The **United Kingdom of Great Britain and Northern Ireland** (since 1922) is situated off the northwest coast of Europe, with an area of 244,110 sq km/94,251 sq mi.

▲ *Windsor Castle, one of the many homes of the UK's monarch.*

UNITED NATIONS

Boutros Boutros Ghali (UN Sec.-Gen. 1992–96, Egyptian) issued 'An Agenda for Peace' on preventive diplomacy, peace-making, peace-keeping and peace-building (1992) and presided over the UN's adoption of the Comprehensive Nuclear Test-Ban Treaty (1996).

Dag Hammarskjöld (UN Sec.-Gen. 1953–61, Swedish), who described himself as 'curator of the secrets of 82 nations', won the Nobel Peace Prize (1961) after dying in an air crash while negotiating over the Congo crisis (1961).

Differences between the UN and League of Nations were: stronger executive powers for the Security Council; extent of specialised agencies (ultimately 15); and requirements that member-states provide armed forces.

Javier Pérez de Cuéllar (UN Sec.-Gen. 1982–91, Peruvian) set up a UN office for Emergency Operations in Africa (1984) to help co-ordinate famine relief efforts. UN peacekeeping operations were awarded the Nobel Peace Prize (1988).

Kofi Annan (UN Sec.-Gen. 1997– , Ghanaian) conducted negotiations following Iraq's invasion of Kuwait (1990), leading to the 'oil-for-food' formula, and negotiated with Saddam Hussein to allow UN inspection of Iraq's secret installations (1997).

Kurt Waldheim (UN Sec.-Gen. 1972–81, Austrian) fell under suspicion during his last years at the UN regarding the nature of his role as a Wehrmacht officer in wartime Yugoslavia.

The name **'United Nations'**, devised by Pres. Franklin D. Roosevelt to describe World War II allies fighting against the Axis Powers, appeared in a joint pledge (1942) not to make a separate peace with the enemy.

The UN, as an international organisation to succeed the discredited **League of Nations**, was discussed at a Foreign Ministers' conference (Moscow, 1943), planned at Dumbarton Oaks, Yalta and San Francisco (1944–45) and established by charter (1945).

U Thant (UN Sec.-Gen. 1961–71, Burmese) played a major diplomatic role during the Cuban crisis, headed a mission to Castro (1962) and formulated a plan to end the Congolese civil war (1962).

UN secretary generals have achieved greater influence as arbitrators than their League predecessors. **Trygve Lie**, first UN Sec.-Gen. (1946–52, Norwegian), mediated in Palestine (1947) and Kashmir (1948).

UNITED STATES OF AMERICA

The **United States of America** date from the Declaration of Independence of 4 Jul. 1776, whereby the 13 British colonies rejected British rule.

The **United States of America (capital: Washington, DC)** are located in North America, between Canada and Mexico, with an area of 9,529,063 sq km/3,679,192 sq mi.

The **population of the United States of America** is 252,177,000 (est. 1991), comprising 80.3% white, 12.1% black and 7.6% other races. 52.7% are Protestant, 26.2% Roman Catholic, 7.6% other Christian, 1.9% Muslim and 1.8% Jewish.

The **United States of America export** machinery and transport equipment, miscellaneous manufactures, chemicals, foodstuffs, live animals and mineral fuels.

With only 5% of the world's land area and less than 7% of its population, the **United States of America** consumes almost 50% of what the world produces.

▼ *The White House, home of the US president.*

UNIVERSE

Apart from the galaxies in the **Local Group**, all the galaxies we can observe display red shift in their spectra, showing they are moving away from us.

Current data suggest that the galaxies are **moving apart** at a rate of 50–100 kps/30–60 mps for every million parsecs (1 parsec = 3.2616 light years) of distance.

The **big bang theory** suggests the universe was formed from a single explosive event that threw material out from a hot super-dense centre about 15 bn years ago.

The further we look into space the greater the **red shifts**; this implies that the more distant galaxies are receding at ever greater speeds.

The most distant detected galaxies and quasars lie 10 bn light years or more from Earth and are drifting further apart as the **universe expands**.

The **steady-state theory** suggests that the universe appears the same wherever and whenever it is viewed. It is expanding by newly created matter. Bondi, Gold and Hoyle expounded this in 1948.

The **universe** is thought to be between 10 and 20 bn years old, and is mostly empty space with galaxies dotted about.

UNIVERSE, LAWS

Bode's law predicted the existence of a planet between Mars and Jupiter which lead to the discovery of asteroids. The law breaks down for Neptune and Pluto.

Edwin Hubble, US astronomer (1889–1953), announced **Hubble's law** in 1929. This states that the galaxies are moving apart at a rate that increases with their distance.

Einstein stated in his **theory of relativity** that the gravitational field of everything in the universe warps time and space so any quantities of light or distance cannot be taken at face value.

Einstein, inventor of the Theory of Relativity. ▶

German astronomer Johann Kepler formed three laws of **planetary motion** in 1609–18. The first states that all planets move about the Sun in elliptical orbits, having the Sun as one of the foci.

Kepler's second law states that the radius vector of each planet sweeps out equal areas in equal time. The third states that the squares of the periods of the planets are proportional to the cubes of their mean distances from the Sun.

Newton showed that the motion of bodies does not have to follow Kepler's elliptical path, but can take on other orbits depending on the total energy of the body.

UNIVERSITIES

Early 12th c Islamic institutions took the form of **religious schools** or court schools in India, China and Japan.

In 1992 the number of universities in the UK doubled: the original 45 were joined by former polytechnics and colleges. This saw the end of the **old binary system**.

The average total **income of English universities** stands at £7 bn per year; over half of this is provided by the state.

The **first European university**, a school of medicine, was founded at Salerno in the 9th c. Pavia, Ravenna and Bologna existed by 1158. The University of Paris was founded by William of Chapeaux c. 1110.

▲ *A medieval scholar.*

The majority of universities passed out of religious control in the 16th–17th c. **Royal patronage** replaced Church influence in most of northern Europe.

The scientific revolution of the 18th c led to the establishment of the **Royal Society** in England and the Academy of Sciences in Russia.

The **total number of universities** in the EU amounts to around 600; a similar number can be found in the US. About a quarter are research institutions.

University College, Oxford was **founded** in 1249. Scholars from Oxford migrated to Cambridge and a university was founded in 1329. The oldest Scottsh universities are St Andrews (1411), Glasgow (1451) and Aberdeen (1494).

Within the European Union there are over 8.5 m. **undergraduates**, compared with the US's 13 m. Growth in student numbers is a global phenomenon.

URANUS

The **rings** around Uranus are charcoal black and are believed to be made up from the debris of former 'moonlets' that have broken up.

Uranus has a **diameter** of 50,800 km/31,600 mi and a mass 14.5 times that of Earth. It has 15 moons and thin equatorial rings, discovered in 1977.

Uranus has an unusual **magnetic field** whose axis is tilted at 60° to the axis of spin and is placed about one-third of the way from the planet's centre to its surface.

Uranus is the **seventh planet** from the Sun and is twice as far out as the sixth planet, Saturn. It was discovered by German-born William Herschel in 1781.

Uranus orbits the Sun every 84 years at an average distance of 2,870 m. km/1,783 m. mi. Its spin axis is at 98° so that one pole points towards the Sun, giving extreme seasons.

Uranus spins from east to west, the opposite of the other planets, except Venus and possibly Pluto. The average **rotation** rate is 16.5 hr.

Voyager 2 found 11 rings made up of rock and dust and 10 small moons in addition to the 5 visible from Earth, around Uranus. Titania, the largest moon, is 1,580 km/980 mi in diameter.

URUGUAY

The **population of Uruguay** is 3,112,000 (est. 1991), comprising 85.9% Spanish-Italian, 3% mestizo, 2.6% Italian, 1.7% Jewish, 1.2% Mulatto and 5.6% other.

Uruguay (capital: Montevideo) lies on the east bank of the Uruguay River between Argentina and Brazil, with an area of 176,215 sq km/68,037 sq mi.

Uruguay became the world's leading soccer nation, winning at the Olympic Games in 1924 and 1928, before winning the first World Cup (against Argentina) in 1930.

Uruguay exports textiles, animals, beef, hides, leather, foodstuffs, beverages, tobacco, plastics and rubber, mainly to Brazil, the US, Germany and Argentina.

Uruguay was discovered by Juan Diaz de Solis in 1516. Colonised by Portugal and later by Spain, it was part of Brazil until the republic was established in 1830.

US CIVIL RIGHTS MOVEMENT

A bitter US Civil Rights confrontation occurred in **Little Rock, Arkansas** (1957) when Pres. Dwight Eisenhower was forced to use troops to achieve school integration.

Dr **Martin Luther King, Jr** organised a 1955 bus boycott protesting against segregation and became leader of the US Civil Rights struggle. He was killed in 1968.

Founded in 1942 the **Congress of Racial Equality** (CORE) became famous during the 1960s US Civil Rights movement for staging 'freedom rides' through segregated southern states.

Growing from US Civil Rights struggles and white obstructionism, Huey P. Newton and Bobby G. Seale organised the **militant Black Panthers** (1966) for African-American defence.

The 1955 Montgomery, Alabama Bus Boycott protesting against US segregation began when **Rosa Parks** refused to surrender her seat to a white man. Bus integration resulted (1956).

The **1965 Civil Rights Act** outlawing housing discrimination marked the culmination of the US Civil Rights movement.

The **Civil Rights movement** in US

The Great Rift valley in Kenya. ▶

worked for full social and political integration for African-Americans in the 1950s and 1960s.

The US Civil Rights movement began with the 1954 Supreme Court decision in ***Brown v. Board of Education*** of Topeka, declaring segregated schools unconstitutional.

VALLEYS

A **fjord** is a U-shaped valley that has been deepened by a glacier and afterwards invaded by the sea. Fjords are common in Scandinavia, Canada, Greenland and Chile.

A **ria** coast is a system of river valleys that has been drowned when the coast sinks or the sea level rises. An example is the Sydney area, Australia.

Death Valley is a desert in California. Its lowest point is 82 m/270 ft below sea level. The valley is a million years old. It was an obstacle to pioneer settlers, hence its name.

Lake Cristobal, Colorado, was formed after the river valley was blocked by the **Slumgullion earth-flow**, an enormous mass of moist volcanic ash moving down from nearby hills.

Some rivers flow in existing **valleys**, but most make their own, deepening the channel as they flow. Rain, air, frost, gravity, plants and animals do most of the widening.

The **Great Rift Valley** runs from Turkey down through East Africa to Mozambique. It is a series of trenches 6,400 km/4,000 mi long and mostly 40-56 km/25-35 mi wide. Mts Kilimanjaro and Kenya are volcanoes in the rift.

VENUS

The carbon dioxide **atmosphere** traps the Sun's heat by the greenhouse effect, raising the surface temperature of Venus to 480°C/900°F. The atmospheric pressure is 90 times that of Earth.

The first artificial object to hit another planet was the Soviet probe *Venera 3* which crashed on Venus, 1 Mar. 1966. Later *Venera* probes successfully landed and analysed surface material.

Venus is cloaked with clouds of sulphuric acid droplets which sweep across from east to west every four days. The **atmosphere** is almost entirely carbon dioxide.

Venus is the **second planet** from the Sun. Its diameter is 12,100 km/7,500 mi and its mass is 0.82 that of the Earth.

Venus **orbits** the Sun every 225 days at an average distance of 108.2 m. km/67.2 m. mi and can approach Earth within 38 m. km/24 m. mi, closer than any other planet.

Venus **rotates** on its axis more slowly than any other planet, once every 243 days, and from east to west, the opposite to other planets (except Uranus and possibly Pluto).

Venus's surface consists mainly of plains and deep impact craters. The largest highland area is Aphrodite Terra: near the equator, it is half the size of Africa, formed by volcanoes.

VIENNA

A Celtic town known as Vindobona, **Vienna** was fortified by the Romans. In 1137 Henry Jasomirgott made it the capital of the duchy of Austria.

Haydn, Mozart, Beethoven and Schubert lived in **Vienna** and composed much of their best music here, but it was Johann Strauss (1825–99) who immortalised the city in his waltzes.

The **population of Vienna** is 1,487,577 (1989 census), compared with 2,031,498 in 1910 when it was the capital of the Habsburg Empire.

Vienna is situated at the eastern foot of the Wiener Wald, on the right bank of the Danube at the eastern end of Austria.

Vienna produces a wide range of luxury goods, notably jewellery, leather, silks and *objets d'art*. It also produces iron and steel, furniture and optical instruments.

VIETNAM

Formerly the French Protectorate of Annam and Tonkin, **Vietnam** became independent in 1945, split in two (1955) and was re-united on 2 Jul. 1976.

Nationalist resistance to the French in **Vietnam** began in 1941 when Nguyen Ai Quoc, a former hotel porter, changed his name to Ho Chi Minh ('he who enlightens').

The **population of Vietnam** is 67,589,000 (est. 1991), comprising 87.1% Vietnamese, 1.8% Tho, 1.5% Chinese, 1.4% Khmer, 1.4% Muong and 5.3% other.

Vietnam (capital: Hanoi) is situated in south-east Asia, bordered by China, Laos and Kampuchea, with an area of 329,566 sq km/127,246 sq mi.

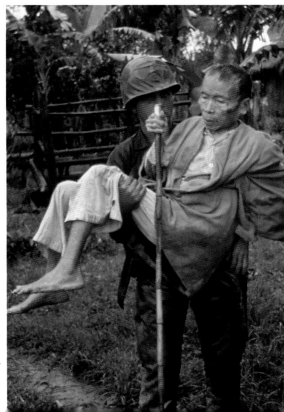

▶ *US marine in South Vietnam.*

VIKINGS

In 789 the *Anglo-Saxon Chronicle* records the first breath of a storm which was to change the face of Britain: 'In this year ... came three ships of Norwegians from Hörthaland.'

In Constantinople, Vikings formed the elite bodyguard of the Byzantine emperors, the feared and famous **Varangian Guard**.

Skilful seafarers, Vikings settled Greenland and Iceland, and from there they sailed as far as the eastern seaboard of North America, which they called **Vinland**.

The **Norn** dialect of Old Norse, spoken by the Vikings, was still widely spoken in the Orkney and Shetland islands well into the 18th c.

The **Vikings** are the Norsemen – Danes, Norwegians and Swedes, who traded and raided throughout northern Europe from about 800 to 1100.

Viking marauders sacked the monastery on the island of **Lindisfarne** in 793, followed by that of Jarrow in 794, and Iona in 795.

Vikings conquered northern France, and these Norsemen, or **Normans**, later raised the invasion fleet which in 1066 brought William the Conqueror to England.

VOLCANIC DISASTERS

A **volcano** is a vent in the Earth's crust from which molten rock, lava, ashes and gases are ejected. They are usually cone shaped.

Andesitic volcanoes are more violent; the molten rock is mostly from plate material and is rich in silica. This makes it very stiff and it solidifies to form high volcanic mountains.

Basaltic volcanoes are quieter and found along rift valleys and ocean ridges. The molten material is derived from the Earth's mantle and quite runny, flowing for long distances and causing low, broad volcanoes.

Izalco volcano in western El Salvador is the most active volcano in central America, having erupted more than 50 times since 1700. It is 1,830 m/6,004 ft high.

Many volcanoes are submarine and occur along mid-ocean ridges. The **highest volcano** is Guallatiri in the

North Island, New Zealand which is 6,060 m/19,900 ft high.

There are more than 1,300 potentially active volcanoes on Earth. Volcanism has also shaped other parts of the **Solar System** including the Moon, the planets Mars, Venus and Jupiter's moon Io.

Volcanoes are closely linked with the movements of lithospheric plates (the top layer of the Earth's structure) especially around **plate boundaries**.

▲ *The eruption of a volcano in Montserrat.*

VOLCANOES

Ngorongoro National Park, Tanzania, sits in the world's biggest crater of an extinct volcano. The crater, formed 250,000–2,500,000 years ago, measures 20 km/12.5 mi across. Between 25,000 and 30,000 animals live there.

The eruption of **Mt Vesuvius**, Italy, in AD 79 destroyed Herculaneum and Pompeii. A quarter of Pompeii's inhabitants escaped, the rest were buried in ash, choked by fumes or crushed.

The Japanese say that everyone should climb **Mt Fuji**, but only once. The mountain, sacred to Buddhists, is a 600,000-year-old volcano. 18 eruptions are known, the last in 1707.

The largest volcanic explosion was on **Krakatau**, Indonesia, in 1883. The noise was heard 3,200 km/2,000 mi away in Australia. Two-thirds of the island disappeared. Tidal waves killed 36,000 people on nearby coasts.

The **puys**, or peaks, in the Auvergne, France, are cones of ancient volcanoes. Some are needle-sharp, others softly rounded. Some churches and castles built on volcanic plugs date from the 11th c.

Volcanic eruptions between 1963 and 1967 created **Surtsey**, off Iceland. Grasses, wildflowers and sedges now grow on the 150-m/490-ft-high island of ash.

▼ *An active volcano in Chile.*

Volcanoes, lava flows, geysers, hot springs and fumaroles are all forms of **igneous activity** (from the Latin *ignis*, 'fire'), caused by heat, chemical reactions, pressure and friction.

WALLS

Hadrian's Wall was a Roman defensive barrier to keep out northern invaders, extending 118 km/73 mi from the Tyne to the Solway.

London Wall was built by the Romans around *Londinium* (London) *c.* AD 200. In medieval times the walls were rebuilt and extended, requiring new gateways in addition to the six Roman ones.

On 9 Nov. 1989 the East German government opened the country's borders with West Germany, and openings were made in the **Berlin Wall** through which East Germans could travel freely to the West.

The **Berlin Wall** was first erected on 12 Aug. 1961 by decree of the East German *Volkskammer* (Peoples' Chamber). The original barbed wire and cinder block wall was later replaced by a series of concrete walls.

The **Great Wall of China** was one of the largest building-construction projects ever carried out, running 6,400 km/4,000 mi. Parts of it date from the 4th c BC.

The **Siegfried Line** was a system of pillboxes and strong-points built along the German western frontier in the 1930s. It was used as a barrier by retreating German troops in 1944.

The **Western Wall** is the only remains of the Second Temple of Jerusalem, built by Herod (37–4 BC) and destroyed by the Romans in AD 70.

The Great Wall of China. ▶

WARS

Discontent with British rule led the 13 American colonies to declare independence. In the **War of Independence**, aided by the French, the Americans defeated the British by 1783.

Eager to prevent an alliance forming against him, Frederick the Great triggered off the **Seven Years' War** by consolidating his hold in the German states.

In the hope of stabilising a weak South Vietnamese government, the US became embroiled in a demoralising struggle in south-east Asia. The **Vietnam War** raged for nineteen years.

Russian and Japanese expansionism in the Far East prompted the beginning of the **Russo-Japanese War**, which resulted in the fall of Port Arthur and the decisive defeat of Russia in 1905.

The **American Civil War** was fought between eleven south-

▲ *Kuwaiti soldiers during the Gulf War.*

ern states and the industrialised north. A bitter and protracted conflict, that set brother against brother, it ended in defeat for the south.

The British manufactured reasons to invade Zululand in 1879. After an initial defeat the British went on to burn Ulundi and capture the Zulu king Cetewayo.

The **Crimean War**, between Russia and the allied powers of Britain, France, Turkey, and Sardinia arose from British and French mistrust of Russia's ambitions in the Balkans.

The **First** (1880–81) **and Second Boer Wars** (1899–1902) were fought by the Orange Free State and the Transvaal to resist British encroachment. In 1910 they joined Natal and the Cape to form the Union of South Africa.

The **Gulf War** was fought between Iraq and a coalition of 28 nations after Iraq annexed Kuwait in 1990. The six-week air offensive was followed by a 100-hour ground war which destroyed the Iraqi army.

The **Napoleonic Wars** were a series of European wars (1803–15) conducted by Napoleon I, following the Revolutionary Wars (1792–1802), aiming for French conquest of Europe.

WARSAW

Conrad, Duke of Mazovia erected a castle on the site of **Warsaw** in the 9th c. Sigismund Augustus made it the capital of Poland in 1550 in preference to Cracow.

The **population of Warsaw** is 1,655,100 (est. 1990), compared with 1,225,451 immediately before the outbreak of World War II.

Uprisings, first by the Jews in the infamous Ghetto (1943) and then by the Poles in 1944, resulted in the destruction of **Warsaw**, painstakingly rebuilt after World War II.

Warsaw is picturesquely located on a lofty terrace overlooking the left bank of the Vistula. The suburb of Praga across the river is connected by bridges.

Warsaw produces iron and steel, machinery and transport equipment. There is a considerable trade in leather goods and footwear as well as food-processing.

WARSAW PACT

As a result of the Sino–Soviet conflict, Albania under Enver Hoxha (1908–85) fell under Chinese influence and withdrew from the **Warsaw Pact** in 1968.

During the **uprisings in Hungary and Poland** (1956) the Warsaw Pact became a target for hostility, particularly its provision for garrisoning Soviet troops in satellite territory.

Intended as a **military alliance** between the USSR and East European communist states, the Warsaw Pact was originally established in response to the admission of West Germany into NATO.

The military structure and agreements of the Warsaw Pact were dismantled early in 1991. A political organisation remained until the **alliance was officially dissolved** in Jul. 1991.

The **signatories** to the Warsaw Pact (1955) were: Albania (withdrew 1968), Bulgaria, Czechoslovakia, East Germany (German Democratic Republic, GDR), Hungary, Poland, Romania and the USSR.

The USSR invoked the Warsaw Pact when it moved troops into Czechoslovakia in Aug. 1968 to quell the **'Prague Spring'** liberalisation movement led by Alexander Dubcek.

The Warsaw Pact (or Eastern European Mutual Assistance Pact) was **initiated** by Nikita Khrushchev and Nikolay Bulganin (1955) on their assumption to power in the USSR after Stalin's death (1953).

With an estimated **military strength** of 6 m. personnel, the Warsaw Pact provided for unified military command and maintenance of Soviet army units within other participating states.

WASHINGTON, DC

Planned exclusively as the seat of the US federal government, **Washington** was laid out by Major Pierre Charles L'Enfant in 1800 and named after the first president.

Washington, coterminous with the District of Columbia, lies on the north-east bank of the River Potomac at the head of tide and navigation, 64 km/40 mi south-west of Baltimore.

The **population of Washington** is 606,900 (est. 1990), rather less than it was in 1840.

Washington's manufactures and commerce are of relatively little importance, although it is the centre for the production of government stores of all kinds.

The White House, **Washington**, residence of the American president, was designed by James Hoban. It was painted white to cover the marks left when it was burned by the British in 1812.

WATER POLO

Hungary hold the record for **most Olympic water polo victories** with six; they were successful in 1932, 1936, 1952, 1956, 1964 and 1976.

The **most goals scored in a water polo international** by an individual are the 13 of Debbie Handley for Australia when they defeated Canada 16–10 in the 1982 World Championships.

The Netherlands are the most successful nation in the FINA **Women's water polo World Cup** having won the trophy on four consecutive occasions between 1988 and 1993.

The **record number of international water polo appearances** is 412 by Aleksey Barkalov (USSR) between 1965 and 1980.

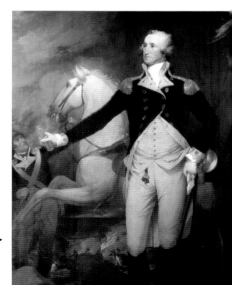

America's first president, George Washington. ▶
◀ *The signing of the Warsaw Pact.*

The UK won four of the first five water polo Olympic tournaments; in 1900, 1908, 1912 and 1920. Club side **Osborne Swimming Club, Manchester** represented the UK in 1900.

Water Polo is played by seven-a-side teams and was **developed in the UK** in the 1870s; it has been an Olympic sport since 1900.

WATER SPEED RECORDS

In Dec. 1964, **Donald Campbell** became the only man ever to break land and water speed records in the same year when he achieved 444.69 kph/276.33 mph on Australia's Lake Dumbleyung.

In Jun. 1967 **Lee Taylor** was ready to challenge the late Donald Campbell's record of 444.69 kph/276.33 mph. He achieved his goal with 458.993 kph/285.213 mph on Lake Guntersville, Alabama.

On 13 Jun. 1930, **Henry Segrave**'s first two runs yielded a new record at 158.93 kph/98.76 mph. Segrave died on the ensuing all-out run; as he reached 185 kph/115 mph *Miss England II* struck something in the water and rolled over.

◄ *Henry Segrave and the ill-fated* **Miss England.**

On 18 Jul. 1932 **Kaye Don** became the first man to travel at two miles a minute on water as he achieved a new record of 192.81 kph/119.81 mph, with a best one-way figure of 193.92 kph/120.50 mph.

On 19 Aug. 1939, on Coniston Water and in *K4*, Sir Malcolm Campbell achieved the least troubled record of his career, a quantum leap to 228.10 kph/141.74 mph.

On 26 May 1978 **Betty Cook** became the first person ever to complete the gruelling 935 km/580 mi race from San Felipe to Lapaz, down the Gulf of California, in one day. She took 12 hr 45 min, averaging 80 kph/50 mph in her 8.8 m/29 ft Scarab monohull.

On 29 Sept. 1952, **John Cobb** was travelling at massive speed (386 kph/240 mph, when the boat nose-dived into Loch Ness. Cobb was killed instantly. Later, the official figure for his run through the mile was given as 332.95 kph/206.89 mph.

On 8 Oct. 1978 **Ken Warby** increased the water speed record by the largest margin in its history, to 511.107 kph/317.596 mph, in a boat built in his back yard.

WEAPONS

Breech-loading firearms increased artillery firepower, and the invention of repeating handguns, rifles and early machine guns increased the volume of small-arms fire.

By the 17th c, the basic small arm was the **smoothbore flintlock**, a gun having a flint in the hammer that set off sparks to ignite the gunpowder.

By the end of the 19th c smokeless powder, the percussion cap, breech-loading weapons, the cylindro-conoidal bullet and various types of **machine gun** were developed.

From the 12th c, as more and more **crossbows** were being used, knights had to wear even tougher, heavier and restricting plate armour.

Gustavus Adolfus introduced the **paper cartridge**, which contained both powder and shot, and he instituted a mixed formation of both cavalry and infantry.

In the 19th c, when generals such as Napoleon Bonaparte came to favour lighter and faster-firing **artillery**, the age of the musket- and rifle-armed infantryman drew to a close.

Mediterranean cultures used easily manoeuvrable galleys to **ram** other vessels; these galleys contained a small number of heavily armed soldiers to protect the ship against attack.

The development of fortifications spurred the creation of more specialised **siege weapons** such as moveable battering rams.

The first artillery pieces, **bombards**, were little more than iron barrels with long metal bars bound together by hoops. Explosive charges spewed rocks and other debris.

The **hand gun** made its first impact at the Battle of Cerignola (1503), when a thin line of arquebusiers mowed down French pikemen and men-at-arms.

▲ *Napoleon favoured fast-firing artillery to heavy muskets.*

WEAVING

By *c.* 2500 BC a **horizontal frame loom** with treadles was apparently in use in east Asia. Fragments of silk fabrics found in China show traces of a twill damask pattern.

Mechanised weaving began in 1733 when John Kay invented the flying shuttle. The steam-powered loom was invented by English clergyman Edmund Cartwright in 1785.

Recent developments are **shuttleless looms** that work at high speed passing the weft through the warp by means of *rapiers* and jets of air or water.

The **earliest evidence** of the use of the **loom** (4400 BC) is a picture of a horizontal two-bar loom on a pottery dish found at al-Badari, Egypt.

The vertical two-bar loom again appears in Egypt (1567–1320 BC). It coincides with more intricate textile patterns, the earliest known **tapestries** (1483–1411 BC) were found in Thutmose IV's tomb at Thebes.

The word **loom** (from Middle English *lome*, 'tool') is applied to any set of devices permitting a warp to be tensioned and a shed to be formed.

Woven cloth is normally longer in one direction than the other. The lengthwise threads are called the warp; the other threads, which are combined with the warp and lie widthwise, are called the weft.

WEIRD FACTS

At the time of the 1983 general election, John Dougrez-Lewis of the **Raving Monster Loony Party** ran for Parliament in Cambridge. Despite changing his name to Tarquin Fintimlinbinwhinbimlin Bus Stop-F'Tang-F'Tang-Ole-Biscuit Barrel, he gained 286 votes.

Condoms break an average of once in every 161 condoms used.

Eddie Levin and Delphine Crha elebrated the breaking of the record for the longest ever **kiss** (17 days 10 ½ hr) in Chicago on 24 Sept. 1984.

From 17–21 Jul. 1989 David Beattie and Adrian Simons travelled a pair of **escalators** for 101 hr at Top Shop, Oxford Street, London. They each travelled 214.34 km/133.19 mi.

On average, men think about **sex** every 9 minutes.

Remy Bricka of Paris, France, walked across the **Atlantic Ocean** on 4.2 m/13 ft 9 in skis in 1988. Leaving Tenerife on 2 Apr. 1988, he covered 5636 km/3502 mi, arriving in Trinidad on 31 May.

The greatest height from which **fresh eggs** have been dropped to earth and remained intact is 198 m/650 ft, by David S. Donoghue from a helicopter on 2 Oct. 1979, on a golf course in Tokyo, Japan.

The late Samuel Riley (b. 1922) of Sefton Park, Merseyside, was found by a disbelieving pathologist to have a **blood alcohol** level of 1,220 mg per 100 ml (15 times the UK legal driving limit of 80 mg of alcohol per 100 ml of blood).

The longest **chewing gum** wrapper chain on record was 18.9 m/59.67 ft in length and was made by Cathy Ushler of Redmond, Washington, US, between 1969 and 1987.

The longest single unbroken **apple peel** on record is one of 52.52 m/172

ft 4 in, peeled by Kathy Wafler of Wolcott, New York, US in 11 hr 30 min at Long Ridge Mall, Rochester, New York, on 16 Oct. 1976. The apple weighed 567 g/20 oz.

William Pitt the Younger (1759–1806), the British PM, once allegedly drank 574 bottles of claret, 854 bottles of Madeira and 2410 bottles of port in a single year.

WILD FLOWERS

About 12,000 different **Wild flowers** have been recorded in the US and Canada alone. Many of them, noted for their beautiful blossom, have been adopted as state or provincial flowers.

Heather is strictly the common ling (*Calluna vulgaris*) but often applied to all species of *Erica*. They are evergreen shrubs of low growth, with clusters of small flowers.

Honeysuckle (genus *Lonicera*) comprise about 175 species of climbing or prostrate shrubs all over the northern hemisphere. They are noted for their large fragrant flowers.

Phlox is a genus of about 60 species, mainly hardy perennials native to the US. Most are tall herbs with magnificent blossom.

The **Columbine** (genus *Aquilegia*) comprise some 75 species of the northern temperate zones. They grow in woods and thickets, alpine meadows and the Rocky Mountains.

The **Harebell** (*Campanula rotundifolia*), also known as witches' thimbles and the Scottish bluebell, has a long, slender stem and drooping bell flowers.

The **Magnolia**, named after Pierre Magnol (1638–1715) is a genus comprising 35 species distributed in China, Japan and the US and noted for their large white flowers.

gradient, is proportional to that difference.

Because of the earth's rotation the air flow from high-pressure areas to low is **deflected** to the right in the northern hemisphere, to the left in the southern hemisphere.

From the equator to latitude 40° the earth's surface has a surplus of radiated energy and from latitude 40° to the poles it emits more energy than it absorbs from the sun. This imbalance is responsible for the **wind movements** over the earth.

Small-scale wind features such as anticyclones cause variations within their dominant circulatory system. In winter 1962–63, an **anticyclone** remained stationary over Scandinavia, carrying bitter east winds to the UK.

WIND

Air movement (wind) takes place when a difference in air pressure exists between two points. The strength of the movement, which runs from high pressure to low, called the **pressure**

Tornadoes and cyclones are destructive high winds. ▶

The Ancient Greeks believed that the god Aeolus kept the winds in his care, locked up in a vast cavern. Winds are endowed with personalities, hence their **names**, such as mistral, chinook, southerly buster, williwaw and brickfielder.

The highest **surface wind speed** recorded was 371 kph/231 mph at Mt Washington, New Hampshire, US, Apr. 1934. At Commonwealth Bay, Antarctica, winds may gust to 320 kph/ 200 mph.

The **trade winds** blow on the equatorial margins of the subtropical high-pressure belts. They are steady and reliable in both direction and speed, originating from high-pressure centres with constant circulation.

The world's largest **wind generator** is the Boeing Mod-5B in Oahu, Hawaii, US. It has 97.5-m/320-ft rotors and produces 3,200 KW when the wind reaches 51 kph/32 mph.

WIND POWER

Cast-iron drives were first introduced to windmills in 1754 by English engineer John Smeaton. The actual **power produced** by these mills was probably only from 10–15 hp.

From Arabia, windmills with vertical sails on horizontal shafts reached Europe (France) in 1180. Builders there began to use fabric-covered, **wood-framed sails**.

▲ *Wind was the main source of power for many centuries.*

Modern wind turbines extract energy from the wind for electricity generation, by rotation of propeller-like blades that drive a generator. Interest was rekindled by the oil crisis of the 1970s.

Vineyards in Spain. ▶

The earliest references to **wind-driven grain mills**, are found in Arabic writings of AD 9th c, and refer to a Persian millwright of AD 644.

The first known **wind device** was described by Hero of Alexandria (AD 1st c). It was modelled on a water-driven paddle wheel and was used to drive a piston pump.

The first **wind-driven sawmill** was built in 1592 in the Netherlands by Cornelis Cornelisz. It was mounted on a raft to allow easy turning into the wind.

Wind-driven pumps continued to be used in large numbers, even in the US, well into the 20th c until low-cost electric power became readily available in rural areas.

WINES

Burgundy is a smaller region but produces many famous wines from two related grape varieties: Pinot Noir for reds and Chardonnay for whites. The best reds come from the Cote d'Or.

Cultivation of the grapevine began several thousand years before Christ, and is mentioned many times in the Old Testament. The Ancient Egyptians made wine; the early Greeks exported it on a considerable scale.

For convenience in commerce, the **Bordeaux** merchants classified their finest red wines as early as 1725, but it was not until 1855 that such a classification, based on the market price for each wine, received official recognition.

From southern Spain comes **sherry**, the most versatile and classic fortified wine. Sherry ranges from the dry manzanilla and fino through the medium-dry amontillado to the sweet oloroso and 'cream' styles.

Mainly light, fruity white wines are made in Germany. The finest of these are made of the **Riesling** grape from three districts on the Rhine: from the Rheingau, Rheinhesse and Rheinpfalz; from the Nahe Valley; and from the Mosel, Saar and Ruwer valleys.

Red wine should be **served** at room temperature, 18–22 C/65–72∞ F. White and rose wines should be at refrigerator temperature, 6–10∞ C/43–50∞ F. Only wines that have thrown a sediment in the bottle, such as vintage port, red Bordeaux and red Burgundy, need be decanted.

The *appellation controlée* (quality control) law came into effect in France (1936) and is now the model for similar legislation in other countries. The law allows, for example, only wine made from grapes grown in the Champagne region, to be called 'champagne'.

The best-known **Italian wines** are from the north; Barolo, the sparkling Asti Spumante and the wines used for vermouth from Piedmont; Chianti from Tuscany; Soave, Valpolicella and Bardolino from Veneto; and Lambrusco, from central Italy.

The **Champagne** region in northern

France produces indisputably the best sparkling wine in the world. Other good sparkling wines are produced in Loire, Burgundy and Savoie regions.

Wines may be either red, white or rose and also dry, medium or sweet. They fall into three basic categories: natural or 'table' wines, sparkling wines and fortified wines.

WOMEN'S EMANCIPATION

Lucretia Coffin Mott, an American reformer, campaigned vigorously for the abolition of slavery and for women's rights. With Elizabeth Cady Stanton she organised the first **women's-rights convention** in the US (1848).

▶ *Mary Wollstonecraft, an early exponent of women's rights.*

Gloria Steinem (b. 1934) is one of the most influential figures of the modern feminist movement. Organiser of the National Women's Political Caucus and the Women's Alliance for Action, she has campaigned for political, economic and sexual liberation of women.

Militant political action among women began in the UK (1903), with the formation of the Women's Social and Political Union (**WSPU**) for the right to vote, under the leadership of Emmeline Pankhurst. Women demonstrated on a massive scale.

In the UK the right for women to **vote** was granted in 1918, although it was confined to women aged 30 and above. In 1928 the voting age was lowered to 21.

Founded in Chicago in 1920, the **League of Women Voters** is an organisation that attempts to further the development of political awareness through political participation. The league consists of more than 1,200 state and local chapters.

The preamble to the United Nations (UN) Charter (1945) referred to **equal rights** for women; in 1948 the UN Commission on the Status of Women was established; and in 1952 the UN General Assembly held a convention on the political rights of women.

During the 1960s a militant feminist trend emerged in the West, encouraged by **feminist studies**, such as *The Second Sex* (1953, Simone de Beauvoir) and *The Feminine Mystique* (1963, Betty Friedan).

▲ *Suffragettes campaigning for women's votes.*

425

The struggle to achieve **equal rights for women** is often thought to have begun, in the English-speaking world, with the publication of Mary Wollstonecraft's *A Vindication of the Rights of Women* (1792).

Emmeline Pankhurst, assisted by her daughters Christabel and Sylvia founded the Women's Social and Political Union (1903). Her followers, called '**suffragettes**' heckled politicians and were frequently arrested for inciting riots.

The USSR and the Netherlands granted **women's suffrage** in 1917; Austria, Czechoslovakia, Poland and Sweden in 1918; and Germany and Luxembourg in 1919. Spain extended the ballot in 1931, France in 1944 and Belgium, Italy, Romania and Yugoslavia in 1946.

In many Middle Eastern countries **universal suffrage** was acquired after World War II, although women remain totally disenfranchised in some countries such as Kuwait.

WORLD RECORDS

At the Atlanta Olympics in Jul. 1996 Donovan Bailey (Canada) ran the **fastest-ever 100 m**, timed at 9.84 seconds.

Bob Beamon won the 1968 **Olympic long-jump title** in the rarefied air of Mexico City with a leap of 8.90 m – 55 cm beyond the existing world record. Beamon's mark stood for an incredible 23 years and 316 days until broken by Mike Powell.

Jesse Owens broke six world records within an hour at the US Olympic trials in 1935. The events were 100 yds, long jump, 200 m/220 yards and 200 m/220 yd hurdles.

Jonathan Edwards became the first British athlete to break the **triple-jump world record**. In Aug. 1995. He extended the record to 18.29 m/60 ft ¼ in.

On 6 May 1954 Roger Bannister (England) finally broke middle-distance running's most elusive record: **the four-minute mile**. At the Oxford University track he clocked 3 minutes 59.4 seconds.

Sergey Bubka (Ukraine) broke the **pole vault world record** 27 times as he dominated the event in the 1980s and 1990s.

YUGOSLAVIA

Formerly a kingdom (1918) and a people's republic (1946), **Yugoslavia** disintegrated in 1991, leaving only Serbia and Montenegro with the autonomous provinces of Kosovo and Voivodina.

Sacred to **Yugoslavia** is Kosovo where the Serbs were decisively defeated by the Turks in 1389. Both Tsar Lazar and Sultan Murad I were killed in battle.

The **population of Yugoslavia** is 10,337,504 (1991 census), comprising 75% Serb, 17.7% Albanian and 7.3% Montenegrin. 80% are Serb Orthodox and 20% Muslim.

Yugoslavia (capital: Belgrade) is in the north-western Balkans, bordered by the Adriatic, with an area of 102,173 sq km/ 39,449 sq mi.

Yugoslavia exports machinery and transport equipment, manufactured goods, chemicals, foodstuffs and mineral fuels, mainly to Russia, Ukraine, Italy, Germany and France.

ZOOLOGY

Zoology is the study of animals, not only individually but in relation to each other, with plants and with the inanimate environment.

Animal Morphology is the study and classification of animals according to their body size, shape, colour, skin, hair, scales, feathers, as well as anatomical and cellular differences.

Conservation began as the preservation or breeding of animals for human welfare. In recent years it has been extended to all forms of life, whether beneficial to man or not.

Ecology is the study of animals as they occur in their natural environment, subdivided into the environment itself and the animal within it.

Embryology is the study of animals in the embryo stage of their development. The groundwork for this was established by T.H. Morgan in *Experimental Embryology* (1927).

Fauna is the term describing the animals or animal life of a region, period or special environment. It is derived from Faunus, a satyr-like deity in Roman mythology.

Heredity is the sum of the qualities transmitted by parents to offspring through a mechanism lying primarily in the chromosomes.

Author Biographies

Ingrid Cranfield read geography at the University of Sydney. She is the author of nine books, including *The Challengers*, a survey of modern British exploration and adventure. She has edited several travel handbooks and other works and contributes frequently to periodicals, encyclopedias and compilations.

Ray Driscoll is a self-confessed sports buff who has contributed to many sports books and football programmes. Among his interests are fishing and pub quizzes. He has the good fortune to reach two Grand Finals of Channel 4's prestigious quiz Fifteen-to-1. During the football season he can be seen cheering on his beloved Chelsea.

Deborah Gill was educated in India and England and has worked in publishing for 15 years, writing on a variety of far-reaching subjects, including fine art and literature. She has written monographs on several artists, including *Magritte, Mucha* and *Klimt*. She is married with two grown-up children, and lives in London.

Dr James Mackay is a journalist and broadcaster, biographer and historian. A former saleroom correspondent of the *Financial Times*, he has also written numerous books on stamps, coins, antiques and other collectables. A history graduate of Glasgow University, he is regarded as the world's leading authority on Robert Burns.

Martin Noble, Oxford-based editor, fiction/arts writer and English graduate was in-house publishing editor (Granada, NEL), freelance from 1979. Novels include: *Private Schulz, Bullshot, Who Framed Roger Rabbit, Ruthless People, Tin Men, Trance Mission*. Contributed to: *The Encyclopedia of Singles, The Reader's Companion to the Twentieth-Century Novel*.

Karen Sullivan was born and educated in Canada and is the author of 12 books on health, nutrition and complementary medicine, including *Vitamins* and *Minerals in a Nutshell, Alternative Remedies* and *The Complete Guide to Pregnancy and Childcare*. She was general editor of the *Complete Illustrated Guide to Natural Home Remedies*. She is health editor of *Northern Woman* magazine, and lectures widely on woman's health and health issues.

Jon Sutherland has written more than 60 books over the past 10 years on a wide range of subjects. These include transport, sport, business education and children's adventure stories. He now lives in Suffolk.

Rana K. Williamson PhD, holds degrees from Southwest Texas State University and Texas Christian University. An historian, she authored *When the Catfish Had Ticks: Texas Drought Humor* and *Putting the Pieces Together: A Technological Guide for Educators*. The native Texan works as a professor and computer consultant in Ft. Worth.

Picture Credits

Allsport: 25, 59, 68, 116, 124 (t), Hulton Deutsch 130 (b), 170, 189 (l), 179, 185, 200, Mike Powell 215, Mark Thompson 270, 295, 331, 380, 426.

Bridgeman Art Library: 120, 212.

Clive Tarling Photography: 124 (b).

Christie's Images: 13, 17, 27, 31 (b), 32, 45, 47, 49, 50, 51, 52, 53, 57, 66, 70 (l), 72, 78 (r), 79, 81 (b), 84, 85, 90, 91, 92, 98, 100, 101, 105, 108, 122 (r), 128, 129, 130 (t), 158, 159, 175, 187, 196, 199, 210, 211, 219, 228, 235, 239, 241, 246, 247, 268, 280, 282, 308, 309, 317, 322, 324 (r), 335 (t), 340, 341, 342, 344, 353, 375, 376 (r), 377, 382, 397, 415.

Foundry Arts: David Banfield 31 (t), 148, 273, 352, 387; Claire Dashwood 277 (b).

Image Select: 24, 58, 113 (b), 193, 237, 255 (b), 261, 284, 305, 317, 345, 374, 379, 400, 406.

Image Select/Ann Ronan: 78 (l), 240 (b), 330, 401.

Image Select/CFCL: 18, 19, 21, 41, 43, 54, 60, 62, 67, 70 (b), 81 (t), 86, 87, 96, 107 (t), 126, 133 (t), 139, 142 (b), 145, 146, 156, 157, 166, 173 (t), 178, 181 (t), 201, 206, 213, 226, 230, 231, 232, 233, 244, 245, 251, 252, 269 (b), 272, 285, 287, 288, 298, 301, 304, 323, 324 (l), 338, 347, 350, 355, 356, 357, 363, 365, 371, 376 (l), 384, 386, 396 (l), 404, 410, 423.

Image Select/Giraudon: 192.

Mary Evans Picture Library: 20, 29 (b), 73, 94, 134, 138, 203, 204, 223, 242, 243, 248, 264, 313 (l), 329, 348, 362, 378, 424.

Pictorial Press Ltd: 11, 12, 15, 16, 102, 118, 163, 276, 277 (t), 296, 339, 349.

Still Pictures: 34, 36 (l), 151, 195, 227, 366, 428; Jecko Vassilev 22, 76 (t), 354, 420 (r); Tony Crocetta 35, 136, 335 (b); Putao 36 (r); Mark Cawardine 37, 61; Delpho 39, 253; Klein/Hubert 64 (t), 76 (b), 99, 312;

Thomas D. Mangelsen 75; Gil Moti 106, 165, 332; Kevin Schafer 121, 137, 143 (l), 171, 172, 184 (t), 186, 209, 302, 333, 358, 393; B & C Alexander 155; Bruno Marielli 161, 169, 420 (l); Fred Bavendam 164, 197, 293; Foto-Unep 208, 292, 385; Neckles-Unep 217, 224; Heine Pedersen 294, 346; Luiz C. Marigo 306 (t); Michael Gunther 306 (b); Daniel Heuclin, 366 (b).

Topham Picturepoint: 10, 22, 26, 29 (t), 40, 46, Associated Press 55, 56, 63, 64 (b), 71, 83, 88 (t), 97, 103, 107 (b), 109, 111, 113 (t), 122 (l), Associated Press 125, 131, 133 (b), 135, 141, 142 (t), 143 (r), 144, 149, 152, 153, 154, 160, 162, 167, 173 (b), 176, 177, 181 (b), 182, 184 (b), 188, 189 (r), 190, 194, 198, 202, Associated Press 205, 207, 214, 216, 225, 236, 238, 240 (t), 249, 250, 254, 255 (t), 259, 262, 263, 265, 266, 269 (t), 274, 278, Associated Press 279, 283, 289, 291, 299, 300, 303, 311, 313 (r), 314, 316, 319, 320, 321, 325, 328, 334, 336, 337, 351, 359, 361, 364, 369, 373, Press Association 381, 383, 388, 389, 391, 392, 394, 396 (t), 399, 403, Associated Press 405, 407, Associated Press 409, 411, 412, 414, 416, 421, 425.

Travel Photo International: 258.

Vandystadt: 256.

Visual Arts Library: 44, 48, 69, 260, 281, 327, 402, 422.

www.aldigital.co.uk/: 119, 220.

Every effort has been made to trace the copyright holders of pictures and we apologise in advance for any omissions. We would be pleased to insert the appropriate acknowledgement in any subsequent edition of this publication.

Index